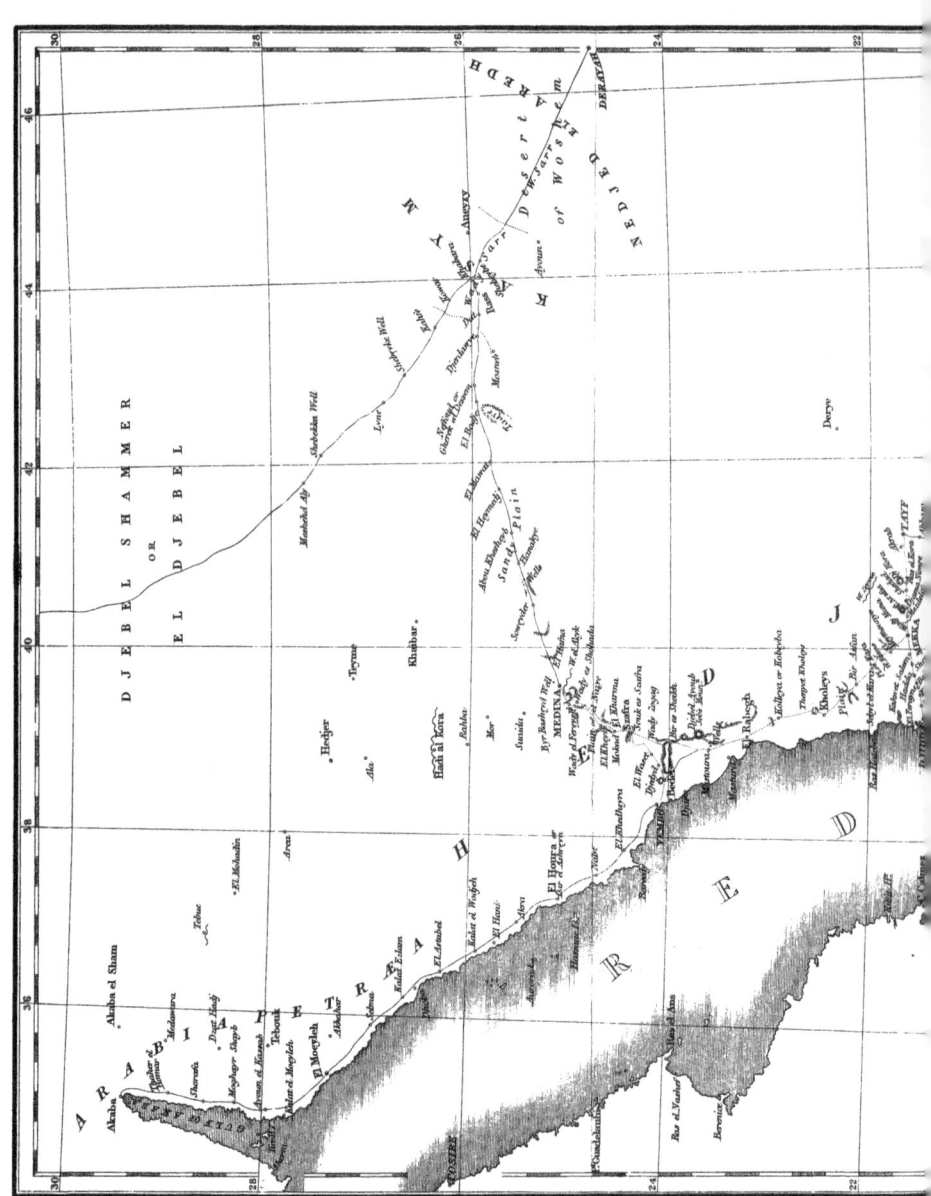

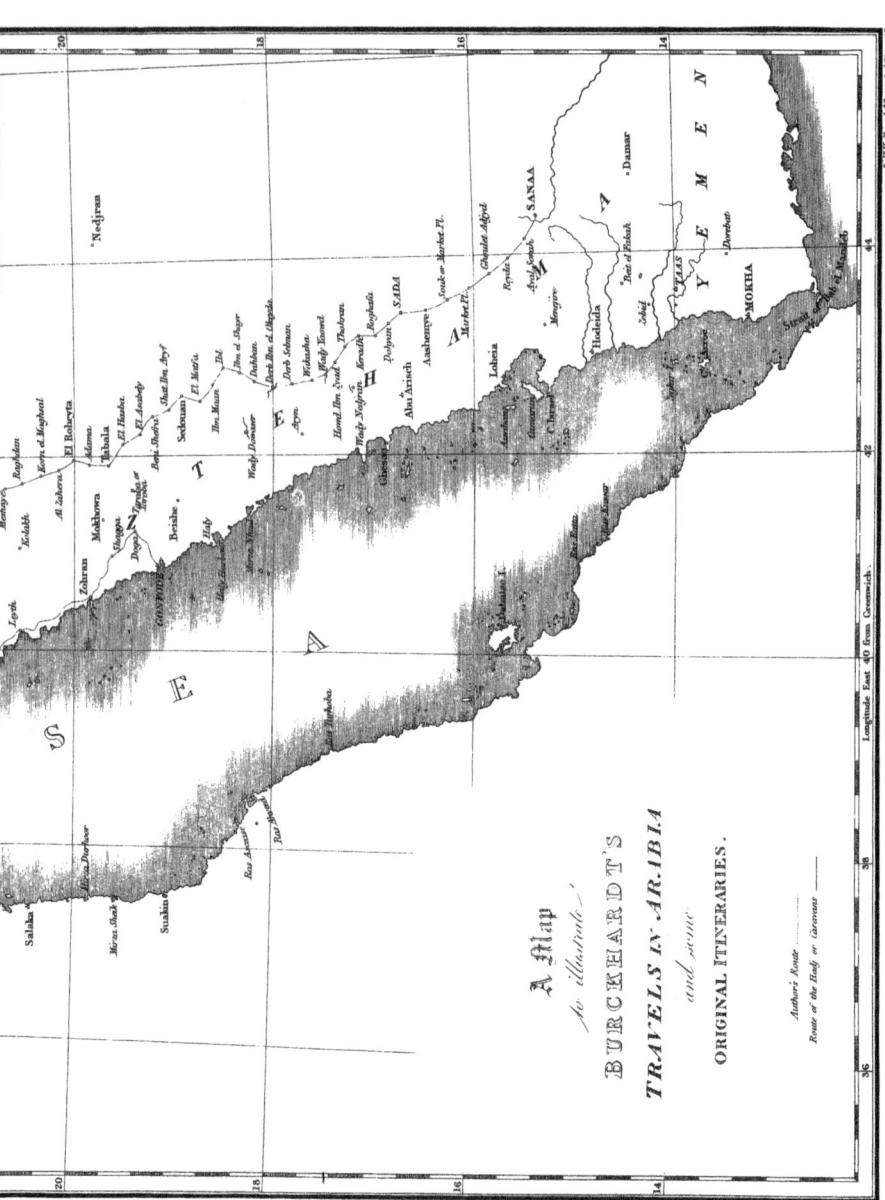

TRAVELS IN
ARABIA

TRAVELS IN
ARABIA

JOHN LEWIS BURCKHARDT

DOVER PUBLICATIONS, INC.
MINEOLA, NEW YORK

Bibliographical Note

This Dover edition, first published in 2020, is a republication of the book originally published under the title *Travels in Arabia: Comprehending an Account of Those Territories in Hedjaz Which the Mohammedans Regard as Sacred* by Henry Colburn, London, in 1829. The four maps appear in their original positions in the book. To view and enlarge the content of the maps online, please see: https://www.doverpublications.com/0486838668.

Library of Congress Cataloging-in-Publication Data

Names: Burckhardt, John Lewis, 1784–1817, author.
Title: Travels in Arabia / John Lewis Burckhardt.
Description: Mineola, New York : Dover Publications, Inc., 2020. | "Originally published under the title Travels in Arabia: Comprehending an Account of Those Territories in Hedjaz Which the Mohammedans Regard as Sacred by Henry Colburn, London, in 1829"—Title page. | Summary: "In 1809, John Lewis Burckhardt disguised himself as an Arab and traveled to sites forbidden to Westerners. His travel diary is rich in ethnographic, cultural, geographic, and political observations"—Provided by publisher.
Identifiers: LCCN 2019025955 | ISBN 9780486838663 (trade paperback)
Subjects: LCSH: Arabian Peninsula—Description and travel.
Classification: LCC DS207 .B94 2020 | DDC 915.304—dc23
LC record available at https://lccn.loc.gov/2019025955

Manufactured in the United States by LSC Communications
83866801
www.doverpublications.com

2 4 6 8 10 9 7 5 3 1
2019

CONTENTS

	PAGE
Preface of the Editor	xiii
The Author's Introduction	xxi
Corrigenda	xxiii
Djidda	1
Route from Djidda to Tayf	53
Residence at Tayf	70
Journey to Mekka	87
Arrival at Mekka	93
Description of Mekka	102
Quarters of Mekka	109
Description of the Beitullah, or Great Mosque, at Mekka	134
Some Historical Notices Concerning the Kaaba, and the Temple of Mekka	162
Description of Several Other Holy Places, Visited by Pilgrims at Mekka, and In Its Neighbourhood	171
Remarks on the Inhabitants of Mekka and Djidda	180
Government of Mekka	219
Climate and Diseases of Mekka and Djidda	240

CONTENTS

	PAGE
The Hadj, or Pilgrimage	246
Journey from Mekka to Medina	291
Medina	317
Description of Medina	321
Account of Some Places of Zyara, or Objects of Pious Visitation in the Neighbourhood of Medina	362
On the Inhabitants of Medina	370
On the Government of Medina	391
Climate and Diseases of Medina	398
Journey from Medina to Yembo	401
Yembo	410
From Yembo to Cairo	426
Appendix	445
Index of Arabic Words	471

LIST OF MAPS

	PAGE
A Map to Illustrate Burckhardt's Travels in Arabia and Some Original Itineraries	Frontispiece
Plan of Mekka	*facing* 102
The Plain of Arafat with the Camp of the Pilgrims	*facing* 266
Plan of Medina	*facing* 321

PREFACE OF THE EDITOR.

SOME years have now elapsed since two distinct portions of Burckhardt's works (his Travels in Nubia and Syria) were offered to the public, and most favourably received; their success being insured not only by instrinsic merit, but by the celebrity of their editor as a scholar and antiquary, a traveller and a geographer. It must not however be inferred, from any delay in publishing the present volume, that its contents are less worthy of notice than those parts which have already proved so interesting and instructive to a multitude of readers. It was always intended that this Journal, and other writings of the same lamented author, should issue successively from the press: " There still remain," says Colonel Leake, in his Preface to the Syrian Journal (p. ii.) " manuscripts sufficient to fill two volumes: one of these will consist of his Travels in Arabia, which were confined to the Hedjaz or Holy Land of the Muselmans, the part least accessible to Christians; the fourth volume will contain very copious remarks on the Arabs of the Desert, and particularly the Wahabys."

Respecting the portion now before the reader, Colonel Leake, in another place, expresses a highly flattering opinion. " Burckhardt," says he, " transmitted to the Association the most accurate and complete account of the Hedjaz, including the cities of Mekka and Medina, which has ever been received in Europe. His knowledge of the Arabic language, and of Mohammedan manners, had enabled him to assume the Muselman character with such success, that he resided at Mekka during the whole time of the pilgrimage, and passed through the various ceremonies of the occasion, without the smallest suspicion having arisen as to his real character." (See the Life of Burckhardt prefixed to his Travels in Nubia, p. lvii. 4to. edition, 1819).

Recommended so strongly, the work of a less eminent traveller would be entitled to our notice: this presents itself with another claim; for the manuscript Journal was partly corrected and prepared for publication by the learned editor of Burckhardt's former writings. But some important literary occupations prevented Colonel Leake from superintending the progress of this volume through the press. His plan, however, has been almost invariably adopted by the actual editor; particularly in expressing with scrupulous fidelity the author's sentiments on all occasions, and in retaining, without any regard to mere elegance of style or selection of terms, his original language, wherever an alteration was not absolutely necessary to reconcile with our system of phraseology and grammatical construction certain foreign idioms which had crept into his English writings.*

---

* It was thought expedient, from circumstances of typographical convenience tending to facilitate and expedite the publication of this volume, that the Arabic characters which in the original manuscript follow immediately certain words, or appear between the lines or in the margin, should here be placed together at the end, as an Index, with references to the pages wherein they occur.

PREFACE OF THE EDITOR. xv

The map prefixed to this volume might almost appear superfluous, since the positions of Djidda, Mekka, Medina, Tayf, and Yembo, the chief places of Hedjaz visited by Burckhardt, are indicated with accuracy in the excellent maps that illustrate his Nubian and Syrian Travels. But as the reader of this volume cannot reasonably be supposed to have constantly at hand, for immediate reference, the two former portions of our author's works, a map is here given, in the construction and delineation of which Mr. Sydney Hall has attended to every suggestion offered by the editor: at whose recommendation the names of places are spelt after Burckhardt's manner, however different from that more usual among us.*

By the editor's advice, also, several places situate beyond the Eastern limits of Hedjaz are included in this map; since Burckhardt, although he did not visit them himself, has given some original itineraries, in which they are mentioned.

That those places do not belong to the region properly denominated Hedjaz, is evident; but how far this region extends eastward cannot easily be determined; and the same difficulty respecting it occurs in various directions. The editor, that he might ascertain by what boundaries we are justified in supposing Hedjaz to be separated from other provinces of Arabia, consulted a multiplicity of authors, both European and Oriental. The result, however, of his inquiry has not proved satisfactory; for to each of the neighbouring countries

---

* Thus in the map as in the letter-press of this volume, *Mekka* might have been spelt *Mecca;* and *Hejaz, Jidda, Nejed,* would as well express the proper sounds of those words as *Hedjaz, Djidda, Nedjed;* and at the same time approximate more closely to the original Arabic orthography, by which our English *j* (as in *Jar, James,* &c.) is represented without the assistance of a *d;* although the prefixing of this letter to the *j* might prevent a Frenchman from pronouncing it as in *jour, jamais,* &c.

certain writers have assigned towns, stations, and districts, which by others of equal authority are placed in Hedjaz.

Such confusion may partly have arisen from the different statements of the number, extent, and names of divisions comprised within the same space; this being occupied, according to European writers, by three great regions, the *Stony*, the *Desert*, and the *Happy* Arabia; while Oriental geographers partition it into two, five, six, seven, or more provinces, under denominations by no means corresponding in signification to the epithets above mentioned, which we have borrowed from the Greeks and Romans.

That it would be a most difficult, or scarcely possible task, to fix precisely the limits of each Arabian province, is acknowledged by that excellent geographer, D'Anville; but he seems disposed to confound the region comprising Mekka, Djidda, and Yembo, (places which, as we know, are unequivocally in Hedjaz,) with Arabia Felix.[*] D'Herbelôt, in one place, declares Hedjaz to be Arabia Petræa,[†] and in another he identifies it with Arabia Deserta.[‡]

Among the Eastern writers, some divide Arabia into two parts, Yemen and Hedjaz; others into five great provinces, Yemen, Hedjaz, Nedjed, Tehaina, and Yemama. Bahrein has also been included;

---

[*] D'Anville, Géographie Ancienne.

[†] See the Bibliothèque Orientale in " Hegiaz ou Higiaz"—" Nom d'une province de l'Arabie, que nous appelons Pierreuse," &c.—Richardson also, in his Arabic and Persian Dictionary, explains Hijaz by " Mecca and the adjacent country, Arabia Petræa;" and Demetrias Alexandrides, who translated some portions of Abulfeda's Geography into Greek, (printed at Vienna, 1807, 8vo.) always renders Hedjaz by 'Αραβία Πετραία.

[‡] " Les Provinces de Tabama et d'Iemamah sont comme au cœur du pays; celle de Hegiaz est devenue la plus célèbre à cause des villes de la Mecque et de Medine, et fait avec les deux dernières que nous avons nommées ce que nous appelons l'Arabie Déserte."— Biblioth. Orient. in " Arab."

and Aroudh is named as an Arabian province, but appears to be the same as Yemama. Hadramaut, Mahrah, Shejr, Oman, and other subdivisions have likewise been reckoned independent provinces by some, while many confound them with the greater regions, Yemen and Hedjaz. To the latter, indeed, are often assigned even the extensive countries of Nedjed, Tehama, and Yemama.

Respecting the boundaries of all these provinces, much embarrassment has arisen from contradictory statements made by several of the most eminent Oriental geographers; Edrisi, Abulfeda, Al Madaieni, Ibn Haukal, Ibn el Vardi, Bakoui, and others. Mr. Rommel, a very ingenious commentator on Abulfeda's " Arabia," is frequently obliged to acknowledge the difficulty of ascertaining where one division begins and another terminates. With regard, more particularly, to the boundaries of Hedjaz, Abulfeda is silent; but it appears that his opinion, so far as Mr. Rommel could collect from incidental accounts of places assigned to this province and adjoining territories, did not in all respects coincide with the statements of other celebrated geographers.*

---

* See " Christophori Rommel Abulfedea Arabiæ Descriptio, commentario perpetuo illustrata," Gottingæ, 1802, 4to. " Ambitum et fines hujus provinciæ Abulfeda designare supersedet.—Al Madaieni hæc profert: ' Hbegiaz est provincia complectens illum tractum montium qui inde ab Yaman expansus usque ad Sham (Syriam) protenditur. In eo tractu sitæ sunt Madinah et Amman'—Cum hoc dissidere Abulfedam non dubium est.— Ibn al Arabi: ' Quod est inter Tehamah et Nagd, illud est Hhegiaz.'—Fusius Ibn Haukal: ' Quod protenditur a limite Serrain urbis sitæ ad mare Kolzum adusque viciniam Madian, et inde reflectendo per limitem tendentem in ortum urbis Hhegr, ad montem Tai transeundo juxta tergum Yamamah ad mare Persicum, hoc totum ad Hhegiaz pertinet.' Et alio loco: ' Hhegiaz ea est provincia, quæ Maccah et Madinah et Yamamah cum earundem territoriis comprehendit.'—Ibn al Vardi Hhegiaz appellat provinciam secus Sinum Arabicum et a regione Habyssiniæ sitam—Bakui eam inter Yaman et Syriam posuisse satis habet, simul longitudinem ejus mensis itinere emetiens."—(pp. 57—58.)

PREFACE OF THE EDITOR.

It may perhaps be asked, why our inquisitive traveller did not learn from some intelligent native the precise extent and limits of Hedjaz? To this question the following passage (written by Burckhardt, near the end of his journal, and probably intended for the Appendix,) may serve as a reply, and show that even the present inhabitants do not agree in their application of the name Hedjaz. " This," says he, " is not used by the Arabian Bedouins in the usual acceptation of the word. They call Hedjaz exclusively the mountainous country, comprehending many fertile valleys south of Tayf, and as far as the dwelling-places of the Asyr Arabs, where the coffee-tree begins to be cultivated abundantly. This is the general application of the term among all the Bedouins of those countries; and the town's-people of Mekka and Djidda also use it in that sense among themselves. But when they converse with foreigners, whose notions they politely adopt, the name Hedjaz is bestowed on the country between Tayf, Mekka, Medina, Yembo, and Djidda. The Bedouins give the name of El Ghor, or the low-land, to the whole province westward of the mountains from Mekka up to Beder and Yembo; while those mountains themselves northward of Tayf are called by them Hedjaz-es'-Shám, or the Northern Hedjaz."*

* This would confirm the derivation of Hedjaz (mentioned by Golius) from *ahhtedjezet*, " quod (provincia Hhegiaz) colligata et constricta montibus sit :" but others derive it from the Arabic word *yehedjez*, because Hedjaz *divides* Nedjed from Tehama, or because it *connects* Yemen with Syria, between which it is situate. As even the shortest note written by Burckhardt must be considered valuable, a few lines, that immediately follow the passage above quoted from his Journal, are here given : " 1 compute the population of the province usually called Hedjaz, comprising the whole territory of the Sherif of Mekka, together with that of Medina and the towns situated therein, and all the Bedouin tribes, at about two hundred and fifty thousand souls; a number which, I am certain, is rather over than under rated; the greater part being the Bedouin inhabitants of the mountains, and principally the strong tribes of Beni Harb."

PREFACE OF THE EDITOR.

On reference to pages 396 and 397, a remark will be found concerning the different application of this name (Hedjaz) among those who inhabit the sea-coast and those Bedouins who occupy the interior country; and it will even appear that doubts have been entertained whether the sacred city Medina does not belong rather to Nedjed than to Hedjaz.

From statements so vague as those above quoted, an attempt to trace exactly the limits of any country must be vain and fallacious: that region, therefore, which borders on the Red Sea, and which the natives, we know, entitle unequivocally *Hedjaz*, is marked in our map, as in almost every other published hitherto, merely with that name, its first letter being placed where the editor supposes Arabia Petræa to terminate, and its last letter where he would separate Hedjaz from Tehama.*

To those who seek the most accurate information respecting places but little known, this work is sufficiently recommended by the name of its author, and of the country which it describes. " The manners of the Hejazi Arabs have continued," says Sir William Jones, " from the time of Solomon to the present age."† " Our notions of Mecca must be drawn," says Gibbon, " from the Arabians. As no unbeliever is permitted to enter the city, our travellers are silent; and the short hints of Thevenot are taken from the suspicious mouth of an African renegado."‡

But the reader of this preface must not be withholden from

---

* Burckhardt (Syrian Travels p. 511.) quotes Makrizi, the Egyptian historian, who says, in his chapter on Aila, (Akaba): " It is from hence that the Hedjaz begins: in former times it was the frontier place of the Greeks, &c."

† Discourse on the Arabs, Asiat. Researches, vol. ii.

‡ Roman Empire, chap. 50. note 18.

perusing Burckhardt's authentic and interesting account of the places which he visited, of the extraordinary ceremonies which he witnessed, and of the people among whom he lived in the character of a Muselman.

Some short notices, written on a detached leaf, but evidently intended by the author as an introduction to his Journal, are given accordingly in the next page: for, that the Arabian Travels should appear under such a form as Burckhardt himself probably wished them to assume, has been throughout a favourite object of the editor,

WILLIAM OUSELEY.

London, January, 1829.

THE AUTHOR'S INTRODUCTION.

In the pages of this Journal I have frequently quoted some Arabian historians, whose works are in my possession. It is now to me a subject of regret that those manuscripts were not with me in the Hedjaz. The two first I purchased at Cairo, after my return from Arabia.

These works are—1. The History of Mekka, entitled *Akhbar Mekka*, a thick quarto volume, by *Aby el Wolyd el Azraky*, who flourished in the year of the Hedjra 223, and has traced the annals of his native city down to that period. This work is particularly interesting on account of its topographical notices, and the author's intimate acquaintance with the state of Arabia before Islám or Mohammedanism. The manuscript appears, from the hand-writing, to be six, or perhaps seven hundred years old.

2. The History of Mekka, entitled *Akd e' themyn*, in three folio volumes, by *Taky ed' dyn el Fasy*, who was himself Kadhy of Mekka. This history comes down to the year of the Hedjra 829, and is com-

prised in the first volume; the other two volumes containing biographical anecdotes of distinguished natives of Mekka.

3. The History of the Mosque of Mekka, with which the history of the town is interwoven, called *El Aalam hy aalam beled Allah el haram*, in one volume quarto. The author was *Kottob ed' dyn el Mekky*, who held high offices at Mekka, and brings the history down to the year 990 of the Hedjra.

4. The History of the Hedjaz, and more particularly of Mekka, by *Asamy*. Of this chronicle I possess only the second volume, a large folio manuscript, comprising historical records from the time of the *Beni Omeya*, to the year (of the Hedjra) 1097. I have not been able to ascertain the title of this work, which abounds with curious and valuable information. The author, *Asamy*, was a native of Mekka.

5. The History of the Temple and Town of Medina. This work is entitled *Khelaset el Wafa*, its author was *Nour ed' dyn Aly Ibn Ahmed e' Samhoudy*,* and it is comprised in one folio volume, bringing the history down to the year 911 of the Hedjra.

* To this writer Burckhardt refers in p. 323, by the letters (V. S.) " Vide Samhoudy."

CORRIGENDA.

Page 12 *for*	Gonfady	*read*	Gonfade.
29	Badingam	. . .	Badinjan.
95	Metzem	. . . .	Meltezem.
109	Hareh	. . . .	Haret.
156	Achmed	. . . .	Ahhmed.
183	Moktar	. . . .	Mokhtar.
232	Yahyn	. . . .	Yahya.
446	Matsa .	. · . .	Matfa.
462	Benezes	. . . .	Aenezes.

⁂ The name of *Kayd Beg*, which frequently occurs, is sometimes spelt in the Ms. *Kait Beg*, and once erroneously *Kail Beg*. On reference to Burckhardt's Nubian Travels, it appears that he entered Djidda on the 18th of July, and not on the 15th, as printed in the first page of this volume through a mistake of the figure 8 for 5; the ink with which he wrote having in many parts of his Journal faded considerably, and become of a pale reddish colour. As far, also, as the faded ink in some places of the Ms. allows the editor (and others who have seen it) to judge, *Mekkawy* is used to express a person of Mekka: in many pages of the Ms. *Mekkan* is distinctly written, but the Arabic derivative *Mekky* occurs only in the Author's Introduction (p. xiv.) Local derivatives similar to *Mekkawy* occur in the various parts of Burckhardt's works: the present volume, and his Syrian and Nubian Travels, exhibit Djiddawy, Yembawy, Kennawy, Dongolawy, Bornawy, Bedjawy, &c. from Djidda, Yembo, Kenne, Dongola, Bornou, Bedja, &c.

TRAVELS

IN

THE HEDJAZ OF ARABIA.

DJIDDA.

My arrival in the Hedjaz was attended with some unfavourable circumstances. On entering the town of Djidda, in the morning of the 15th of July, 1814, I went to the house of a person on whom I had a letter of credit, delivered to me, at my departure from Cairo, in January, 1813, when I had not yet fully resolved to extend my travels into Arabia. From this person I met with a very cold reception; the letter was thought to be of too old a date to deserve notice: indeed, my ragged appearance might have rendered any one cautious how he committed himself with his correspondents, in paying me a large sum of money on their account; bills and letters of credit are, besides, often trifled with in the mutual dealings of Eastern merchants; and I thus experienced a flat refusal, accompanied, however, with an offer of lodgings in the man's house. This I accepted for the first two days, thinking that, by a more intimate acquaintance I might convince him that I was neither an adventurer nor impostor; but finding him inflexible, I removed to one of the numerous public

Khans in the town, my whole stock of money being two dollars and a few sequins, sewed up in an amulet which I wore on my arm. I had little time to make melancholy reflections upon my situation; for on the fourth day after my arrival, I was attacked by a violent fever, occasioned, probably, by indulging too freely in the fine fruits which were then in the Djidda market; an imprudence, which my abstemious diet, for the last twelve months, rendered, perhaps, less inexcusable, but certainly of worse consequence. I was for several days delirious; and nature would probably have been exhausted, had it not been for the aid of a Greek captain, my fellow passenger from Souakin. He attended me in one of my lucid intervals, and, at my request, procured a barber, or country physician, who bled me copiously, though with much reluctance, as he insisted that a potion, made up of ginger, nutmeg, and cinnamon, was the only remedy adapted to my case. In a fortnight after, I had sufficiently recovered to be able to walk about; but the weakness and languor which the fever had occasioned, would not yield to the damp heat of the atmosphere of the town; and I owed my complete recovery to the temperate climate of Tayf, situated in the mountains behind Mekka, where I afterwards proceeded.

The Djidda market little resembled those Negro markets, where a single dollar would purchase two or three weeks' provision of dhourra and butter. The price of every thing had risen here to an unusual height, the imports from the interior of Arabia having entirely ceased, while the whole population of the Hedjaz, now increased by a Turkish army and its numerous followers, and a host of pilgrims who were daily coming in, wholly depended for its supply upon the imports from Egypt. My little stock of money was therefore spent during my illness, and before I was sufficiently recovered to walk out. The Greek captain, though he had shown himself ready to afford me the common services of humanity, was not disposed to trust to the honour or respectability of a man whom he knew to be entirely destitute of money. I was in immediate want of a sum sufficient to defray my daily expenses, and, no other means being left to procure it, I was compelled to sell my slave: I regretted much the necessity for parting with him, as I knew he had some affection for me, and he was very desirous to remain with me. During my preceding journey he had proved himself a faithful and useful companion; and although I have since had several other slaves in my possession, I never found one equal to him. The Greek captain sold him for me, in the slave-market of Djidda, for forty-eight dollars.*

The present state of the Hedjaz rendered travelling through it, in the disguise of a beggar, or at least for a person of my outward appearance, impracticable; and the slow progress of my recovery made me desirous of obtaining comforts: I therefore equipped myself anew, in the dress of a reduced Egyptian gentleman, and immediately wrote to Cairo for a supply of money; but this I could hardly receive in less than three or four months. Being determined, however, to remain in the Hedjaz until the time of the pilgrimage in the following November, it became necessary for me to find the means of procuring subsistence until my funds should arrive. Had I been disappointed in all my hopes, I should then have followed the example of numbers of the poor Hadjis, even those of respectable families, who earn a daily subsistence, during their stay in the Hedjaz, by manual labour; but before I resorted to this last expedient, I thought I might try another. I had indeed brought with me a letter of introduction from Seyd Mohammed el Mahrouky,† the first merchant

---

* This slave cost me sixteen dollars at Shendy; thus, the profits of sale on *one* slave defrayed almost the whole expense of the four months' journey through Nubia, which I had performed in the spring.

† The original characters of these and other names, both of persons and places, are given in the Index of Arabic words at the end of this volume.

in Cairo, to Araby Djeylany, the richest merchant of Djidda; but this I knew could be of no use, as it was not a letter of credit; and I did not present it.* I determined therefore, at last, to address the Pasha, Mohammed Aly, in person. He had arrived in the Hedjaz at the close of the spring of 1813, and was now resident at Tayf, where he had established the head-quarters of the army, with which he intended to attack the strongholds of the Wahabis. I had seen the Pasha several times at Cairo, before my departure for Upper Egypt, and had informed him in general terms of my travelling madness (as he afterwards jocularly termed it himself at Tayf). I should here observe that, as the merchants of Upper Egypt are in general poor, and none of them strictly honour a bill or obligation by immediate payment, I had found it necessary, during my stay there, in order to obtain a supply of money, to request my correspondent at Cairo to pay the sum which I wanted into the Pasha's treasury, and to take an order from him upon his son, Ibrahim Pasha, then governor of Upper Egypt, to repay me the amount. Having therefore already had some money dealings with the Pasha, I thought that, without being guilty of too much effrontery, I might now endeavour to renew them in the Hedjaz, and the more so, as I knew that he had formerly expressed rather a favourable opinion of my person and pursuits. As soon, therefore, as the violence of my fever had subsided, I wrote to his physician, an Armenian of the name of Bosari, whom I had also known at Cairo, where I had heard much in his favour, and who was then with his master at Tayf. I begged him to represent my unfortunate situation to the Pasha, to inform him that my letter of credit upon Djidda had not been honoured, and to ask him whether he would accept a bill upon

---

* I afterwards became acquainted with Djeylany, at Mekka; and what I saw of him, convinced me that I was not mistaken in the estimation I had formed of his readiness to assist a stranger.

my correspondent at Cairo, and order his treasurer at Djidda to pay the amount of it.

Although Tayf is only five days distant from Djidda, yet the state of the country was such, that private travellers seldom ventured to cross the mountains between Mekka and Tayf; and caravans, which carried the letters of the people of the country, departed only at intervals of from eight to ten days; I could not, therefore, expect an answer to my letter in less than twenty days. During this period I passed my leisure hours at Djidda, in transcribing the journal of my travels in Nubia; but I felt the heat at this season so oppressive, especially in my weak state, that, except during a few hours early in the morning, I found no ease but in the cool shade of the great gateway of the Khan in which I lodged; where I passed the greater part of the day, stretched upon a stone bench. Bosari's correspondent at Djidda, through whom I had sent my letter to Tayf, had meanwhile mentioned my name to Yahya Effendi, the physician of Tousoun Pasha, son of Mohammed Aly, now governor of Djidda, who had been in Upper Egypt while I was there, but I had not seen him. This physician, when at Cairo, had heard my name mentioned as that of a traveller; and understanding now, that I came from the Black countries, he was curious to see me, and desired Bosari's friend to introduce me to him. He received me politely, invited me repeatedly to his house, and, in the course of further explanation, became acquainted with my wants, and the steps I had taken to relieve them. He happened at this time to be preparing for a journey to Medina with Tousoun Pasha, and was sending back all his unnecessary baggage to Cairo; with this he was also desirous to transmit to his family his last year's savings, amounting to three thousand piastres (about 100*l*.), and he was so kind as to offer me the money for a bill upon Cairo, payable at sight; an advantage which, he well knew, the merchants of Djidda never insure to those who take their bills. Such an offer would not be considered as conferring any obligation in the commercial towns of Europe; but in the East, and under the circumstances in which I was placed, it was extraordinary. Yahya Effendi added, that some of his friends had given me a flattering character while at Cairo, and that he could not, therefore, entertain the slightest doubt of my solvency and respectability, in which opinion he had been confirmed on reading the letter of credit I had brought with me. As the issue of my application to the Pasha at Tayf was uncertain, I readily and gratefully accepted Yahya's proposal; the money was immediately paid to me, the bills drawn, and a few days after, my obliging friend departed with Tousoun Pasha for Medina, where I had the pleasure of seeing him again early in the following year.

I was now in possession of a sum sufficient to banish all apprehension of suffering from poverty before the arrival of fresh supplies from Egypt, whatever might be the consequence of my application to the Pasha; but Yahya Effendi was no sooner gone, than I received a somewhat favourable answer to the letter I had written to Tayf. Bosari, it appeared, had been rather unwilling to urge my request to the Pasha, afraid, perhaps, that he might himself become a sufferer, should I forfeit my word. The Pasha, however, had heard of my being at Djidda, through another person in his suite, whom I had seen there, and who had arrived at Tayf; and hearing that I was walking about in rags, he immediately despatched a messenger, with two dromedaries, to the collector of customs at Djidda, Seyd Aly Odjakly, in whose hands was the management of all the affairs of the town, with an order to furnish me a suit of clothes, and a purse of five hundred piastres as travelling money; accompanied with a request that I should repair immediately to Tayf, with the same messenger who had brought the letter. In a postscript, Seyd Aly Odjakly was enjoined to order the messenger to take me by the upper road to Tayf, which leaves Mekka to the south, the lower and more usual road passing through the middle of that town.

The invitation of a Turkish Pasha is a polite command; whatever, therefore, might be my reluctance to go at this time to Tayf, I could not avoid, under the present circumstances, complying with the Pasha's wishes; and, notwithstanding the secret aversion I had to receive a present at his hands instead of a loan, I could not refuse to accept the clothes and money, without hurting the pride and exciting the resentment of a chief, whose good graces it was now my principal aim to conciliate.* I likewise understood the meaning of the postscript, although Seyd Aly was not aware of it; but, on this point, I flattered myself I should be a match for the Pasha and his people.

As the invitation was very pressing, I left Djidda in the evening of the same day on which the messenger arrived, after supping with Seyd Aly, in company with a great number of Hadjis from all parts of the world; for the fast of Ramadhan had already commenced, and during this month everybody displays as much hospitality and splendour as he possibly can, particularly in the supper after sun-set. Distrusting in some measure the Pasha's intentions, I thought it necessary to carry a full purse to Tayf; I therefore changed the whole of the three thousand piastres which I had received from Yahya Effendi into gold, and put it in my girdle. A person who has money has little to fear among Osmanlis,

* Some persons, perhaps, consider it an honour to receive presents from Pashas; but I think differently. I know that the real motive of a Turk in making presents, is either to get double the value in return, (which could not be the case with me,) or to gratify his own pride in showing to his courtiers that he deigns to be liberal towards a person whom he holds infinitely below him in station or worth. I have often witnessed the sneers of the donor and his people on making such presents; and their sentiments are sometimes expressed by the saying, " Look, he has thrown a morsel to this dog!" Few Europeans may, perhaps, agree with me in this respect, but *my* knowledge authorises me to form this opinion; and the only advice which I can give to travellers who would not lower themselves in the estimation of Turkish grandees, is to be always ready, on similar occasions, to return the supposed favour two-fold. As for myself, I had but seldom occasion to make presents during my travels; and this was the only one that I was ever obliged to accept.

except the loss of it; but I thought that I might stand in need of what I had, either as a bribe, or to facilitate my departure from Tayf. I was, however, fortunately mistaken in both these conjectures.

I shall add here some remarks on Djidda and its inhabitants. The town is built upon a slightly rising ground, the lowest side of which is washed by the sea. Along the shore it extends in its greatest length for about fifteen hundred paces, while the breadth is no where more than half that space. It is surrounded on the land-side by a wall, in a tolerable state of repair, but of no strength. It had been constructed only a few years since by the joint labours of the inhabitants themselves, who were sensible that they possessed no protection against the Wahabis in the ancient half-ruined wall, built, A.H. 917, by Kansoue el Ghoury, Sultan of Egypt.[*] The present structure is a sufficient barrier against Arabs, who have no artillery. At every interval of forty or fifty paces, the wall is strengthened by watch-towers, with a few rusty guns. A narrow ditch was also carried along its whole extent, to increase the means of defence; and thus Djidda enjoys, in Arabia, the reputation of being an impregnable fortress. On the sea-shore, in front of the town, the ancient wall remains, but in a state of decay. At the northern extremity, near the spot where the new wall is washed by the sea, stands the Governor's residence; and at the southern extremity is a small castle, mounting eight or ten guns. There is, besides, a battery, to guard the entrance from the side of the sea, and command the whole harbour. Here is mounted an immense old piece of ordnance, which carries a ball of five hundred pounds, and is so celebrated all over the Red Sea, that the very fame of it is a protection to Djidda. The approach into the town from the sea is by two quays, where small boats discharge the cargoes of the large ships, these being obliged to

---

[*] See Kotobeddin, History of Mekka.

anchor in the roadstead, about two miles from shore; none but the vessels called *say*, (the smallest that navigate the Red Sea,) approaching close to the shore. The quays are shut every evening about sunset; thus all communication is prevented, at night, between the town and the shipping.

On the land side Djidda has two gates; the Báb Mekka on the east side, and Báb el Medina on the north. A small gate in the south wall has lately been filled up. The area inclosed by the new wall (about three thousand paces in circuit) and the sea, is not entirely covered with buildings. A broad piece of open ground extends the whole length of the interior of the wall; and there is, besides, a good deal of waste ground near the Báb el Medina, and on the southern extremity. Having traversed this open space in coming from the gate, you enter the suburbs, comprising only huts formed of reeds, rushes, and brushwood, and encircling the inner town, which consists of stone buildings. The huts are chiefly inhabited by Bedouins, or poor peasants and labourers, who live here completely after the Bedouin fashion. Similar quarters for people of this description may be found in every town of Arabia. The interior of Djidda is divided into different districts. The people of Sowakin, who frequent this place, reside near the Báb el Medina; their quarters are called Haret è Sowakiny. Here they live in a few poor houses, but principally under huts, to which the lowest class of people frequently resort, as many public women reside here, and those who sell the intoxicating beverage called Boosa. The most respectable inhabitants have their quarters near the sea, where a long street, running parallel to the shore, appears lined with shops, and affords many khans constantly and exclusively frequented by the merchants. Djidda is well built; indeed, better than any Turkish town of equal size that I had hitherto seen. The streets are unpaved, but spacious and airy; the houses high, constructed wholly of stone, brought for the greater part from the sea-shore, and consisting of madrepores and other marine fossils. Almost every house has two stories, with many small windows and wooden shutters. Some have bow-windows, which exhibit a great display of joiners' or carpenters' work. There is, generally, a spacious hall at the entrance, where strangers are received, and which, during the heat of the day, is cooler than any other part of the house, as its floor is kept almost constantly wet. The distribution of rooms is nearly the same as in the houses of Egypt and Syria; with this difference, however, that in Djidda there are not so many large and lofty apartments as in those countries, where but few houses, at least of the natives, have two stories, whilst the rooms on the ground-floor are sometimes of a considerable height. It thus happens that, in many houses of the Hedjaz, the only cool spot is the entrance-hall ; and here, at noon, the master, with all his male attendants, hired servants or slaves, may be seen enjoying the siesta.* As building is very expensive in this country, little is adapted for outward show beyond the lattice-work of the bow-windows; this frequently is painted with most gaudy colours, both on the outside and inside. In many houses the lawful wife of a man occupies one part, and his female Abyssinian slaves are lodged in their own distinct apartments; convenience, therefore, in the building, is more studied than size or beauty ; yet, in Egypt, many ordinary houses have spacious and handsome rooms.

Uniformity in architecture is not observed at Djidda. Some houses are built with small, others with large square stones, the smooth side outwards, and the interior filled up with mud. Sometimes the walls are entirely of stone ; many have, at intervals of about three feet, thin layers of planks placed in the wall, and these, the

* Although the cool breeze comes only from the north, yet the Arabians do not seem to take so much advantage of it in their houses as the Egyptians, whose principal rooms are generally so contrived as to open towards the north. The large ventilators constructed on the terraces of houses in Egypt, and which diffuse a current of air through all the lower apartments, are unknown in the Hedjaz.

Arabs imagine, tend to increase its strength. When the walls are plastered, the wood is left of its natural colour, which gives to the whole a gay and pleasing appearance, as if the building had been ornamented with so many bands; but the dazzling white of the walls during sun-shine is extremely distressing to the eyes. Most of the gateways have pointed arches; some few round; and the latter are seen, though less frequently, over the gates of private houses in every part of Egypt. No buildings of ancient date are observed in Djidda, the madrepore being of such a nature that it rapidly decays when exposed to the rain and moist atmosphere prevalent here.* Besides many small mosques, there are two of considerable size: one of these was built by Sherif Serour, predecessor of the last reigning Sherif Ghaleb. The Governor's habitation, in which the Sherif himself frequently resided, is a paltry building; such, likewise, is that in which dwells the collector of the customs. There are some well-built public khans in the town, with good accommodation, where the foreign merchants reside during their short stay here. In these khans are large open squares with arched passages, which afford a cool shade to the merchants for the greater part of the day. Except during the monsoon, when Djidda is extremely crowded with people, private lodgings may easily be procured in the most distant quarters of the town. The best private dwellings of Djidda belong to the great mercantile establishment of Djeylani, who, with his family, occupies a small square behind the principal street. This square is composed of three large buildings, the most commodious and costly private houses in all the Hedjaz. Every house of moderate size has its cistern; but as the rains are not sufficiently regular or abundant to fill the cisterns from the tops of the houses, (as

* In general, it may be said that Djidda is a modern town; for its importance as a market of Indian goods can only be traced to the beginning of the fifteenth century, although it had been known in the most ancient times of Arabian history as the harbour of Mekka.

throughout Syria,) they are often supplied with water from pools formed outside of the town in rainy seasons.

Of these cisterns, the water is very inadequate to the consumption of Djidda, and is reckoned a delicacy. Much of the drinking water is drawn from some wells a mile and a half distant on the southern side; water, indeed, may be found every where at a depth of fifteen feet, but it is generally of a bad taste, and in some places scarcely drinkable. Two only of the wells afford water that can be called sweet; but even this is considered heavy,* and, if suffered to stand twenty-four hours in a vessel, it becomes full of insects. The good water of these two wells being scarce and dear, cannot always be procured without the assistance of powerful friends; in fact, not more than from two to three hundred persons are ever able to obtain it, while the rest of the inhabitants must content themselves with the water supplied by other wells; and to this the constant ill-health of the people may chiefly be ascribed. As Djidda has the name of a Turkish fortress, we might suppose that the wells would have been protected by a fort; but the Turks have neglected this precaution, and when, in December, 1814, the people apprehended that the Wahabis were advancing on the side of Gonfady, the Governor of Djidda, in great haste, filled the few cisterns belonging to the government houses with water from the wells, and for several days withheld that necessary of life from all the inhabitants, as every water-camel was employed by him. Several of the wells are private property, and yield to their owners a considerable income.

The town of Djidda is without gardens, or vegetation of any kind except a few date-trees adjoining one of the mosques; even outside the town the whole country is a barren desert, covered

* *Heavy* and *light*, applied to water, are expressions common in most languages of the East, where both natives and foreigners, from the vast quantity which they consume, become more refined in their taste regarding it than the people of our northern climates.

on the sea-shore with a saline earth, and higher up with sand : here are found some shrubs and a few low acacia trees. The number of wells around the town might be considerably augmented, and water obtained for the purposes of irrigation; but the inhabitants of Djidda consider their residence as merely temporary, and, like all the other people of the Hedjaz, devote their whole attention to commerce and the acquisition of riches: on this account they are much less inclined to rural enjoyments or occupations than any other race of Moslems that I ever saw.

Beyond the Báb Mekka, and close to the town, are several huts, through the midst of which lies the road to Mekka. These huts are inhabited by the camel-drivers who traffic between that city and Djidda; by poor Bedouins, who earn a livelihood by cutting wood at a considerable distance in the mountains; and by Negro Hadjis, who adopt the same means of supporting themselves during their stay at Djidda. Here is held the market for live cattle, wood and charcoal, fruits and vegetables in wholesale. Coffee also is sold in many booths in this place, frequented for a short time, at an early hour, by the inferior class of merchants, who resort hither to learn the news from Mekka, whence the post arrives every morning soon after sunrise. About a mile beyond these huts, eastward of the town, is the principal burial-ground, containing the tombs of several sheikhs; but there are smaller cemeteries within the walls. About two miles northward of the town, is shown the tomb of Howa (Eve), the mother of mankind; it is, as I was informed, a rude structure of stone, about four feet in length, two or three feet in height, and as many in breadth; thus resembling the tomb of Noah, seen in the valley of Bekaa, in Syria.

During the predominance of the Wahabis, Djidda had been in a declining state; many of its buildings had gone to ruin; no one constructed a new house; trade was much depressed, in consequence of the pilgrimage from Turkey having been discontinued, and the unwillingness of the merchants to bring their goods hither for sale. Since the recovery of the holy cities, however, and the re-establishment of the pilgrimage, together with the daily arrival of soldiers, and a number of merchants and followers of the army, the town has quickly recovered its former condition, and is now as flourishing as at any former period. The number of its inhabitants may be estimated, generally, at from twelve to fifteen thousand; but in the months preceding the pilgrimage, and again during the summer months corresponding with the monsoon winds, there is a great influx of strangers, which increases the above number perhaps one-half.

The inhabitants of Djidda, like those of Mekka and Medina, are almost exclusively foreigners. The descendants of the ancient Arabs who once peopled the town, have perished by the hands of the governors, or have retired to other countries. Those who can be truly called natives are only a few families of sherifs, who are all learned men, and attached to the mosques or the courts of justice; all the other Djiddawys (people of Ddjidda) are foreigners or their descendants. Of the latter, those from Hadramaut and Yemen are the most numerous: colonies from every town and province of those countries are settled in Djidda, and keep up an active commerce with their native places. Upwards of a hundred Indian families (chiefly from Surat, and a few from Bombay,) have also established themselves here; and to these may be added some Malays and people of Maskat. The settlers from Egypt, Syria, Barbary, European Turkey, and Anatolia, may be still recognised in the features of their descendants, who are all mixed in one general mass, and live and dress in the same Arab manner. The Indians alone remain a distinct race in manners, dress, and employment. There are no Christians settled in Djidda; but a few Greeks from the islands of the Archipelago occasionally bring merchandize to this market from Egypt. In the time of the sherifs they were much molested, compelled to wear a particular dress, and prohibited from approaching the Mekka gate; but the Turks having become masters of the Hedjaz, abolished these restrictions, and a Christian now enjoys complete liberty here : if he dies, he is not buried on shore, (this being sanctified ground, belonging to the holy city,) but upon some one of the small islands in the bay of Djidda. Jews were formerly the brokers of this town ; but they were driven out, about thirty or forty years since, by Serour, the predecessor of Ghaleb, some of them having offended by their misconduct. They all retired to Yemen or to Sanaa. During the monsoons some Banians visit Djidda in the Indian ships : but they always return with them, and none are settled here.

The mixture of races in Djidda is an effect of the pilgrimage, during which rich merchants visit the Hedjaz with large adventures of goods: some of these not being able immediately to settle their accounts, wait till another year; during this period, they cohabit, according to the custom of the country, with some Abyssinian slaves, whom they soon marry; finding themselves at last with a family, they are induced to settle in the country. Thus every pilgrimage adds fresh numbers to the population not only of Djidda, but of Mekka also, which is indeed very necessary, as in both towns the number of deaths is far greater than that of births.

The people of Djidda are almost entirely engaged in commerce, and pursue no manufactures or trades but those of immediate necessity. They are all either sea-faring people, traders by sea, or engaged in the traffic with Arabia. Djidda derives its opulence not only from being the port of Mekka, but it may be considered as that of Egypt, of India, and of Arabia ; all the exports of those countries destined for Egypt first passing through the hands of the Djidda merchants. Hence, it is probably richer than any town of the same size in the Turkish dominions. Its Arabian name, which means " rich," is therefore perfectly well bestowed. The two greatest merchants in the place, Djeylany and Sakkat, both of Maggrebin *

---

* Maggrebin, " inhabitants of the West," is the name given by all the Eastern Arabs to the natives of the Barbary States.

origin, and whose grandfathers first settled here, are known to possess from one hundred and fifty to two hundred thousand pounds sterling. Several Indians have acquired capitals nearly equal, and there are upwards of a dozen houses possessing from forty to fifty thousand pounds sterling. Wholesale trade is carried on here with greater facility and profit, and with less intrigue and fraud, than any where I have seen in the Levant; the principal reason of which is, that almost all the bargains are made for ready money, very little or no credit being given. This, however, is not to be understood as implying any thing favourable to the character of the merchants, who are as notorious for their bad faith as they are for their large fortunes; but the nature of the trade, and the established usage, render it a less troublesome and intriguing business here than in any other country of the East.

The commerce of Djidda may be divided into two principal branches—the coffee trade, and the Indian trade; with both of which that of Egypt is connected. Ships laden with coffee arrive from Yemen all the year round, without being restricted to any particular season. During the voyage, they sail constantly near the coast, and are thus enabled to take advantage of the land breezes during the season when notherly winds prevail, and render the voyage difficult in mid-channel. They dispose of their cargoes for dollars, which are almost the only article that the merchants of Yemen take in return. The coffee trade is liable to great fluctuations, and may be considered a species of lottery, in which those only embark who have large capitals at their command, and who can bear occasionally great losses. The price of coffee at Djidda, being regulated by the advices from Cairo, varies almost with the arrival of every ship from Suez. The price at the latter place depending upon the demand for Mocha coffee in Turkey, is thus equally fluctuating. When I arrived at Djidda, coffee-beans were at thirty-five dollars a hundred-weight; three weeks after they fell to twenty-four dollars, in consequence of the peace between England and America, and the expectation that West-India coffee would be again imported in large quantities at Smyrna and Constantinople. From the hazardous nature of this trade, there are many merchants who will not engage in it, except as agents; others send the coffee on their own account to Cairo, where the chief part of the trade is in the hands of the Hedjaz merchants residing there. Within the last six years, the coffee trade between Arabia and the Mediterranean has suffered greatly by the importation of West-India coffee into the ports of Turkey. These were formerly supplied exclusively with Mocha coffee; the use of which has been almost entirely superseded in European Turkey, Asia Minor, and Syria, by that of the West Indies. The Pasha of Egypt, however, has hitherto strictly prohibited the importation of West-India coffee into his dominions.

The trade in India goods is much safer, and equally profitable. The fleets, principally from Calcutta, Surat, and Bombay, reach Djidda in the beginning of May, when they find the merchants already prepared for them, having collected as many dollars and sequins as their circumstances admit, that they may effect bargains in wholesale at the very first arrival of the ships. Large sums are also sent hither by the Cairo merchants to purchase goods on their account; but the cargoes for the greater part are bought up by the merchants of Djidda, who afterwards send them to Cairo to be sold for their own advantage. The India fleets return in June or July, when the prices of every article brought by them immediately rise;* and it commonly occurs that, on the very day when the last ships sail, ten per cent. profit may be obtained upon the first price. The merchants, however, unless pressed for money, do not sell at this time, but keep their goods in warehouses for four or five

* The ships from Bengal leave Djidda in June, those from Surat and Bombay in July or the beginning of August. The Maskat and Bassora shipping, and the slave vessels from the Mozambique coast, arrive at the same time.

months, during which the price continues to rise; so that if they choose to wait till the January or February following, they may calculate with great security upon a gain of from thirty to forty per cent; and if they transport a part of their goods to Mekka for sale to the Hadj, their profits are still greater. It is the nature of this commerce that renders Djidda so crowded during the stay of the fleet. People repair hither from every port on the Red Sea, to purchase at the first hand; and the merchants of Mekka, Yembo, and Djidda, scrape together every dollar they possess, to lay them out in these purchases.* Another cause of the India trade with Djidda being more safe and profitable is, the arrival of the merchant-ships but once in the year, at a stated period, and all within a few weeks: there is, therefore, nothing to spoil the market; the price of goods is settled according to the known demand and quantity of imports; and it is never known to fall till the return of the next fleet. In the coffee trade it was the reverse.

In Syria and Egypt it is the work of several days, and the business of three or four brokers, to conclude a bargain between two merchants to the amount of a thousand dollars. At Djidda sales and purchases are made of entire ships' cargoes in the course of half an hour, and the next day the money is paid down. The greater part of the merchandize thus bought is shipped for Suez, and sold at Cairo, whence it finds its way into the Mediterranean. The returns are made either in goods, which are disposed of chiefly in the Hedjaz, or in dollars and sequins, large quantities of which are carried off annually by the Indian fleet: this principally causes the scarcity of silver in Egypt. The coffee ships

* Some time after the Indian fleet had sailed from Djidda, I was present when a merchant of great property and respectability called upon an acquaintance of mine to borrow one hundred dollars, saying, he had laid out every farthing of his money in India goods which he did not wish yet to sell, and had, in the mean while, no money left for his daily expenses. This occurs, I understood, very frequently among them.

from Yemen take a few articles of Egyptian manufacture in return, as Mellayes, (blue-striped cotton cloths,) linen stuffs for shirts, and glass beads; but their chief sales are mostly for cash. If Suez were to participate in the direct Indian trade, the present flourishing state of Djidda would, no doubt, be greatly diminished, and the town would become merely what its position renders it, the harbour of the Hedjaz, instead of being, as it now is, the port of Egypt. It was natural that the sherifs of Mekka, who had the customs in their own hands, should endeavour, by every means in their power, to make Djidda an emporium for the Indian trade, the custom-duties on which formed the principle source of their income. Suez, however, is not a place where large capitals are always found ready to make purchases; even Cairo could not, at least immediately, engage in this trade with advantage, were it transferred to Suez; for, according to old customs, from which Orientals seldom like to depart, ready money is almost unknown in the commercial transactions of that city; India goods are in consequence never sold there except at very long credit. Undoubtedly cash might in time have found its way to Suez, as it now does to Djidda; but the channel of trade was such, that a fleet of ships coming direct from India to Suez, would hardly have been able to dispose of their cargoes either with profit or within due time. Another cause also contributed to favour the harbour of Djidda: the India ships, although most of them sail under the English flag, are entirely manned and commanded by the people of the country, Arabs and Lascars;* and they have adopted the same coasting navigation that is followed in every part of the Red

* No English captain had been at Djidda for five years, when, in 1814, the Resoul, Captain Boag, from Bombay, arrived laden with rice. The ships are not navigated by Englishmen, and very few English merchants resident in India have ever speculated in the trade of the Red Sea, which is carried on almost exclusively with the capitals of Muselman merchants of Djidda, Maskat, Bombay, Surat, and Calcutta. The Americans seldom visit any other harbour in this sea than that of Mekka.

Sea. They never venture out to sea, and must, therefore, necessarily pass Djidda and Yembo, both harbours of the Sherif, who could easily oblige them to anchor in his ports and pay duties, as he is known to have done with many coffee ships bound direct for Suez from Yemen. These causes, however, no longer exist; for Mohammed Aly, Pasha of Egypt, having possession of the harbours and custom-houses of the Hedjaz, might transfer the customs of Djidda to Suez, and thence open a direct communication with India. The chief obstacles to such a change which have hitherto presented shemselves, are the jealousy and false representations of the merchants of Djidda, and the Pasha's ignorance of his own real interests, added perhaps to the fear of displeasing his sovereign; he has it, notwithstanding, in contemplation to change the system, after the example of a very respectable English house at Alexandria, which had, in concert with its correspondents at Bombay, in 1812, when the Hedjaz was not yet in the Pasha's hands, concluded a treaty with him for allowing English ships to come direct to Suez, and for insuring the protection of merchandize across the Desert to Cairo. The reports of the Wahabi war, and of hostile cruisers in the Red Sea, prevented the merchants from taking advantage of the treaty till 1815, when a large ship was despatched from Bombay to Suez. The Pasha, however, who was at Mekka when she touched at Djidda, in direct violation of his engagements, stopped the ship, prohibited her proceeding to Suez, compelled the captain to sell the cargo at a loss, while the plague was raging in the town, and exacted the same duties as are taken on country ships, in contravention of the stipulations existing between Great Britain and the Porte. This affair, which created great disgust amongst the Europeans in Egypt, might easily have been remedied by retaliation upon the Pasha's ships trading to Malta, which would have taught him to respect the British flag wherever he might meet it. The British officers, however, from an erroneous conception perhaps of his power and importance, and from a wish to remain upon a friendly footing with him, instead of evincing any displeasure, preferred submitting silently to the outrage; forgetting that the favour of a Turkish ruler can never be bought by conciliation, but can only be obtained by an attitude of defiance. In consequence of all this, the merchants were obliged to make a second treaty with the Pasha, which was formally ratified. His first demand was, that the ships should pay at Suez the joint customs of that port and Djidda, which would have been equivalent to about 12 per cent.; but he contented himself, at last, with a promise of 9 per cent. upon all imports into Suez from India, which was six per cent. more than the usual duty paid by European merchants in the ports of the Grand Signior. This arrangement, it is supposed, will lead to the opening of an active trade. The Pasha himself is disposed to speculate on his own account; and the first adventure he sent to Bombay, in the spring of 1816, was to bring him, in return, a richly caparisoned elephant, destined as a present to his sovereign at Constantinople. Still, however, I am afraid he will as little respect the second treaty as he did the first; for his avarice, if not effectually checked, knows no bounds, and he can at any time exact additional imposts, as far as the profits of this new commercial route can bear them, by threatening the security of the road from Suez to Cairo, the Bedouins of the neighbouring Desert being completely at his command.

The former master of Djidda, Sherif Ghaleb, was actively engaged in the Indian trade; he had two ships, of four hundred tons each, employed in it, besides many smaller vessels in the coffee trade to Yemen; indeed, he was a shrewd speculator in all branches of the Red Sea trade. He oppressed the merchants of Djidda by heavy duties and his own powerful competition; but he was never known to practise extortion upon them. If he borrowed money, he repaid it at the stipulated time, and never ventured to levy extraordinary contributions from individuals, although he did it from the whole community, by increasing the duties in an arbitrary manner. It was the well-known security which property enjoyed under his government that induced foreign merchants to visit the port of Djidda, even when Ghaleb was reduced to great distress by the Wahabis. His conduct, however, in this respect, was not caused by any love of justice, for he governed most despotically; but he well knew that, if the merchants should be frightened away, his town would sink into insignificance. Towards the close of his government, the duty upon coffee was increased by him from two and a half to five dollars per quintal, or to about fifteen per cent. The duty upon India goods was from six to ten per cent., according to their quality. If Ghaleb could not immediately sell the coffee or India goods imported on his account, he distributed the cargoes of his ships among the native merchants of the place at the current market-price, in quantities proportioned to the supposed property of each merchant, who was thus forced to become a purchaser for ready money. In this respect Ghaleb was not singular; for in Egypt the present Pasha frequently distributes his coffee among the merchants; with this difference, however, from the practice of Ghaleb, that the price which he exacts is always above the real market-price.

Business in Djidda is conducted through the intervention of brokers, who are for the most part Indians of small property and bad reputations.

The number of ships belonging to Djidda is very great. Taking into account all the small vessels employed in the Red Sea trade, two hundred and fifty perhaps may be calculated as belonging either to merchants of the town, or to owners, who navigate them, and who consider the port as their principal home. The different names given to these ships, as Say, Seume, Merkeb, Sambouk, Dow, denote their size; the latter only, being the largest, perform the voyage to India. The ships are navigated chiefly by people from Yemen, from the Somawly coast (opposite to Aden, between Abyssinia and Cape Guardafui,) and by slaves, of which latter three or four are generally found in every ship. The crew receive a certain sum for the voyage, and every sailor is, at the same time, a petty trader on his own account; this is another cause of the resort of foreigners to Djidda during the trade winds, for persons with the smallest capitals can purchase goods in retail, at the first hand, from the crews of these ships. No vessels of any kind are now constructed at Djidda, so scarce has timber become; indeed, it is with difficulty that means are found to repair a ship. Yembo is subject to the same inconvenience. Suez, Hadeyda, and Mokha, are the only harbours in the Red Sea where ships are built. The timber used at Suez is transported thither overland from Cairo, and comes originally from the coast of Asia Minor :* that employed at Hadeyda and Mokha comes partly from Yemen, and partly from the African coast. Many ships are purchased at Bombay and Maskat; but those built at Suez are most common in the sea north of Yemen. There has been a great want of shipping at Djidda during the last three years, as the Pasha had seized a great number of ships, and obliged their owners to transport provisions, ammunition, and baggage, from Egypt to the Hedjaz, for which he pays a very low freight. During my stay at Djidda, scarcely a day passed without some arrival by sea, chiefly from Yembo and Cosseir ; and there were constantly forty or fifty ships in the harbour. An officer, entitled Emir al Bahhr, acts as harbour-master, and takes from each ship a certain sum for anchorage. This was an office of considerable dignity in the time of the sherif, but it has now sunk into insignificance. I was somewhat surprised to find that, in so well-frequented a port as Djidda, there were no pleasure-boats of any kind in the harbour, nor even any regular public boatmen ; but I learned that this proceeded from the jea-

* The canvas used all over the Red Sea is of Egyptian manufacture. The cordage is of the date-tree. Ships coming from the East Indies have cordage made of the cocoa-nut tree, of which a quantity is also brought for sale.

lousy of the custom-house officers, who forbid all craft of this description, and even insist that the ships' boats should return to the ships after sunset.

Djidda carries on no trade by land, except with Medina and Mekka. A caravan departs for Medina once in forty or fifty days, principally with India goods and drugs, and is always augmented by a crowd of pilgrims who wish to visit Mohammed's tomb. These caravans consist of from sixty to one hundred camels, and are conducted by the Harb Bedouins. The intercourse, however, between Djidda and Medina is more commonly carried on by the intermediate route of Yembo, whither merchandize is sent by sea. Besides the caravans above mentioned, others depart for Mekka almost every evening, and at least twice a week, with goods and provisions; and during the four months preceding the Hadj, when every ship that arrives brings pilgrims to Djidda, this intercourse farther increases, and caravans then set out regularly from the gate called Báb Mekka every evening after sunset. The loaded camels take two nights to perform the journey, resting midway at Hadda during the day; but, in addition to these, a small caravan of asses, lightly laden, starts also every evening, and performs the journey of fifteen or sixteen hours in one night, arriving regularly at Mekka early in the morning.* It is by the ass-caravan that letters are conveyed between the two towns. In time of peace, caravans are occasionally met with on the sea-coast, towards Yemen, and the interior of Tehama, to Mokhowa, whence corn is imported. (V. Appendix on the Geography of the Hedjaz.)

The following enumeration of the different shops in the principal commercial street of Djidda, may throw some light on the

* When camels abound, the hire of one from Djidda to Mekka is from twenty to twenty-five piastres. In time of scarcity, or at the approach of the Hadj, from sixty to seventy piastres are paid. During my stay, the hire of an ass from Djidda to Mekka was twenty piastres. These prices would be considered enormous in any other part of the Levant. Only fifteen piastres are paid for a camel from Cairo to Suez, which is double the distance between Djidda and Mekka.

trade of the town, as well as on the mode of living of its inhabitants. The shops (as in all parts of Turkey) are raised several feet above ground, and have before them, projecting into the street, a stone bench, on which purchasers seat themselves; this is sheltered from the sun by an awning usually made of mats fastened to high poles. Many of the shops are only six or seven feet wide in front; the depth is generally from ten to twelve feet, with a small private room or magazine behind.

There are twenty-seven coffee-shops. Coffee is drunk to excess in the Hedjaz; it is not uncommon for persons to drink twenty or thirty cups in one day, and the poorest labourer never takes less than three or four cups. In a few of the shops may be had keshre, made from the skin of the bean, which is scarcely inferior in flavour to that made from the bean itself. One of the shops is frequented by those who smoke the *hashysh*, or a preparation of hemp-flowers mixed with tobacco, which produces a kind of intoxication. Hashysh is still more used in Egypt, especially among the peasants.*

In all these shops the Persian pipe is smoked, of which there

---

* Of the hemp-flowers, they use for this purpose the small leaves standing round the seed, (called *sheranek*.) The common people put a small quantity of them upon the top of the tobacco with which their pipes are filled. The higher classes eat it in a jelly or paste (*maadjoun*) made in the following manner:—a quantity of the leaves is boiled with butter for several hours, and then put under a press; the juice so expressed is mixed with honey and other sweet drugs, and publicly sold in Egypt, where shops are kept for that purpose. The Hashysh paste is politely termed *bast*, and those who sell it *basty* (i. e. cheerfulness). On the occasion of a festival to celebrate the marriage of a son of one of the principal grandees at Cairo, when all the different crafts of the town were represented in a showy procession, the *basty*, although exercising a business prohibited and condemned by the law, was among the most gaudy. Many persons of the first rank use the *bast* in some shape or other; it exhilarates the spirits, and raises the imagination as violently as opium. Some persons also mix the paste with seeds of the *Bendj*, which comes from Syria.

are three different sorts. 1. The *Kedra*, which is the largest, and rests upon a tripod; it is always neatly worked, and found only in private houses. 2. The *Shishe* (called in Syria *Argyle*), of a smaller size, but, like the former, joined to a long serpentine tube (called *lieh*), through which the smoke is inhaled. 3. The *Bury*. This consists of an unpolished cocoa-nut shell, which contains water; a thick reed answers the purpose of the serpentine tube: this pipe is the constant companion of the lower classes, and of all the sailors of the Red Sea, who indulge most inordinately in using it. The tobacco smoked in the two former of these pipes comes from the Persian gulf; the best is from Shiraz. An inferior sort (called *tombak*) comes from Basra and Baghdad; the leaf is of a light yellow colour, and much stronger in taste than common tobacco; it is, therefore, previously washed to render it milder. The *tombak* used in the *Bury* comes from Yemen, and is of the same species as the other, but of an inferior quality. The trade in this article is very considerable, its consumption in the Hedjaz being almost incredibly great; large quantities are also shipped for Egypt. The common pipe is little used in the Hedjaz, except by Turkish soldiers and Bedouins. The tobacco is of Egyptian growth, or from Sennar, whence it is carried to Sowakin. Very little good Syrian tobacco finds its way across the Red Sea.

The coffee-houses are filled with people during the whole day; and in front a shed is generally erected, under which persons also sit. The rooms, benches, and small low chairs, are very filthy, and form a contrast to the neatness and elegance observable in the coffee-houses of Damascus. Respectable merchants are never seen in a coffee-house; but those of the third class, and sea-faring people, make it their constant resort. Every person has his particular house, where he meets those who have business with him. An Arab, who cannot afford to ask his friend to dine, invites him from the coffee-house, when he sees him pass, to enter and take a cup, and is highly offended if the invitation be rejected. When his friend enters, he orders the waiter to bring him a cup, and the waiter, in presenting it, exclaims aloud, so that every one in the place may hear him, *djebba!* (gratis). An Arab may cheat his creditors, or be guilty of bad faith in his dealings, and yet escape public censure; but he would be covered with infamy, if it were known that he had attempted to cheat the coffee-house waiter of his due. The Turkish soldiers have done their utmost in this respect to increase the contempt in which they are held by the Arabs. I never saw in the coffee-houses of the Hedjaz any of those story-tellers who are so common in Egypt, and still more in Syria. The Mangal * is generally played in all of them, and the Dama, " a kind of draughts," differing somewhat from the European game; but I never happened to see chess played in the Hedjaz, though I heard that it is not uncommon, and that the sherifs in particular are fond of it.

Near to almost every coffee-shop a person takes his stand, who sells cooled water in small perfumed jars.†

Twenty-one butter-sellers, who likewise retail honey, oil, and vinegar. Butter forms the chief article in Arab cookery, which is more greasy than even that of Italy. Fresh butter, called by the Arabs *zebde*, is very rarely seen in the Hedjaz. It is a common practice amongst all classes to drink every morning a coffee-cup full of melted butter or *ghee*, after which coffee is taken. They regard it as a powerful tonic, and are so much accustomed to it from their earliest youth, that they would feel great inconvenience in discontinuing the use of it. The higher classes content themselves

---

* See Niebuhr's Travels.

† The Orientals often drink water before coffee, but never immediately after. I was once recognised in Syria as a foreigner or European, in consequence of having called for water just after I had taken coffee. "If you were of this country," said the waiter, "you would not spoil the taste of the coffee in your mouth by washing it away with water."

with *drinking* the quantity of butter, but the lower orders add a half-cup more, which they *snuff* up their nostrils, conceiving that they prevent foul air from entering the body by that channel. The practice is universal as well with the inhabitants of the town as with the Bedouins. The lower classes are likewise in the habit of rubbing their breasts, shoulders, arms, and legs, with butter, as the negroes do, to refresh the skin. During the war, the import of this article from the interior had almost entirely ceased; but even in time of peace, it is not sufficient for the consumption of Djidda; some is, therefore, brought also from Sowakin; but the best sort, and that which is in greatest plenty, comes from Massowah, and is called here *Dahlak* butter: whole ships' cargoes arrive from thence, the greater part of which is again carried to Mekka. Butter is likewise imported from Cosseir; this comes from Upper Egypt, and is made from buffaloes' milk; the Sowakin and Dahlak ghee is from sheep's milk.

The Hedjaz abounds with honey in every part of the mountains. The best comes from those which are inhabited by the Nowaszera Bedouins, to the south of Tayf. Among the lower classes, a common breakfast is a mixture of ghee and honey poured over crumbs of bread as they come quite hot from the oven. The Arabs, who are very fond of paste, never eat it without honey.

The oil used for lamps is that of Sesamum (Seeredj, brought from Egypt). The Arabs do not use oil for culinary purposes, except in frying fish, or with broken paste to be given to the poor. Salad, of which the northern Turks are so fond, is never seen on an Arabian table.

Eighteen vegetable or fruit-stands. The number of these has now greatly increased, on account of the Turkish troops, who are great devourers of vegetables. All the fruits come from Tayf, behind Mekka, which is rich in gardens. I found here in July grapes of the best kind, with which the mountains behind Mekka abound; pomegranates of middling quality; quinces, which have not the harsh taste of those in Europe, and may be eaten raw; peaches; lemons of the smallest size only, like those of Cairo; bitter oranges; bananas—these do not grow at Tayf, but are brought by the Medina road principally from Safra, Djedeyda, and Kholeys. These fruits last till November. In March, water melons are brought from Wady Fatmé, which are said to be small, but of a good flavour. The Arabs eat little fruit except grapes; they say it produces bile, and occasions flatulency, in which they are probably not mistaken. The fruit sold at Djidda is particularly unwholesome; for having been packed up at Tayf in an unripe state, it acquires a factitious maturity by fermentation during the journey. The Turks quarrel and fight every morning before the shops, in striving to get the fruits, which are in small quantities and very dear. Vegetables are brought to Djidda from Wady Fatmé, six or eight miles distant to the north, which also supplies Mekka. The usual kinds are Meloukhye, Bamye, Portulaca egg-plants, or Badingans, cucumbers, and very small turnips, of which the leaves are eaten, and the root is thrown away as useless. Radishes and leeks are the only vegetables regularly and daily used in Arab cookery; they are very small, and the common people eat them raw with bread. In general, the Arabs consume very few vegetables, their dishes being made of meat, rice, flour, and butter. In these fruit-shops, tamarind (called here *Hōmar*) is also sold; it comes from the East Indies, not in cakes, like that from the negro countries, but in its natural form, though much decomposed. When boiled in water, it constitutes a refreshing beverage, and is given to sick people boiled with meat into a stew.

Eight date-sellers. Of all eatables used by the Arabs, dates are the most favourite; and they have many traditions from their prophet, showing the pre-eminence of dates above all other kinds of food. The importation of dates is uninterrupted during the whole year. At the end of June, the new fruit (called *ruteb*) comes in: this lasts for two months, after which, for the remainder of the year, the date-paste, called *adjoue*, is sold. This is formed by pressing the dates, when fully ripe, into large baskets so forcibly as to reduce them to a hard solid paste or cake, each basket weighing generally about two hundred weight; in this state the Bedouins export the adjoue; in the market it is cut out of the basket and sold by the pound. This adjoue forms a part of the daily food among all classes of people. In travelling, it is dissolved in water, and thus affords a sweet and refreshing drink. There are upwards of twelve different sorts of adjoue; the best comes from Taraba, behind Tayf (now occupied by the Wahabis.) The most common kind at present in the market is that from Fatmé; and the better sort, that from Kheleys, and Djedeyde, on the road to Medina. During the monsoon, the ships from the Persian gulf bring adjoue from Basra for sale, in small baskets, weighing about ten pounds each; this kind is preferred to every other. The East-India ships, on their return, take off a considerable quantity of the paste, which is sold to great profit among the muselmans of Hindostan.

Four pancake-makers, who sell, early in the morning, pancakes fried in butter; a favourite breakfast.

Five bean-sellers. These sell for breakfast also, at an early hour, Egyptian horse-beans boiled in water, which are eaten with ghee and pepper. The boiled beans are called *mudammes*; they form a favourite dish with the people of Egypt, from whom the Arabs have adopted it.

Five sellers of sweetmeats, sugar-plums, and different sorts of confectionary, of which the Hedjaz people are much fonder than any Orientals I have seen; they eat them after supper, and in the evening the confectioners' stands are surrounded by multitudes of buyers. The Indians are the best makers of them. I saw no articles of this kind here that I had not already found in Egypt; the *Baklawa*, *Gnafe*, and *Ghereybe*, are as common here as at Aleppo and Cairo.

Two *kebab* shops, where roasted meat is sold; these are kept by Turks, the *kebab* not being an Arab dish.

Two soup-sellers, who also sell boiled sheep's heads and feet, and are much visited at mid-day.

One seller of fish fried in oil, frequented by all the Turkish and Greek sailors.

Ten or twelve stands where bread is sold, generally by women; the bread has an unpleasant flavour, the meal not having been properly cleansed, and the leaven being bad. A loaf of the same size as that which at Cairo is sold for two paras, costs here, though of a much worse quality, eight paras.

Two sellers of *leben*, or sour milk, which is extremely scarce and dear all over the Hedjaz. It may appear strange that, among the shepherds of Arabia, there should be a scarcity of milk, yet this was the case at Djidda and Mekka; but, in fact, the immediate vicinity of these towns is extremely barren, little suited to the pasturage of cattle, and very few people are at the expense of feeding them for their milk only. When I was at Djidda, the rotolo or pound of milk (for it is sold by weight) cost one piastre and a half, and could only be obtained by favour. What the northern Turks called *yoghort*, and the Syrians and Egyptians *leben-hamed*,* does not appear to be a native Arab dish; the Bedouins of Arabia, at least, never prepare it.

Two shops, kept by Turks, where Greek cheese, dried meat, dried apples, figs, raisins, apricots, called *kammared'din*, &c. are sold at three times the price paid in Cairo. The cheese comes from Candia, and is much in request among all the Turkish troops. An indifferent sort of cheese is made in the Hedjaz; it is extremely white, although salted, does not keep long, and is not by any means very nutritive. The Bedouins themselves care little for cheese; they either drink their milk, or make it into butter. The dried meat sold in these shops is the salted and smoked beef of Asia Minor, known all over Turkey by the name of *bastorma*, and

---

* Very thick milk, rendered sour by boiling and the addition of a strong acid.

much relished by travellers. The Turkish soldiers and the Hadjis are particularly fond of it, but the Arabs never can be induced to taste it; many of them, observing that it differs in appearance from all other meat with which they are acquainted, persist in regarding it as pork, and the estimation in which they hold the Turkish soldiery and their religious principles is not likely to remove their prejudices on this head. All the dried fruits above mentioned, except the apricots, come from the Archipelago; the latter are sent from Damascus all over Arabia, where they are considered a luxury, particularly among the Bedouins. The stone is extracted and the fruit reduced to a paste, and spread out upon its leaves to dry in the sun. It makes a very pleasant sauce when dissolved in water. On all their marches through the Hedjaz, the Turkish troops live almost entirely upon biscuit and this fruit.

Eleven large shops of corn-dealers, where Egyptian wheat, barley, beans, lentils, dhourra,* Indian and Egyptian rice, biscuits, &c. may be purchased. The only wheat now sold in the Hedjaz comes from Egypt. In time of peace, there is a considerable importation from Yemen into Mekka and Djidda, and from Nedjed to Medina; but the imports from Egypt are by far the most considerable, and the Hedjaz may truly be said to depend upon Egypt for corn. The corn-trade was formerly in the hands of individuals, and the Sherif Ghaleb also speculated in it; but at present, Mohammed Aly Pasha has taken it entirely into his own hands, and none is sold either at Suez or Cosseir to private persons, every grain being shipped on account of the Pasha. This is likewise the case with all other provisions, as rice, butter, biscuits, onions, of which latter great quantities are imported. At the time of my residence in the Hedjaz, this country not producing a sufficiency, the Pasha sold the grain at Djidda for the price of

* Or *durra*, from Sowakin, which comes from Taka, in the interior of Nubia, and a small-grained sort from Yemen, are also sold here.

from one hundred and thirty to one hundred and sixty piastres per *erdeb*, and every other kind of provision in proportion; the corn cost him twelve piastres by the erdeb in Upper Egypt, and including the expense of carriage from Genne to Cosseir, and freight thence to Djidda, twenty-five or thirty piastres. This enormous profit was alone sufficient to defray his expenses in carrying on the Wahaby war; but it was little calculated to conciliate the good-will of the people. His partisans, however, excused him, by alleging that, in keeping grain at high prices, he secured the Bedouins of the Hedjaz in his interest, as they depend upon Mekka and Djidda for provisions, and they were thus compelled to enter into his service, and receive his pay, to escape starvation. The common people of the Hedjaz use very little wheat; their bread is made either of durra or barley-flour, both of which are one-third cheaper than wheat; or they live entirely upon rice and butter. This is the case also with most of the Bedouins of Tehama, on the coast. The Yemen people in Djidda eat nothing but durra. Most of the rice used at Djidda is brought as ballast by the ships from India. The best sort comes from Guzerat and Cutch: it forms the chief article of food among the people of the Hedjaz, who prefer it to the rice from Egypt, because they think it more wholesome than the former, which is used exclusively by the Turks and other strangers from the northward. The grain of the Indian rice is larger and longer than the common sort of Egypt, and is of a yellowish colour; whereas the latter has a reddish tint; but the best sorts of both are snow-white. The Indian rice swells more in boiling than the Egyptian, and is for this reason preferred by the Arabs, as a smaller quantity of it will fill a dish; but the Egyptian rice is more nutritive. The Indian rice is rather cheaper, and is transported from Djidda to Mekka, Tayf, Medina, and thence as far as Nedjed. A mixture of equal portions of rice and lentils, over which butter is poured, forms a favourite preparation with the middle class, and generally their only dish at supper.* I found, in every part of the Hedjaz, that the Bedouins, when travelling, carried no other provision than rice, lentils, butter, and dates. The importation of biscuits from Egypt has of late been very considerable, for the use of the Turkish army. The Arabians do not like and seldom eat them even on board their ships, where they bake their unleavened cake every morning in those small ovens which are found in all the ships of every size that navigate the Red Sea.

Salt is sold by the corn-dealers. Sea-salt is collected near Djidda, and is a monopoly in the hands of the sherif. The inhabitants of Mekka prefer rock-salt, which is brought thither by the Bedouins from some mountains in the neighbourhood of Tayf.

Thirty-one tobacco-shops, in which are sold Syrian and Egyptian tobacco, tombac, or tobacco for the Persian pipe, pipe-heads and pipe-snakes, cocoa-nuts, coffee-beans, keshre, soap, almonds, Hedjaz raisins, and some other articles of grocery. The Egyptian tobacco, sometimes mixed with that of Sennar, is the cheapest, and in great demand throughout the Hedjaz. There are two sorts of it: the leaf of one is green, even when dry; this is called *ribbé*, and comes from Upper Egypt: the other is brown-leaved, the best sort of which grows about Tahta, to the south of Siout. During the power of the Wahabys, tobacco could not be sold publicly; but as all the Bedouins of the Hedjaz are passionately fond of it, persons sold it clandestinely in their shops, not as tobacco or *dokhan*, but under the name of " the wants of a man." Long snakes for the Persian pipe, very prettily worked, are imported from Yemen. Cocoa-nuts are brought from the East Indies, as well as from the south-eastern coast of Africa and the Somawly country, and may

---

* This dish is known in Syria, and called there *medjeddereh*, because the lentils in the rice look like a person's face marked with the small-pox, or *djedreh*.

be had quite fresh, at low prices, during the monsoon. The people of Djidda and Mekka appear to be very fond of them. The larger nuts, as already mentioned, are used for the *boury*, or common Persian pipe, and the smallest for snuff-boxes.

Soap comes from Suez, whither it is carried from Syria, which supplies the whole coast of the Red Sea with it. The soap-trade is considerable, and, for the greater part, in the hands of the merchants from Hebron, (called in Arabic *el Khalyl* or the *Khalylis*,) who bring it to Djidda, where some of them are always to be found. The almonds and raisins come from Tayf and the Hedjaz mountains; large quantities of both are exported, even to the East Indies. The almonds are of most excellent quality; the raisins are small and quite black, but very sweet. An intoxicating liquor is prepared from them.

Eighteen druggists. These are all natives of the East Indies, and mostly from Surat. In addition to all kinds of drugs, they sell wax candles, paper, sugar, perfumery, and incense; the latter is much used by the inhabitants of the towns, where all the respectable families perfume their best rooms every morning. Mastic and sandal-wood, burnt upon charcoal, are most commonly used for this purpose. Spices of all sorts, and heating drugs, are universally used in the Hedjaz. Coffee is rarely drunk in private houses without a mixture of cardamoms or cloves; and red pepper, from India or Egypt, enters into every dish. A considerable article of trade among the druggists of Djidda and Mekka consists in rose-buds, brought from the gardens of Tayf. The people of the Hedjaz, especially the ladies, steep them in water, which they afterwards use for their ablutions; they also boil these roses with sugar, and make a conserve of them. The sugar sold in the druggists' shops is brought from India; it is of a yellowish white colour, and well refined, but in powder. A small quantity of Egyptian sugar is imported, but the people here do not like it; in general, they prefer every thing that comes from India, which they conceive to be of a superior quality; in the same manner as English produce and manufactures are preferred on the continent of Europe. The Indian druggists are all men of good property; their trade is very lucrative, and no Arabs can rival them in it. At Mekka, also, and at Tayf, Medina, and Yembo, all the druggists are of Indian descent; and although they have been established in the country for several generations, and completely naturalized, yet they continue to speak the Hindu language, and distinguish themselves in many trifling customs from the Arabs, by whom they are in general greatly disliked, and accused of avarice and fraud.

Eleven shops where small articles of Indian manufacture are sold, such as china-ware, pipe-heads, wooden spoons, glass beads, knives, rosaries, mirrors, cards, &c. These shops are kept by Indians, mostly from Bombay. Very little European hardware finds its way hither, except needles, scissors, thimbles, and files; almost every thing else of this kind comes from India. The earthenware of China is greatly prized in the Hedjaz. The rich inhabitants display very costly collections of it, disposed upon shelves in their sitting-rooms, as may be remarked also in Syria. I have seen, both at Mekka and Djidda, china dishes brought to table, measuring at least two feet and a half in diameter, carried by two persons, and containing a sheep roasted entire. The glass beads exported from Djidda are chiefly for the Souakin and Abyssinian market; they are partly of Venetian and partly of Hebron manufacture. The Bedouin women of the Hedjaz likewise wear them; though bracelets, made of black horn, and amber necklaces, seem to be more in fashion among them. It is in these shops that the agate beads, called reysh,* are sold, which come from Bombay, and are used in the very heart of Africa. A kind of red beads, made of wax, are seen here in great quantities; they come from India, and are

* See Travels in Nubia, article Shendy.

mostly destined for Abyssinia. Of rosaries, a great variety is sold: those made of *yosser** are the most costly; it is a species of coral which grows in the Red Sea. The best sort is found between Djidda and Gonfode, is of a deep black colour, and takes a fine polish. Strings of one hundred beads each are sold at from one to four dollars, according to their size. They are made by the turners of Djidda, and are much in demand for the Malays. Other rosaries, (also brought from India,) made of the odoriferous *kalambac*, and of the sandal-wood, are in great demand throughout Egypt and Syria. Few pilgrims leave the Hedjaz without taking from the holy cities some of these rosaries, as presents to their friends at home.

Eleven clothes-shops. In these various articles of dress are sold every morning by public auction. The greater part of those dresses are of the Turkish fashion, adopted by merchants of the first and second classes, with some trifling national variations in the cut of the clothes. During the period of the Hadj, these shops are principally frequented for the purchase of the Hiram or Ihram, that mantle in which the pilgrimage is performed, and which consists generally of two long pieces of white Indian cambric. Here, too, the Hedjaz Bedouins come to buy the woollen abbas, or Bedouin cloaks, brought from Egypt, on which country they entirely depend for this article; and thus they seem to possess the same indolent character as most people of the Hedjaz; for it is customary with the wives of other Bedouins to fabricate their own abbas. Here, also, they bring Turkish carpets of an inferior quality, which form an indispensable article of furniture for the tent of a Sheikh. In these shops are likewise retailed all other imports from Egypt necessary for dress, as mellayes, cotton quilts, linen for shirts, shirts dyed blue, worn by the peasants, red and yellow slip-

---

* From this, the principal lane of Djidda is called *Hosh Yosser*.

pers, used by the more opulent merchants, and by all the ladies, red caps, all kinds of cloth dresses, second-hand cashmere shawls, muslin shawls, &c. &c.

Six large shops of Indian piece-goods: French cloth, cashmere shawls, &c. belonging to respectable merchants, whose clerks here sell by retail. Almost all the principal merchants carry on also a retail business in their own houses, except the great Indian merchants established here, who deal in nothing but Indian piece-goods. The other merchants of Djidda engage in every branch of commerce. I once saw the brother of Djeylany quarrelling with a Yembo pedlar about the price of a *mellaye*, worth about fifteen shillings; but this is the case also in Egypt and Syria, where the most wealthy native merchants sell in retail, and enter into all the minute details of business, and yet without keeping any large establishment of clerks or accomptants, which their mode of conducting business renders little necessary. A Turkish merchant never keeps more than one accompt-book; into this he copies from a pocket-book his weekly sales and purchases. They have not that extensive correspondence which European merchants are obliged to keep up; and they write much less, though perhaps more to the purpose, than the latter. In every town with which they traffic, they have one friend, with whom they annually balance accounts. Turkish merchants, with the exception of those living in sea-ports, generally pursue but one branch of trade; maintaining a correspondence with the town only from whence they obtain their merchandize, and with that to which they transport it. Thus, for instance, the great Baghdad merchants of Aleppo, men with from thirty to forty thousand pounds in capital, receive goods from their friends at Baghdad, and then send them from Aleppo to Constantinople. I have known many of them who kept no clerk, but transacted the whole of their business themselves. At Cairo, the Syrian merchants trade in the stuffs of Damascus and Aleppo, and are altogether unconnected with the Maggrebin, Syria, and Djidda merchants.

Mercantile transactions are farther simplified by the traders employing chiefly their own capital, commission business being much less extensive than it is in Europe. When a merchant consigns a considerable quantity of goods to a place, he sends a partner with them, or perhaps a relative, if he have no partner resident in the place. Banking concerns and bills of exchange are wholly unknown among the natives, which saves them much trouble. In those towns where European factories are established, bills may be found, but they are hardly current with the natives, among whom assignments only are customary.

The practice followed equally by Mahomedan, Christian, and Jewish merchants, in the East, of never drawing an exact balance of the actual state of their capital, is another cause that renders the details of book-keeping less necessary here than in Europe. For the same reason that a Bedouin never counts the tents of his tribe, nor the exact number of his sheep, nor a military chief the exact number of his men, nor a governor the number of inhabitants of his town, a merchant never attempts to ascertain the exact amount of his property; an approximation only is all that he desires. This arises from a belief that counting is an ostentatious display of wealth, which heaven will punish by a speedy diminution.

The Eastern merchant seldom enters into hazardous speculations, but limits his transactions to the extent of his capital. Credit to a great amount is obtained with difficulty, as affairs of individuals are in general much more publicly known than in Europe; failures are, therefore, of rare occurrence; and when a man becomes embarrassed either from an unsuccessful speculation or inevitable losses, his creditors forbear to press their demands, and are generally paid after a few years' patience;

thereby saving the merchant's credit, and preventing the consequences of bankruptcy.

On the other hand, however, the Eastern merchants are liable to the imputation of uncertainty in their payments, which they often delay beyond the stipulated periods. Even the most respectable among them do not hesitate to put off the payment of a debt for months; and it may be stated as a general rule in Egypt and Syria, that assignments are never fully paid till after a lapse of nearly double the time named. But this, I was often assured by the best informed people here, has only become the practice within the last twenty or thirty years, and is a consequence of the universal decay of commerce and diminution of capital in the Levant. At Djidda, as I have already observed, almost all bargains are made for ready money.

Three sellers of copper vessels. A variety of well-tinned copper vessels may be found in every Arabian kitchen. Even the Bedouins have one capacious boiler, at least, in every tent. The whole of these come from Egypt. The most conspicuous article of this description is the *abrik*, or water-pot, with which the Muselman performs his ablutions. No Turkish pilgrim arrives in the Hedjaz without one of these pots, or at least he purchases one at Djidda. There are found, also, in the market a few copper vessels from China, brought hither by the Malays; but they are not tinned, and though the copper seems to be of a much finer quality than that of Anatolia, which is brought from Cairo, the Arabs dislike to use it.

Four barbers' shops. The barbers are at once the surgeons and physicians of this country. They know how to let blood, and to compound different sorts of aperient medicines. The few Arabians whose beards are longer and thicker than those of their countrymen usually are, take great pains in keeping them neatly cut, so that not a hair may project beyond another. The mustachios are always cut closely, and never allowed to hang over the lips; in this they differ from the northern Turks, who seldom touch their thick bushy mustachios with scissors. The barbers' shops are frequented by loungers of the lower classes, who resort thither to hear the news, and amuse themselves with conversation. In one of these shops I found established a seal-engraver of Persian origin; he had a good deal of business, for a pilgrim, after he has performed his visits to the holy places, usually adds to the name on his seal the words *El Hadjy*, or " The Pilgrim."

Four tailors. Many others live in various parts of the town; they are mostly foreigners. Tousoun Pasha's court-tailor was a Christian of Bosnia, and exercised authority over all the other tailors in the town; who complained bitterly of being subjected, not only to the commands and insults, but often to the stick of this Christian.

Five makers of *nâl*, or sandals. There is not one shoe-maker in the Hedjaz. Those who wear shoes or slippers buy them of the merchants by whom they are imported from Egypt.

The shape of the sandals used throughout Arabia differs in every province; and to those delineated by Niebuhr, a dozen other forms might be added. Some are peculiar to certain classes: a merchant, for instance, would not wear the sandals of a mariner. This is the case in Turkey with regard to shoes, of which each province and class has its particular shape. Egypt and Abyssinia furnish the thick leather used in making sandals.

Three shops where water-skins brought from Sowakin and Egypt are sold and repaired. The greater part of the Hedjaz is furnished with water-skins from Sowakin; they are in great request, being very light, and sewed with much neatness. A Sowakin water-skin will last, in daily use, about three or four months.

Two turners, who bore pipe-tubes, and make beads, &c.

Three sellers of sweet-oils or essences, civet, aloe-wood, balsam of Mekka, and rose-water from Fayoum in Egypt. The civet and Mekka balsam can seldom be bought pure, except at first hand. The Habesh or Abyssinian merchants bring the civet in large cow-horns; they sold it at four piastres per drachm in the year 1814. Musk also is sold in these shops, the best at two dollars per metkal. It is brought hither by the Indian and Persian Hadjys.

One watchmaker, a Turk. All the Mekka and Djidda merchants wear watches, many of which are of good English manufacture; they are brought either from India, or by the Hadjys from Constantinople. As it often happens that the Turkish pilgrims want money in the Hedjaz, they are sometimes compelled to dispose of their most valuable articles; the watch is always the first, then the pistols and sabre, and lastly the fine pipe, and best copy of the Korán: all these articles are consequently very common in the auction-markets of Djidda and Mekka.

One seller of Turkish and Persian tobacco-pipes. The latter come principally from Baghdad. The wealthy often display in their sitting-rooms a whole range of the finest *nargils*: these cost as much as one hundred dollars a piece.

Seven money-dealers, or *seráfs*. They sit upon benches in the open street, with a large box before them containing the money. Formerly, these seráfs were all Jews, as is still the case, with few exceptions, at Cairo, Damascus, and Aleppo; but since the Sherif-Serour drove the Jews out of the Hedjaz, the Djiddawys themselves have taken up the profession, to which their natural disposition and habits incline them. There is usually at each stand a partnership of them, comprising half a dozen individuals. A large amount of cash is required to carry on the business; but it is very profitable. The value of money changes here more rapidly than in any part of the East with which I am acquainted. The price of dollars and sequins fluctuates almost daily, and the seráfs are always sure to be gainers. During the stay of the Indian fleet, the value of a dollar becomes very high. While I was at Djidda, it rose to eleven and twelve piastres. After the departure of the fleet, when there is no immediate demand for dollars, the price falls; in January, 1815, it was at nine piastres. The gold coins vary in proportion. Formerly the old current coins of the Hedjaz were Venetian and Hungarian sequins, Spanish dollars, and money coined at Constantinople. Egyptian coins were wholly excluded;* but since the arrival of the troops of Mohammed Ali Pasha, all the Cairo coins have been forcibly put into circulation, and the Cairo silver money is now next in estimation to the Spanish dollar. The Pasha of Egypt, who enjoys the right of coining money in the name of the Sultan, has lately much abused this privilege. In 1815, he farmed out the mint for a yearly sum of seven millions of piastres, which is, at the present rate of exchange, about two hundred thousand pounds sterling, obliging the people to take the dollar at eight of his piastres, although it is well known to be now worth twenty-two or twenty-three. In the Hedjaz he has not the same means of enforcing his despotic measures to their full extent; and thus it happens that in the interior of the country, where the Turkish troops are placed, the value of the dollar is eighteen or nineteen piastres. The Bedouins, however, refuse to take the Egyptian piastres, even at a depreciation, and will receive nothing but dollars; a determination to which the Pasha himself has been frequently obliged to yield.

The *párá*, or smallest Turkish coin, (here called *diwany*,) is current all over the Hedjaz, and in great request, from its being of more intrinsic value than the piastre, though coined like them at Cairo. Forty párás make a piastre; but in the time of the Hadj, when small change is necessary for the immense daily traffic of the pilgrims, the seráfs gave twenty-five párás only in

---

* According to the historians of Mekka, it appears that the sherifs there assumed the privilege of coining their own money, in the name of the Sultan of Constantinople, as late as the seventeenth century; but this is now abandoned.

change for the piastre. A few Indian rupees are seen in the Djidda market, but they have no currency. I never met with any money coined by the Imám of Yemen.

In the same great street of shops are ten large *okales*, always full of strangers and goods. Most of them were formerly the property of the sherif; they now belong to the Pasha, who levies an annual rent on the merchants. In Syria these buildings are called *khans;* in the Hedjaz *hosh*, which, in the dialect of Egypt, means a court-yard.

In a street adjoining the great market-place live a few artisans, blacksmiths, silversmiths, carpenters, some butchers, &c. most of them natives of Egypt.

The reader will perceive, by the foregoing pages, that Djidda depends for its commodities entirely on importations either from Egypt or the East Indies; and this is the case even to the most trifling article. The want of hands, and the high price of manual labour, but still more the indolence and want of industry inherent in the natives of the Hedjaz, have hitherto prevented them from establishing any kind of manufactory, except of the most indispensable articles. In this respect they offer a contrast to the Syrian and Egyptian Arabs, who in general are industrious, and who, in spite of the obstacles often thrown in their way by the government, have nevertheless established several manufactures, which render them, in some parts of the country, entirely independent of foreign supplies. The inhabitants of the Hedjaz appear to have only two occupations; commerce, and the pasture of cattle. The first engrosses the mind of almost every town-inhabitant, not excepting even the *olemas*, or learned men. Every one endeavours to employ whatever capital he possesses in some advantageous traffic, that he may live without much bodily exertion; for these people seem to be as averse to the latter as they are eager to endure all the anxieties and risks inseparable from the former. It is even difficult to find persons who will perform the common labour of porters, &c.: those who follow similar occupations are for the most part foreigners from Egypt or Syria, and negro pilgrims, who thus earn a very comfortable livelihood, and generally make but a temporary stay at Djidda. The only race of Arabians whom I have found more industrious than the others, are the people of Hadramaut, or, as they are called, El Hadáreme. Many of them act as servants in the merchants' houses, as door-keepers, messengers, and porters, in which latter character they are preferred to all others for their honesty and industry. Almost every considerable town in the East has its particular race of porters: at Aleppo, the Armenians of the mountains of Asia Minor are in request for this office; at Damascus, the people of Mount Libanus; at Cairo, the Berábera Nubians; at Mekka and Djidda, the Hadáreme, who, like those of Syria, are mountaineers. It is well known that similar qualifications recommend my countrymen, the Alpine mountaineers, to the same offices at Paris. There is another striking similarity among the natives of all these countries; they generally return home with their gains, and pass the remainder of their days with their families. Notwithstanding this source, there is a great and almost absolute want of free servants in the Hedjaz. No man who has been born in one of the holy cities, will act as a menial servant, unless he be driven to it by the fear of dying from want of food; and no sooner is he in good condition, than he ceases to labour, and either turns pedlar or beggar. The number of beggars at Mekka and Djidda is very great, and it is a common remark among the merchants of the latter place, that a Djiddawy will never work while he can possibly maintain himself by begging. Mendicity is much encouraged by the pilgrims, who are fond of displaying their charity on first touching holy ground at this place.

Respecting the people of Djidda and their character, I shall have occasion to make further observations in describing the inhabitants of Mekka, whom generally they resemble. In fact, all the respectable families have houses at both places, and frequently pass from one to the other.

Djidda is governed by a pasha of three tails, who takes precedence of most others, from the connexion of this place with the holy cities; but the government of it is an honour little esteemed by the Turkish grandees, who have always regarded Djidda as a place rather of exile than of preferment, and it has often been conferred on disgraced statesmen. The Pasha styles himself not only Wály or governor of Djidda, but of Sowakin and Habesh; and in support of this title, keeps custom-house officers at Sowakin and Massoua, which, prior to the government of Mohammed Aly, were entirely dependent on the sherif.

The pashalik of Djidda was reduced to perfect insignificance by the power of the sherif of Mekka; and the title had become merely an honorary distinction, enjoyed by the individual on whom it had been bestowed, while he resided in some provincial town of Turkey or at Constantinople, without ever attempting to take possession of his government. There was, however, an exception in 1803, when, after the total evacuation of Egypt by the French, Sherif Pasha went to Djidda with a body of four or five hundred soldiers; but like all his predecessors, he became the mere instrument of Sherif Ghaleb, and in 1804 his career was terminated by sudden death—the fate of many former Pashas both of Djidda and of Mekka.

According to the orders of the Sultan, whose nominal supremacy over the Hedjaz was recognised until the last Wahaby conquest, the revenue arising from the customs collected at Djidda should have been divided equally between the Pasha and the sherif of Mekka, while the former was to have exclusively the command of the town. When the Turks began to subdue Asia, the sherif received only one third of this revenue, and it was not until the year of the Hedjira 1042 that he obtained the half.* Subse-

* Vide Asámi, History of the Hedjaz.

quently, however, the sherif not only usurped the government of Djidda, but also applied the customs wholly to his own use, the Pasha being rendered altogether dependent upon his bounty.

Soon after the death of Sherif Pasha, the Sherif Ghaleb was obliged to surrender Mekka to the Wahabys, having been besieged, the preceding year, in Djidda, by Saoud. He then openly declared himself a proselyte to the Wahaby faith, and a subject of the Wahaby chief, though he still retained full possession of Djidda and the produce of its customs, which formed the principal part of his income. The Wahabys did not enter the town, which ostensibly declared in favour of their doctrines. The Turkish soldiers were now obliged to retire towards Egypt, or elsewhere; and from that period till 1811 all Turkish authority was entirely excluded from the Hedjaz.

In 1811, Mohammed Aly Pasha commenced his operations against the Wahabys, by sending a body of troops under the command of his son Tousoun Bey, who was defeated in the passes between Yembo and Medina. A second, in 1812, was more successful: while Tousoun, in September of that year, took Medina, Mustafa Bey, the Pasha's brother-in-law, proceeded directly with the cavalry under his command to Djidda, Mekka, and Tayf; all which surrendered, almost without bloodshed. The Sherif Ghaleb, who, from the moment he began to apprehend the probable success of Aly's expedition, had entered into a secret correspondence with Egypt, now openly declared himself a friend to the Turks, who entered Djidda as friends. The title of Pasha of Djidda was soon after conferred by the Porte upon Tousoun, as a reward for his services. The details of this war will be given in another place; I shall, therefore, only mention here, that after the Osmanlys, or Turks, entered Djidda, a quarrel arose between the Pasha and the sherif respecting the customs, which were to be divided between them, but which the Pasha, being now superior in power, kept wholly to himself. He sent the sherif as prisoner to Turkey, and since that event, the town has continued wholly at his disposal, the new sherif, Yahya, being a servant in the pay of Tousoun.

Djidda, in the time of Sherif Ghaleb, was governed either by himself, when he resided there, or, during his absence, by an officer called Vizir, under whose orders the police of the town was placed; while the collection of the customs *(gumruk)* was entrusted to another officer, called the *gumrukdjy;* and the police of the harbour to the *Emir el Bahhr*, or the "Chief of the Sea," a title equivalent to "harbour-master." In later times the vizir was a black slave of Ghaleb, and much detested for his pride and despotic conduct. Ghaleb seldom resided in Djidda, his continual intrigues with the Bedouins, and his schemes against the Wahaby tribes, requiring his presence in the more central position of Mekka.

The form of government which existed under Ghaleb has not been changed by the Osmanlys. It happened that Tousoun Pasha could seldom reside in his capital, being placed under the command of his father, who received from the Porte the entire direction of the Hedjaz war, and the disposal of all the resources of that country. Tousoun was more usefully employed in moving about with the troops under his command, till he returned to Cairo in the autumn of 1815. Since the year 1812, a military commander has always resided in the town, with a garrison of two or three hundred men, which the Pasha takes care to change every three or four months. The collection of the customs, the entire regulation of civil affairs, the correspondence with Cairo and Mekka, the conveyance of troops, stores, and government merchandize between Egypt and Djidda, and the Pasha's treasury, are in the hands of this commander, whose name is Seyd Ali Odjakly. His father was from Asia Minor, and belonged to the corps of Janissaries (Odjak), whence his son takes the epithet of Odjakly. He is disliked by the merchants of Djidda, because they remember his selling nuts in the streets about twenty years ago. In the time of Sherif Ghaleb, he was employed by him in his private commercial affairs; and as he possesses great talents and activity, joined to a good knowledge of the Turkish language, Mohammed Ali could with difficulty have pitched upon a person more competent to fill the post which he now holds.

The public revenue of Djidda arises almost exclusively from the customs, called here *ashour*, or tithes. This ought legally to be, as I was informed, ten per cent. upon all imported goods; but, in consequence of abuses which have been long practised, some articles of merchandize are charged much higher, while others pay less. During the latter period of the sherif's power, coffee was charged at five dollars the quintal, which may be computed as fifteen to twenty per cent. Spices pay somewhat less than ten per cent.; India piece-goods something more. Great irregularity, therefore, exists in levying the customs; and it is in the power of the officer of customs to favour his friends without incurring any responsibility.

After the sherif had embraced the Wahabi doctrine, his income was greatly diminished; because Saoud, the chief of the Wahabis, insisted that the goods of all his followers should pass duty-free, and thus the greater part of the coffee trade became exempt. I heard from a person who had means of knowing the truth, and who had no motive for concealing it from me, that the amount of customs collected at Djidda in 1814 was four hundred thousand dollars, equal to eight thousand purses, or four millions of piastres, which would give an annual importation of about four millions of dollars, a sum certainly below rather than above the truth. Customs are levied after the same rate at the two gates of the town, called Bab Mekka and Bab el Medina, upon all provisions coming from the interior of the country, principally cattle, butter, and dates, which, in time of peace, when the communication with the interior is uninterrupted, becomes a matter of importance. Except these, the people of the town pay no imposts whatever.

During my residence, the Turks had made Djidda the principal depôt for their army. A large magazine of corn belonging to the Pasha, received almost daily supplies from Egypt, and caravans were every day despatched to Mekka and Tayf; the commerce of the town also was much increased by the wants of the army and its followers. The police of the place was well regulated; and the Pasha had given the strictest injunctions to his troops that they should not commit excesses, as he well knew that the high-minded Arabians do not so quietly submit to ill-treatment as the enslaved Egyptians: whenever quarrels happened between Arabs and Turks, the former generally had the advantage. No *avanies* (or wanton act of oppression and injustice) had, under any pretence, been exercised upon individuals, except in the occupation of a few of the best houses by the Pasha as lodgings for his wives. The merchants suffered, however, as in the sherif's time, from the arbitrary rates of customs, and from the necessity of frequently purchasing all kinds of merchandize from the Pasha, who, while he was in the Hedjaz, seemed to be as eager in his mercantile as he was in his military pursuits. But after an impartial view of the merits and demerits of both governments, it may be said that the people of Djidda have certainly gained by the Osmanlys; yet, strange to mention, not an Arab could be found, whether rich or poor, sincerely attached to his new masters; and the termination of the sherif's government was universally regretted. This must not be attributed wholly to the usual levity of a mob, which is found among the subjects of the Porte, even in a greater degree than among those of any European nation. The Ottoman governors or Pashas are continually changing, and every new one becoming a supreme ruler, gives ample cause for complaints and private hatred and disgust; while their rapid succession inspires the people with the hope of being soon rid of their present despot, an event to which they look forward with pleasure, as the first months of a new governor are generally marked by clemency and justice.

The Arabians are a very proud, high-spirited nation; and this may be said even of those who inhabit the towns, however corrupted the true Bedouin character may be among this degenerate race. They despise every nation that does not speak the Arabic language, or that differs in manners; they have, besides, been accustomed, for many years, to look upon Turks as a very inferior people, who, whenever they entered the Hedjaz, were overawed by the power of the sherif. The rigid ceremonial of a Turkish court was not adapted to the character and established notions of Mohammed Aly's new subjects. The sherif, in the height of his power, resembled a great Bedouin Sheikh, who submits to be boldly and often harshly addressed. A Turkish Pasha is approached with the most abject forms of servitude. "Whenever the Sherif Ghaleb wanted a loan of money," observed one of the first merchants of the Hedjaz to me, " he sent for three or four of us; we sat in close discourse with him for a couple of hours, often quarrelling loudly, and we always reduced the sum to something much less than was at first demanded. When we went to him on ordinary business, we spoke to him as I now speak to you; but the Pasha keeps us standing before him in an humble attitude, like so many Habesh (Abyssinian) slaves, and looks down upon us as if we were beings of an inferior creation. I would rather," he concluded, " pay a fine to the sherif than receive a favour from the Pasha."

The little knowledge which the Turks possess of the Arabic language, their bad pronunciation of it even in reciting prayers from the Koran, the ignorance of Arabia and its peculiarities which they betray in every act, are so many additional causes to render them hateful or despicable in the eyes of the Arabs. The Turks return an equal share of contempt and dislike. Whoever does not speak the language of the Turkish soldier, or does not dress like one, is considered as a *fellah*, or boor, a term which they have been in the habit of applying to the Egyptian peasants, as beings in the lowest state of servitude and oppression. Their hatred of the Arabian race is greater, because they cannot indulge their tyrannical disposition with impunity, as they are accustomed to do in Egypt, being convinced by experience that an Arabian, when struck, will strike again. The Arabians particularly accuse the Turks of treachery, in seizing the sherif and sending him to Turkey after he had declared for the Pasha, and permitted Djidda and Mekka to be occupied by the Turkish troops, who, they assert, would never, without the assistance of the sherif, have been able to make any progress in Arabia, much less to acquire a firm footing therein.

The term *khayn*, " treacherous," is universally applied to every Turk in Arabia, with that proud self-confidence of superiority, in this respect, for which the Arabs are deservedly renowned. The lower classes of the Arabs have discovered a fanciful confirmation of their charge against the Turks in one of the Grand Signor's titles, *Khán*, an ancient Tatar word, which in Arabic signifies " he betrayed," being the preterite of the verb *ykhoun*, " to betray." They pretend that an ancestor of the Sultan having betrayed a fugitive, received the opprobrious appellation of " el Sultan Khán," (" the Sultan has been treacherous;") and that the title is merely retained by his successors from their ignorance of the Arabic language.

Whenever the power of the Turks in the Hedjaz declines, which it will when the resources of Egypt are no longer directed to that point by so able and so undisturbed a possessor of Egypt as Mohammed Ali, the Arabs will avenge themselves for the submission, light as it is, which they now reluctantly yield to their conquerors; and the reign of the Osmanlis in the Hedjaz will probably terminate in many a scene of bloodshed.

ROUTE FROM DJIDDA TO TAYF.*

On the 24th of August, 1814, (11th of Ramadhán, A. H. 1230.) I set out from Djidda, late in the evening, with my guide and twenty camel-drivers of the tribe of Harb, who were carrying money to Mekka for the Pasha's treasury. After having left the skirts of the town, where the road passes by mounds of sand, among which is the cemetery of the inhabitants, we travelled across a very barren, sandy plain, ascending slightly towards the east; there are no trees in it, and it is strongly impregnated with salt to about two miles from the town. After three hours' march, we entered a hilly country, where a coffee-hut stands near a well named *Raghâme*. We continued in a broad and winding valley amongst these hills, some sandy and some rocky, and, at the end of five hours and a half, stopped for a short time at the coffee-hut and well called *El Beyádhye*. Of these wells the water is not good. From thence, in one hour and a half, (seven hours in all,) we reached a similar station called *El Feráyne*, where we overtook a caravan of pilgrims, who were accompanying goods and provisions destined for the army: they had quitted Djidda before us in the evening. The coffee-huts are miserable structures, with half-

* I was unable to take any bearings during this excursion, as the only compass which I possessed, and which had served me throughout my Nubian journey, had become useless, and no opportunity offered of replacing it till December in this year, when I obtained one from a Bombay ship which arrived at Djidda.

ruined walls, and coverings of brushwood; they afford nothing more than water and coffee. Formerly, it is said, there were twelve coffee-houses on this road, which afforded refreshments of every kind to the passengers between Djidda and the holy city; but as the journey is now made chiefly during the night, and as the Turkish soldiers will pay for nothing unless by compulsion, most of these houses have been abandoned. The few that still remain are kept by some of the Arabs of the Lahyan tribe, (a branch of the Hodheyl Arabs,) and Metarefe, whose families are Bedouins, and live among the hills with their flocks. From Ferayne the valley opens, and the hills, diverging on both sides, increase considerably in height. At the end of eight hours, about sun-rise we reached Bahhra, a cluster of about twenty huts, situated upon a plain nearly four hours in length and two in breadth, extending eastward. At Bahhra there is plenty of water in wells, some sweet and some brackish. In a row of eight or ten shops are sold rice, onions, butter, dates, and coffee-beans, at thirty per cent. in advance of the Djidda market-price. This is what the Arabs call a *souk*, or market, and similar places occur at every station in this chain of mountains as far as Yemen. Some Turkish cavalry was stationed at Bahhra to guard the road. After travelling for two hours farther over the plain, we halted, at ten hours from Djidda, at Hadda, a souk, similar to the above Between Bahhra and Hadda, upon an insulated hillock in the plain, are the ruins of an ancient fortification.

August 25th. — The caravan from Djidda to Mekka rests during the day at Bahhra or at Hadda, thus following the common practice of the Hedjaz Arabs, who travel only by night. This is done in winter as well as in summer, not so much for the purpose of avoiding the heat as to afford the camels time for feeding, these animals never eating by night. Such nocturnal marches are most unfavourable to the researches of a traveller, who thus crosses the country at a time when no objects can be observed;

and during the day, fatigue and the desire of sleep render every exertion irksome.

We alighted at Hadda, under the shed of a spacious coffee-hut, where I found a motley crew of Turks and Arabs, in their way to or from Mekka, each extended upon his small carpet. Some merchants from Tayf had just brought in a load of grapes; and, although I felt myself still weak from the fever, I could not withstand this temptation, and seized a few of them ; for the baskets were no sooner opened than the whole company fell upon them, and soon devoured the entire load; the owner, however, was afterwards paid. It is at Hadda that the inhabitants of Djidda, when making a pilgrimage to Mekka, put on the *ihram*, or pilgrim's cloak. By the Muselman law, every one is obliged to assume it, whatever may be his rank, who enters the sacred territory of Mekka, whether on pilgrimage or for other purposes ; and he is enjoined not to lay it aside till after he has visited the temple. Many persons, however, transgress this law; but an othodox Mekkan never goes to Djidda without carrying his ihram with him, and on his return home, he puts it on at this place. In the afternoon some of the Turkish soldiers who were here put on this garment, with the prescribed ceremonies, which consist in an ablution, or, if the pilgrim choose, an entire purification, an audible avowal of the act of investment, a prayer of two *rikats*, and the recital of pious exclamations called *telbye*. This being a time of war, the soldiers continued to wear their arms over the cloak.

In the afternoon, the coffee-house keeper dressed the provisions I had brought, as well as those belonging to many others of the company. There was great disorder in the place, and nobody could attempt to sleep. Soon after our arrival, a troop of soldiers passed, and pitched their tents a little farther on the plain ; they then entered the coffee-huts, and took away all the sweet water, which had been procured from a well about half-an-hour distant, and kept at Hadda in large jars. The huts of the few miserable inhabitants, thus exposed to all the casualties attending the continual passage of troops, are formed with brushwood, in the shape of a flattened cone, and they receive light only through the entrance; here the whole family lives huddled together in one apartment. The numerous coffee-huts are spacious sheds, supported by poles, with the coffee-waiter's hearth placed in one corner. They are infested by great numbers of rats, bolder than any I ever saw.

We left Hadda about five o'clock in the evening. The road continuing over the plain, the soil is sandy, in some parts mixed with clay, and might, I think, be easily cultivated by digging wells. At one hour from Hadda, we saw on our left, in the plain, some date-trees: here, as I understood, flows a small rivulet, which in former times irrigated some fields. The trees are at present neglected. We now left the plain, and diverging a little southward from our easterly course, again entered a hilly country, and reached, at two hours from Hadda, another coffee-hut, called Shemeysa. Behind it is the Djebel Shemeysa, or mountain of Shemeysa, from which, according to the historians of Mekka, was extracted the marble of many columns in the mosque of that holy city. In the mountain, near the hut, is a well. From Shemeysa we rode in a broad valley overspread with deep sands, and containing some thorny trees. At four hours from Hadda, we passed Kahwet Salem, or Salem's coffee-shop, and a well; there we met a caravan coming from Mekka. The mountains nearly close at this place, leaving only a narrow straight valley, crossed at intervals by several other valleys. We then proceeded as far as Hadjalye, a coffee-house, seven hours distant from Hadda, with a large well near it, which supplies the camel-drivers of the Syrian pilgrim caravan, on the way to and from Mekka.

Not having enjoyed a moment's sleep since we quitted Djidda, I lay down on the sands, and slept till day-break, while my companions pursued their road to Mekka. My guide only remained with me; but his fears for the safety of his camels would not allow him to close his eyes. The route from Djidda to Mekka is always frequented by suspicious characters; and as every body travels by night, stragglers are easily plundered. Near Hadjalye, are the ruins of an ancient village, built with stone; and in the Wady are traces of former cultivation.

August 26th.—At half an hour from Hadjalye, we came to a small date plantation, surrounded by a wall. From hence the road to Mekka lies to the right, and enters the town by the quarter called Djerouel. My guide had orders to conduct me by a by-road to Tayf, which passes in the north of Mekka; it branches off at Hadda, crosses the road from Mekka to Wady Fatmé, and joins the great road from Mekka to Tayf, beyond Wady Muna. Just before we left Hadda, my guide, who knew nothing further respecting me than that I had business with the Pasha at Tayf, that I performed all the outward observances of a Moslem pilgrim, and that I had been liberal to him before our departure, asked me the reason of his having been ordered to take me by the northern road. I replied, that it was probably thought shorter than the other. "That is a mistake," he replied; "the Mekka road is quite as short, and much safer; and if you have no objection, we will proceed by it." This was just what I wished, though I had taken care not to betray any anxiety on the subject; and we accordingly followed the great road, in company with the other travellers. Instead, however, of taking me the usual way, which would have carried me through the whole length of the town, he, having no curiosity to gratify, conducted me, without my being aware of it, by a short cut, and thus deprived me of an opportunity of seeing Mekka fully at this time.

From the date plantation beyond Hadjalye, we reached in half an hour the plain where the Syrian pilgrim-caravan usually encamps, and which has taken the name of Sheikh Mahmoud, from the tomb of a saint so called, built in the midst of it. It is encompassed by low mountains; is from two to three miles in length, and one in breadth; and is separated from the valley of Mekka by a narrow chain of hills, over which a road has been cut through the rocks, with much labour. By this road we ascended, and on the summit of the hill passed two watch-towers, built on each side of the road by the Sherif Ghaleb. As we descended on the other side, where the road is paved, the view of Mekka opened upon us; and at an hour and a half from Hadjalye, we entered the eastern quarter of the town, near the Sherif's palace (marked 50 in the plan). The great body of the town lay on our right, hidden, in part, by the windings of the valley. As I knew that I should return to Mekka, I did not press my guide to allow me a full view of the city, since we should, for that purpose, have been obliged to ride back about two miles in a contrary direction. I repressed my curiosity, therefore, and followed him, reciting those ejaculations which are customary on entering the holy city.

I travelled several times afterwards between Mekka and Djidda, in both directions. The caravan's rate of march is here very slow, scarcely exceeding two miles an hour. I have ridden from Mekka to Djidda upon an ass in thirteen hours. The distance may, perhaps, be fairly estimated at sixteen or seventeen hours' walk, or about fifty-five miles; the direction a trifle to the northward of east.

On turning to our left, we passed, a little farther on, the great barracks of the Sherif; and in the suburbs called El Moabede, we alighted at the house of an Arab, with whom my guide happened to be acquainted. It was now the fast of Ramadhán; but travellers are exempted by law from observing it. The woman of the house, whose husband was absent, prepared us a breakfast, for which we paid her, and remained in the house till after mid-day; we then remounted our camels, and turning by the Sherif's garden-house, situated at the eastern extremity of the suburbs, we took the high road to Wady Muna. Winding valleys, of greater or less breadth, covered with sands, and almost wholly destitute of vegetation, with hills on both sides, equally barren, lead to Muna. At half an hour from the garden-house of the Sherif, the country opens a little to the left. There the canal passes which supplies Mekka with sweet water; and we saw, about two miles distant, at the extremity of the opening, a conical mountain, called *Djebel el Nour*, considered holy by the pilgrims, as will be subsequently mentioned. We passed on our right, in an hour and a half, a large tank, built of stones. This, in the time of the Hadj, is filled with water from the canal, which passes close by it. I believe this to be the place called Sebyl-es-Sett. One of the side-valleys between Mekka and Muna is called Wady Mohsab. El Fasy, the historian of Mekka, says that there were formerly sixteen wells between that city and Muna. At the end of two hours, after having ascended a little by a paved causeway formed across the valley, which is about forty yards in breadth, we entered Wady Muna. Near the causeway we saw a small field, irrigated by means of a brackish well, where a few miserable Bedouins raised onions and leeks for the market at Mekka. I shall give hereafter a more detailed description of Wady Muna, where the Hadj remains three days after its return from Arafat.

We continued our route among the ruined houses of Muna, passed the short columns, at which the pilgrims throw stones, then the Sherif's palace, and issued into the open country, which continues thence towards Mezdelife, distant three hours and three quarters from Mekka. This name is given to a small mosque, now almost in ruins, close to which is a tank or reservoir of water. Here a sermon is preached from a high platform in front of the mosque, to the pilgrims after their return from Arafat. El Fasy, the historian, says that this mosque was built in A. H. 759. It is often called Moshár el Haram; but, according to the same author, this name belongs to a small hill at the extremity of the valley of Mezdelife, which bears also the appellation of El Kazeh. From Mezdelife two roads lead to Arafat; the one on the left along the plain or valley called Dhob; the other leads straight across the mountain, and joins the former near the Aalameyn. We proceeded along the great road in the valley. At four hours and a quarter the mountains again close, and a narrow pass called El Mazomeyn or El Medyk leads across them for half an hour, after which the view opens upon the plain of Arafat. At the end of four hours and three quarters, we passed, in this plain, a tank called *Bir Basan*, constructed of stone, with a small chapel adjoining. Here the country opens widely to the north and south. Eastward, the mountains of Tayf are seen for the first time in their full height.* At five hours we reached El Aalameyn, two stone structures standing one on each side of the road, from eighty to one hundred paces from each other, and between them the pilgrims must pass in going, and more particularly in returning from Arafat. They are of coarse masonry, plaistered white, and the annexed outline represents their form.

Fasy says that there were formerly three, that they were built in A. H. 605, and that one had fallen. Of those now remaining one is entire, the other half ruined. At five hours and a quarter we passed to our right a large insulated mosque in a state of decay, called Djama Nimre, or Djama Ibrahim, built as it now stands by the Sultan Kail, Bey of Egypt. The low mountain of

* On my return from Tayf to Mekka, when I was completely my own master, I drew up a much more detailed and accurate description of the road than this given here; but I accidentally lost the papers containing it; the present, therefore, is written from memory, and the few short notes which I hastily made during the route to Tayf.

Arafat was now to our left at the extremity of the plain, about two miles distant. We proceeded, without stopping, over the plain, which is covered with shrubs of considerable height, and low acacia trees: from these it is prohibited to take even the smallest branch, this being holy ground. On attaining the eastern limits of the plain, we reached, at five hours and three quarters, the canal of Mekka, issuing from the mountainous ground. Near it is a small tank, and in its vicinity a cluster of Arab huts similar to those at Hadda, and bearing the name of *Kahwet Arafat*, or the coffee-house of Arafat. They are inhabited chiefly by Beni Koreysh, who cultivate vegetables in a valley extending from hence towards the south. We rested here some hours; a caravan from Tayf, composed of mules and asses, arrived at the same time.

From Kahwet Arafat, the road becomes rocky, and the mountains nearly close, and are intersected by valleys which cross the road in every direction. Acacia-trees grow here in great abundance. At seven hours and a half we again entered upon sandy ground, in a valley called Wady Noman, where, towards the south, are some wells, and a few plantations cultivated by the Arab tribes of Kebákeb and Ryshye. At eight hours and a half we passed an encampment of the Bedouin tribe of Hodheyl, where dogs attacked our camels so fiercely that I had much difficulty, though mounted, to defend myself from their teeth. At eight hours and three quarters we passed a cluster of huts and coffee-shops, called *shedad*, with wells of very good water. At nine hours and a half, it being a cloudy and extremely dark night, we lost our way in following the windings of a side valley, and being unable to regain the right road, we lay down on the sand and slept till daybreak.

August 27th.—We found ourselves close to the road, and proceeding, we began to ascend, in half an hour, the great chain of mountains. From Djidda to this place, our route, though generally between hills and mountains, had been constantly over flat ground, in valleys, with an ascent almost imperceptible to the traveller, and the existence of which became visible only in viewing the country from the summit of the mountains now before us. The lower hills are seldom higher than four or five hundred feet. The lowest range above Djidda is calcareous; but its rocks soon change into gneiss, and a species of granite, with schorl in the place of feldspath, accompanied by predominant masses of quartz, and some mica. This rock continues along the road, with few variations, as far as the vicinity of Djebel Nour, to the eastward of Mekka, where granite begins. I learned at Mekka, that, south of Hadda, some hours distant, a mountain yields fine marble, which served for the pavement of the great mosque. The mountains forming the valley of Muna are composed of this red and grey granite, and continue so from thence to this higher chain, mixed in a few places with strata of grunstein. The lower chain of the high ridge which we were now ascending, again, consists of grey granite; towards the middle I found it of all colours, mixed with strata of grunstein, trappe, and porphyry schistus, the latter much decayed: at the summit of the ridge, red granite occurred again; its surface had been completely blackened by the sun's rays.

We ascended by a road, still bad, although Mohammed Ali Pasha had recently caused it to be repaired. The country around was very wild, being covered with large blocks of loose stones, carried down by the winter torrents, and interspersed with a few acacia and nebek trees. At one hour we came to a building of loose stones, called *Kaber Er'-rafyk*, i. e. the Companion's tomb. The following tradition concerning it was related by my guide. In the last century, a Bedouin returning from the Hadj was joined, beyond the gates of Mekka, by a traveller going the same road with himself; they reached this spot in company, when one of them felt himself so ill, that he was unable to proceed farther, and on the following day the small-pox broke out on his body. In this situation his companion would not abandon him. He built two huts with boughs of acacia-trees, one for his friend, the other for himself; and continued to nurse him, and solicit alms for his benefit from passing travellers, until he recovered. But in turn, he himself became ill of the same disease, and was nursed by his convalescent companion with equal kindness, though not with equal success; for he died, and was interred by his friend on this spot, where his tomb serves as a monument of Bedouin generosity, and inculcates benevolence even towards the casual companions of the road.

At one hour and a half, still ascending, we reached some huts built among the rocks, near a copious spring; they are named *Kahwet Kora*, from the mountains which collectively bear the name of Djebel Kora. I found here a Turkish soldier, charged with the transport of provisions for the Pasha's army over the mountain. This being the shortest road from Mekka to Tayf, caravans are continually passing. The camel-loads are deposited at this place, and then forwarded to the summit of the mountain on mules and asses, of which about two hundred are kept here. On the mountain camels are prepared for carrying the loads to Tayf. The more northern road to Tayf, of which I shall speak hereafter, is passable for camels all the way; but it is by one day longer than this.

The huts of Kora are constructed between the rocks, on the slope of the mountain, where there is scarcely any level surface. The inhabitants are Hodheyl Bedouins. In two or three huts nothing could be procured but coffee and water. The Turkish soldier had lately incurred the Pasha's displeasure, having stolen and sold the camel of a Hodheyl woman, who had gone to lay her complaint before his master, the Pasha, at Tayf. The soldier treated me with much civility, when he learned that I was going to visit the Pasha, and begged me to intercede in his behalf; this, however, I declined to do, telling him that I was myself a solicitor for my own concerns. We remained till mid-day at this pleasant spot, from whence there is a fine prospect over the lower country. A large nebek-tree, near the spring which drizzles down the rocks, afforded me shade, and a delicious cool breeze allayed the sultry heat which we had endured ever since our departure from Djidda. Leaving Kora, we found the road very steep, and, although it had lately been repaired, so bad, that a mounted traveller could hardly hope to reach the summit without alighting. Steps had been cut in several places, and the ascent rendered less steep, by conducting it, in many windings, to the top : half a dozen spacious resting-places had also been formed on the side of the mountain, where the caravans take breath, there being no where so much as eight square feet of level ground. The same spring, which comes from near the top, is crossed several times. I met many of the Hodheyl Bedouins, with their families and flocks of sheep, near the road. One of them gave me some milk, but would not take any money in return; the sale of milk being considered by these Bedouins as a scandal, though they might derive great profits from it at Mekka, where one pound of milk is worth two piastres. I conversed freely with the men, and with the wife of one of them. They seemed a race of hardy mountaineers, and, although evidently poor, have a more robust and fleshy appearance than the northern Bedouins, which I ascribe chiefly to the healthiness of the climate, and the excellence of the water. The Beni Hodheyl, famous in the ancient history of Arabia, were nominally subject to the Sherif of Mekka, in whose territory they live; but they were in fact quite independent, and often at war with him.

We were full two hours in ascending from the coffee-huts to the summit of the mountain, from whence we enjoyed a beautiful prospect over the low country. We discerned Wady Muna, but not Mekka; and as far as the eye could reach, winding chains of hills appeared upon a flat surface, towards the north and south, with narrow stripes of white sand between them, without the slightest verdure. Close to our right rose a peak of the mountain

Kora, called Nakeb el Ahmar, from four to five hundred feet higher than the place where we stood, and appearing to overtop all the neighbouring chain. Towards the north, the mountain, about thirty miles distant, seemed to decrease considerably in height; but southward it continues of the same height. After half an hour's ride from the summit, we came to a small village called Ras el Kora. Finding myself much fatigued, I insisted upon sleeping here, with which my guide reluctantly complied, as he had received orders to travel expeditiously.

August 28th.—The village and neighbourhood of Ras el Kora is the most beautiful spot in the Hedjaz, and more picturesque and delightful than any place I had seen since my departure from Lebanon, in Syria. The top of Djebel Kora is flat, but large masses of granite lie scattered over it, the surface of which, like that of the granite rocks near the second cataract of the Nile, is blackened by the sun. Several small rivulets descend from this peak, and irrigate the plain, which is covered with verdant fields and large shady trees on the side of the granite rocks. To those who have only known the dreary and scorching sands of the lower country of the Hedjaz, this scene is as surprising as the keen air which blows here is refreshing. Many of the fruit-trees of Europe are found here, — figs, apricots, peaches, apples, the Egyptian sycamore, almonds, pomegranates; but particularly vines, the produce of which is of the best quality. There are no palm-trees here, and only a few nebek-trees. The fields produce wheat, barley, and onions; but the soil being stony, these do not succeed so well as the fruits. Every *beled*, as they here call the fields, is enclosed by a low wall, and is the property of a Hodheyl Bedouin. When Othman el Medhayfe took Tayf from the Sherif, this place was ruined, the fields were destroyed, and many of the walls had not yet been rebuilt.

After having passed through this delightful district, for about half an hour, just as the sun was rising, when every leaf and blade of grass was covered with a balmy dew, and every tree and shrub diffused a fragrance as delicious to the smell as was the landscape to the eye, I halted near the largest of the rivulets, which, although not more than two paces across, nourishes upon its banks a green Alpine turf, such as the mighty Nile, with all its luxuriance, can never produce in Egypt. Some of the Arabs brought us almonds and raisins, for which we gave them biscuits; but although the grapes were ripe, we could not obtain any, as they are generally purchased while on the vines by the merchants of Tayf, who export them to Mekka, and keep them closely watched by their own people till they are gathered. Here a Turkish soldier, complimented with the title of Aga, was stationed under a tent, to forward the provisions coming from the lower station to Tayf. I observed with some astonishment, that not a single pleasure-house was built on this high platform. Formerly, the Mekka merchants had their country-seats at Tayf, which stand in a situation as desert and melancholy, as this is cheerful and luxuriant; but none of them ever thought of building a cottage here; a new proof of the opinion which I have long entertained, that orientals, especially the Arabs, are much less sensible of the beauties of nature than Europeans. The water of Ras el Kora is celebrated throughout the Hedjaz for its excellence. While Mohammed Ali remained at Mekka and at Djidda, he received a regular supply of Nile water for drinking, sent from Egypt, by every fleet, in large tin vessels; but on passing this place, he found its water deserving of being substituted for the other: a camel comes here daily from Tayf for a load of it.

The houses of the Hodheyl, to whom these plantations belong, are scattered over the fields in clusters of four or five together. They are small, built of stones and mud, but with more care than might be expected from the rude hands of the occupants. Every dwelling comprises three or four rooms, each of which being separated from the others by a narrow open space, forms, as it were, a small detached cottage. These apartments receive no light but from the entrance; they are very neat and clean, and contain Bedouin furniture, some good carpets, woollen and leathern sacks, a few wooden bowls, earthen coffee-pots, and a matchlock, of which great care is taken, it being generally kept in a leathern case. At night I reposed upon a large well-tanned cow-skin : the covering was formed of a number of small sheep-skins neatly sewed together, similar to those used in Nubia. The Hodheyl told me, that before the Wahabys came, and obliged them to pay tribute for their fields, they knew no land-tax, but, on the contrary, received yearly presents from the sherifs, and from all the Mekkawys who passed this way to Tayf. Ras el Kora extends from east to west about two and a half or three miles, and is about a mile in breadth. According to the statements of the Arabs, many spots towards the south, where Bedouin tribes, like the Hodheyl, cultivate the soil in detached parts of the mountain, are equally fertile and beautiful as that which we saw in the chain above mentioned.

We left the Ras, which will be remembered by me as long as I am sensible to the charms of romantic scenery, and rode for about one hour over uneven barren ground, with slight ascents and descents, till we came to a steep declivity, to walk down which occupied us half an hour, and double that time would be necessary for ascending it. The rock is entirely composed of sand-stone. From the summit of the declivity just mentioned, Tayf is seen in the distance. At half an hour from the foot of the mountain, we entered a fertile valley, called Wady Mohram, extending from N.W. to S.E. Like the upper district, it is full of fruit-trees; but the few cultivated fields are watered from wells, and not by running streams. A village, which the Wahabys had almost wholly ruined, stands on the slope, with a small tower constructed by the inhabitants to secure the produce of their fields against the invasion of enemies.

Here begins the territory of Tayf, and of the Arab tribe of Thekyf, who, in former times, were often at war with their neighbours the Hodheyl. The Wady is denominated Mohram, from the circumstance, that here the pilgrims and visitors going from the eastward to Mekka, invest themselves with the *ihram* before noticed. There is a small ruined stone tank close by the road. The caravan of the Yemen pilgrims, called Hadj el Kebsy, whose route lies along these mountains, used always to observe the ceremony here, and the tank was then filled with water for ablution. The husbandmen of Mohram draw the water from their wells in leathern buckets suspended from one end of an iron chain, passed round a pulley, and to the other end they yoke a cow, which, for want of a wheel, walks to a sufficient distance from the well to draw up the bucket, when she is led back to resume the same course. The cows I saw here, like all those of the Hedjaz, are small, but of a stout, bony make: they have generally only short stumps of horns, and a hump on the back, just over the shoulder, about five inches in height and six in length, much resembling in this respect the cows which I saw on the borders of the Nile in Nubia. According to the natives, the whole chain of mountains from hence southward, as far as the country where the coffee-plantations begin, is intersected by similar cultivated valleys at some distance from each other, the intermediate space consisting chiefly of barren rocky soil.

From Wady Mohram we again crossed uneven, mountainous ground, where I found sand-stone and silex. Acacia trees are seen in several sandy valleys, branching out from the road. At two hours and a half from Wady Mohram we ascended, and at the top of the hill saw Tayf lying before us. We reached it in three hours and a half from Wady Mohram, after having crossed the barren sandy plain which separates it from the surrounding hills. The rate of our march from Mekka, when we were quite alone upon our dromedaries, and able to accelerate their pace at pleasure, was not less than three miles and a quarter per hour. I therefore calculate from Mekka to the foot of Djebel Kora, about thirty-two miles; to its top, ten miles; and from thence to Tayf, thirty miles, making in the whole seventy-two miles. The bearing of the road from Arafat to Tayf is about twelve or fifteen degrees of the compass, to the southward of that from Mekka to Arafat; but having had no compass with me, I cannot give the bearing with perfect accuracy.

RESIDENCE AT TAYF.

I ARRIVED at Tayf about mid-day, and alighted at the house of Bosari, the Pasha's physician, with whom I had been well acquainted at Cairo. As it was now the fast of Ramadhan, during which the Turkish grandees always sleep in the day-time, the Pasha could not be informed of my arrival till after sun-set. In the mean while, Bosari, after the usual Levantine assurances of his entire devotion to my interests, and of the sincerity of his friendship, asked me what were my views in coming to the Hedjaz. I answered, to visit Mekka and Medina, and then to return to Cairo. Of my intention respecting Egypt he seemed doubtful, begged me to be candid with him as with a friend, and to declare the truth, as he confessed that he suspected I was going to the East Indies. This I positively denied; and in the course of our conversation, he hinted that if I really meant to return to Egypt, I had better remain at head-quarters with them, till the Pasha himself should proceed to Cairo. Nothing was said about money, although Bosari was ignorant that my pecuniary wants had been relieved at Djidda.

In the evening Bosari went privately to the Pasha at his women's residence, where he only received visits from friends or very intimate acquaintances. In half an hour he returned, and told me that the Pasha wished to see me rather late that evening in his public room. He added, that he found seated with the Pasha the Kadhy of Mekka, who was then at Tayf for his health; and that the former, when he heard of my desire to visit the holy cities, observed jocosely, " it is not the beard * alone which proves a man to be a true Moslem;" but turning towards the Kadhy, he said, " you are a better judge in such matters than I am." The Kadhy then observed that, as none but a Moslem could be permitted to see the holy cities, a circumstance of which he could not possibly suppose me ignorant, he did not believe that I would declare myself to be one, unless I really was. When I learnt these particulars, I told Bosari that he might return alone to the Pasha; that my feelings had already been much hurt by the orders given to my guide not to carry me through Mekka; and that I certainly should not go to the Pasha's public audience, if he would not receive me as a Turk.

Bosari was alarmed at this declaration, and in vain endeavoured to dissuade me from such a course, telling me that he had orders to conduct me to the Pasha, which he could not disobey. I however adhered firmly to what I had said, and he reluctantly went back to Mohammed Aly, whom he found alone, the Kadhy having left him. When Bosari delivered his message, the Pasha smiled, and answered that I was welcome, whether Turk or not. About eight o'clock in the evening I repaired to the castle, a miserable, half-ruined habitation of Sherif Ghaleb, dressed in the new suit which I had received at Djidda by the Pasha's command. I found his highness seated in a large saloon, with the Kadhy on one hand, and Hassan Pasha, the chief of the Arnaut soldiers, on the other; thirty or forty of his principal officers formed a half-circle about the sofa on which they sat; and a number of Bedouin sheikhs were squatted in the midst of the semicircle. I went up to the Pasha, gave him the "Salam Aleykum," and kissed his hand. He made a sign for me to sit down by the side of the

---

* I wore a beard at this time, as I did at Cairo, when the Pasha saw me.

Kadhy, then addressed me very politely, inquired after my health, and if there was any news from the Mamelouks in the Black country which I had visited; but said nothing whatever on the subject most interesting to me. Amyn Effendi, his Arabic dragoman, interpreted between us, as I do not speak Turkish, and the Pasha speaks Arabic very imperfectly. In about five minutes he renewed the business with the Bedouins, which I had interrupted. When this was terminated, and Hassan Pasha had left the room, every body was ordered to withdraw, except the Kadhy, Bosari, and myself. I expected now to be put to the proof, and I was fully prepared for it; but not a word was mentioned of my personal affairs, nor did Mohammed Aly, in any of our subsequent conversations, ever enter further into them than to hint that he was persuaded I was on my way to the East Indies. As soon as we were alone, the Pasha introduced the subject of politics. He had just received information of the entrance of the allies into Paris, and the departure of Bonaparte for Elba; and several Malta gazettes, giving the details of these occurrences, had been sent to him from Cairo. He seemed deeply interested in these important events, chiefly because he laboured under the impression that, after Bonaparte's downfall, England would probably seek for an augmentation of power in the Mediterranean, and consequently invade Egypt.

After remaining for two or three hours with the Pasha in private conversation, either speaking Arabic to him, through the medium of the Kadhy, who, though a native of Constantinople, knew that language perfectly, or Italian, through Bosari, who was an Armenian, but had acquired a smattering of that tongue at Cairo, I took my leave, and the Pasha said that he expected me again on the morrow at the same hour.

August 29th.—I paid a visit to the Kadhy before sun-set, and found him with his companion and secretary, a learned man of Constantinople. The Kadhy Sádik Effendi was a true eastern courtier, of very engaging manners and address, possessing all that suavity of expression for which the well-bred natives of Stamboul are so distinguished. After we had interchanged a few complimentary phrases, I mentioned my astonishment on finding that the Pasha had expressed any doubts of my being a true Moslem, after I had now been a proselyte to that faith for so many years. He replied that Mohammed Aly had allowed that he (the Kadhy) was the best judge in such matters; and added, that he hoped we should become better acquainted with each other. He then began to question me about my Nubian travels. In the course of conversation literary subjects were introduced: he asked me what Arabic books I had read, and what commentaries on the Koran and on the law; and he probably found me better acquainted, with the titles, at least, of such works than he had expected, for we did not enter deeply into the subject. While we were thus conversing, the call to evening prayers announced the termination of this day's fast. I supped with the Kadhy, and afterwards performed the evening prayers in his company, when I took great care to chaunt as long a chapter of the Koran as my memory furnished at the moment; after which we both went to the Pasha, who again sat up a part of the night in private conversation with me, chiefly on political affairs, without ever introducing the subject of my private business.

After another interview, I went every evening, first to the Kadhy, and then to the Pasha; but, notwithstanding a polite reception at the castle, I could perceive that my actions were closely watched. Bosari had asked me if I kept a journal; but I answered that the Hedjaz was not like Egypt, full of antiquities, and that in these barren mountains I saw nothing worthy of notice. I was never allowed to be alone for a moment, and I had reason to suspect that Bosari, with all his assurances of friendship, was nothing better than a spy. To remain at Tayf for an indeterminate period, in the situation I now found myself, was little desirable; yet I could not guess the Pasha's intentions with respect to me. I was evidently considered in no other light than as a spy sent to this country by the English government, to ascertain its present state, and report upon it in the East Indies. This, I presume, was the Pasha's own opinion: he knew me as an Englishman, a name which I assumed during my travels (I hope without any discredit to that country), whenever it seemed necessary to appear as an European; because at that time none but the subjects of England and France enjoyed in the East any real security: they were considered as too well protected, both by their governments at home and their ministers at Constantinople, to be trifled with by provincial governors. The Pasha, moreover, supposed me to be a man of some rank, for every Englishman travelling in the East is styled " My lord;" and he was the more convinced of this by a certain air of dignity which it was necessary for me to assume in a Turkish court, where modesty of behaviour and affability are quite out of place. Afraid as he then was of Great Britain, he probably thought it imprudent to treat me ill, though he did nothing whatever to forward my projects. As far as he knew, I could have only the five hundred piastres which he had ordered for me at Djidda, and which were not sufficient to pay my expenses for any length of time in the Hedjaz. Nothing was said to me either by him or Bosari of taking my bill upon Cairo, as I had requested him to do; but this favour I did not again solicit, having money enough for the present, and expecting a fresh supply from Egypt.

To remain for any length of time at Tayf, in a sort of polite imprisonment, was little to my taste; yet I could not press my departure without increasing his suspicions. This was manifest after my first interview with the Pasha and the Kadhy, and I knew that the reports of Bosari might considerably influence the mind of Mohammed. Under these circumstances, I thought the best course was to make Bosari tired of me, and thus induce him involuntarily to forward my views. I therefore began to act at his house with all the petulance of an Osmanly. It being the Ramadhan, I fasted during the day, and at night demanded a supper apart; early on the following morning I called for an abundant breakfast, before the fast re-commenced. I appropriated to myself the best room which his small house afforded; and his servants were kept in constant attendance upon me. Eastern hospitality forbids all resentment for such behaviour; I was, besides, a great man, and on a visit to the Pasha. In my conversations with Bosari, I assured him that I felt myself most comfortably situated at Tayf, and that its climate agreed perfectly with my health; and I betrayed no desire of quitting the place for the present. To maintain a person in my character for any length of time at Tayf, where provisions of all kinds were much dearer than in London, was a matter of no small moment; and a petulant guest is everywhere disagreeable. The design, I believe, succeeded perfectly; and Bosari endeavoured to persuade the Pasha that I was a harmless being, in order that I might be the sooner dismissed.

I had been six days at Tayf, but seldom went out, except to the castle in the evening, when Bosari asked whether my business with the Pasha was likely to prevent me much longer from pursuing my travels, and visiting Mekka. I replied that I had no business with the Pasha, though I had come to Tayf at his desire; but that my situation was very agreeable to me, possessing so warm and generous a friend as he, my host. The next day he renewed the subject, and remarked that it must be tiresome to live entirely among soldiers, without any comforts or amusements, unacquainted besides, as I was, with the Turkish language. I assented to this; but added, that being ignorant of the Pasha's wishes, I could determine on nothing. This brought him to the point I wished. " This being the case," said he, " I will, if you like, speak to his Highness on the subject." He did so in the evening, before I went to the castle; and the Pasha told me, in the course of conversation, that as he understood I wished to pass the last days of Ramadhan at Mekka, (a suggestion originating with Bosari,) I had better join the party of the Kadhy, who was going there to the feast, and who would be very glad of my company. This was precisely such a circumstance as I wished for. The departure of the Kadhy was fixed for the 7th of September, and I hired two asses, the usual mode of conveyance in this country, in order to follow him.

As it was my intention to proceed afterwards to Medina, where Tousoun Pasha, the son of Mohammed Aly, was governor, I begged Bosari to ask the Pasha for a firman or passport, authorising me to travel through all the Hedjaz, together with a letter of recommendation to his son. In reply, Bosari told me that the Pasha did not like to interfere personally in my travels; that I might act as I pleased, on my own responsibility; and that my knowledge of the language rendered a passport unnecessary. This was equivalent to telling me, " Do what you please; I shall neither obstruct nor facilitate your projects," which, indeed, was as much, at present, as I could well expect or desire.

On the 6th of September I took my leave of the Pasha, who told me at parting, that if ever my travels should carry me to India, I might assure the English people there that he was much attached to the interests of the India trade. Early on the 7th the Kadhy sent me word that he should not set out till evening, would travel during the night, and hoped to meet me at Djebel Kora, midway to Mekka. I therefore left Tayf alone, as I had entered it, after a residence of ten days. At parting, Bosari assured me of his inviolable attachment to my interest; and I blessed my good stars, when I left the precincts of the town, and the residence of a Turkish court, in which I found it more difficult to avoid danger, than among the wild Bedouins of Nubia.

During my stay at Tayf, I had five or six interviews with the

Pasha; and the following extracts from my journal will show the general result of what passed between us on those different occasions:—

Q. Sheikh Ibrahim, I hope you are well.

A. Perfectly well, and most happy to have the honour of seeing you again.

Q. You have travelled much since I saw you at Cairo. How far did you advance into the negro country?

To this question I replied, by giving a short account of my journey in Nubia.

Q. Tell me, how are the Mamelouks at Dongola?

I related what the reader will find in my Nubian Travels.

Q. I understand that you treated with two of the Mamelouk Beys at Ibrim; was it so?

The word *treated* (if the dragoman rightly translated the Turkish word), startled me very much; for the Pasha, while he was in Egypt, had heard that, on my journey towards Dongola, I had met two Mamelouk Beys at Derr; and as he still suspected that the English secretly favoured the Mamelouk interest, he probably thought that I had been the bearer of some message to them from government. I therefore assured him that my meeting with the two Beys was quite accidental; that the unpleasant reception which I experienced at Mahass was on their account; and that I entertained fears of their designs against my life. With this explanation the Pasha seemed satisfied.

Q. Let us only settle matters here with the Wahabys, and I shall soon be able to get rid of the Mamelouks. How many soldiers do you think are necessary for subduing the country as far as Senaar?

A. Five hundred men, good troops, might reach that point, but could not keep possession of the country; and the expenses would scarcely be repaid by the booty.

Q. What do those countries afford?

A. Camels and slaves; and, towards Senaar, gold, brought from Abyssinia; but all this is the property of individuals. The chiefs or kings in those countries do not possess any riches.

Q. In what state are the roads from Egypt to Senaar?

A. I described the road between Asouan and Shendy, and from Souakin to the same place.

Q. How did you pass your time among the Blacks?

A. I related some laughable stories, with which he seemed greatly amused.

Q. And now, Sheikh Ibrahim, where do you mean to go?

A. I wish to perform the Hadj, return to Cairo, and then proceed to visit Persia.—(I did not think it advisable to mention my design of returning into the interior of Africa.)

Q. May God render the way smooth before you! but I think it folly and madness to travel so much. What, let me ask, is the result of your last journey?

A. Men's lives are predestined; we all obey our fate. For myself, I enjoy great pleasure in exploring new and unknown countries, and becoming acquainted with different races of people. I am induced to undertake journies by the private satisfaction that travelling affords, and I care little about personal fatigue.

Q. Have you heard of the news from Europe?

A. Only some vague reports at Djidda.

The Pasha then gave me an account of the events which ended in Bonaparte's banishment to Elba, after the entrance of the allies into Paris. Bonaparte, he said, behaved like a coward; he ought to have sought for death, rather than expose himself in a cage to the laughter of the universe. The Europeans, he said, are as treacherous as the Osmanlys; all Bonaparte's confidants abandoned him—all his generals, who owed to him their fortunes.

He was eager in his inquiries about the political relations between Great Britain and Russia, and whether it was not likely that war might break out between them, on account of the hostile intentions of the latter towards the Porte. (On this point he had received false intelligence.) His only fear seemed to be that the English army, which had been employed in the south of France, and in Spain, would now be at liberty to invade Egypt. "The great fish swallow the small," he said; "and Egypt is necessary to England, in supplying corn to Malta and Gibraltar." I reasoned with him in vain on this subject, and perceived that the dragoman did not always interpret my answers correctly, from the fear of contradicting the well-known opinions of his master. These opinions, indeed, were deeply rooted, and had been fostered by the French mission in Egypt. "I am the friend of the English," he continued. (This addressed by a Turk to a Christian, means only that he fears him, or wants his money.) "But to tell you the truth, among great men we see many compliments, and very little sincerity. My hope is, that they will not fall upon Egypt during my stay in the Hedjaz; if I am there myself, I shall at least have the satisfaction of fighting personally for my dominions. Of the Sultan I am not afraid, (this he repeatedly asserted, but I much doubt his sincerity,) and I shall know how to outwit him in all his measures. An army from Syria can never attack Egypt by land in very large bodies, from the want of camels; and separate corps are easily destroyed as soon as they have passed the desert."

I took the liberty of telling him that he was like a young man in possession of a beautiful girl; although sure of her affection, he would always be jealous of every stranger. "You say well," he replied. "I certainly love Egypt with all the ardour of a lover; and if I had ten thousand souls, I would willingly sacrifice them for its possession."

He asked me in what state I had found Upper Egypt; and whether his son Ibrahim Pasha (the governor) was liked there. I replied, in the language of truth, that all the chiefs of villages hated him (for he had compelled them to abandon their despotic treatment of their fellow-peasants); but that the peasants themselves were much attached to him. (The fact is, that instead of being oppressed, as formerly, by the Mamelouk Beys and Kashefs, as well as by their own Sheikhs, they have at present only one tyrant, the Pasha himself, who keeps his governors of districts in perfect order.)

Mohammed Aly wished to know my opinion respecting the number of troops necessary for defending Egypt against a foreign army. I answered, that I knew nothing of war, but from what I had read in books. "No, no;" he exclaimed, "you travellers always have your eyes open, and you inquire after every thing." He persisted in his question; and being thus forced to reply, I said that twenty-five thousand chosen troops would probably be able to resist any attack. "I have now thirty-three thousand," said he: —a false assertion, for I am quite certain that he had at that time not more than sixteen thousand men, dispersed over Egypt and the Hedjaz.

He would next explain to me the *Nizam Djedyd*, or new system of discipline and military regulations. He said it was only the avidity of the chiefs, and not the dislike of the common soldiers, that obstructed the institution of a well-organised army in Turkey, and opposed the mustering necessary to prevent the officers from imposing on the public treasury. "But I shall make a regular corps of negro soldiers," he added. This his predecessor Khurshid Pasha had attempted, but with little success. The subject of the Nizam Djedyd was resumed as soon as Mohammed Aly returned to Egypt from this expedition; but the revolt of his soldiers, who plundered his own capital, obliged him to abandon the undertaking, which had been badly planned. In the defence of Egypt, he said, he should principally use his cavalry and horse-artillery; the former should destroy all the provisions in advance of the enemy, as the Russians had lately done; and the latter would harass them on all sides, without ever attempting to make a stand.

During my stay at Tayf, letters arrived from Constantinople, across the Desert, by way of Damascus, bringing to the Pasha a Turkish translation of the treaty of peace concluded at Paris. After having read it several times, he ordered his Turkish writer to explain it to me in Arabic, word for word. This occupied us in a private apartment several hours. I then returned to the audience, and was desired by the Pasha to tell him my opinion of the treaty. Referring to a Turkish atlas, copied from European maps, and printed at Constantinople, he made me point out to him the new limits of Belgium, the islands Mauritius and Tobago, the position of Genoa, &c. &c. With respect to the latter place, a curious mistake occurred. It had been stated to me that *Genoa* was ceded to the Swedes, which I could not credit. Upon inquiry, I found that *Geneva* and Switzerland were meant; a town and country which, I am sorry to say, were not comprised in the geographical knowledge of a Turkish viceroy. The mistake, however, was easily made; for in Turkish, Geneva is written like Genoua, and Sweden is pronounced Shwit.

The Pasha observed that much yet remained to be done, before all differences between the parties could be settled; and I clearly saw how impatiently he looked forward to a war among the European powers, which would relieve him from any apprehensions for his own safety, and at the same time occasion a great demand for corn at Alexandria.

With respect to Bonaparte, he seemed quite certain that the English would one day seize him in Elba. "Have the English, then," he exclaimed, "fought for nothing these twenty years? They have only got Malta, and a few other islands!" He was impressed with the fear that there were secret articles in the peace, which assigned to them the possession of Egypt. The notion of their having re-established the balance of power in Europe, and secured their own safety and independence, did not enter into his mind. "They should not leave Spain," he continued, "without being handsomely paid by the Spaniards; and why now abandon Sicily?" That the English were guided in their policy by the laws of honour, and a sense of the general good of Europe, he could not comprehend. "A great king," he exclaimed, with much warmth, "knows nothing but his sword and his purse; he draws the one to fill the other; there is no honour among conquerors!" —a frank avowal of the sentiments which guide even the most petty of the Turkish rulers.

Mohammed Aly had some notions of the English parliament; the name of Wellington was familiar to him. "He was a great general," he said; but he doubted whether, if his Lordship had commanded such bad soldiers as the Turkish troops are, he would have been able to do with them as much as he (the Pasha) had done in conquering Egypt and the Hedjaz. He betrayed great anxiety about the fate and future possession of Corfu and the Seven Islands. On the one hand, he wished the Russians to make war on the Porte, and to drive the Sultan out of Europe; on the other, he feared that, if the Russians should seize Turkey in Europe, the English would not remain quiet spectators, but would take their share of the Turkish empire, which he was firmly persuaded would be no other than the province of Egypt.

I am still ignorant of the Pasha's real opinion concerning my sincerity in professing the Mohammedan faith. He certainly treated me as a muselman, and I flattered myself that the boldness of my conduct at Tayf had convinced him that I was a true proselyte. As to the Kadhy, who was a shrewd Constantinopolitan, most people supposed that the Porte had sent him to watch the proceedings of Mohammed Aly, and give information accordingly to the Sultan; and it struck me that his behaviour towards myself was connected with an intention of accusing the Pasha, on his return to Constantinople, of having protected a Christian in his visit to the holy cities, a crime which would be considered unpardonable in a Pasha. Mohammed Aly, after his return to Cairo, (where, contrary to his expectations, he again found me, and where I only saw him once,) took frequent opportunities, and indeed seemed anxious, to convince Mr. Salt and Mr. Lee, His Majesty's and the Levant Company's consuls, as well as several English travellers of note who passed through Cairo, that he knew perfectly well, in the Hedjaz, that I was no Moslem, but that his friendship for the English nation made him overlook the circumstance, and permit me to impose upon the Kadhy. He entertained a notion, suggested to him by some of his Frank counsellors at Cairo, that, in some future account of my travels, I might perhaps boast of having imposed upon him, like Aly Bey el Abassi, whose work had just been received at Cairo, and who declares that he deceived not only the Pasha, but all the olemas, or learned men, of Cairo. To Mohammed Aly it was of more consequence not to be thought a fool than a bad muselman.

Notwithstanding these declarations of the Pasha to the English gentlemen, which were made in private, and certainly were not occasioned by any imprudent speeches of mine, I continued to live, after my return to Cairo, without molestation, as a Moslem, in the Turkish quarter. I have to thank him for his polite reception of me at Tayf, and for his having thrown no obstacles in the way of my travels through the Hedjaz.

I was at Mekka in December, and at Medina in the April following, when the Pasha was at both places; but I did not think it necessary or advisable to wait upon him at either place, where I was otherwise wholly unknown. My practice in travelling has been to live as retired as possible; and, except during my short visit to Tayf, where circumstances forced me to appear somewhat conspicuously, I was known only in the Hedjaz as a hadjy, or pilgrim, a private gentleman from Egypt, one with whom no person was acquainted but the few officers of the Pasha whom I had seen at Tayf.

My information respecting Tayf is very scanty, and was not

committed to paper until after I had left the town. I was never suffered to be alone during my stay there. I had no acquaintances from whom much could be learned; and during the fast of Ramadhan, few individuals of the higher classes, among whom I lived, stir out of their houses in the day-time.

The town of Tayf is situated in the midst of a sandy plain, about four hours in circuit, overgrown with shombs, and encompassed by low mountains, called Djebal Ghazoan. These are subordinate ridges of the great chain, which, continuing for four or five hours farther east, are then lost in the plain. Tayf is an irregular square, of thirty-five minutes quick walking in circumference; it is inclosed with a wall and a ditch, newly constructed by Othman el Medhayfe. The wall has three gates, and is defended by several towers; but it is much less solid than the walls of Djidda, Medina, and Yembo, being in few places more than eighteen inches thick. On the west side, within the town, and forming a part of its wall, stands the castle, upon a rocky elevated site. It was built by Sherif Ghaleb, and has no claim to the title of a castle, except that it is larger than the other buildings in the town, and that its stone walls are stronger. Though it is now half ruined, Mohammed Aly had made this castle his head-quarters. The houses of the town are mostly small, but well built with stone: the sitting-rooms are on the upper floor; at least I saw no saloons on the ground-floor, as usual in Turkey. The streets are broader than those in most eastern towns. The only public place is in front of the castle, a large open space which serves for a market.

At present, Tayf may be described as in a state of ruin, for but few houses are in complete repair. Many of the buildings were destroyed by the Wahabys, when they took the town, in 1802; and as it has been almost abandoned since that period, every thing is hastening to decay. I saw two small mosques; the best, that of the Henoud, or Indians. The tomb of El Abbas, which had a good dome over it, and was often visited by pilgrims, has been entirely destroyed by the Wahabys. Excepting four or five buildings, now inhabited by the principal officers of the Pasha, I saw none above the most common size.

Tayf is supplied with water from two copious wells, one of which is within the walls, and the other just before one of the gates. The water is well-tasted, but heavy. The town is celebrated all over Arabia for its beautiful gardens; but these are situated at the foot of the mountains which encircle the sandy plain. I did not see any gardens, nor even a single tree within the walls; and the immediate neighbourhood is entirely destitute of verdure, which renders a residence here as melancholy as in any other city of Arabia. The nearest gardens appeared to be on the S. W. side, at the distance of about half or three quarters of an hour : on that side also stands a deserted suburb, separated from the town, with some date-trees among its ruins; it was abandoned long before the invasion of the Wahabys.

I did not visit any of the gardens. In some of them are small pavilions, where the people of Tayf pass their festive hours; the most noted of them are Wady Methna, Wady Selame, and Wady Shemal. The gardens are watered by wells and by rivulets, which descend from the mountains. Numerous fruit-trees are found here, together with fields of wheat and barley. The fruits which I tasted at Tayf were grapes of a very large size and delicious flavour, figs, quinces, and pomegranates; but all the other sorts mentioned at Djebel Kora are likewise found here. The gardens of Tayf are renowned also for the abundance of their roses, which, like the grapes, are transported to all parts of the Hedjaz. To these gardens all the great merchants of Mekka formerly retired in summer; and here the Sherif himself often passed a part of the hot season : they had all their houses and establishments here, and therefore lost considerable property, when Tayf was plundered by the Wahabys.

The indigenous inhabitants of Tayf are Arabs, of the tribe of

Thekyf,* who have become settlers: in their possession are all the gardens adjoining the town, and most of the provision-shops within its walls. A few Mekkawys are also settled here, but the far greater part of the foreigners are Indians by origin. As at Djidda, these people, although born in Arabia, and in some instances established here for several generations, still preserve the dress and manners of the Indian Muselmans: some of them are merchants; but the greater part are druggists, whose trade is of much more importance in the Hedjaz than in other countries, from the general predilection of all classes for drugs, perfumes, &c. There are, I believe, no wholesale merchants in Tayf; I counted in all about fifty shops. Before the Wahaby invasion, this was a commercial town, to which the Arabs of the country around, at the distance of many days' journey, resorted, that they might purchase articles of dress; while those of the mountains brought caravans of wheat and barley: it was also a considerable *entrepôt* for coffee, brought on camels from the mountains of Yemen by Bedouins, who thus eluded the heavy duties levied in the harbours of the Arabian coast. Every thing denotes great misery in the town. At present, the only imports from the interior are dates, brought by the Ateybe Arabs from the many fruitful plantations in their territory. The principal streets abound with beggars, amongst whom are many Indians, who must often be exposed to perish from absolute hunger; for, during my residence, it required at least two piastres, (which, according to the actual exchange, was equal to about one-sixth of a dollar, or ten-pence) to procure bread enough for a man's daily subsistence. Caravans of provisions arrived every week, but the want of camels did not allow of a sufficient importation from the coast to lower the price of food; and although the common class lived principally upon dates, and thus

---

* Of the Thekyf tribes are El Hamde, Beni Mohammed, and Themale.—Vide Assamy.

consumed none of the provisions brought hither from Mekka; yet I learned from good authority that there was only a supply for ten days in Tayf for the Turkish army.

In the time of the Sherif, this town was governed by an officer of his appointment, named Hakem, himself a sherif, and who narrowly escaped the sword of the Wahabys. He has been restored to his office by Mohammed Aly; but it is at present merely honorary. Several sherif families of Mekka are settled here; and the mode of living, the dress, and manners, appear to be the same as at Mekka; but I had few opportunities of making observations on this subject.

September 7th. I set out early in the morning from Tayf for Mekka, by the same road which I had come. There is, as I have already mentioned, a more northern route, by which caravans may avoid the difficulties of passing Djebel Kora. The first station from Mekka, on that road, is Zeyme, short of which, about ten miles, are several steep ascents. Zeyme is a half-ruined castle, at the eastern extremity of Wady Lymoun, with copious springs of running water. Wady Lymoun is a fertile valley, which extends for several hours in the direction of Wady Fatmé; it has many date-plantations, and formerly the ground was cultivated; but this, I believe, has ceased since the Wahaby invasion: its fruit-gardens, too, have been ruined. This is the last stage of the Eastern-Syrian Hadj route, or that which lies to the east of the Great Hedjaz chain, running from Medina to Mekka. To the S. E. or E. S. E. of Wady Lymoun, is another fertile valley, called Wady Medyk, where some sherifs are settled, and where Sherif Ghaleb possessed landed property.

From Zeyme, the road to Tayf leads, on the second day, from Mekka to Seyl, a rivulet so called, flowing across a plain, which is without trees, but affords abundance of rich pasture. At Seyl, the road enters a mountainous tract, through which is a difficult and very narrow passage of about six hours. The station of this day is Akrab, situated in the upper plain, at about three hours' distance from Tayf, to the northward, and on the same level with it: thus a traveller reaches Tayf on the fourth day from Mekka. This route was now impassable, except to large and well-protected caravans, the hostile Arabs of the Ateybe tribe having frequently made inroads on that side, and plundered small caravans.

Not far from Tayf I overtook three Arnaut soldiers, each, like myself, mounted on an ass. At Tayf they had exchanged their money, getting thirteen piastres of the Cairo mint for one Spanish dollar, which at Djidda was worth but eleven; they had, therefore, made a common purse of one thousand dollars, and travelled from Djidda to Tayf, whenever the road was secure, for the sake of the two piastres which they gained upon each dollar. They carried the money, sewed in bags, upon their asses; and having forgotten, perhaps, to leave out any cash for travelling expenses, they joined me, finding that my travelling sack was well stocked with provisions, and left me to pay for our joint expenses on the road, whenever we stopped at the coffee-huts. But they were good-humoured companions, and the expense was not thrown away.

In passing by Wady Mohram, I assumed the *ihram*, as being now for the first time about to visit Mekka and its temple. The ihram consists of two pieces of linen, or woollen, or cotton cloth, one of which is wrapped round the loins, and the other thrown over the neck and shoulders, so as to leave part of the right arm uncovered. Every garment must be laid aside before this is put on. Any piece of stuff will answer the purpose; but the law ordains that there shall be no seams in it, nor any silk or ornaments; and white is considered preferable to any other colour. White Indian cambric is usually employed for the purpose; but rich hadjys use, instead of it, white Cashmere shawls, which have not flowered borders. The head remains totally uncovered. It is not permitted to have the head shaved, in conformity with the oriental habits, until it is permitted also to lay aside the ihram.

The instep must likewise be uncovered: those, accordingly, who wear shoes, either cut a piece out of the upper leather, or have shoes made on purpose, such as the Turkish hadjys usually bring with them from Constantinople. Like most of the natives, I wore sandals while dressed in the ihram.

Old-age and disease are excuses for keeping the head covered; but this indulgence must be purchased by giving alms to the poor. The sun's rays become extremely troublesome to persons bareheaded; but although the law forbids that the head should be protected by any thing in immediate contact with it, there is no prohibition against the use of umbrellas, and with these most of the northern hadjys are provided, while the natives either brave the sun's rays, or merely tie a rag to a stick, and make a little shade, by turning it towards the sun.

Whether assumed in summer or in winter, the ihram is equally inconvenient and prejudicial to health, particularly among the northern Mohammedans, who, accustomed to thick woollen clothes, are at this period obliged to leave them off for many days; yet the religious zeal of some who visit the Hedjaz is so ardent, that if they arrive even several months previous to the Hadj, they vow on taking the ihram, in approaching Mekka, not to throw it off till after the completion of their pilgrimage to Arafat; and thus they remain for months covered, night and day, only with this thin cloak;* for the law forbids any other covering even at night; but with this few hadjys strictly comply.

When the ancient Arabs performed their pilgrimage to the idols at Mekka, they also took the ihram; but that pilgrimage was fixed to a certain period of the year, probably autumn; for although the Arabs computed by lunar months, they inserted one month every

---

* The Arabian historians relate that Haroun Errashid and his wife Zobeyda once performed the pilgrimage on foot, from Baghdad to Mekka, clothed only with the ihram; that at every station of the caravan there was a castle, with apartments splendidly furnished; and that the whole road was covered daily with carpets, on which they walked.

three years; and thus the month of the pilgrimage did not vary in its season, as at present. The intercalation of a month, established two hundred years before Islam, was prohibited by the Koran, which ordained that the same pilgrimage should be continued, in honour of the living God, which had before been performed in honour of idols, but that it should be fixed to a lunar month; thus its period became irregular, and in the space of thirty-three years was gradually changed from the depth of winter to the height of summer.

The person covered by the ihram, or, as he is called, El Mohrem, is not obliged to abstain from particular kinds of food, as ancient Arabians, who, during the time of wearing it, did not taste butter among other things; but he is enjoined to behave decently, not to curse, or quarrel, not to kill any animal, not even a flea on his body, nor to communicate with the other sex. The ihram of the women consists of a cloak which they wrap completely about them, with a veil so close that not even their eyes can be seen: according to the law, their hands and ankles must be covered, but this rule they generally disregard.

Although my companions, the soldiers, were going to Mekka, as well as myself, they did not think it necessary to take the ihram, which, as I have already said, the law prescribes at all times of the year to every one travelling towards the sacred city.

We remained an hour on the delightful summit of Djebel Kora, and towards the evening descended the mountain. A shower of rain obliged us to seek shelter in a spacious cavern by the side of the road, which is used on similar occasions by shepherds of the Hodheyl tribe; and we arrived after sun-set at the coffee-huts, before mentioned, on the mountain-side, where the caravans from Mekka alight. Here we kindled a large fire, and hired an earthen pot of the Arabs, in which we boiled some rice for our supper. The long day's march, the rain, and my light covering, brought on a slight fever; but I kept myself well covered during the night, and was in good health the next morning. The change of air, during my journey to Tayf, and the comparatively cooler climate of that place had already completely recovered me from the effects of my severe illness at Djidda. During the night, the Kadhy of Mekka arrived from Tayf.

September 8th. At day-break, I went to visit the Kadhy, whom I found smoking his pipe and drinking coffee; availing himself of the privilege granted to travellers in Ramadhan, of dispensing with the fast. According to our agreement at Tayf, I was to join him here on his way to Mekka; I could not therefore avoid joining him; but I was extremely averse to continuing with him, because he would probably carry me to his house at Mekka, where I should be again placed in a situation similar to that which had proved so uncomfortable at Tayf. He seemed, however, willing to avoid the trouble and expense of a guest; for when I expressed some apprehensions that my tired ass would be unable to keep pace with his fine mule, he immediately answered, that he hoped, at all events, to meet me again at Mekka. I departed, therefore, with the soldiers, leaving the Kadhy to repose a little longer. We passed the mid-day hours at the coffee-hut called Shedad, where several Bedouins were amusing themselves by shooting at a mark. They gave proofs of great dexterity, often hitting a piastre, which I placed at about forty yards' distance. Except coffee and water, nothing is to be procured in any of the huts on this road; the coffee is not served up in single cups, as usual in most parts of the Levant; but, whoever asks for it, has a small earthen pot of hot coffee set before him, containing from ten to fifteen cups: this quantity the traveller often drinks three or four times a day. These pots are called *mashrabe*. (See their form in the outlines annexed.)

Into the mouth of the pot is stuck a bunch of dry herbs, through which the liquid is poured. I have already noticed the immoderate use of coffee in this part of Arabia, and it is said to prevail still more in the south, and towards the vicinity of the coffee country.

On the road from Shedad, which lies along the lower plains, between sharp mountains, we were surprised by a most violent shower of rain and hail, which obliged us to halt. In a very short time the water poured down in torrents from the mountains; and when the hail ceased, after about an hour, we found that the rain, which still continued, had covered the Wady Noman with a sheet of water three feet deep, while streams of nearly five feet in breadth crossed the road with an impetuosity which rendered it impossible for us to pass them. In this situation we could neither advance nor retreat, knowing that similar currents would have been formed in our rear; we therefore took post on the side of the mountain, where we were sure of not being washed away, and where we could wait in security till the subsiding of the storm. The mountains, however, soon presented on their sides innumerable cascades, and the inundation became general; while the rain, accompanied with thunder and lightning, continued with undiminished violence. I saw the Kadhy, who had quitted Shedad soon after us, at some distance, separated from our party by a deep torrent, while several of his women, mounted upon mules, were also obliged to remain at a distance from him. We continued in this disagreeable situation for about three hours, when the rain ceased and the torrents soon diminished; but our asses could with difficulty be brought to attempt the slippery ground still covered with water, and we were at last obliged to alight and drive them before us, till we reached a more elevated surface. The Kadhy and his whole party were under the necessity of doing the same. Night now overtook us, and the cloudy sky involved us in complete darkness; but after an adventurous walk of three or four hours, stumbling or falling almost at every step, we reached the coffee-houses of Arafat, to the great satisfaction of my companions, the soldiers, who had entertained apprehensions for their money-bags. I was not less pleased myself, being much in want of a fire after such a drenching, with only the scanty covering of the ihram.

The coffee-houses, unfortunately, had also been inundated; we could not find a dry place on which to sit, and with some difficulty a fire was lighted in one of the small and more weather-proof huts of the Arabs, into which the Kadhy, with a few of his people and myself, crept, and boiled our coffee; in another hut were his women, crying from the severity of the cold. He not wishing that they should be exposed to the consequences of such a night's lodging, mounted again, after a stay of half an hour, and proceeded towards Mekka, leaving me and my party in possession of the fire, by the side of which, after some time, we contrived to make ourselves comfortable.

September 9th. We set out early, and found that the storm of yesterday had not extended farther than the plain of Arafat. Such storms and inundations are frequent in this country, where the seasons seem to be much less regular than in other places under the same latitude. I heard that in the Upper Mountains, and at Tayf, the rainy season, although not so regular as under the tropics in Africa, is yet more steady than in the low country of Mekka and Djidda, where, even in the midst of summer, the sky is often clouded by storms and rain. The historians of Mekka have recorded several dreadful inundations in that city; the most disastrous occurred in the years of the Hedjira 80, 184, 202, 280, 297, 549, 620, 802, 829. In some of these, the whole town of Mekka, and the Temple, as high as the black stone, were under water, and in all of them many houses were destroyed and lives lost. Assamy gives the details of an inundation which devastated Mekka in A. H. 1039, or in the year 1626 of our era, when five hundred lives were lost, and the Kaaba in the Temple was destroyed. Another dreadful inundation happened in 1672.

I arrived at Mekka about mid-day, when my companions went in search of their acquaintance among the soldiers, and left me to shift for myself, without knowing a single individual in the town, and without being recommended to any body but the Kadhy, whom, as I have already said, I wished to avoid.

Whoever enters Mekka, whether pilgrim or not, is enjoined by the law to visit the Temple immediately, and not to attend to any worldly concern whatever, before he has done so. We crossed the line of shops and houses, up to the gates of the mosque, where my ass-driver took his fare and set me down: here I was accosted by half a dozen *metowef*, or guides to the holy places, who knew, from my being dressed in the ihram, that I intended to visit the Kaaba. I chose one of them as my guide, and, after having deposited my baggage in a neighbouring shop, entered the mosque at the gate called Bab-es'-Salam, by which the new-comer is recommended to enter. The ceremonies to be performed in visiting the mosque are the following:—1. Certain religious rites to be practised in the interior of the temple; 2. The walk between Szafa and Meroua; 3. The visit to the Omra. These ceremonies ought to be repeated by every Moslem whenever he enters Mekka from a journey farther than two days' distance, and they must again be more particularly performed at the time of the pilgrimage to Arafat. I shall here describe them as briefly as possible; a full detail and explanation of the Mohammedan law on this subject would be extremely tedious; indeed there exist many voluminous works in Arabic which treat of nothing else.

1. *Rites to be performed in the Interior of the Temple.*

At the entrance, under the colonnade, some prayers are recited on first sight of the Kaaba, and then two *rikats*, or four prostrations addressed to the divinity, in thanks for having reached the holy spot, and in salutation of the mosque itself; after which the pilgrim approaches the Kaaba by one of the paved ways to it, through the open area in which it stands. In passing under the insulated arch in front of the Kaaba, called Bab-es'-Salam, certain prayers are said. Other prayers are recited in a low voice, and the visitor then places himself opposite to the black stone of the Kaaba, and prays two *rikats*; at the conclusion of which, the stone is touched with the right hand, or kissed, if there is no great pressure of people. The devotee then begins the *Towaf*, or walk round the Kaaba, keeping that building on his left hand. This ceremony is to be repeated seven times; the three first are in a quick pace, in imitation of the Prophet, whose enemies having reported that he was dangerously ill, he contradicted them by running thrice round the Kaaba at full speed. Every circuit must be accompanied with prescribed prayers, which are recited in a low voice, and appropriated to the different parts of the building that are passed: the black stone is kissed or touched at the conclusion of each circuit, as well as another stone, walled in at one corner of the black stone. When the seven circuits are finished, the visiter approaches the wall of the Kaaba, between the black stone and the door of the building, which space is called El Metzem. There, with widely outstretched arms, and with his breast closely pressed against the wall, he beseeches the Lord to pardon his sins. He then retires towards the neighbouring Mekam Ibrahim, and there prays two *rikats*, called Sunnet-et-towaf, after which he repairs to the adjoining well of Zemzem; and, after a short pious address in honour of the well, drinks as much of the water as he wishes, or as he can on occasions when the crowd is very great; and this completes the ceremonies to be observed within the temple.

I may here add, that the *Towaf* is a Muselman ceremony not exclusively practised in the temple at Mekka. In the summer of 1813, I was present at the annual festival of the patron saint of Kenne, in Upper Egypt, called Seid Abderrahman el Kennawy. Many thousands of the people of the country were assembled on the plain, in which stands the saint's tomb, at a distance of one mile from the town. Each person, as he arrived, walked seven times round the small mosque which contains the tomb; and when the new covering intended to be laid over it for that year was brought in solemn procession, the whole assembly followed it seven times round the building, after which it was placed upon the tomb.

2. Walk between Szafa and Meroua.

My guide, who, during the whole of the ceremonies above mentioned, had been close at my heels, reciting all the necessary prayers, which I repeated after him, now led me out of the mosque by the gate called Bab-es'-Szafa. About fifty yards from the S. E. side of the mosque, on a slightly ascending ground, stand three small open arches, connected by an architrave above, having below three broad stone steps leading up to them.

This is called the Hill of Szafa: here, standing on the upper step, with his face turned towards the mosque, which is hidden from view by intervening houses, the pilgrim raises his hands towards heaven, addresses a short prayer to the Deity, and implores his assistance in the holy walk, or Say, as it is called; he then descends, to begin the walk, along a level street about six hundred paces in length, which the Arabian historians call Wady Szafa, leading towards Meroua, which is at its farther extremity, where stands a stone platform, elevated about six or eight feet above the level of the street, with several broad steps ascending to it. The visiter is enjoined to walk at a quick pace from Szafa to Meroua; and for a short space, which is marked by four stones or pilasters, called El Myleyn el Akhdereyn, built into the walls of the houses on both sides, he must run. Two of these stones seemed to be of a green colour; they exhibit numerous inscriptions; but these are so high in the walls, that it would be difficult to read them. Prayers are recited uninterruptedly in a loud voice during this walk. Persons who are unwell may ride, or be borne in a litter. On reaching Meroua, the pilgrim ascends the steps, and, with uplifted hands, repeats a short prayer like that of Szaffa, to which place he must now return. The walk between the two places is to be repeated seven times, concluding at Meroua; four times from Szaffa to Meroua; and three times from Meroua to Szaffa.

3. *The Visit to the Omra.*

In the vicinity of Meroua are many barbers' shops; into one of these the pilgrim enters, having completed the Say, and the barber shaves his head, reciting a particular prayer, which the pilgrim repeats after him. The Hanefys, one of the four orthodox sects of Moslims, shave only one-fourth part of the head; the other three-fourths continuing untouched till they return from the Omra. After the ceremony of shaving is finished, the visitor is at liberty to lay aside the ihram, and put on his ordinary dress; or, if he choose, he may go immediately from thence to the Omra, in which case he still wears the ihram, and says only two rikats on setting out. This, however, is seldom done, as the ceremonies of the Towaf and Say are sufficiently fatiguing to render repose desirable on their completion; the visitor, therefore, dresses in his usual clothes; but the next or any following day, (the sooner the better,) he resumes the ihram, with the same ceremonies as are observed on first assuming it, and then proceeds to the Omra, a place one hour and a half from Mekka. Here he repeats two rikats in a small chapel, and returns to the city, chanting all the way the pious ejaculations called Telby, beginning with the words, "Lebeyk, Alla humma, Lebeyk." He must now again perform the Towaf and the Say, have his head completely shaved, and lay aside the ihram, which closes those ceremonies. A visit to the Omra is enjoined by the law as absolutely necessary; but many individuals, notwithstanding, dispense with it. I went thither, on the third day after my arrival in the city, performing the walk in the night-time, which is the fashion during the hot season.

At the time of the Hadj, all these ceremonies must be repeated after returning from Wady Muna, and again on taking leave of Mekka. The Towaf, or walk round the Kaaba, should also be performed as often as convenient; and few foreigners live at Mekka, who do not make it a point to execute it twice daily; in the evening and before day-break.

Prior to the age of Mohammed, when idolatry prevailed in Arabia, the Kaaba was regarded as a sacred object, and visited with religious veneration by persons who performed the Towaf nearly in the same manner as their descendants do at present. The building, however, was, in those times, ornamented with three hundred and sixty idols, and there was a very important difference in the ceremony; for men and women were then obliged to appear in a state of perfect nudity, that their sins might be thrown off with their garments. The Mohammedan Hadj or pilgrimage, and the visit to the Kaaba, are, therefore, nothing more than a continuation and confirmation of the ancient custom. In like manner, Szafa and Meroua were esteemed by the old Arabians as holy places, which contained images of the gods Motam and Nehyk; and here the idolaters used to walk from the one place to the other, after their return from the pilgrimage to Arafat. Here, if we may believe Mohammedan tradition, Hadjer, the mother of Ismayl, wandered about in the Desert, after she had been driven from Abraham's house, that she might not witness the death of her infant son, whom she had laid down almost expiring from thirst; when the angel Gabriel appearing, struck the ground with his foot, which caused the well of Zemzem immediately to spring forth. In commemoration of the wanderings of Hadjer, who in her affliction had gone seven times between Szafa and Meroua, the walk from one place to the other is said to have been instituted.

El Azraky relates that, when the idolatrous Arabs had concluded the ceremonies of the Hadj at Arafat, all the different tribes that had been present, assembled, on their return to Mekka, at the holy place called Szafa, there to extol, in loud and impassioned strains, the glory of their ancestors, their battles, and the fame of their nation. From each tribe, in its turn, arose a poet who addressed the multitude. "To our tribe," exclaimed he, "belonged such and such eminent warriors and generous Arabs; and now," he added, "we boast of others." He then recited their names, and sang their praises; concluding with a strain of heroic poetry, and an appeal to the other tribes, in words like the following :—"Let him who denies the truth of what I have said, or who lays claim to as much glory, honour, and virtue as we do, prove it here!" Some rival poet then arose, and celebrated in similar language the equal or superior glory attached to his own tribe, endeavouring, at the same time, to undervalue or ridicule his rival's pretensions.

To allay the animosity and jealousies produced by this custom; or, perhaps, to break the independent spirit of his fierce Bedouins, Mohammed abolished it by a passage in the Koran, which says:— "When you have completed the rites of the pilgrimage, remember God, as you formerly were wont to commemorate your forefathers, and with still greater fervency." Thus, probably, was removed the cause of many quarrels; but, at the same time, this stern lawgiver destroyed the influence which the songs of those rival national bards exercised over the martial virtues and literary genius of their countrymen.

The visit of the Omra was likewise an ancient custom. Mohammed retained the practice; and it is said that he frequently recited his evening prayers on that spot.

Having completed the fatiguing ceremonies of the Towaf and Say, I had a part of my head shaved, and remained sitting in the barber's shop, not knowing any other place of repose. I inquired after lodgings, but learned that the town was already full of pilgrims, and that many others, who were expected, had engaged apartments. After some time, however, I found a man who offered me a ready-furnished room: of this I took possession, and having no servant, boarded with the owner. He and his family, consisting of a wife and two children, retired into a small, open court-yard, on the side of my room. The landlord was a poor man from Medina, and by profession a Metowaf, or *cicerone*. Although his mode of living was much below that of even the second class of Mekkawys, yet it cost me fifteen piastres a day; and I found, after we parted, that several articles of dress had been pilfered from my travelling sack; but this was not all: on the feast-day he invited me to a splendid supper, in company with half a dozen of his friends, in my room, and on the following morning he presented me with a bill for the whole expense of this entertainment.

The thousands of lamps lighted during Ramadhan in the great mosque, rendered it the nightly resort of all foreigners at Mekka; here they took their walk, or sat conversing till after midnight. The scene presented altogether a spectacle which (excepting the absence of women) resembled rather an European midnight assemblage, than what I should have expected in the sanctuary of the Mohammedan religion. The night which closes Ramadhan, did not present those brilliant displays of rejoicing that are seen in other parts of the East; and the three subsequent days of the festival are equally devoid of public amusements. A few swinging machines were placed in the streets to amuse children, and some Egyptian jugglers exhibited their feats to multitudes assembled in the streets; but little else occurred to mark the feast, except a display of gaudy dresses, in which the Arabians surpass both Syrians and Egyptians.

I paid the visit, customary on occasion of this feast, to the Kadhy, and at the expiration of the third day, (on the 15th of September,) set out for Djidda, to complete my travelling equipments, which are more easily procured there than at Mekka. On my way to the coast, I was nearly made prisoner at Bahra by a flying corps of Wahabys. My stay at Djidda was prolonged to three weeks, chiefly in consequence of sore legs; a disease very prevalent on this unhealthy coast, where every bite of a gnat, if neglected, becomes a serious wound.

About the middle of October I returned to Mekka, accompanied by a slave whom I had purchased. This boy had been in the caravan with which I went from the Black Country to Sowakin, and was quite astonished at seeing me in a condition so superior to that in which he had before known me. I took with me a camel-load of provisions, mostly flour, biscuit, and butter, procured in Djidda at one third of the price demanded at Mekka, where, immediately on my arrival, I hired decent apartments in a quarter of the town not much frequented, called Haret el Mesfale. I had here the advantage of several large trees growing before my windows, the verdure of which, among the barren and sun-burnt rocks of Mekka, was to me more exhilarating than the finest landscape could have been under different circumstances. At this place I enjoyed an enviable freedom and independence, known only to the Kadhy and his followers, who soon after took their departure. The Pasha and his court remained at Tayf till the days of the Hadj. I frequented only such society as pleased me, and, mixing with a crowd of foreign pilgrims from all parts of the world, I was not liable to impertinent remarks or disagreeable inquiries. If any question arose about my origin (a circumstance that rarely happened in a place which always abounds with strangers), I stated myself to be a reduced member of the Mamelouk corps of Egypt, and found it easy to avoid those persons whose intimate knowledge of that country might perhaps have enabled them to detect the falsehood. But there was little to be apprehended even from the consequences of such detection; for the assumption of a false character is frequent among all eastern travellers, and especially at Mekka, where every one affects poverty in order to escape imposition, or being led into great expenses. During all my journies in the East, I never enjoyed such perfect ease as at Mekka; and I shall always retain a pleasing recollection of my residence there, although the state of my health did not permit me to benefit by all the advantages that my situation offered. I shall now proceed to describe the town, its inhabitants, and the pilgrimage, and then resume the narrative of my travels.

DESCRIPTION OF MEKKA.*

Mekka is dignified among the Arabs with many lofty-sounding titles. The most common are Om el Kora (the mother of towns);

---

* EXPLANATION OF THE PLAN.

1. The Quarter of Djerouel.
2. The Quarter el Báb.
3. The Quarter el Shebeyka.
4. The Quarter el Khandaryse.
5. The Quarter el Hedjla.
6. A house of the Sherif.
7. The Quarter called Souk-es'-Sogheyr.
8. Quarter called el Mesfale.
9. Quarter called Báb el Omra.
10. Quarter called Shamye.
11. Quarter called Soeyga.
12. Quarter called Garara.
13. House of the family of Djeylany.
14. A Quarter half-ruined, inhabited by poor people.
15. Quarter called Rakoube.
16. Wady el Naga.
17. Principal palace of the Sherif.
18. Quarter called el Soleymanye.
19. Quarter called Shab Aamer.
20. The Street el Hadadeyn.
21. Quarter called el Málá.
22. A small Mesdjed or Mosque.
23. Quarter called el Múmele.
24. Quarter called Ghazze.
25. Quarter called Shab el Mouled.
26. Quarter called Souk el Leyl.
27. Quarter called el Modaa.
28. 28. Two Corn Magazines.
29. El Meroua.
30. El Messa.
31. Quarter called Zogág el Hadjar.
32. Mouled Sitna Fatme.
33. The Street called Derb el Syny.
34. Quarter called Geshashye.
35. Quarter called Shab Aly.
36. Es' Szafa.
37. Two houses of the Sherif.
38. Wells of brackish water in different parts of the town.
39. Quarter called el Djyád.
40. Huts occupied by the Sherif's slaves.
41. The Sherif's palace, called Beit es Sade
42. The great Castle.
43. A ruined Quarter.
44. Ruined Khan of the Yemen pilgrims.
45. Birket Mádjen, a tank for the Yemen pilgrims.
46. Some cultivated fields.
47. Birket es Shámy.
48. Birket el Masry.
49. Cultivated fields.
50. A house of the Sherif.
51. Mekam Abon Taleb.
52. A large stone trough, filled with water of the Canal.
53. Paved road to Sheikh Mahmoud.
54. Sheikh Mahmoud, at the encamping place of the Syrian pilgrims.
55. The Tomb of Khadidje, wife of Mohammed.
56. A large palace of the Sherif, serving as barracks.
57. Suburbs called Moábede.
58. A public fountain supplied by water of the Canal.
59. A Summer-house of the Sherif, with a garden.
60. A Well.
61. The great Mosque, called El Haram.
62. The House of the Kadhy, annexed to the Mosque.
63. The Tomb of Seyd Ageyl, a great merchant, annexed to the Mosque.
64. Apartments originally belonging to a public school, where the Pashas who come to Mekka reside.
65. The Mountain called Djebel Hindy.
66. The Mountain called Djebel Lala, or Djebel Kokeykan.
67. Djebel Abou Kobeys.
68. The highest summit of the mountains of Mekka, called Khandame.
69. Djebel Omar.
a. Round Watch-towers in different parts.
b. Baths in different quarters.
c. Burial-grounds; the one called Kebour Shebeyka; the other Kebour el Málá.
d. Small encampment of Bedouins.
e. Public Fountains supplied by water of the Canal.

to face p. 102.

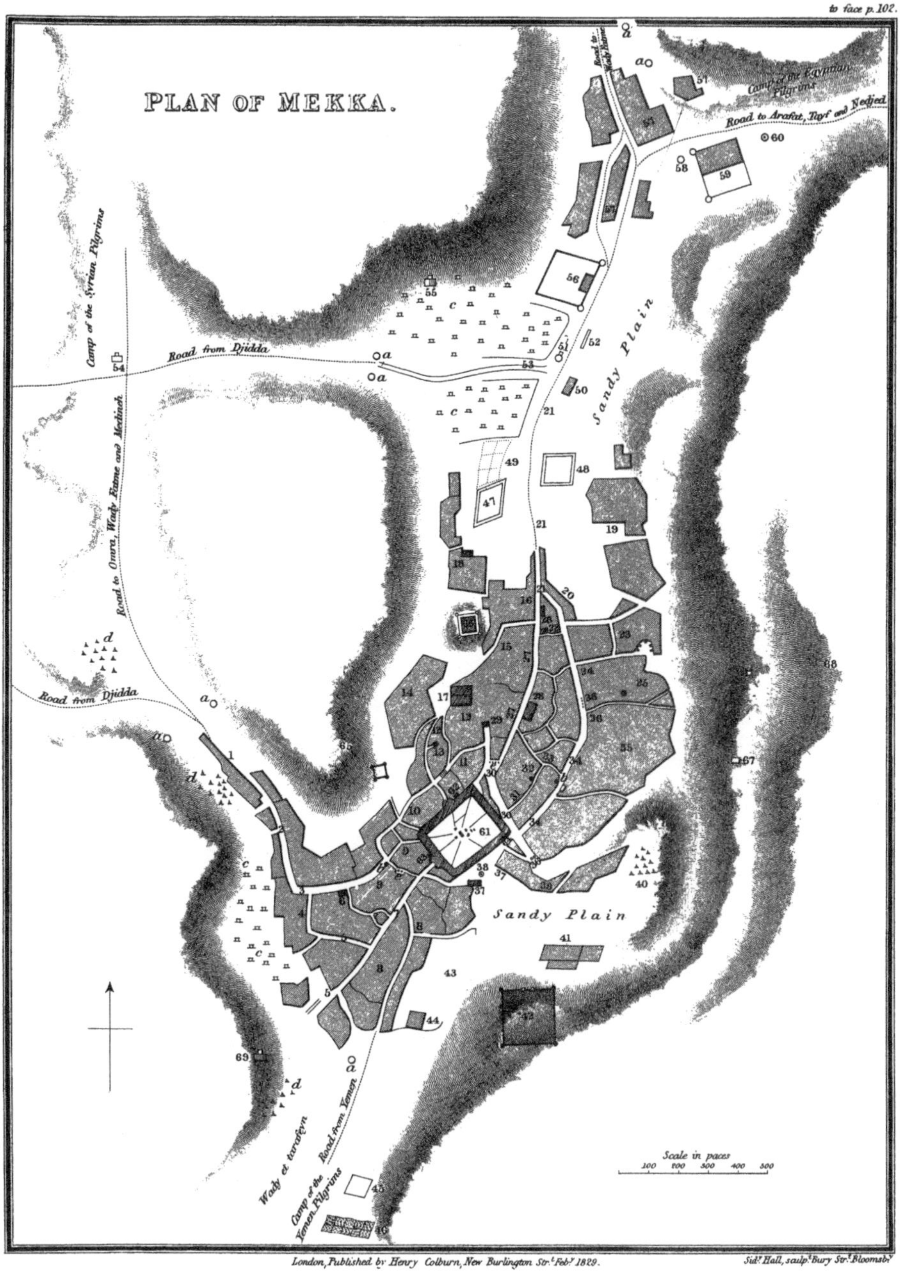

London, Published by Henry Colburn, New Burlington Str.t Feb.y 1829.

Sid.y Hall, sculp.t Bury Str.t Bloomsb.y

DESCRIPTION OF MEKKA. 103

El Mosherefe (the noble); Beled al Ameyn (the region of the faithful). Firuzabádi, the celebrated author of the Kamus, has composed a whole treatise on the different names of Mekka. This town is situated in a valley, narrow and sandy, the main direction of which is from north to south; but it inclines towards the north-west near the southern extremity of the town. In breadth this valley varies from one hundred to seven hundred paces, the chief part of the city being placed where the valley is most broad. In the narrower part are single rows of houses only, or detached shops. The town itself covers a space of about fifteen hundred paces in length, from the quarter called El Shebeyka to the extremity of the Mala; but the whole extent of ground comprehended under the denomination of Mekka, from the suburb called Djerouel (where is the entrance from Djidda) to the suburb called Moabede (on the Tayf road), amounts to three thousand five hundred paces. The mountains inclosing this valley (which, before the town was built, the Arabs had named Wady Mekka or Bekka) are from two to five hundred feet in height, completely barren and destitute of trees. The principal chain lies on the eastern side of the town: the valley slopes gently towards the south, where stands the quarter called El Mesfale (the low place). The rain-water from the town is lost towards the south of Mesfale in the open valley named Wady el Tarafeyn. Most of the town is situated in the valley itself; but there are also parts built on the sides of the mountains, principally of the eastern chain, where the primitive habitations of the Koreysh, and the ancient town appear to have been placed.

Mekka may be styled a handsome town: its streets are in general broader than those of eastern cities; the houses lofty, and built of stone; and the numerous windows that face the streets give them a more lively and European aspect than those of Egypt or Syria, where the houses present but few windows towards the exterior. Mekka (like Djidda) contains many houses three stories high; few at Mekka are white-washed; but the dark grey colour of the stone is much preferable to the glaring white that offends the eye in Djidda. In most towns of the Levant the narrowness of a street contributes to its coolness; and in countries where wheel-carriages are not used, a space that allows two loaded camels to pass each other is deemed sufficient. At Mekka, however, it was necessary to leave the passages wide, for the innumerable visitors who here crowd together; and it is in the houses adapted for the reception of pilgrims and other sojourners, that the windows are so contrived as to command a view of the streets.

The city is open on every side; but the neighbouring mountains, if properly defended, would form a barrier of considerable strength against an enemy. In former times it had three walls to protect its extremities; one was built across the valley, at the street of Mala; another at the quarter of Shebeyka; and the third at the valley opening into the Mesfale. These walls were repaired in A. H. 816 and 828, and in a century after some traces of them still remained.*

The only public place in the body of the town is the ample square of the great mosque; no trees or gardens cheer the eye; and the scene is enlivened only during the Hadj by the great number of well-stored shops which are found in every quarter. Except four or five large houses belonging to the Sherif, two *medreses* or colleges (now converted into corn magazines), and the mosque, with some buildings and schools attached to it, Mekka cannot boast of any public edifices, and in this respect is, perhaps, more deficient than any other eastern city of the same size. Neither khans, for the accommodation of travellers, or for the deposit of merchandize, nor palaces of grandees, nor mosques, which adorn every quarter of other towns in the East, are here to be seen; and we may perhaps attribute this want of splendid buildings to the veneration which its inhabitants entertain for their temple; this prevents them from constructing any edifice which might possibly pretend to rival it.

The mode of building is the same as that adopted at Djidda, with the addition of windows looking towards the street; of these many project from the wall, and have their frame-work elaborately

* See Azraky, Fasy, and Kotobeddyn.

carved, or gaudily painted. Before them hang blinds made of slight reeds, which exclude flies and gnats while they admit fresh air. Every house has its terrace, the floor of which (composed of a preparation from lime-stone) is built with a slight inclination, so that the rain-water runs off through gutters into the street; for the rains here are so irregular that it is not worth while to collect the water of them in cisterns, as is done in Syria. The terraces are concealed from view by slight parapet walls; for throughout the east it is reckoned discreditable that a man should appear upon the terrace, whence he might be accused of looking at women in the neighbouring houses, as the females pass much of their time on the terraces, employed in various domestic occupations, such as drying corn, hanging up linen, &c. The Europeans of Aleppo alone enjoy the privilege of frequenting their terraces, which are often beautifully built of stone; here they resort during the summer evenings, and often to sup and pass the night. All the houses of the Mekkawys, except those of the principal and richest inhabitants, are constructed for the accommodation of lodgers, being divided into many apartments, separated from each other, and each consisting of a sitting-room and a small kitchen. Since the pilgrimage, which has begun to decline, (this happened before the Wahaby conquest,) many of the Mekkawys, no longer deriving profit from the letting of their lodgings, found themselves unable to afford the expense of repairs; and thus numerous buildings in the out-skirts have fallen completely into ruin, and the town itself exhibits in every street houses rapidly decaying. I saw only one of recent construction; it was in the quarter of El Shebeyka, belonged to a sherif, and cost, as report said, one hundred and fifty purses; such a house might have been built at Cairo for sixty purses.

The streets are all unpaved; and in summer time the sand and dust in them are as great a nuisance as the mud is in the rainy season, during which they are scarcely passable after a shower; for in the interior of the town the water does not run off, but remains till it is dried up. It may be ascribed to the destructive rains, which, though of shorter duration than in other tropical countries, fall with considerable violence, that no ancient buildings are found in Mekka. The mosque itself has undergone so many repairs under different sultans, that it may be called a modern structure; and of the houses, I do not think there exists one older than four centuries; it is not, therefore, in this place, that the traveller must look for interesting specimens of architecture or such beautiful remains of Saracenic structures as are still admired in Syria, Egypt, Barbary, and Spain. In this respect the ancient and far-famed Mekka is surpassed by the smallest provincial towns of Syria or Egypt. The same may be said with respect to Medina, and I suspect that the towns of Yemen are generally poor in architectural remains.

Mekka is deficient in those regulations of police which are customary in Eastern cities. The streets are totally dark at night, no lamps of any kind being lighted; its different quarters are without gates, differing in this respect also from most Eastern towns, where each quarter is regularly shut up after the last evening prayers. The town may therefore be crossed at any time of the night, and the same attention is not paid here to the security of merchants, as well as of husbands, (on whose account principally, the quarters are closed,) as in Syrian or Egyptian towns of equal magnitude. The dirt and sweepings of the houses are cast into the streets, where they soon become dust or mud according to the season. The same custom seems to have prevailed equally in ancient times; for I did not perceive in the skirts of the town any of those heaps of rubbish which are usually found near the large towns of Turkey.

With respect to water, the most important of all supplies, and that which always forms the first object of inquiry among Asiatics, Mekka is not much better provided than Djidda; there are but few cisterns for collecting rain, and the well-water is so brackish that it is used only for culinary purposes, except during the time of the pilgrimage, when the lowest class of hadjys drink it. The famous well of Zemzem, in the great mosque, is indeed sufficiently copious to supply the whole town; but, however holy, its water is heavy to the taste and impedes digestion; the poorer classes besides have not permission to fill their water-skins with it at pleasure. The best water in Mekka is brought by a conduit from the vicinity of Arafat, six or seven hours distant. The present government, instead of constructing similar works, neglects even the repairs and requisite cleansing of this aqueduct. It is wholly built of stone; and all those parts of it which appear above ground, are covered with a thick layer of stone and cement. I heard that it had not been cleaned during the last fifty years; the consequence of this negligence is, that the most of the water is lost in its passage to the city through apertures, or slowly forces its way through the obstructing sediment, though it flows in a full stream into the head of the aqueduct at Arafat. The supply which it affords in ordinary times is barely sufficient for the use of the inhabitants, and during the pilgrimage sweet water becomes an absolute scarcity; a small skin of water (two of which skins a person may carry) being then often sold for one shilling—a very high price among Arabs.

There are two places in the interior of Mekka where the aqueduct runs above ground; there the water is let off into small channels or fountains, at which some slaves of the Sherif are stationed, to exact a toll from persons filling their water-skins. In the time of the Hadj, these fountains are surrounded day and night by crowds of people quarrelling and fighting for access to the water. During the late siege the Wahabys cut off the supply of water from the aqueduct; and it was not till some time after, that the injury which this structure then received, was partially repaired.

The history of this aqueduct, a work of vast labour and magnitude, is given by the Arabian historians at great length. Zebeyda, the wife of Haroun-er'-Rashid, first carried the spring, called Ayn Noman, from its source in Djebel Kora to the town. The spring of Ayn Arf from the foot of Djebel Shamekh to the north of Djebel Kora, which watered the fertile valley called Wady Honeyn, was next brought to join the Ayn Noman; and, finally, four other sources were added to the aqueduct—El Beroud, Zafaran, Meymoun, and Ayn Meshash.

Subsequently it seems to have been obstructed; but in A. H. 643 it was repaired by Kokeboury, King of Arbela; again in 762, by order of Sultan Sayd Khadanbede; and a third time, but not completely, in 811, by the Sherif Hassan Ibn Adjelan, then reigning. Kaiabey, Sultan of Egypt, expended a large sum upon it in 879; and in 916, Kansoue el Ghoury, one of the last of the Zirkassian kings of Egypt, contributed to its repair: but the aqueduct was still often obstructed; and whenever that happened, the Mekkawys and Hadjys were exposed to great privations. In 931, Sultan Soleyman attempted to construct it anew; but the design was not completed. At last, his son, Selym Ibn Soleyman, or Selim II., after many years labour, and at enormous expense, excavated a passage through the rocks behind Arafat, and formed a new conduit, which alone now subsists. He succeeded in bringing water very abundantly to the town, in A.H. 979. The whole length of the aqueduct is seven or eight hours.

There is a small spring which oozes from under the rocks behind the great palace of the Sherif, called Beit el Sad; it is said to afford the best water in this country, but the supply is very scanty. The spring is inclosed, and appropriated wholly to the Sherif's family.

Beggars, and infirm or indigent hadjys, often intreat the passengers in the streets of Mekka for a draught of sweet water; they particularly surround the water-stands, which are seen in every corner, and where, for two paras in the time of the Hadj, and for one para, at other times, as much water may be obtained as will fill a jar.

I shall now proceed to describe the different quarters of Mekka, reserving an account of the great mosque to the last; and then add some notices respecting the inhabitants and government.

QUARTERS OF MEKKA.

At the entrance from the side of Djidda, in turning round the angle of a sandy and gravelly valley, the traveller sees two round watch-towers. They were constructed by the Sherif Ghaleb for the defence of his capital. Similar towers are seen at the other entrances of the town, and they are sufficiently spacious to contain about twenty men. As the hills approach very closely at the entrance of the city, these towers command the passage. Here, it appears, was formerly a gate, the threshold of which only is now remaining, close to a small building, where the officers of the Sherif collected the duties on merchandize, &c. carried into the town. Here, also, is a row of shops, and low, ruined dwelling-houses, known by the appellation of Hareh, or the quarter El Djerouel. It comprises an encampment to the right, in which the Bedouins live who carry on the transport trade between Mekka and Djidda; they belong to the tribes of Harb, Metrefy, and Lahawy.

Beyond the Djerouel, the name of the street changes to that of Haret el Bab. This is a broad street, with several good houses, and leads into the quarter of El Shebeyka, which extends principally to the right, and is so called because the followers of Mohammed, in their wars with the Koreysh, were here attacked and closely pressed by their enemies. There are many good houses in Shebeyka, which is one of the cleanest and airiest quarters in the town. Many of the people of Djidda reside in it; and here also the Sherif Ghaleb has a good house, where his family, consisting of several young children and a grown-up daughter, continued to dwell after his deposition. The main street is lined with coffee-shops, from which the post sets out every evening, on asses, with the letters for Djidda. This is the only post for letters that I have seen in the East, besides that established among the Europeans at Cairo, between that city and Alexandria; but the delivery of letters is there much less regular than it is at Mekka, where it is duly performed, and at the trifling expense of two paras upon each letter, and as much more for the person who distributes the letters received from Djidda.

In the coffee-shops just mentioned, live also the caravan-brokers, through whose agency the Bedouins let out their camels for the journey to Djidda and Medina.

On the western side of the Shebeyka, towards the mountain, is a large burying-ground, in which are dispersed huts and tents of Bedouins, and some miserable dwellings of the lowest class of public women: this is called El Khandaryse. Although tradition says that great numbers of the friends and adherents of Mohammed lie buried here, yet it has become unfashionable to deposit the dead in it; and all of the first and second classes of Mekkawys use the extensive cemeteries lying on the north of the town. There are few shops in the Shebeyka; and it does not contain many foreign inmates during the Hadj, being inhabited by persons in easy circumstances, who consider it disgraceful to let out apartments.

In proceeding from the Shebeyka along the broad street, northerly, we come to a bath, which, though by far the best of the three in Mekka, is inferior to those of other Asiatic cities, from the scarcity of water; it was built in A. H. 980, by Mohammed Pasha, the vizier of Sultan Soleyman II., and is one of the best structures in the town.* It is frequented principally by foreigners, the native Arabs being little accustomed to the use of the bath, and choosing to perform the ablutions prescribed by their religion at their own dwellings.

The bath, together with several by-streets leading to the mosque, forms the quarter called Haret Bab el Omra, which is inhabited by

---

* Vide Kotobeddyn.

a number of the guides called Metowef, and is full of pilgrims, especially of those from Turkey. The streets are narrow, and excessively dirty; but the hadjys prefer the quarter, because it is the cheapest in the vicinity of the mosque, near which they are anxious to reside, that they may be sure of not missing the prayers; or, (as they add) that, if disturbed in their sleep, they may have the temple close at hand to dispel their bad dreams. Men are seen, in the middle of the night, running to the mosque in their sleeping-clothes; here they perform the walk round the Kaba, kiss the black stone, utter a short prayer, drink of the water of Zemzem, and then return to their beds. Near to the gate of the mosque called Bab Omra, from which this quarter takes its name, is a spacious building, originally a public school, but now occupied by Hassan Pasha, governor of Mekka. It is probably the Medrese mentioned by El Fasy, as having been built near Bab el Omra, in A. H. 814, by the orders of Mansour Ghyath Eddyn Atham Shah, the Lord of Bengal. In A. H. 519, the governor of Aden also ordered a Medrese to be built in this neighbourhood, which was called Dar-es'-Selsalè. In this quarter is one of the fountains of sweet water derived from the canal, and there are several wells of brackish water.

Returning from hence to the Shebeyka, and then turning southerly along different streets, composed of good buildings, but which are rapidly falling to decay, we descend by a slight slope into the street called Souk-es'-Sogheyr, or the little market, which terminates at the gate of the great mosque, called Bab Ibrahim. The houses on both sides of this street are low, and inhabited by the lower classes. There is a continued range of shops, in which are sold all sorts of provisions, but principally grain, butter, and dates. In some of the shops locusts are sold by measure. The Souk is frequented chiefly by Bedouins of the southern part of Arabia, who bring hither charcoal. Some poor Negro pilgrims of Africa take up their abode also in the miserable huts and ruined houses of this part of the town, and have here established a market for firewood, which they collect in the surrounding mountains.

The extremity of Souk-es'-Sogheyr, towards the mountain, is called Haret el Hadjela, or Hadjela b'il Tekyet Sadek; where stand a few tolerably good houses, inhabited by the eunuchs who guard the mosque, and who live there with their *wives*, for they are all married to black slaves. This is the lowest part of the town; and whenever great floods, during the rainy season, inundate the valley, the water rushes through this street, in its way to the open country. Some remains of the aqueduct are visible here; for when it was kept in good repair, its water, after supplying the town, was conducted this way into the southern valley, where it served to irrigate some fields.

The Souk-es'-Sogheyr is sometimes comprehended in the Mesfale, or " low place," the name of the quarter on the east and south sides of the Souk; but that name is more commonly applied exclusively to the latter district. The Mesfale is tolerably well built, and, like the Shebeyka, contains a few new houses; but that part of it which lies towards the great castle-hill is now almost entirely in ruins. It is inhabited by Arab and Bedouin merchants, who travel in time of peace to Yemen, principally to Mokhowa, from whence they import grain, coffee-beans, and dried grapes. It is also the residence of many poor Indians, established at Mekka; these let out their houses to their countrymen, who visit this city in the time of the Hadj. In the ruined dwellings, Negro pilgrims take up their temporary abode; some of these are settled in Mekka, and their wives prepare the intoxicating liquor made from durra, and called *bouza*, of which the meaner inhabitants are very fond. It was in the Mesfale, as I have already mentioned, that I took up my lodging on returning from Djidda, at first in the house of a Maggrebyn settler, from which I soon afterwards removed into that of a Yemen merchant close by. The person, whose apartment I hired, was from Szana in Yemen, a Metowef or guide by profession, and who occupied the first floor of the house, from which he removed, during my stay, into a corner on the ground-floor; the other parts of the dwelling were inhabited by the Maggrebyn landlord and his family, by a village sheikh from

Egypt, who had come to the Hadj, accompanied by several fellahs, by a poor man from the Afghan country, or territory El Soleymanye, as it is now usually called; and by a hadjy or pilgrim from one of the Greek islands. In the house of the Yemen merchant, I found myself among a party of Maggrebyn pilgrims belonging to the Berber nation, or the Shilhy, who had come by sea to Egypt. There are few houses in this part of the town, where the same strange mixture of nations is not to be met with.

On the southern extremity of the Mesfale is a large ruined khan, which, even when new, must have been a mean building. It was destined for the accommodation of the pilgrim-caravan, which formerly arrived by land from Yemen, along the coast. Another Yemen pilgrim-caravan came along the mountains.

In issuing from the town on this side, we discover a watch-tower standing in the plain, similar in construction to those at the Djerouel entrance. A broad valley leads from hence, in a southern direction, to the small village of Hosseynye, two or three hours distant, where are some date-trees. Here the Sherif Ghaleb had a small pleasure-garden and a country-house; and he kept here a herd of buffaloes, brought from Egypt; but they did not prosper. From Hosseynye a road leads to Arafat, passing to the S. and S. E. of Mekka, two or three hours distant from which, on that road, is the small fertile valley and Arab settlement of Aabedye. The valley just mentioned is called El Tarafeyn; one mile beyond the present skirts of the city may be traced the ruins of former habitations; among them are several large, deep, and well-built cisterns, which, with little labour, might again be rendered fit for their original purpose of collecting rain-water. At a mile and a half from the city is a large stone tank, called Birket Madjen, built for the supplying of water to the Yemen caravan; I found some water in it, but it is falling rapidly to decay. Beyond this tank, the people of the Mesfale cultivate a few fields of cucumbers and different vegetables, immediately after the fall of the rains, when the ground has been copiously irrigated. Many Bedouin huts and tents of the tribes of Faham and Djehadele are scattered over this valley: their inhabitants earn a livelihood by collecting in the mountains grass and wild herbs, which they sell, when dry, in the Mekka market, twisted into bundles: they serve to feed horses, camels, and asses; but are so scarce and dear, that the daily feed for a horse costs from two to three piastres. These Bedouins also rear a few sheep; but although poor, they keep themselves quite distinct from the lower classes of the Mekkawys, whom they scorn to imitate in their habits of mendicity. Some few of them are water-carriers in the city.

On one summit of the western chain of the valley of Tarafeyn, just in front of the Mesfale, stood, prior to the invasion of the Wahabys, a small building with a dome, erected in honour of Omar, one of Mohammed's immediate successors, and therefore called Mekam Seydna Omar. It was completely ruined by the Wahabys.

Nearly on the summit of the opposite mountain stands the Great Castle, a very large and massy structure, surrounded by thick walls and solid towers. It commands the greatest part of the town, but is commanded by several higher summits. I heard that this castle owes its origin to the Sherif Serour, the predecessor of Ghaleb; but I believe it to be of a more ancient date. It is often mentioned by Asamy, in his history, as early as the fourteenth century; but he does not say who built it. No person might enter without permission from the governor of Mekka, and I did not think it either prudent, or worth the trouble, to apply for that favour. Ghaleb considerably strengthened and thoroughly repaired the building, and mounted it with heavy guns. It was said that he had made its principal magazines bomb-proof. It contains a large cistern and a small mosque; and might accommodate a garrison of about one thousand men. To Arabs it is an impregnable fortress; and so it is considered by the Mekkawys; even against Europeans, it might offer some resistance. The approach is by a steep narrow path.

Below the castle-hill, upon a small plain between the mountain and the Djebel Kobeys, stands the great palace of the reigning sherif, called Beit es' Sade. This, too, is said to have been built by Serour; but I find it mentioned by Asamy in the account of transactions that occurred two hundred years ago. Its walls are very high and solid, and seem to have been intended for an outwork to the castle above it, with which, according to the reports of the Mekkawys, there is a subterranean communication. It is an irregular pile of building, and comprises many spacious courts and gloomy chambers, which have not been inhabited since Sherif Ghaleb fled before the enemy to Djidda: he then attempted to destroy it by fire; but it was too strongly built. The Turks, under Mohammed Aly, have converted it into a magazine of corn. In the adjacent plain, which was formerly the place of exercise for the Sherif's troops, I found a herd of camels, with the encampment of their drivers, who make a journey weekly to Djidda or Tayf. Here also many poor hadjys, who could not pay for lodgings, had erected their miserable tents, formed of a few rags spread upon sticks. The soldiers were busily occupied in destroying all the remaining ceilings of the palace, in quest of fire-wood.

In a narrow inlet in the mountain, to the north of the palace, and adjoining the above-mentioned plain, are numerous low huts built of brush-wood, the former abodes of Sherif Ghaleb's slaves, who served as soldiers in his guard. The greater part of them fled after the Sherif's capture; and the huts now form barracks for about two hundred Arab soldiers, in the service of his successor, Sherif Yahya.

In turning from hence towards the mosque, on the right hand, we come to a small quarter, built on the declivity of the mountain, in which are many half-ruined houses: it is called Haret el Djyad, and is inhabited by poor people, and several of the lower servants of the Sherif's household. Asamy says that it derives its name from having been the post occupied by the horsemen who accompanied Toba, King of Yemen, in his expedition against Mekka; an event celebrated among the Moslim writers, for the miraculous destruction of the army. This is certainly one of the most ancient quarters of the town.

Close by the mosque, on either side of the entrance to the above-mentioned plain, stands a palace of the Sherif; the northern consists of two stately houses, connected together, which are occupied by Sherif Yahya: his women reside in the opposite southern building, which was erected by Sherif Ghaleb, who in this favourite residence spent the greater part of his time, induced by its vicinity to the mosque, its central situation, and the large open space which it commands.

Continuing from this place, in a northern direction, parallel with the mosque, we enter the long street called Mesaa. The small by-streets to the right, in approaching the Mesaa, form the quarter of El Szafa, which takes its name from the holy place Szafa, already described. The houses surrounding this place are handsome buildings, and here the richest foreigners, in the time of the pilgrimage, take up their abode. In a large house here resides the Aga of the eunuchs belonging to the temple, together with all the eunuch boys, who are educated here, till they attain a sufficient age to allow of their living in private lodgings.

We now turn into the Mesaa, the straightest and longest street in Mekka, and one of the best built. It receives its name from the ceremony of the Say, which is performed in it, and which I have already described: from this circumstance, and its being full of shops, it is the most noisy and most frequented part of the town. The shops are of the same description as those enumerated in the account of Djidda, with the addition of a dozen of tin-men, who make tin bottles of all sizes, in which the pilgrims, upon their return, carry the water of Zemzem to their homes. The shops are generally magazines on the ground-floor of the houses, before which a stone bench is reared. Here the merchant sits, under the shade of a slight awning of mats fastened to long poles; this custom prevails throughout the Hedjaz. All the houses of the Mesaa are rented by Turkish pilgrims. On the arrival of a party of hadjys from Djidda, which happens almost every morning, for four or five months of the year, their baggage is usually deposited in this street, after which they pay their visit to the mosque, and then go in quest of lodgings; and in this manner I found the street crowded almost every day with new comers, newsmongers, and guides.

About the time of my stay at Mekka, the Mesaa resembled a Constantinopolitan bazar. Many shops were kept by Turks from Europe or Asia Minor, who sold various articles of Turkish dress, which had belonged to deceased hadjys, or to those who, being deficient in cash, had sold their wardrobe. Fine swords, good English watches, and beautiful copies of the Koran, the three most valuable articles in a Turkish pilgrim's baggage, were continually offered for sale. Constantinopolitan pastry-cooks sold here pies and sweetmeats in the morning; roasted mutton, or kebabs, in the afternoon; and in the evening, a kind of jelly called *mehalabye*. Here, too, are numerous coffee-houses, crowded from three o'clock in the morning until eleven o'clock at night. The reader will be surprised to learn, that in two shops intoxicating liquors are publicly sold during the night, though not in the day-time: one liquor is prepared from fermented raisins, and although usually mixed with a good deal of water, is still so strong, that a few glasses of it produce intoxication. The other is a sort of *bouza*, mixed with spices, and called *soubye*. This beverage is known (although not made so strong) at Cairo.

The Mesaa is the place of punishment: there capital offenders are put to death. During my stay, a man was beheaded, by sentence of the Kadhy, for having robbed a Turkish pilgrim of about two hundred pounds sterling; this was the only instance of the kind which came to my knowledge, though thieves are said to abound in Mekka, while the Hadj continues. The history of Mekka, however, affords many instances of the most cruel punishments: in A. D. 1624, two thieves were flayed alive in this street; in 1629, a military chief of Yemen, who had been made prisoner by the reigning Sherif, had both his arms and shoulders perforated in many places, and lighted tapers put into the wounds; one of his feet was turned up, and fastened to his shoulder by an iron hook, and in this posture he was suspended two days on a tree in the Mala, till he died. The destruction of a man's sight, no uncommon punishment in other parts of the east, seems never to have been inflicted by the Hedjaz governors.

In the Mesaa, and annexed to the mosque, stands a handsome building, erected in A. H. 882, by Kaid Bey, Sultan of Egypt, in which he established a large public school, with seventy-two different apartments; he also furnished it with a valuable library. The historian Kotobeddyn, who, one hundred years afterwards, was librarian here, complains that only three hundred volumes remained in his time, the rest having been stolen by his unprincipled predecessors.

On the northern extremity of the Mesaa is the place called Merowa, the termination of the Say, as already described; this, as it now stands, was built in A. H. 801. Behind it is shown a house which was the original habitation of El Abbas, one of the many uncles of Mohammed. Near the Merowa are the barbers' shops, in which pilgrims have their heads shaved after performing the Say. Here, too, public auctions are held every morning, where wearing-apparel, and goods of every description, are offered to the highest bidder: for the sake of the Turkish pilgrims, their language is used on these occasions; and there is scarcely a boy at Mekka who is not thus acquainted with, at least, the Turkish numerals. Near this place, too, is a public fountain, the work of the Othman Emperor Soleyman Ibn Selym: it is supplied from the Mekka aqueduct, and is crowded the whole day by hadjys, who come to fill their water-skins.

Eastward of the Mesaa, near its extremity at the Merowa, branches off a street called Soueyga, or the Little Market, which runs almost parallel with the east side of the mosque. Though narrow, it is the neatest street in the town, being regularly cleaned and sprinkled with water, which is not the case with any of the others. Here the rich India merchants expose their piece-goods for sale, and fine Cashmere shawls and muslins. There are upwards of twenty shops, in which are sold perfumes, sweet oils, Mekka balsam, (in an adulterated state,) aloe-wood, civet, &c. Few pilgrims return to their homes without carrying some presents for their families and friends; these are usually beads, perfumes, balm of Mekka, aloe-wood, which last is used throughout the east, in small pieces, placed upon the lighted tobacco in the pipe, producing an agreeable odour.

In other shops are sold strings of coral, and false pearls, rosaries made of aloe, sandal or kalembac wood, brilliant necklaces of cut cornelians, cornelians for seal-rings, and various kinds of China ware. These shops are all kept by Indians, and their merchandize is entirely of Indian production and manufacture. Against these Indians much prejudice is entertained in Arabia, from a general opinion that they are idolaters, who comply in outward appearance only with the rites of Mohammedism: they are supposed to be of the Ismayley sect; those mysterious devotees, of whom I have given some account in my journey to Lebanon,* and whose name is, at Mekka, applied to those Indians. About a dozen of them reside here; the others arrive annually at the pilgrimage; they buy up old gold and silver, which they remit to Surat, from whence most of them come. Some have lived at Mekka for ten years, scrupulously performing every religious ceremony; they rent a large house, in which they live together, never allowing other strangers to occupy any part of it, even should several of the apartments be untenanted. Contrary to the practice of all other Mohammedans, these Indians never bring their women to the pilgrimage, although they could well afford the expense; and those residing, for however long a period, at Mekka have never been known to marry there; which is the more remarkable, as other natives of India, who live here for any length of time, usually take wives, although they may have been already married at home.

The same stories are prevalent respecting them, which are told of the Syrian Ismayleys, to my account of whom I must refer the reader.† My endeavours to collect authentic information on the subject of their secret doctrines were as fruitless here as they had

---

* See Travels in Syria, &c.
† See Travels in Syria and the Holy Land.

been in Syria, where it was vaguely reported that the chief seat of the Ismayleys was in India, and that they kept up regular correspondence between that country and Syria. A sect of "Light-extinguishers" is said to exist in India, as well as in Mesopotamia, and to them the Ismayleys of Syria and those of Mekka may, perhaps, belong. Those whom I saw at Mekka have rather the features of Persians than of Indians, and are taller and stouter men than Indians in general.*

About the middle of the Soueyga, where the street is only four paces in breadth, are stone benches on each side. Here Abyssinian male and female slaves are exposed for sale; and as beauty is an universal attraction, these benches are always surrounded by hadjys, both old and young, who often pretend to bargain with the dealers, for the purpose of viewing the slave-girls, during a few moments, in some adjoining apartment. Many of these slaves are carried from hence to the northern parts of Turkey. The price of the handsomest was from one hundred and ten to one hundred and twenty dollars.

At the extremity of the Soueyga, the street is covered with a high vaulted roof of stone, supported on each side by several massy buildings, serving as warehouses to the wealthy merchants; they were the work of one Mohammed, Pasha of Damascus, who lived several centuries ago, and now belong to the mosque. This, being the coolest spot in the town during mid-day, is on that account the most frequented. In the Soueyga all the gentlemen hadjys take their morning and evening lounge, and smoke their pipes. I formed an acquaintance with one of the perfume-sellers, and daily passed an hour in the morning, and another in the afternoon, seated on the bench before his shop, smoking my nargyle, and treating my friend with coffee. Here I heard the news:—whether any great hadjy had arrived the preceding night; what law-suits had been carried before

---

* The people here mentioned by our author were probably some Parsees from Surat or Bombay.

the Kadhy; what was going forward in Mohammed Aly's army; or what great commercial bargains had been concluded. Sometimes European news would be discussed, such as the last fortunes of Bonaparte; for the pilgrims who arrived from Constantinople and Greece were continually bringing news from Europe. I usually spent the early part of each morning, and the later part of the evening, in walking about the town, and frequenting the coffee-houses in its extremities, whereI might meet with Bedouins, and, by treating them with a cup of coffee, soon engage them to talk about their country and their nation. During the mid-day hours I staid at home : the first part of the night I passed in the great square of the mosque, where a cooling breeze always reigns; here, seated upon a carpet, which my slave spread for me, I indulged in recollections of far distant regions, while the pilgrims were busily engaged in praying and walking round the Kaaba.

At the eastern extremity of the Soueyga, the street changes its name into that of Shamye, which is applied also to several by-streets on either side, those on the right leading towards the mountain, and those on the left towards the mosque. At the further end the Shamye joins the quarter of Shebeyka and Bab el Omar. This is a well-built part of the town, chiefly inhabited by rich merchants, or by olemas attached to the mosque. There are few shops in the main street except during the pilgrimage, when many are opened, in which the Syrian merchants display the produce and manufactures of their country; a circumstance from which it derives its name. In these shops are found silk stuffs from Damascus and Aleppo; cambric manufactured in the district of Nablous; gold and silver thread from Aleppo; Bedouin handkerchiefs, called *keffie*, of Baghdad and Damascus fabric; silk from Lebanon; fine carpets from Anadolia and the Turkman Bedouins; abbas from Hamah; dried fruits and the kammereddyn from Damascus; pistacios from Aleppo, &c. Among all the Syrians at Mekka, I could never discover any individual whom I had known in his own country, except the son of the chief of Palmyra, who, however, did not recognise me. He had come with two or three hundred camels, to transport the baggage of the Pasha of Damascus.

In returning through the Shamye towards the Soueyga, we find, on the north side of these streets, a quarter called Garara, the most reputable of the town, and perhaps the best built, where the wealthiest merchants have their houses. The two first merchants of the Hedjaz, Djeylany and Sakkat, live here for the greater part of the year, and only go to Djidda (where they also have establishments,) when the arrival of the Indian fleet demands their presence at that place. In the quarter of Garara, the women of Mohammed Aly Pasha, with a train of eunuchs attached to them, have now taken up their abode. The houses are all two or three stories high, many of them gaudily painted, and containing spacious apartments. Here Sherif Ghaleb built a palace, the finest of all those he possessed at Mekka, and resided in it principally during the winter months, when he divided his time between this mansion and that near the mosque. Some military chiefs have now taken up their quarters in this palace, which will soon be ruined. It is distinguished from the other houses of Mekka only by its size, and the number of windows; having neither a fine portico, nor any other display of architecture.

Near the palace, upon a hill which may be described as within the town, Ghaleb built a fort, flanked by strong towers, but of much smaller size than the great castle. When the Turkish army advanced towards the Hedjaz, he mounted it with guns, and stored it well with provisions; but the garrison, like that of the castle, dispersed immediately after he was made prisoner. The hill upon which it stands is known by the name of Djebel Lala, and is often mentioned by Arabian poets. Opposite to this hill, in a S.E. direction, upon the summit of a mountain beyond the precincts of the town, stands another small fort, which was also repaired by Ghaleb. It is called Djebel Hindy, from the circumstance of a great sheikh or devotee from Cashmere having been buried there. The tower is now inhabited by a few Indian families, who enjoy the advantage of an excellent cistern for rain-water. This mountain is also called by the present Mekkawys "Djebel Keykaan"—an appellation more ancient probably than that of Mekka itself. Azraky, however, places the Djebel Keykaan more to the north, and says that the name is derived from the cries and the clashing of arms of the Mekkawy army, which was stationed there, when the Yemen army, under Toba, had taken possession of the hill of Djyad. Between the two castle-hills, the space is filled with poor, half-ruined houses, which are principally inhabited by the lowest class of Indians established at Mekka.

In turning eastward from the Garara, and passing the quarter called Rekoube, which, in point of building, nearly equals the Garara, although it is not reckoned so genteel a residence, we arrive at the great street called Modaa, which is a continuation of the Mesaa, and then retrace our steps through the latter to the vicinity of El Szafa, that we may survey the eastern quarters of the town.

Near the Szafa branches off a broad street, running almost parallel with the Modaa, to the east of it, called Geshashye. Here, among many smaller dwellings, are several well-built, and a few lofty edifices; a number of coffee-houses; several gunsmiths' shops; and a bath. Here resides the Hakem, or superintendant of the police, who is the first officer under the Sherif at Mekka. Part of the street is built on the lower declivity of the eastern mountain, called Djebel Kobeys, to which narrow, dirty, and steep lanes lead up on that side. The Geshashye is a favourite quarter of the pilgrims, being broad, airy, and open to the northerly winds. I lived here during the last days of Ramadhan, in September, 1814, when I first arrived at Mekka from Tayf.

This street, as it proceeds, adopts the name of Haret Souk el Leyl, which comprises an extensive quarter on the East, where the Moled e' Nebby, or Prophet's birth-place, is shown, and which adjoins the Moamele, or establishment of the potteries. The by-streets close to the Moled are denominated Shab el Moled, or "Rocks of the Moled," the ground which rises here being covered with stones.

The Moamele lies on the side of Djebel Kobeys, and comprises about a dozen furnaces, of which the chief productions are jars, especially those used in carrying the water of the celebrated well Zemzem. These Moamele jars, although prettily wrought, are too heavy, differing in this respect from the beautiful pottery of Upper Egypt and Baghdad, which are so slight that an empty jar may be thrown down by a mere puff of wind. The Moamele alone supplies all the Hedjaz, at present, with these water-vessels; and few hadjys return to their homes without some jars, as specimens of Mekkawy ingenuity.

Farther on, the Souk el Leyl takes the name of El Ghazze, and so are called both sides of the main street, which still forms a continuation of the Geshashye. Several deep wells of brackish water are situated in this street. Here also are found the shops of carpenters, upholsterers from Turkey, undertakers, who make the seryrs, or stands, upon which the Mekkawys sleep, as well as those on which they are carried to the grave. Wholesale dealers in fruits and vegetables, which are brought from Tayf and Wady Fatme, here dispose of their stock to the retail dealers early in the morning. At the northern end of the Ghazze, where the street widens considerably, is held a daily market of camels and cows. On the east side, towards the mountain, and partly on its declivity, stands the quarter called Shab Aly, adjoining the Shab el Moled : here is shown the venerated place of Aly's nativity. Both these quarters, called Shab, (i.e. rock,) are among the most ancient parts of the town, where the Koreysh formerly lived; they are even now inhabited principally by sherifs, and do not contain any shops. The houses are spacious, and in an airy situation.

Beyond the cattle-market in the Ghazze, the dwelling-houses terminate, and low shops and sheds occupy both sides of the street. This part is called Souk el Haddadeyn; and here blacksmiths and Turkish locksmiths have their shops. A little further, the street opens into that called Mala, which is itself a continuation of the Modaa, and forms the division between the eastern and western parts of the town, running due north along the slightly ascending slope of the valley. The Modaa and the Mala, (which latter means the High Place, in opposition to the Mesfale, or the low quarter,) are filled with shops on both sides. Here are found grocers, druggists, corn-merchants, tobacconists, haberdashers, sandal-makers, and a great number of dealers in old clothes. In the Modaa is a large corn magazine, formerly a public school; and there is another in the Mala. From these, the provision-caravans for the Turkish army at Tayf take their departure: public auctions are held in this place every morning. At the northern end of the Mala is a market, whither Bedouins from all quarters bring their sheep for sale. Here, also, are the butchers' shops, in which beef, mutton, and camels' flesh are sold; and in the same street is a small chapel, or Mesdjed,* for daily prayers, the great mosque being distant; but the Friday's prayers are always said in the latter. Towards this northern end of the Mala, where it joins the Souk el Haddadeyn, the stone houses terminate, and are succeeded by a single row of low shops and stands on each side, where provisions are sold to the eastern Bedouins, who come to Mekka for grain. Here is a coffee-house, called Kahwet el Hashashein, where are sold the intoxicating preparations of *hashysh* and *bendj*, which are mixed and smoked with tobacco. This house is frequented by all the lowest and most disorderly persons of the town. Sherif Ghaleb had imposed a heavy tax on the sale of hashysh, in order to discourage a practice directly violating the law.

The Mala is known also under the appellation of Haret el Naga, which is derived from the ancient name of Wady el Naga, given to this part of the valley of Mekka.

In the by-streets of the Modaa the richest Indian traders have their houses; here they receive customers, being too proud to open public shops or warehouses. An Indian of this quarter, originally from Surat, called El Shamsy, was esteemed the wealthiest man in the Hedjaz; yet his mercantile concerns were much less extensive than those of Djeylany, and several others. Though possessing

* I believe this to be the Mesdjed mentioned by historians under the name of Mesdjed Rayet. El Azraky speaks of four or five other mosques at Mekka in his time.

several hundred thousand pounds sterling, this man bargained with me personally for nearly an hour and a half about a muslin shawl, not worth more than four dollars!

In the Modaa, a high, broad mole or embankment was thrown across the valley, with an iron gate, by Omar Ibn el Khatab, to resist the torrents flowing in this direction towards the mosque, during heavy rains. Some vestiges of it remained till the fourteenth century. While it existed, the pilgrims on arriving at Mekka used to enjoy from its summit the first sight of the Kaaba; there also they recited prayers, from which circumstance the street takes its name, Modaa meaning "place of prayers."

Between the Modaa and Mala, on the one side, and the Ghazze and Geshashye on the other, are several quarters consisting of tolerable buildings, but of extremely dirty and narrow streets, from which the filth is never removed, and fresh air is always excluded. Here we find the Zokak e Seiny, or "Chinese street," where gold and silversmiths have their shops. They work in the coarsest manner, but are very much employed, principally in making silver rings for men and women—ornaments very generally used among the Arabs. To the south of this quarter is the Zokak el Hadjar (called also Zokak el Merfek), or the "street of the stone," which comprises the birth-place of Fatme, the daughter of Mohammed; and of Abou Beker, the prophet's successor in the Khalifat. This street takes its name from the hadjar, or stone, which used miraculously to greet Mohammed with the salutation of "Salam aleyk," whenever he passed this way on his return from the Kaaba. It has been mute since the days of the prophet, but is still shown, projecting a little from the wall of a house, which, in honour of it has been white-washed.

We now return towards the Mala, a little beyond the spot where it joins the Ghazze. The shops terminate, and a broad, sandy plain commences, on which there are only a few detached coffee-houses. This may be called the extremity of the town. What lies farther towards the north, must be considered as forming part of the suburbs. Continuing along the plain, we find on each side of the road large birkets, or reservoirs of water, for the accommodation of the pilgrim-caravans: they can be filled from the aqueduct which passes this way towards the town. Of these birkets, one is for the Egyptian caravan; another for the Syrian: they were constructed in A. H. 821, are entirely cased with stone, and continue in a state of perfect repair. Similar monuments of the munificent Turkish Sultans are found at every station of the Hadj, from Medina as far as Damascus and Aleppo. Some of those which I saw to the southward of Damascus, appeared more solid in their construction than the birkets of Mekka: that appropriated to the Egyptian pilgrims is about one hundred and sixty feet square, and from thirty to thirty-five feet in depth. When the birket contains from eight to ten feet of water, the supply is deemed sufficient for the caravan. These reservoirs are never completely filled. As the aqueduct furnishes water but scantily, adjoining to the western birket are some acres, irrigated by means of a well, and producing vegetables. Near it, also, is a small mosque, called Djama è Soleymanye, in a state of decay, and no longer used for religious purposes; but serving, at present, to lodge a few Turkish soldiers. It belongs to the quarter named El Soleymanye, which extends from Djebel Lala close to the western mountain, as far as the cemeteries beyond the birkets. It does not contain any good houses; and I heard that it derives its name from the Soleymanye, as the Muselmans call the people of Kandahar, Afghanistan, Cashmere, and several other countries on this side of the Indus. It is said that some descendants of those people who were the original settlers, still reside here, mixed with many Indians. It appears, however, from Kotobeddyn's history, that Sultan Solyman erected, about A. H. 980, a mosque in this quarter. The mosque at least may be supposed to have borrowed its name from the founder. The inhabitants of Soleymanye are Muselmans of the Hanefy sect, the first of the four orthodox divisions, and not disciples of Aly, like the Persians; many of whom come yearly to the Hadj of Mekka, either by sea from Bombay or Bassora, or by land, travelling as dervises, along the southern provinces of

Persia to Baghdad, and through Mesopotamia and Syria to Egypt. I have seen many who had come by that route; they appeared to be men of a much better and more vigorous character than the generality of Indians.

Opposite to this quarter El Soleymanye, on the eastern mountain, and adjoining the Ghazze and Shab Aly, is a half-ruined district, called Shab Aamer, inhabited by Bedouin pedlars of the Thekyf and Koreysh tribes, and by a few poor sherif families. In this quarter are some large mills, worked by horses, for the Turkish governor: the town, I believe, does not contain any others of considerable size. It is the custom at Mekka to use hand-mills, which are usually turned by the slaves of the family, or, among the poorer classes, by the women. Here, also, are the only places in Mekka (or perhaps in the Hedjaz) where linen and cotton are dyed with indigo and saffron: woollen cloth is not dyed here.

As numbers of the public women reside at Shab Aamer, this quarter is not ranked among the most respectable in Mekka. Sherif Ghaleb imposed a regular tax upon those females, and required an additional payment from such of them as, in the time of the pilgrimage, followed the hadjys to Arafat. A similar tax is levied at Cairo, and in all the great provincial towns of Egypt. Mekka abounds with the frail sisterhood, whose numbers are increased during the Hadj by adventurers from foreign countries. They are somewhat more decorous than the public women in Egypt, and never appear in the streets without veils. Among them are many Abyssinian slaves, whose former masters, according to report, share the profits of their vocation. Some are slaves belonging to Mekkawys.

The Arabian poets make frequent allusions to Shab Aamer; thus Ibn el Faredh says:—

> "Is Shab Aamer, since we left it, still inhabited?
> Is it to this day the place of meeting for lovers?" *

* See Sir William Jones's Comment. de Poës. Asiat., on the subject of a poem by Ibn Faredh, which abounds with local allusions to Mekka.

Proceeding from the birkets northward over the plain, we come to an insulated house, of good size and construction, belonging to the Sherif, in which some of Ghaleb's favourites once resided. Opposite to this building, a paved causeway leads towards the western hills, through which is an opening that seems artificial. El Azraky applies the name Djebel el Hazna to this part of the mountain; and says that the road was cut through the rock by Yahia Ibn Khold Ibn Barmak. On the other side of the opening, the road descends into the plain of Sheikh Mahmoud, so named from the tomb of a saint, round which the Syrian pilgrims generally encamp. Sherif Ghaleb erected upon the hill, on both sides of the narrow road, which is formed in rude steps, (whether natural or artificial, it would be difficult to say,) two watch-towers, similar to those already described. On both sides of the causeway, in the valley of Mekka, extend the burying-grounds, where most of the inhabitants of the city have their family tombs.

A little beyond the Sherif's house just mentioned, and at the termination of the Mala, stands the tomb of Abou Taleb, an uncle of Mohammed, and father of Aly. The Wahabys reduced the building which covered the tomb to a mere heap of rubbish; and Mohammed Aly Pasha has not thought fit to rebuild it. Abou Taleb is the great patron of the city; and there are many persons at Mekka who, though they would have little scruple in breaking an oath taken before God, yet would be afraid of invoking the name of Abou Taleb in confirmation of a falsehood. "I swear by the Mosque"—" I swear by the Kaaba," are ejaculations constantly used by the Mekkawys to impose upon strangers; but to swear by Abou Taleb is a more serious imprecation, and is seldom heard upon such occasions. Opposite to the ruined tomb stands a public fountain, consisting of a trough built of stone, fifty or sixty feet in length, which is daily filled with water from the aqueduct. Near it grow a few trees.

No buildings are seen beyond the fountain, till we come to a large palace of the Sherif, which is surrounded by high walls flanked with towers, and contains within the inclosure a spacious court-yard. In the time of the Sherif it was well garrisoned, and during his wars with the Wahabys he often resided here, as he could set out from hence upon a secret attack or expedition, without its becoming immediately known in the city. The building now serves as a barrack for the Turkish soldiers.

To the north of this palace lies the quarter or suburb called Moabede, which consists partly of low and ill-built stone houses, and partly of huts constructed of brushwood; it is wholly inhabited by Bedouins, who have become settlers here, for the purpose of carrying on a traffic, principally in corn, dates, and cattle, between the town and their native tribes. I have seen among them Arabs of the tribes of Koreysh, Thekyf, Hodheyl, and Ateybe; and it was said that, in time of peace, individuals of all the great tribes of the Desert, and of Nedjed, are occasionally found here. They live, as I have already observed in speaking of those who occupy another part of Mekka, much in the same manner as they would do in the Desert. Their houses contain no furniture but such as is to be found under the tent of a wealthy Bedouin. Being at a distance from the great mosque, they have enclosed a square space with low walls, where such of them as pretend to any regularity in their devotions (which seldom happens among Bedouins), recite their prayers upon the sand, according to the custom of the Desert.

The Turkish governor of Mekka has not thought proper to place here any of his soldiers, for which the suburb is much indebted to him. The Moabede is, by its situation, and the pursuits of its inhabitants, so much separated from the city, that a woman here had not entered the town for the last three years, as she herself assured me; although the Bedouin females walk about the valley with freedom.

The valley of Mekka has here two outlets: on the north side is a narrow passage, defended by two watch-towers: it leads to Wady Fatmé. At the eastern extremity, the Moabede is terminated by a garden and pleasure-house of the Sherif, where Ghaleb used frequently to pass the hours of noon. The garden is enclosed by high walls and towers, and forms a fortified post in advance of the town. It contains date and nebek and a few other fruit-trees, the verdure and shade of which must be particularly agreeable. In the time of Ghaleb, the entrance was always open to the people of Mekka. The house is badly built, and is not one of Ghaleb's works. During his last wars with the Wahabys, the latter obtained possession of this residence, and fought for several weeks with the soldiers of Mekka, who were posted at the neighbouring palace or barrack to the south; and who, having laid a mine, and blown up a part of the walls, forced the Wahabys to retreat. Ghaleb subsequently repaired the damage. Some Turkish soldiers now live in the house, which is already half ruined by them. A public fountain of sweet water, no longer in use, with a pretty cupola built over it, stands on one side of the garden; on the other is a large well of brackish water: many such are dispersed over the Moabede.

The road from Mekka, eastward, towards Arafat and Tayf, passes by this house; at a short distance beyond it the valley widens, and here the Egyptian Hadj establishes its encampment, part of which generally stretches over the plain towards the birket. Formerly, the Syrian caravan used to encamp at the same place. Between the garden-house and the palace or barrack just mentioned, the aqueduct of Mekka is conducted above ground for about one hundred paces, in a channel of stone, plaistered on the inside, and rising four feet above the surface. This is the only place in the valley of Mekka where it is visible.

As soon as we pass these extreme precincts of Mekka, the Desert presents itself; for neither gardens, trees, nor pleasure-houses, line the avenues to the town, which is surrounded on every side by barren sandy valleys, and equally barren hills. A stranger placed on the great road to Tayf, just beyond the turn of the hill, in the immediate neighbourhood of the Sherif's garden-house, would think himself as far removed from human society as if he were in the midst of the Nubian Desert. But this may be wholly ascribed to the apathy of the inhabitants, and their indifference for agricultural pursuits. Numerous wells, dispersed throughout the town, prove that water may be easily obtained at about thirty feet below the surface.

In Arabia, wherever the ground can be irrigated by wells, the sands may be soon made productive. The industry of a very few years might thus render Mekka and its environs as remarkable for gardens and plantations, as it now is for absolute sterility. El Azraky speaks of gardens in this valley, and describes different springs and wells that no longer exist, having probably been choked up by the violent torrents. El Fasy likewise affirms that in his days the town contained no less than fifty-eight wells. But, in the earliest times of Arabian history, this place was certainly barren; and the Koran styles it accordingly " the valley without seeds." Azraky further says, that before houses were constructed here by the Kossay, this valley abounded with acacias and various thorny trees.

Nothing is more difficult than to compute exactly the population of eastern towns, where registers are never kept, and where even the number of houses can scarcely be ascertained. To judge from appearances, and by comparison with European towns, in which the amount of population is well known, may be very fallacious. The private habitations in the East are generally (though the Hedjaz forms an exception to this rule) of one story only, and therefore contain fewer inmates in proportion than European dwellings. On the other hand, Eastern towns have very narrow streets, are without public squares or large market-places, and their miserable suburbs are in general more nurously peopled than their principal and best streets. Travellers, however, in passing rapidly through towns, may be easily deceived, for they see only the bazars and certain streets, in which the greater part of the male population is usually assembled during the day. Thus it happens that recent and respectable authorities have stated two hundred thousand souls as the population of Aleppo; four hundred thousand as that of Damascus; and three hundred thousand as that of Cairo. My estimate of the population of the three great Syrian towns is as follows:—Damascus two hundred and fifty thousand; Hamah (of which, however, I must speak with less confidence) from sixty to one hundred thousand; and Aleppo, daily dwindling into decay, between eighty and ninety thousand. To Cairo I would allow at most two hundred thousand. As to Mekka, which I have seen both before and after the Hadj, and know, perhaps, more thoroughly than any other town of the East, the result of my inquiries gives between twenty-five and thirty thousand stationary inhabitants, for the population of the city and suburbs; besides from three to four thousand Abyssinian and black slaves: its habitations are capable of containing three times this number. In the time of Sultan Selym I. (according to Kotobeddyn, in A. H. 923) a census was taken of the inhabitants of Mekka, previous to a gratuitous distribution of corn among them, and the number was found to be twelve thousand, men, women, and children. The same author shows that, in earlier times, the population was much more considerable; for when Abou Dhaher, the chief of the Carmatis, (a heretic sect of Moslims) sacked Mekka, in A. H. 314, thirty thousand of the inhabitants were killed by his ferocious soldiers.

DESCRIPTION OF THE BEITULLAH, OR GREAT MOSQUE, AT MEKKA.

WHERE the valley is wider than in other interior parts of the town, stands the mosque, called Beitullah, or El Haram, a building remarkable only on account of the Kaaba, which it encloses; for there are several mosques in other places of the East nearly equal to this in size, and much superior to it in beauty.

The Kaaba stands in an oblong square, two hundred and fifty paces long, and two hundred broad, none of the sides of which run quite in a straight line, though at first sight the whole appears to be of a regular shape. This open square is enclosed on the eastern side by a colonnade: the pillars stand in a quadruple row: they are three deep on the other sides, and united by pointed arches, every four of which support a small dome, plastered and whitened on the outside. These domes, according to Kotobeddyn, are one hundred and fifty-two in number. Along the whole colonnade, on the four sides, lamps are suspended from the arches. Some are lighted every night, and all during the nights of Ramadhan. The pillars are above twenty feet in height, and generally from one foot and a half to one foot and three quarters in diameter; but little regularity has been observed in regard to them. Some are of white marble, granite, or porphyry, but the greater number are of common stone of the Mekka mountains. El Fasy states the whole at five hundred and eighty-nine, and says they are all of marble, excepting one hundred and twenty-six, which are of common stone, and three of composition. Kotobeddyn reckons five hundred and fifty-five, of which, according to him, three hundred and eleven are of marble, and the rest of stone taken from the neighbouring mountains; but neither of these authors lived to see the latest repairs of the mosque, after the destruction occasioned by a torrent, in A. D. 1626. Between every three or four columns stands an octagonal one, about four feet in thickness. On the east side are two shafts of reddish gray granite, in one piece, and one fine gray porphyry column with slabs of white feldspath. On the north side is one red granite column, and one of fine-grained red porphyry: these are probably the columns which Kotobeddyn states to have been brought from Egypt, and principally from Akhmim (Panopolis), when the chief El Mohdy enlarged the mosque, in A.H. 163. Among the four hundred and fifty or five hundred columns, which form the enclosure, I found not any two capitals or bases exactly alike: the capitals are of coarse Saracen workmanship; some of them, which had served for former buildings, by the ignorance of the workmen have been placed upside down upon the shafts. I observed about half a dozen marble bases of good Grecian workmanship. A few of the marble columns bear Arabic or Cufic inscriptions, in which I read the dates 863 and 762. (A.H). A column on the east side exhibits a very ancient Cufic inscription, somewhat defaced, which I could neither read nor copy. Those shafts, formed of the Mekka stone, cut principally from the side of the mountain near the Shebeyka quarter, are mostly in three pieces, but the marble shafts are in one piece. Some of the columns are strengthened with broad iron rings or bands, as in many other Saracen buildings of the East: they were first employed here by Ibn Dhaher Berkouk, King of Egypt, in rebuilding the mosque, which had been destroyed by fire in A. H. 802.

This temple has been so often ruined and repaired, that no traces of remote antiquity are to be found about it. On the inside of the great wall which encloses the colonnades, a single Arabic inscription is seen, in large characters, but containing merely the names of Mohammed and his immediate successors: Abou Beker, Omar, Othman, and Aly. The name of Allah, in large characters, occurs also in several places. On the outside, over the gates, are long inscriptions, in the Solouth character, commemorating the names of those by whom the gates were built, long and minute details of which are given by the historians of Mekka. The inscription on the south side, over Bab

Ibrahim, is most conspicuous; all that side was rebuilt by the Egyptian Sultan El Ghoury, in A. H. 906. Over the Bab Aly and Bab Abbas is a long inscription, also in the Solouth character, placed there by Sultan Murad Ibn Soleyman, in A. H. 984, after he had repaired the whole building. Kotobeddyn has given this inscription at length; it occupies several pages in his history, and is a monument of the Sultan's vanity. This side of the mosque having escaped destruction in 1626, the inscription remains uninjured.

Some parts of the walls and arches are gaudily painted, in stripes of yellow, red, and blue, as are also the minarets. Paintings of flowers, in the usual Muselman style, are no where seen; the floors of the colonnades are paved with large stones badly cemented together.

Seven paved causeways lead from the colonnades towards the Kaaba, or holy house, in the centre. They are of sufficient breadth to admit four or five persons to walk abreast, and they are elevated about nine inches above the ground. Between these causeways, which are covered with fine gravel or sand, grass appears growing in several places, produced by the Zemzem water dozing out of the jars, which are placed in the ground in long rows during the day. The whole area of the mosque is upon a lower level than any of the streets surrounding it. There is a descent of eight or ten steps from the gates on the north side into the platform of the colonnade, and of three or four steps from the gates, on the south side.

Towards the middle of this area stands the Kaaba; it is one hundred and fifteen paces from the north colonnade, and eighty-eight from the south. For this want of symmetry we may readily account, the Kaaba having existed prior to the mosque, which was built around it, and enlarged at different periods. The Kaaba is an oblong massive structure, eighteen paces in length, fourteen in breadth, and from thirty-five to forty feet in height. I took the bearing of one of its longest sides, and found it to be N. N. W. ¼ W. It is constructed of the grey Mekka stone, in large blocks of different sizes, joined together in a very rough manner, and with bad cement. It was entirely rebuilt as it now stands in A. D. 1627: the torrent, in the preceding year, had thrown down three of its sides; and preparatory to its re-erection, the fourth side was, according to Asamy, pulled down, after the olemas, or learned divines, had been consulted on the question, whether mortals might be permitted to destroy any part of the holy edifice without incurring the charge of sacrilege and infidelity.

The Kaaba stands upon a base two feet in height, which presents a sharp inclined plane; its roof being flat, it has at a distance the appearance of a perfect cube. The only door which affords entrance, and which is opened but two or three times in the year, is on the north side, and about seven feet above the ground. In entering it, therefore, wooden steps are used—of them I shall speak hereafter. In the first periods of Islam, however, when it was rebuilt in A. H. 64, by Ibn Zebeyr, chief of Mekka, the nephew of Aysha, it had two doors even with the ground-floor of the mosque. The present door (which, according to Azraky, was brought hither from Constantinople in 1633,) is wholly coated with silver, and has several gilt ornaments. Upon its threshold are placed every night various small lighted wax candles, and perfuming-pans, filled with musk, aloe-wood, &c.

At the North-east corner of the Kaaba, near the door, is the famous "Black Stone;" it forms a part, of the sharp angle of the building, at four or five feet above the ground. It is an irregular oval, about seven inches in diameter, with an undulated surface, composed of about a dozen smaller stones of different sizes and shapes, well joined together with a small quantity of cement, and perfectly smoothed: it looks as if the whole had been broken into many pieces by a violent blow, and then united again. It is very difficult to determine accurately the quality of this stone, which has been worn to its present surface by the millions of touches and kisses it has received. It appeared to me like a lava, containing several small extraneous particles, of a whitish and of a yellowish substance. Its colour is now a deep reddish brown, approaching to black: it is surrounded on all sides by a border, composed of a substance which I took to be a close cement of pitch and gravel, of a similar, but not quite the same brownish colour. This border serves to support its detached pieces; it is two or three inches in breadth, and rises a little above the surface of the stone. Both the border and the stone itself are encircled by a silver band, broader below than above and on the two sides, with a considerable swelling below, as if a part of the stone were hidden under it. The lower part of the border is studded with silver nails.

In the south-east corner of the Kaaba, or, as the Arabs call it, Roken el Yemány, there is another stone, about five feet from the ground; it is one foot and a half in length, and two inches in breadth, placed upright, and of the common Mekka stone. This the people walking round the Kaaba touch only with the right hand: they do not kiss it.

On the north side of the Kaaba, just by its door, and close to the wall, is a slight hollow in the ground, lined with marble, and sufficiently large to admit of three persons sitting. Here it is thought meritorious to pray: the spot is called El Madjen, and supposed to be that where Abraham and his son Ismayl kneaded the chalk and mud which they used in building the Kaaba; and near this Madjen, the former is said to have placed the large stone upon which he stood while working at the masonry. On the basis of the Kaaba, just over the Madjen, is an ancient Cufic inscription; but this I was unable to decipher, and had no opportunity of copying it. I do not find it mentioned by any of the historians.

On the west side of the Kaaba, about two feet below its summit, is the famous Myzab, or water-spout, through which the rain-water collected on the roof of the building is discharged, so as to fall upon the ground; it is about four feet in length, and six inches in breadth, as well as I could judge from below, with borders equal in height to its breadth. At the mouth, hangs what is called the beard of the Myzab, a gilt board, over which the water falls. This spout was sent hither from Constantinople in A. H. 981, and is *reported* to be of pure gold. The pavement round the Kaaba, below the Myzab, was laid down in A. H. 826, and consists of various coloured stones, forming a very handsome specimen of mosaic. There are two large slabs of fine *verde-antico* in the centre, which, according to Makrizi,* were sent thither as

---

* See, in his work, the chapter " On the Excellencies of Egypt."

presents from Cairo, in A. H. 241. This is the spot where, according to Mohammedan tradition, Ismayl, the son of Ibrahim, or Abraham, and his mother Hagar, are buried; and here it is meritorious for the pilgrim to recite a prayer of two rikats. On this west side is a semicircular wall, the two extremities of which are in a line with the sides of the Kaaba, and distant from it three or four feet, leaving an opening which leads to the burying-place of Ismayl. The wall bears the name of El Hatym, and the area which it encloses is called Hedjer, or Hedjer Ismayl, on account of its being separated from the Kaaba: the wall itself, also, is sometimes so called; and the name Hatym is given by the historians to the space of ground between the Kaaba and the wall on one side, and the Bir Zemzem and Makam Ibrahim on the other. The present Mekkawys, however, apply the name Hatym to the wall only.

Tradition says that the Kaaba once extended as far as the Hatym, and that this side having fallen down just at the time of the Hadj, the expenses of repairing it were demanded from the pilgrims, under a pretence that the revenues of government were not acquired in a manner sufficiently pure to admit of their application towards a purpose so sacred, whilst the money of the hadjys would possess the requisite sanctity. The sum, however, obtained from them, proved very inadequate: all that could be done, therefore, was to raise a wall, which marked the space formerly occupied by the Kaaba. This tradition, although current among the Metowefs, is at variance with history, which declares that the Hedjer was built by the Beni Koreysh, who contracted the dimensions of the Kaaba; that it was united to the building by Hadjadj, and again separated from it by Ibn Zebeyr. It is asserted by Fasy, that a part of the Hedjer, as it now stands, was never comprehended within the Kaaba. The law regards it as a portion of the Kaaba, inasmuch as it is esteemed equally meritorious to pray in the Hadjer as in the Kaaba itself; and the pilgrims who have not an opportunity of entering the latter, are permitted to affirm upon oath that they have prayed in the Kaaba, although they may have only prostrated themselves within the enclosure of the Hatym.

The wall is built of solid stone, about five feet in height, and four in thickness, cased all over with white marble, and inscribed with prayers and invocations, neatly sculptured upon the stone in modern characters. These and the casing are the work of El Ghoury, the Egyptian Sultan, in A. H. 917, as we learn from Kotobeddyn. The walk round the Kaaba is performed on the outside of the wall—the nearer to it the better.

The four sides of the Kaaba are covered with a black silk stuff, hanging down, and leaving the roof bare.* This curtain, or veil, is called *kesoua*, and renewed annually at the time of the Hadj, being brought from Cairo, where it is manufactured at the Grand Seignior's expense.† On it are various prayers interwoven in the same colour as the stuff, and it is, therefore, extremely difficult to read them. A little above the middle, and running round the whole building, is a line of similar inscriptions, worked in gold thread. That part of the kesoua which covers the door is richly embroidered with silver. Openings are left for the Black Stone, and the other in the south-east corner, which thus remain uncovered. The kesoua is always of the same form and pattern; that which I saw on my first visit to the mosque, was in a decayed state, and full of holes. On the 25th of the month Zul' Kade the old one is taken away, and the Kaaba continues without a cover for fifteen days. It is then said that *El Kaaba Yehrem*, "The Kaaba has assumed the ihram," which lasts until the tenth of Zul Hadje, the day of the return of the pilgrims from Arafat to Wady Muna, when the new kesoua is put on. During the first days, the new covering is tucked up by cords fastened to the roof, so as to leave the lower part of the building exposed: having remained thus for some days, it is let down, and covers the whole structure, being then tied to strong brass

---

* The Wahabys, during the first year of their residence at Mekka, covered the Kaaba with a red kesoua, worked at El Hassa, of the same stuff as the fine Arabian Abbas.

† During the first century of Islam, the kesoua was never taken away, the new one being annually put over the old. But the Mekkawys at length began to fear that the Kaaba might yield under such an accumulation, and the Khalif El Mohdy Abou Abdallah removed the coverings in A. H. 160. (See Makrizy.)

rings in the basis of the Kaaba. The removal of the old kesoua was performed in a very indecorous manner; and a contest ensued among the hadjys and people of Mekka, both young and old, about a few rags of it. The hadjys even collect the dust which sticks to the walls of the Kaaba, under the kesoua, and sell it, on their return, as a sacred relic. At the moment the building is covered, and completely bare, (*uryan*, as it is styled,) a crowd of women assemble round it, rejoicing with cries called "Walwalou."

The black colour of the kesoua, covering a large cube in the midst of a vast square, gives to the Kaaba, at first sight, a very singular and imposing appearance; as it is not fastened down tightly, the slightest breeze causes it to move in slow undulations, which are hailed with prayers by the congregation assembled around the building, as a sign of the presence of its guardian angels, whose wings, by their motion, are supposed to be the cause of the waving of the covering. Seventy thousand angels have the Kaaba in their holy care, and are ordered to transport it to Paradise, when the trumpet of the last judgment shall be sounded.

The clothing of the Kaaba was an ancient custom of the Pagan Arabs. The first kesoua, says El Azraky, was put on by Asad Toba, one of the Hamyarite kings of Yemen: before Islam it had two coverings, one for winter and the other for summer. In the early ages of Islam it was sometimes white and sometimes red, and consisted of the richest brocade. In subsequent times it was furnished by the different Sultans of Baghdad, Egypt, or Yemen, according as their respective influence over Mekka prevailed; for the clothing of the Kaaba appears to have always been considered as a proof of sovereignty over the Hedjaz. Kalaoun, Sultan of Egypt, assumed to himself and successors the exclusive right, and from them the Sultans at Constantinople have inherited it. Kalaoun appropriated the revenue of the two large villages Bysous and Sandabeir, in Lower Egypt, to the expense of the kesoua; and Sultan Solyman Ibn Selym subsequently added several others; but the Kaaba has long been deprived of this resource.*

* Vide Kotobeddyn and Asamy.

Round the Kaaba is a good pavement of marble, about eight inches below the level of the great square; it was laid in A. H. 981, by order of the Sultan, and describes an irregular oval; it is surrounded by thirty-two slender gilt pillars, or rather poles, between every two of which are suspended seven glass lamps, always lighted after sun-set. Beyond the poles is a second pavement, about eight paces broad, somewhat elevated above the first, but of coarser work; then another, six inches higher, and eighteen paces broad, upon which stand several small buildings; beyond this is the gravelled ground, so that two broad steps may be said to lead from the square down to the Kaaba. The small buildings just mentioned, which surround the Kaaba, are the five Makams, with the well of Zemzem, the arch called Bab-es'-Salam, and the Mambar.

Opposite the four sides of the Kaaba stand four other small buildings, where the Imaums of the orthodox Mohammedan sects, the Hanefy, Shafey, Hanbaly, and Maleky, take their station, and guide the congregation in their prayers. The Makam el Malaky, on the south, and that of Hanbaly, opposite the Black Stone, are small pavilions, open on all sides, and supported by four slender pillars, with a light sloping roof, terminating in a point, exactly in the style of Indian pagodas. The Makam el Hanefy, which is the largest, being fifteen paces by eight, is open on all sides, and supported by twelve small pillars; it has an upper story, also open, where the Mueddin who calls to prayers, takes his stand. This was first built in A. H. 923, by Sultan Selym I.; it was afterwards rebuilt by Khoshgeldy, governor of Djidda, in 947; but all the four Makams, as they now stand, were built in A. H. 1074.*
The Makam-es-Shafey is over the well Zemzem, to which it serves as an upper chamber.

Near their respective Makams, the adherents of the four different sects seat themselves for prayers. During my stay at Mekka, the Hanefys always began their prayer first; but according to Muselman custom the Shafeys should pray first in the mosque; then the Hanefys, Malekys, and Hanbalys. The prayer of the Magreb is an exception, which they are all enjoined to utter together.† The Makam el Hanbaly

---

* Vide Kotobeddyn and Asamy.   † Vide Fasy.

is the place where the officers of government, and other great people, are seated during prayers ; here the Pasha and the Sherif are placed ; and, in their absence, the eunuchs of the temple. These fill the space under this Makam in front, and behind it the female hadjys, who visit the temple, have their places assigned, to which they repair principally for the two evening prayers, few of them being seen in the mosque at the three other daily prayers : they also perform the towaf, or walk round the Kaaba, but generally at night, though it is not uncommon to see them walking in the day-time among the men.

The present building which encloses Zemzem, stands close by the Makam Hanbaly, and was erected in A. H. 1072 :* it is of a square shape, and of massive construction, with an entrance to the north, opening into the room which contains the well. This room is beautifully ornamented with marbles of various colours ; and adjoining to it, but having a separate door, is a small room with a stone reservoir which is always full of Zemzem water : this the hadjys get to drink by passing their hand with a cup through an iron grated opening, which serves as a window, into the reservoir, without entering the room. The mouth of the well is surrounded by a wall five feet in height, and about ten feet in diameter. Upon this the people stand, who draw up the water, in leathern buckets, an iron railing being so placed as to prevent their falling in. In El Fasy's time there were eight marble basins in this room, for the purpose of ablution.

From before dawn till near midnight, the well-room is constantly filled with visitors. Every one is at liberty to draw up the water for himself, but the labour is generally performed by persons placed there on purpose, and paid by the mosque : they expect also a trifle from those who come to drink, though they dare not demand it. I have been more than once in the room a quarter of an hour before I could get a draught of water, so great was the crowd. Devout hadjys sometimes mount the wall, and draw the bucket for several hours, in the hope of thus expiating their evil deeds.

Before the Wahaby invasion, the well Zemzem belonged to the

* Vide Asamy.

Sherif; and the water becoming thus a monopoly, was only to be purchased at a high price; but one of Saoud's first orders, on his arrival at Mekka, was to abolish this traffic, and the holy water is now dispensed gratis. The Turks consider it a miracle that the water of this well never diminishes, notwithstanding the continual draught from it: there certainly is no diminution in its depth; for by an accurate inspection of the rope by which the buckets are drawn up, I found that the same length was required both at morning and evening to reach the surface of the water. Upon inquiry, I learned from one of the persons who had descended in the time of the Wahabys to repair the masonry, that the water was *flowing* at the bottom, and that the well is therefore supplied by a subterraneous rivulet. The water is heavy to the taste, and sometimes in its colour resembles milk; but it is perfectly sweet, and differs very much from that of the brackish wells dispersed over the town. When first drawn up, it is slightly tepid, resembling, in this respect, many other fountains of the Hedjaz.

Zemzem supplies the whole town, and there is scarcely one family that does not daily fill a jar with the water: this only serves, however, for drinking or for ablution, as it is thought impious to employ water so sacred for culinary purposes or on common occasions. Almost every hadjy, when he repairs to the mosque for evening prayer has a jar of the water placed before him by those who earn their livelihood by performing this service. The water is distributed in the mosque to all who are thirsty for a trifling fee, by water-carriers with large jars upon their backs: these men are also paid by charitable hadjys for supplying the poorer pilgrims with this holy beverage immediately before or after prayers.

The water is regarded as an infallible cure for all diseases; and the devotees believe that the more they drink of it, the better their health will be, and their prayers the more acceptable to the Deity. I have seen some of them at the well swallowing such a quantity of it as I should hardly have thought possible. A man who lived in the same house with me, and who was ill of an intermittent fever, repaired every evening to Zemzem, and drank of the water till he was almost fainting, after which he lay for several hours extended upon his back on the pavement near the Kaaba, and then returned to renew his draught. When by this practice he was brought to the verge of death, he declared himself fully convinced that the increase of his illness proceeded wholly from his being unable to swallow a sufficient quantity of the water! Many hadjys, not content with drinking it merely, strip themselves in the room, and have buckets of it thrown over them, by which they believe that the heart is purified as well as the outer body. Few pilgrims quit Mekka without carrying away some of this water in copper or tin bottles, either for the purpose of making presents, or for their own use in case of illness, when they drink it, or for ablution after death. I carried away four small bottles, with the intention of offering them as presents to the Mohammedan kings in the Black countries. I have seen it sold at Suez by hadjys returning from Mekka at the rate of one piastre for the quantity that filled a coffee-cup.

The chief of Zemzem is one of the principal olemas of Mekka. I need not remind the reader that Zemzem is supposed to be the spring found in the wilderness by Hagar, at the moment when her infant son Ismayl was dying of thirst. It seems probable that the town of Mekka owes its origin to this well; for many miles round, no sweet water is found, nor is there in any part of the adjacent country so copious a supply.

On the north-east side of Zemzem stand two small buildings, one behind the other, called El Kobbateyn; they are covered by domes painted in the same manner as the mosque, and in them are kept water-jars, lamps, carpets, mats, brooms, and other articles used in the very mosque. These two ugly buildings are injurious to the interior appearance of the building, their heavy forms and structure being disadvantageously contrasted with the light and airy shape of the Makams. I heard some hadjys from Greece, men of better taste than the Arabs, express their regret that the Kobbateyn should be allowed to disfigure the mosque. Their contents might be deposited in some of the buildings adjoining the mosque, of which they form no essential part, no religious importance being attached to them. They were built by Khoshgeldy, governor of Djidda, A.H. 947: one is called

Kobbet el Abbas, from having been placed on the site of a small tank said to have been formed by Abbas, the uncle of Mohammed.

A few paces west of Zemzem, and directly opposite to the door of the Kaaba, stands a ladder or staircase, which is moved up to the wall of the Kaaba, on the days when that building is opened, and by which the visitors ascend to the door: it is of wood, with some carved ornaments, moves on low wheels, and is sufficiently broad to admit of four persons ascending abreast. The first ladder was sent hither from Cairo in A. H. 818, by Moay-ed Abou el Naser, King of Egypt; for in the Hedjaz it seems there has always been so great a want of artizans, that whenever the mosque required any work, it was necessary to have mechanics brought from Cairo, and even sometimes from Constantinople.

In the same line with the ladder, and close by it, stands a lightly-built, insulated, and circular arch, about fifteen feet wide and eighteen feet high, called Bab-es'-Salam, which must not be confounded with the great gate of the mosque bearing the same name. Those who enter the Beitullah for the first time, are enjoined to do so by the outer and inner Bab-es'-Salam : in passing under the latter, they are to exclaim, " O God, may it be a happy entrance !" I do not know by whom this arch was built, but it appears to be modern.

Nearly in front of the Bab-es'-Salam, and nearer to the Kaaba than any of the other surrounding buildings, stands the Makam Ibrahim. This is a small building, supported by six pillars about eight feet high, four of which are surrounded from top to bottom by a fine iron railing, which thus leaves the space beyond the two hind pillars open : within the railing is a frame about five feet square, terminating in a pyramidal top, and said to contain the sacred stone upon which Ibrahim (Abraham) stood when he built the Kaaba, and which, with the help of his son Ismayl, he had removed from hence to the place called Madjen, already mentioned. The stone is said to have yielded under the weight of the patriarch, and to preserve the impression of his foot still visible upon it; but no hadjy has ever seen it, as the frame is always entirely covered with a brocade of red silk richly embroidered. Persons are constantly seen before the railing, invoking the good offices of

Ibrahim; and a short prayer must be uttered by the side of the Makam, after the walk round the Kaaba is completed. It is said that many of the Sahabe, or first adherents of Mohammed, were interred in the open space between this Makam and Zemzem, from which circumstance it is one of the most favourite places of prayer in the mosque. In this part of the area, the Khalif Soleyman Ibn Abd el Melek, brother of Wolyd, built a fine reservoir, in A. H. 97, which was filled from a spring east of Arafat; but the Mekkawys destroyed it after his death, on the pretence that the water of Zemzem was preferable.*

On the side of Makam Ibrahim, facing the middle part of the front of the Kaaba, stands the Mambar or pulpit of the mosque; it is elegantly formed of fine white marble, with many sculptured ornaments, and was sent as a present to the mosque in A. H. 969, by Sultan Soleyman Ibn Selym:† a straight narrow staircase leads up to the post of the Khatyb, or preacher, which is surmounted by a gilt polygonal pointed steeple, resembling an obelisk. Here a sermon is preached on Fridays, and on certain festivals; these, like the Friday sermons of all mosques in the Mohammedan countries, are usually of the same tenor, with some slight alterations upon extraordinary occasions. Before the Wahabys invaded Mekka, prayers were added for the Sultan and the Sherif; but these were forbidden by Saoud. Since the Turkish conquest, however, the ancient custom has been restored; and on Fridays, as well as at the end of the first daily evening prayers, the Sultan, Mohammed Aly Pasha, and Sherif Yahya are included in the formula. The right of preaching in the Mambar is vested in several of the first olemas in Mekka; they are always elderly persons, and officiate in rotation. In ancient times, Mohammed himself, his successors, and the Khalifes, whenever they came to Mekka, mounted the pulpit, and preached to the people.

The Khatyb, or preacher, appears in the Mambar wrapped in a white cloak, which covers his head and body, and with a stick in his

---

* Vide Makrizi's Treatise—" Manhadj myn el Kholafa."
† The first Mambar was sent from Cairo in A. H. 818, together with the steps above mentioned, by Moay-ed, King of Egypt. See Asamy.

hand; a practice observed also in Egypt and Syria, in memory of the first age of Islam, when the preachers found it necessary to be armed, from fear of being surprised. As in other mosques, two green flags are placed on each side of him.

About the Mambar, the visitors of the Kaaba deposit their shoes; as it is neither permitted to walk round the Kaaba with covered feet, nor thought decent to carry the shoes in the hand, as is done in other mosques. Several persons keep watch over the shoes, for which they expect a small present; but the vicinity of the holy temple does not intimidate the dishonest, for I lost successively from this spot three new pairs of shoes; and the same thing happens to many hadjys.

I have now described all the buildings within the enclosure of the Temple.*

The gravel-ground, and part of the adjoining outer pavement of the Kaaba, is covered, at the time of evening prayers, with carpets of from sixty to eighty feet in length, and four feet in breadth, of Egyptian manufacture, which are rolled up after prayers. The greater part of the hadjys bring their own carpets with them. The more distant parts of the area, and the floor under the colonnade, are spread with mats, brought from Souakin; the latter situation being the usual place for the performance of the mid-day and afternoon prayers. Many of these mats are presented to the mosque by the hadjys, for which they have in return the satisfaction of seeing their names inscribed on them in large characters.

At sun-set, great numbers assemble for the first evening prayer: they form themselves into several wide circles, sometimes as many as

* The ground-plan of the Temple given by Aly Bey el Abbassi is perfectly correct. This cannot be said of his plan of Mekka, nor of his different *views* in the Hedjaz: a comparison of my description with his work will show in what points I differ from him, as well in regard to the temple, as to the town and its inhabitants. His travels came to my hands after I had returned from Arabia. The view of the mosque given by d'Ohsson, in his valuable work, is tolerably correct, except that the Kaaba is too large in proportion to the rest of the building. The view of the town of Mekka, on the contrary, is very unfaithful. That in Niebuhr, which was copied from an ancient Arabic drawing, is less accurate than d'Ohsson's. The original seems to have been taken before the last alterations made in the buildings of the Temple.

twenty, around the Kaaba as a common centre before which every person makes his prostration; and thus, as the Mohammedan doctors observe, Mekka is the only spot throughout the world in which the true believer can, with propriety, turn during his prayers towards any point of the compass. The Imám takes his post near the gate of the Kaaba, and his genuflexions are imitated by the whole assembled multitude. The effect of the joint prostrations of six or eight thousand persons, added to the recollection of the distance and various quarters from whence they come, and for what purpose, cannot fail to impress the most cool-minded spectator with some degree of awe. At night, when the lamps are lighted, and numbers of devotees are performing the Towaf round the Kaaba, the sight of the busy crowds—the voices of the Metowefs, intent upon making themselves heard by those to whom they recite their prayers—the loud conversation of many idle persons—the running, playing, and laughing of boys, give to the whole a very different appearance, and one more resembling that of a place of public amusement. The crowd, however, leaves the mosque about nine o'clock, when it again becomes the place of silent meditation and prayer, to the *few* visitors who are led to the spot by sincere piety, and not worldly motives or fashion.

There is an opinion prevalent at Mekka, founded on holy tradition, that the mosque will contain any number of the faithful; and that if even the whole Mohammedan community were to enter at once, they would all find room in it to pray. The guardian angels, it is said, would invisibly extend the dimensions of the building, and diminish the size of each individual. The fact is, that during the most numerous pilgrimages, the mosque, which can contain, I believe, about thirty-five thousand persons in the act of prayer, is never half filled. Even on Fridays, the greater part of the Mekkawys, contrary to the injunctions of the law, pray at home, if at all, and many hadjys follow their example. I could never count more than ten thousand individuals in the mosque at one time, even after the return from Arafat, when the whole body of hadjys were collected, for a few days, in and about the city.

At every hour of the day persons may be seen under the colonnade, occupied in reading the Koran and other religious books; and here many poor Indians, or negroes, spread their mats, and pass the whole period of their residence at Mekka. Here they both eat and sleep; but cooking is not allowed. During the hours of noon, many persons come to repose beneath the cool shade of the vaulted roof of the colonnade; a custom which not only accounts for the mode of construction observed in the old Mohammedan temples of Egypt and Arabia, but for that also of the ancient Egyptian temples, the immense porticoes of which were probably left open to the idolatrous natives, whose mud-built houses could afford them but an imperfect refuge against the mid-day heats.

It is only during the hours of prayer that the great mosques of these countries partake of the sanctity of prayer, or in any degree seem to be regarded as consecrated places. In El Azhar, the first mosque at Cairo, I have seen boys crying pancakes for sale, barbers shaving their customers, and many of the lower orders eating their dinners, where, during prayers, not the slightest motion, nor even whisper, diverts the attention of the congregation. Not a sound but the voice of the Imam is heard during prayers in the great mosque at Mekka, which at other times is the place of meeting for men of business to converse on their affairs, and is sometimes so full of poor hadjys, or of diseased persons lying about under the colonnade, in the midst of their miserable baggage, as to have the appearance of an hospital rather than a temple. Boys play in the great square, and servants carry luggage across it, to pass by the nearest route from one part of the town to the other. In these respects, the temple of Mekka resembles the other great mosques of the East. But the holy Kaaba is rendered the scene of such indecencies and criminal acts, as cannot with propriety be more particularly noticed. They are not only practised here with impunity, but, it may be said, almost publicly; and my indignation has often been excited, on witnessing abominations which called forth from other passing spectators nothing more than a laugh or a slight reprimand.

In several parts of the colonnade, public schools are held, where young children are taught to spell and read: they form most noisy.

groups, and the schoolmaster's stick is in constant action. Some learned men of Mekka deliver lectures on religious subjects every afternoon under the colonnade, but the auditors are seldom numerous. On Fridays, after prayer, some Turkish olemas explain to their countrymen assembled around them a few chapters of the Koran, after which each of the audience kisses the hand of the expositor, and drops money into his cap. I particularly admired the fluency of speech of one of these olemas, although I did not understand him, the lecture being delivered in the Turkish language. His gesticulations, and the inflexions of his voice, were most expressive; but like an actor on the stage, he would laugh and cry in the same minute, and adapt his features to his purpose in the most skilful manner. He was a native of Brusa, and amassed a considerable sum of money.

Near the gate of the mosque called Bab-es'-Salam, a few Arab Sheikhs daily take their seat, with their ink-stand and paper, ready to write, for any applicant, letters, accounts, contracts, or any similar document. They also deal in written charms, like those current in the Black countries, such as amulets, and love-receipts, called "Kotob muhbat o kuboul." They are principally employed by Bedouins, and demand an exorbitant remuneration.

Winding-sheets (*keffen*), and other linen washed in the waters of Zemzem, are constantly seen hanging to dry between the columns. Many hadjys purchase at Mekka the shroud in which they wish to be buried, and wash it themselves at the well of Zemzem, supposing that, if the corpse be wrapped in linen which has been wetted with this holy water, the peace of the soul after death will be more effectually secured. Some hadjys make this linen an article of traffic.

Mekka generally, but the mosque in particular, abounds with flocks of wild pigeons, which are considered to be the inviolable property of the temple, and are called the Pigeons of the Beitullah. Nobody dares to kill any of them, even when they enter the private houses. In the square of the mosque, several small stone basins are regularly filled with water for their use; here also Arab women expose to sale, upon small straw mats, corn and durra, which the pilgrims purchase, and throw to the pigeons. I have seen some of the public women take this mode of exhibiting themselves, and of bargaining with the pilgrims, under pretence of selling them corn for the sacred pigeons.

The gates of the mosque are nineteen in number, and are distributed about it, without any order or symmetry. I subjoin their names, as they are usually written upon small cards by the Metowefs: in another column are the names by which they were known in more ancient times, principally taken from Azraky and Kotoby.

Modern Names.		Ancient Names.
Bab-es'-Salam, composed of 3 smaller gates, or arches.		Bab beni Sheybe.
Bab el Neby	2	Bab el Djenaiz, The dead being carried through it to the mosque, that prayers may be said over their bodies.
Bab el Abbas Opposite to this the house of Abbas once stood.	3	Bab Sertakat.
Bab Aly	3	Bab Beni Hashem.
Bab el Zeyt Bab el Ashra	2	Bab Bazan.
Bab el Baghle	2	
Bab el Szafa	5	Bab Beni Makhzoum.
Bab Sherif	2	Bab el Djyad.
Bab Medjahed	2	Bab el Dokhmase
Bab Zoleykha	2	Bab Sherif Adjelan (who built it.)
Bab Om Hany So called from the daughter of Aby Taleb.	2	
Bab el Wodaa Through which the pilgrim passes in taking his final leave of the temple.	2	Bab el Hazoura
Bab Ibrahim *	1	Bab el Kheyatyn, or Bab Djomah.

* So called, not from Abraham, but from a tailor who had his shop near it.

THE BEITULLAH. 153

Modern Names.		Ancient Names.
Bab el Omra	1	
Through which the pilgrims issue to visit the Omra. Also called Beni Saham.		
Bab Ateek	1	Bab Amer Ibn el Aas, or Bab el Sedra.
Bab el Bastye	1	Bab el Adjale.
Bab el Kotoby*	1	Bab Zyade Dar el Nedoua.
Bab Zyade	3	
Bab Dereybe	1	Bab Medrese.
Total number of arches	39	

The principal of these gates are :—on the north side, Bab-es-Salam, by which every pilgrim enters the mosque; Bab Abbas; Bab el Neby, by which Mohammed is said to have always entered the mosque; Bab Aly. On the east side, Bab el Zeyt, or Bab el Ashra, through which the ten first Sahabe, or adherents of Mohammed, used to enter; Bab el Szafa; two gates called Biban el Sherif, opposite the palaces of the Sherif. On the south side, Bab Ibrahim, where the colonnade projects beyond the straight line of the columns, and forms a small square; Bab el Omra, through which it is necessary to pass, on visiting the Omra. On the west side, Bab el Zyade, forming a projecting square similar to that at Bab Ibrahim, but larger. Most of these gates have high pointed arches; but a few round arches are seen among them, which, like all the arches of this kind in the Hedjaz, are nearly semicircular. They are without any ornament, except the inscription on the exterior, which commemorates the name of the builder; and they are all posterior in date to the fourteenth century. As each gate consists of two or three arches, or divisions, separated by narrow walls, these divisions are counted in the enumeration of the gates leading into the Kaaba, and thus make up the number thirty-nine. There being no doors to the gates, the mosque is consequently open at all

---

* Taking its name from the famous author of a History of Mekka, who lived in an adjoining lane, and opened this small gate into the mosque.

times. I have crossed at every hour of the night, and always found people there, either at prayers, or walking about.

The outside walls of the mosque are those of the houses which surround it on all sides. These houses belonged originally to the mosque; the greater part are now the property of individuals, who have purchased them; they are let out to the richest hadjys, at very high prices, as much as five hundred piastres being given, during the pilgrimage, for a good apartment, with windows opening into the mosque. Windows have, in consequence, been opened in many parts of the walls, on a level with the street, and above that of the floor of the colonnades. Hadjys living in these apartments are allowed to perform the Friday's prayers at home; because, having the Kaaba in view from the windows, they are supposed to be in the mosque itself, and to join in prayer those assembled within the temple. Upon a level with the ground-floor of the colonnades, and opening into them, are small apartments formed in the walls, having the appearance of dungeons: these have remained the property of the mosque, while the houses above them belong to private individuals. They are let out to watermen, who deposit in them the Zemzem jars; or to less opulent hadjys, who wish to live in the mosque. Some of the surrounding houses still belong to the mosque, and were originally intended for public schools, as their name of Medrese implies: they are now all let out to hadjys. In one of the largest of them, Mohammed Aly Pasha lived; in another Hassan Pasha *

Close to Bab Ibrahim is a large Medrese, now the property of Seyd Ageyl, one of the principal merchants of the town, whose warehouse opens into the mosque. This person, who is aged, has the repu-

---

* One of the finest Medreses in Mekka, built by order of Kail Beg, Sultan of Egypt, in A. H. 888, in the side of the mosque fronting the street Masaa, has also become a private building, after having been deprived of its revenue by the peculation of its guardians. Besides the Medreses, there were other buildings of less extent erected by different Sultans of Egypt and Constantinople for similar purposes, called Rebat, where poor pilgrims might reside, who chose to study there; but these have shared the fate of the Medreses, and are now either the private property of Mekkawys, or let to individuals on long leases by the mosque, and used as common lodging-houses.

tation of great sanctity; and it is said that the hand of Sherif Ghaleb, when once in the act of collaring him, for refusing to advance some money, was momentarily struck with palsy. He has every evening assemblies in his house, where theological books are read,* and religious topics discussed.

Among other buildings forming the enclosure of the Mesjed, is the Mehkam, or house of justice, close by the Bab Zyade: it is a fine, firmly-built structure, with lofty arches in the interior, and has a row of high windows looking into the mosque. It is inhabited by the Kadhy. Adjoining to it stands a large Medrese, inclosing a square, known by the name of Medrese Soleymanye, built by Sultan Soleyman, and his son Selym II., in A. H. 973. It is always well filled with Turkish hadjys, the friends of the Kadhy, who disposes of the lodgings.

The exterior of the mosque is adorned with seven minarets, irregularly distributed:—1. Minaret of Bab el Omra; 2. of Bab el Salam; 3. of Bab Aly; 4. of Bab el Wodaa; 5. of Medrese Kail Beg; 6. of Bab el Zyade; 7. of Medreset Sultan Soleyman. They are quadrangular or round steeples, in no way differing from other minarets. The entrance to them is from the different buildings round the mosque, which they adjoin. A beautiful view of the busy crowd below is obtained by ascending the most northern one.

It will have been seen by the foregoing description, that the mosque of Mekka differs little in its construction from many other buildings of the same nature in Asia. The mosque of Zakaria at Aleppo, the great mosque called El Amouy at Damascus, and the greater number of the larger mosques at Cairo, are constructed exactly

---

* The cousin of this man is the famous pirate Syd Mohammed el Ageyl, who has committed many outrages upon European ships in the Red Sea, and even insulted the English flag. In the beginning of 1814 he was called to Djidda, with offers to enter the service of Mohammed Aly Pasha, who, it was then thought, had some hostile intentions against Yemen. The Pasha made him considerable presents, either in the hope of engaging him in his service, or of securing his friendship; but the pirate declined his proposals. He has amassed great wealth; has establishments in almost every harbour of the Red Sea; and is adored by his sailors and soldiers for his great liberality. Like his cousin at Mekka, he has succeeded in making people believe that he is endowed with supernatural powers.

upon the same plan, with an arched colonnade round an open square. None is more like it than the mosque of Touloun, at Cairo, built in A. H. 263; and that of Ammer, situated between Cairo and Old Cairo, upon the spot where Fostat once stood: it was built by Ammer Ibn el Aas, in the first years of the conquest of Egypt; it has an arched fountain in the midst, where at Mekka stands the Kaaba; but is only one-third as large as the mosque of Mekka. The history of Beitullah (or God's house) has exercised the industry of many learned Arabians: it is only in latter times that the mosque has been enlarged; many trees once stood in the square, and it is to be regretted that others have not succeeded them.

The service of the mosque occupies a vast number of people. The Khatybs, Imams, Muftis, those attached to Zemzem, the Mueddins who call to prayers, numbers of olemas, who deliver lectures, lamp-lighters, and a crowd of menial servants, are all employed about the Beitullah. They receive regular pay from the mosque, besides what they share of the presents made to it by hadjys, for the purpose of distribution; those not made for such purpose, are reserved for the repairs of the building. The revenue of the mosque is considerable, although it has been deprived of the best branches of its income.

There are few towns or districts of the Turkish empire in which it does not possess property in land or houses; but the annual amount of this property is often withheld by provincial governors, or at least it is reduced, by the hands through which it passes, to a small proportion of its real value. El Is-haaky, in his History of Egypt, states, that in the time of Sultan Achmed, the son of Sultan Mohammed, (who died in A. H. 1027,) Egypt sent yearly to Mekka two hundred and ninety-five purses, destined principally for the mosque, and forty-eight thousand and eighty erdebs of corn. Bayazyd Ibn Sultan Mohammed Khan (in 912) fixed the income of Mekka and Medina, to be sent from Constantinople, at fourteen thousand ducats per annum, in addition to what his predecessors had already ordered; and Sultan Solyman Ibn Selym I. increased the annual income of Mekka, sent from Constantinople, which his father Selym had fixed at seven thousand erdebs of corn, to ten thousand erdebs, and five thousand for the inhabitants of

Medina.* He likewise fixed the *surra* from Constantinople, or, as it is called, the Greek surra, at thirty-one thousand ducats per annum.† Almost all the revenues derived from Egypt were sequestrated by the Mamelouk Beys; and Mohammed Aly has now seized what remained. Some revenue is yet drawn from Yemen, called Wakf el Hamam, and a little is brought in annually by the Hadj caravans. At present, therefore, the mosque of Mekka may be called poor in comparison with its former state.‡ Excepting a few golden lamps in the Kaaba, it possesses no treasures whatever, notwithstanding the stories prevalent to the contrary; and I learnt from the Kadhy himself, that the Sultan, in order to keep up the establishment, sends at present four hundred purses annually, as a present to the Kaaba; which sum is partly expended in the service of the mosque, and partly divided among the servants belonging to it.

The income of the mosque must not be confounded with that of a number of Mekkawys, including many of the servants, which they derive from other pious foundations in the Turkish empire, known by the name of Surra, and of which a great part still remains untouched. The donations of the hadjys, however, are so ample as to afford abundant subsistence to the great numbers of idle persons employed about the mosque; and as long as the pilgrimage exists, there is no reason to apprehend their wanting either the necessaries or the luxuries of life.

The first officer of the mosque is the Nayb el Haram, or Hares el Haram, the guardian who keeps the keys of the Kaaba. In his hands are deposited the sums bestowed as presents to the building, and which he distributes in conjunction with the Kadhy: under his directions,

* See Kotobeddyn.

† See Assamy. These surras (or purses) were first instituted by Mohammed Ibn Sultan Yalderem, in A.H. 816.

‡ The princes of India have frequently given proofs of great munificence towards the mosque at Mekka. In A.H. 798, large presents in money and valuable articles were sent by the sovereigns of Bengal and Cambay; those of Bengal, especially, are often mentioned as benefactors by Asamy.

also, the repairs of the building are carried on.* I have been assured, but do not know how truly, that the Nayb el Haram's yearly accounts, which are countersigned by the Sherif and Kadhy, and sent to Constantinople, amount to three hundred purses, merely for the expenses of the necessary repairs, lighting, carpets, &c., and the maintenance of the eunuchs belonging to the temple. This officer happens at present to be one of the heads of the three only families descended from the ancient Koreysh who remain resident at Mekka. Next to him, the second officer of the mosque in rank is the Aga of the eunuchs, or, as he is called, Agat el Towashye. The eunuchs perform the duty of police officers in the temple;† they prevent disorders, and daily wash and sweep, with large brooms, the pavement round the Kaaba. In time of rain, I have seen the water stand on the pavement to the height of a foot; on such occasions many of the hadjys assist the eunuchs in removing it through several holes made in the pavement, which, it is said, lead to large vaults beneath the Kaaba, though the historians of Mekka and of the temple make no mention of them. The eunuchs are dressed in the Constantinopolitan *kaouk*, with wide robes, bound by a sash, and carry a long stick in their hands. The engraving of their dress given by d'Ohsson is strikingly correct; as are, in general, all the representations of costume in that work, which I had an opportunity of comparing with the original.‡ The number of eunuchs now exceeds forty, and they are supplied by Pashas and other grandees, who send them, when young, as presents to the mosque: one hundred dollars are sent with each as an outfit. Mohammed Aly presented ten young eunuchs to the mosque. At present there

* The honour of keeping the keys of the Kaaba, and the profits arising from it, were often subjects of contention among the ancient Arabian tribes.

† The employment of slaves or eunuchs in this mosque is of very ancient date. Mawya Ibn Aly Sofyan, a short time after Mohammed, first ordered slaves for the Kaaba.—Vid. Fasy.

‡ This excellent work is the only perfect source of information respecting the laws and constitution of the Turkish empire; but it must not be forgotten that the practices prevalent in the provinces are, unfortunately, often in direct contravention of the spirit and letter of the code of law, as explained by the author.

are ten grown-up persons, and twenty boys; the latter live together in a house, till they are sufficiently instructed to be given in charge to their elder brethren, with whom they remain a few years, and then set up their own establishments. Extraordinary as it may appear, the grown-up eunuchs are all married to black slaves, and maintain several male and female slaves in their houses as servants. They affect great importance; and in case of quarrels or riots, lay freely about them with their sticks. Many of the lower classes of Mekka kiss their hands on approaching them. Their chief, or Aga, whom they elect among themselves, is a great personage, and is entitled to sit in the presence of the Pasha and the Sherif. The eunuchs have a large income from the revenues of the mosque, and from private donations of the hadjys; they also receive regular stipends from Constantinople, and derive profit from trade; for, like almost all the people of Mekka, and even the first clergy, they are more or less engaged in traffic; and their ardour in the pursuit of commercial gain is much greater than that which they evince in the execution of their official duties, being equalled only by the eagerness with which they court the friendship of wealthy hadjys.

Most of the eunuchs, or Towashye, are negroes; a few were copper-coloured Indians. One of the former is sometimes sent to the Soudan countries, to collect presents for the Kaaba. The fate of a eunuch of this description is mentioned by Bruce. Some years since a Towashye obtained permission to return to Soudan, on presenting another person to the mosque in his stead. He then repaired to Borgo, west of Darfour, and is now the powerful governor of a province.

Whenever negro hadjys come to Mekka, they never fail to pay assiduous court to the Towashyes. A Towashye, after having been once attached to the service of the Kaaba, which confers on him the appellation of Towashye el Neby (the Prophet's eunuch), can never enter into any other service.

In the time of Ramadhan, (the last days of which month, in 1814, I passed at Mekka,) the mosque is particularly brilliant. The hadjys, at that period, (which happened to be in the hottest time of the year,) generally performed the three first daily prayers at home, but assembled in large crowds in the mosque, for their evening devotions. Every one then carried in his handkerchief a few dates, a little bread and cheese, or some grapes, which he placed before him, waiting for the moment of the call to evening prayers, to be allowed to break the fast. During this period of suspense, they would politely offer to their neighbours a part of their meal, and receive as much in return. Some hadjys, to gain the reputation of peculiar charitableness, were going from man to man, and placing before each a few morsels of viands, followed by beggars, who, in their turn, received these morsels from those hadjys before whom they had been placed. As soon as the Imam on the top of Zemzem began his cry of "Allahou Akbar," (God is most great!) every one hastened to drink of the jar of Zemzem water placed before him, and to eat something, previous to joining in the prayer; after which they all returned home to supper, and again revisited the mosque, for the celebration of the last evening orisons. At this time, the whole square and colonnades were illuminated by thousands of lamps; and, in addition to these, most of the hadjys had each his own lantern standing on the ground before him. The brilliancy of this spectacle, and the cool breeze pervading the square, caused multitudes to linger here till midnight. This square, the only wide and open place in the whole town, admits through all its gates the cooling breeze; but this the Mekkawys ascribe to the waving wings of those angels who guard the mosque. I witnessed the enthusiasm of a Darfour pilgrim, who arrived at Mekka on the last night of Ramadhan. After a long journey across barren and solitary deserts, on his entering the illuminated temple, he was so much struck with its appearance, and overawed by the black Kaaba, that he fell prostrate close by the place where I was sitting, and remained long in that posture of adoration. He then rose, burst into a flood of tears, and in the height of his emotion, instead of reciting the usual prayers of the visitor, only exclaimed, "O God, now take my soul, for this is Paradise!"

The termination of the Hadj gives a very different appearance to the temple. Disease and mortality, which succeed to the fatigues endured on the journey, or are caused by the light covering of the ihram, the unhealthy lodgings at Mekka, the bad fare, and sometimes absolute want, fill the mosque with dead bodies, carried thither to receive the Imam's prayer, or with sick persons, many of whom, when their dissolution approaches, are brought to the colonnades, that they may either be cured by a sight of the Kaaba, or at least have the satisfaction of expiring within the sacred enclosure. Poor hadjys, worn out with disease and hunger, are seen dragging their emaciated bodies along the columns; and when no longer able to stretch forth their hand to ask the passenger for charity, they place a bowl to receive alms near the mat on which they lay themselves. When they feel their last moments approaching, they cover themselves with their tattered garments; and often a whole day passes before it is discovered that they are dead. For a month subsequent to the conclusion of the Hadj, I found, almost every morning, corpses of pilgrims lying in the mosque; myself and a Greek hadjy, whom accident had brought to the spot, once closed the eyes of a poor Mogrebyn pilgrim, who had crawled into the neighbourhood of the Kaaba, to breathe his last, as the Moslems say, " in the arms of the prophet and of the guardian angels." He intimated by signs his wish that we should sprinkle Zemzem water over him; and while we were doing so, he expired: half an hour afterwards he was buried. There are several persons in the service of the mosque employed to wash carefully the spot on which those who expire in the mosque have lain, and to bury all the poor and friendless strangers who die at Mekka.

SOME HISTORICAL NOTICES CONCERNING THE KAABA, AND THE TEMPLE OF MEKKA;

EXTRACTED FROM THE WORKS OF EL AZRAKY, EL FASY, KOTOBEDDYN, AND ASAMY, WRITERS MORE PARTICULARLY MENTIONED IN THE INTRODUCTION.

MOHAMMEDAN mythology affirms that the Kaaba was constructed in heaven, two thousand years before the creation of this world, and that it was there adored by the angels, whom the Almighty commanded to perform the Towaf, or walk round it. Adam, who was the first true believer, erected the Kaaba upon earth, on its present site, which is directly below the spot that it occupied in heaven. He collected the stones for the building from the five holy mountains : Lebanon, Tor Syna (Mount Sinai), El Djoudy (the name given by Muselmans to the mountain on which the ark of Noah rested after the deluge), Hirra, or Djebel Nour, and Tor Zeyt (the mountain to which, as I believe, an allusion is made in the ninety-fifth chapter of the Koran). Ten thousand angels were appointed to guard the structure from accidents : but they seem, from the history of the holy building, to have been often remiss in their duty. The sons of Adam repaired the Kaaba; and after the deluge, Ibrahim (Abraham), when he had abandoned the idolatry of his forefathers, was ordered by the Almighty to reconstruct it. His son Ismayl, who from his infancy resided with his mother Hadjer (Hagar) near the site of Mekka, assisted his father, who had come from Syria to obey the commands of Allah : on digging, they found the foundations which had been laid by Adam. Being in want of a stone to fix into the corner of the building as a mark from whence the Towaf, or holy walk round it, was to commence, Ismayl went in search of one. On his way towards Djebel Kobeys, he met the angel Gabriel, holding in his hand the famous black stone. It was then of a refulgent bright colour, but became black, says El Azraky, in consequence of its having suffered repeatedly by fire, before and after the introduction of Islam. Others say its colour was changed by the sins of those who touched it. At the day of judgment, it will bear witness in favour of all those who have touched it with sincere hearts, and will be endowed with sight and speech.

After the well of Zemzem was miraculously created, and before Ibrahim began to build the Kaaba, the Arab tribe of Beni Djorham, a branch of the Amalekites, settled here, with the permission of Ismayl and his mother, with whom they lived. Ismayl considered the well as his property; but having intermarried with the Djorham tribe, they usurped, after his death, the possession both of the well and the Kaaba. During their abode in this valley, they rebuilt or thoroughly repaired the Kaaba; but the well was choked up by the violence of torrents, and remained so for nearly one thousand years. The tribe of Khozaa afterwards kept possession of the Kaaba for three hundred years; and their successors, of the tribe of Kossay Ibn Kelab, again rebuilt it; for being constantly exposed to the devastations of torrents, it was often in need of repair. It had hitherto been open at the top: they roofed it; and from this period its history becomes less involved in fable and uncertainty.

An Arab of Kossay, named Ammer Ibn Lahay, first introduced idolatry among his countrymen; he brought the idol, called Hobal, from Hyt, in Mesopotamia,* and set it up at the Kaaba. Idolatry then spread rapidly; and it seems that almost every Arab tribe chose its own god or tutelar divinity; and that, considering the Kaaba as a Pantheon common to them all, they frequented it in pilgrimage. The date-tree, called Ozza, says Azraky, was worshipped by the tribe of

---

* See El Azraky.

Khozaa; and the Beni Thekyf adored the rock called El Lat; a large tree, called Zat Arowat, was revered by the Koreysh; the holy places, Muna, Szafa, Meroua, had their respective saints or demi-gods; and the historians give a long list of other deities. The number of idols increased so much, that one was to be found in every house and tent of this valley; and the Kaaba was adorned with three hundred and sixty of them, corresponding probably to the days of the year.

The tribe of Kossay were the first who built houses round the Kaaba; in these they lived during the day, but in the evening they always returned to their tents, pitched upon the neighbouring mountains. The successors of the Beni Kossay at Mekka, or Bekka, (the name then applied to the town,) were the Beni Koreysh. About their time the Kaaba was destroyed by fire; they rebuilt it of wood, of a smaller size than it had been in the time of the Kossay, but indicating by the wall Hedjer (already described) its former limits. The roof was supported within by six pillars; and the statue of Hobal, the Arabian Jupiter, was placed over a well, then existing within the Kaaba. This happened during the youth of Mohammed. All the idols were replaced in the new building; and El Azraky adduces the ocular testimony of several respectable witnesses, to prove a remarkable fact, (hitherto, I believe, unnoticed,) that the figure of the Virgin Mary, with the young Aysa (Jesus) in her lap, was likewise sculptured as a deity upon one of the six pillars nearest to the gate.

The grandfather of Mohammed, Abd el Motalleb Ibn Hesham, had restored the well of Zemzem by an excavation some time before the burning of the Kaaba.

When the victorious Mohammed entered the town of his fathers, he destroyed the images in the temple, and abolished the idolatrous worship of his countrymen; and his Mueddin, the negro Belal, called the Moslems to prayers from the top of the Kaaba.

The Koreysh had built a small town round the Kaaba, which they venerated so much that no person was permitted to raise the roof of his house higher than that of the sacred structure. The pilgrimage to this holy shrine, which the pagan Arabs had instituted, was confirmed by Islam.

Omar Ibn Khatab first built a mosque round the Kaaba. In the year of the Hedjra 17, having purchased from the Koreysh the small houses which enclosed it, and carried a wall round the area, Othman Ibn Affan, in A. H. 27, enlarged the square; and in A. H. 63, when the heretic and rebel Yezyd was besieged at Mekka by Abdallah Ibn Zebeyr, the nephew of Aysha, the Kaaba was destroyed by fire, some say accidentally, while others affirm it to have been done by the slinging machines directed against it by Yezyd from the top of Djebel Kobeys, where he had taken post. After his expulsion, Ibn Zebeyr enlarged the enclosure of the wall by purchasing some more houses of the Mekkawys, and by including their site, after having levelled them, within the wall. He also rebuilt the Kaaba upon an enlarged scale, raising it from eighteen pikes (its height under the Koreysh) to twenty-seven pikes, or nearly equal to what it was in the time of the Beni Kossay. He opened two doors into it, level with the surface of the area, and constructed a double roof, supported by three instead of six pillars, the former number. This new building was twenty-five pikes in length, twenty in breadth on one side, and twenty-one on the other. In the interior, the dry well, called Byr Ahsef, still remained, wherein the treasures were deposited, particularly the golden vessels that had been presented to the Kaaba. It was at this period that the structure took the name of Kaaba, which is said to be derived from *kaab*, a die or cube, the form which the building now assumed. Its former title was the House of God, (Beitullah,) or the Old House, a name still often applied to it.

Twenty years after the last-mentioned date, El Hadjadj Ibn Yousef el Thakafy, then governor of Mekka, disliking the enlarged size of the Kaaba, reduced it to the proportions it had in the time of the Koreysh, cutting off six pikes from its length; he also restored the wall called Hedjer, which Ibn Zebeyr had included within the building. The size then given to the edifice is the same as that of the present structure, it having been scrupulously adhered to in all the repairs or re-erections which subsequently took place.

Towards the end of the first century of the Hedjra, Wolyd Ibn Abd el Melek was the first who reared columns in the mosque. He caused their capitals to be covered with thin plates of gold, and incurred a great expense for decorations: it is related that all the golden ornaments which he gave to the building were sent from Toledo in Spain, and carried upon mules through Africa and Arabia.

Abou Djafar el Mansour, one of the Abassides, in A. H. 139, enlarged the north and south sides of the mosque, and made it twice as large as it had been before, so that it now occupied a space of forty-seven pikes and a half in length. He also paved the ground adjoining the well of Zemzem with marble.

The Khalife El Mohdy added to the size of the mosque at two different periods; the last time, in A. H. 163, he bought the ground required for these additions from the Mekkawys, paying to them twenty-five dinars for every square pike. It was this Khalife who brought the columns from Egypt, as I have already observed. The improvements which he had begun, were completed by his son El Hady. The roof of the colonnade was then built of *sadj*, a precious Indian wood. The columns brought from Egypt by El Mohdy, were landed at one day's journey north of Djidda; but some obstacles arising, they were not all transported to Mekka, some of them having been abandoned on the sands near the shore. I mention this for the sake of future travellers, who, on discovering them, might perhaps consider them as the vestiges of some powerful Greek or Egyptian colony.

The historians of Mekka remark, and not without astonishment, that the munificent Khalife Haroun er Rasheid, although he repeatedly visited the Kaaba, added nothing to the mosque, except a new pulpit, or mambar.

A. H. 226. During the Khalifat of Motasem b'illah, the well of Zemzem was covered above: it had before been enclosed all round, but not roofed.

A. H. 241. The space between the Hedjer and the Kaaba was laid out with fine marbles. At that time there was a gate leading into the space enclosed within the Hedjer.

The Khalife El Motaded, in A. H. 281, put the whole mosque into a complete state of repair: he rebuilt its walls; made new gates, assigning to them new names; and enlarged the building on the west side, by adding to it the space formerly occupied by the celebrated Dar el Nedowa; an ancient building of Mekka, well known in the history of the Pagan Arabs, which had always been the common council-house of the chiefs of Mekka. It is said to have stood near the spot where the Makam el Hanefy is now placed.

In A. H. 314, or, according to others, 301, Mekka and its temple experienced great disasters. The army of the heretic sect of the Carmates, headed by their chief, Abou Dhaher, invaded the Hedjaz, and seized upon Mekka: fifty thousand of its inhabitants were slain during the sack of the city, and the temple and the Kaaba were stripped of all their valuable ornaments. After remaining twenty-one days, the enemy departed, carrying with them the great jewel of Mekka, the black stone of the Kaaba. During the fire which injured the Kaaba, in the time of Ibn Zebeyr, the violent heat had split the stone into three pieces, which were afterwards joined together again, and replaced in the former situation, surrounded with a rim of silver; this rim was renewed and strengthened by Haroun er Rasheid.

The Carmates carried the stone to Hedjer,* a fertile spot in the Desert, on the route of the Syrian caravan, north of Medina, which they had chosen as one of their abodes. They hoped that all the moslems would come to visit the stone, and that they should thus succeed to the riches which the pilgrims from every part of the world had brought to Mekka. Under this impression, Abou Dhaher refused an offer of fifty thousand dinars as a ransom for the stone; but after his death, the Carmates, in A. H. 339, voluntarily sent it back, having been convinced by experience that their expectations of wealth, from the possession of it, were ill founded, and that very few moslems came to Hedjer for the purpose of kissing it. At this time it was in two pieces, having been split by a blow from a Carmate during the plunder of Mekka.

Seventy years after its restoration to its ancient seat, the stone

---

* Asamy says that the stone was carried to El Hassa, near the Persian Gulf, a town which had been recently built by Abou Dhaher. I find, in the Travels of Ibn Batouta, a town in the province of El Hassa, called Hedjer.

suffered another indignity: Hakem b'amr Illah, the mad king of Egypt, who had some intentions of claiming divine honours for himself, sent, in A. H. 413, an Egyptian with the pilgrim caravan to Mekka, to destroy the stone. With an iron club concealed beneath his clothes, the man approached it, and exclaimed, "How long shall this stone be adored and kissed? There is neither Mohammed nor Aly to prevent me from doing this, and to-day I shall destroy this building!" He then struck it three times with his club. A party of horsemen, belonging to the caravan in which he had travelled from Egypt, were ready at the gates of the mosque to assist the lithoclast, as soon as he should have executed his task; but they were not able to protect him from the fury of the populace. He was slain by the dagger of a native of Yemen; the horsemen were pursued; and the whole Egyptian caravan was plundered on the occasion.

Upon inspection, it was found that three small pieces, of the size of a man's nail, had been knocked off by the blows; these were pulverised, and their dust kneaded into a cement, with which the fractures were filled up. Since that time, the stone has sustained no further misfortune, except in the year 1674, when it was found, one morning, besmeared with dirt, together with the door of the Kaaba; so that every one who kissed it, retired with a sullied face. The author of this sacrilegious joke was sought in vain; suspicion fell upon some Persians, but the fact could not be proved against them.*

The sanctity of the stone appears to have been greatly questioned by one of the very pillars of Islam. El Azraky gives the testimony of several witnesses, who heard Omar Ibn Khatab exclaim, while standing before it:—"I know thou art a mere stone, that can neither hurt nor help me; nor should I kiss thee, had I not seen Mohammed do the same."

In A. H. 354, the Khalife El Mokteder built the vestibule near the gate of the mosque, called Bab Ibrahim, which projects beyond the straight line of the columns, and united in it two ancient gates, called

* See Asamy for these details.

Bab Beni Djomah and Bab el Khayatein. From that time no further improvements were made for several centuries.

In A. H. 802, a fire completely destroyed the north and west sides of the mosque: two years after, it was rebuilt at the expense of El Naszer Feradj Ibn Dhaher Berkouk, Sultan of Egypt. The wood necessary for that purpose was transported partly from Egypt and partly from Tayf, where the tree Arar, a species of cypress or juniper, furnished good timber.

In A. H. 906, Kansour el Ghoury, Sultan of Egypt, rebuilt the greater part of the side of Bab Ibrahim; and to him the Hedjaz owes several other public edifices.

In A. H. 959, in the reign of Solyman Ibn Selim I., Sultan of Constantinople, the roof of the Kaaba was renewed.

In A. H. 980, the same Sultan rebuilt the side of the mosque towards the street Mosaa, and caused all the domes to be raised which cover the roof of the colonnades. He also placed the fine pavement, which is now round the Kaaba, and a new pavement all around the colonnades.

In A. H. 984, his son Murad repaired and partly rebuilt the three other sides, that had not been touched by him.

In the year 1039, (or 1626 of our era,) a torrent from Djebel Nour rushed into the town, and filled the mosque so rapidly, that all the persons then within it were drowned; whatever books, fine copies of the Koran, &c. &c. were left in the apartments round the walls of the building, were destroyed; and a part of the wall before the Kaaba, called Hedjer, and three sides of the Kaaba itself, were carried away. Five hundred souls perished in the town. In the following year the damage was repaired, and the Kaaba rebuilt, after the side which had escaped the fury of the torrent had been pulled down.

In 1072, the building over the well Zemzem was erected, as it now stands; and in 1074, the four Makams were built anew.

After this time, the historians mention no other material repairs or changes in the mosque; and I believe none took place in the eighteenth century. We may, therefore, ascribe the building, as it now appears, almost wholly to the munificence of the last Sultans of Egypt, and their successors, the Osmanly Sultans of Constantinople, since the fifteenth and sixteenth centuries.

In the autumn of 1816, several artists and workmen, sent from Constantinople, were employed in the Hedjaz to repair all the damage caused by the Wahabys in the chapels of the saints of that country, as well as to make all the repairs necessary in the mosques at Mekka and Medina.

DESCRIPTION OF SEVERAL OTHER HOLY PLACES,

VISITED BY PILGRIMS AT MEKKA, AND IN ITS NEIGHBOURHOOD.

DURING the time of the Wahabys, no person dared to visit these places without exposing himself to their hostility; and all the buildings which had been erected on these spots were ruined by them, or their domes were, at least, destroyed.

In the town are shown:—

Mouled el Neby, the birth-place of Mohammed, in the quarter named from it. In the time of Fasy a mosque stood near it, called Mesdjed el Mokhtaba. During my stay, workmen were busily employed in re-constructing the building over the Mouled upon its former plan. It consists of a rotunda, the floor of which is about twenty-five feet below the level of the street, with a staircase leading down to it. A small hole is shown in the floor, in which Mohammed's mother sat when she was delivered of him. This is said to have been the house of Abdillah, Mohammed's father.

Mouled Setna Fatme, or the birth-place of Fatme, the daughter of Mohammed, is shown in a good stone building, said to have been the house of her mother Khadidje, in the street called Zogag el Hadjar. A staircase leads down to the floor of this building, which, like that of the former, is considerably below the street. This small edifice includes two holy places: in one is a hole, similar to that in the Mouled el Neby, to mark the place where Fatme was born; and just by is another, of smaller depth, where she is said to have turned her hand-mill, or *rahha*, after she was grown up. In an apartment near this, a narrow cell is shown, where Mohammed used to sit, and receive from the angel Gabriel the leaves of the Koran brought from heaven. This place is called Kobbet el Wahy.

Mouled el Imam Aly, in the quarter called Shab Aly. This is a small chapel, in the floor of which a hole marks the spot where Aly, the cousin of Mohammed, is said to have been born.

Mouled Seydna Abou Beker, a small chapel, just opposite to the stone which gave a salutation, "Salam Aleykum," to Mohammed whenever he passed it. No sacred spot is here shown; but its floor is covered with very fine Persian carpets.

All these Mouleds had undergone complete repair since the retreat of the Wahabys, except that of Mohammed, on which the workmen were still employed. The guardianship of these places is shared by several families, principally Sherifs, who attend by turns, with a train of servants. At every corner of the buildings are spread white handkerchiefs, or small carpets, upon which visitors are expected to throw some money; and the gates are lined with women, who occupy their seats by right, and expect a contribution from the pilgrim's purse. The value of a shilling, distributed in paras at each of the Mouleds, fully answers the expectation of the greedy and the indigent.

Mouled Abou Taleb, in the Mala, is completely destroyed, as I have already said; and will, probably, not be rebuilt.

Kaber Setna Khadidje: the tomb of Khadidje, the wife of Mohammed, the dome of which was broken down by the Wahabys, and is not yet rebuilt; it is regularly visited by hadjys, especially on Friday mornings. It lies in the large burial-ground of the Mala, at the declivity of the western chain; is enclosed by a square wall, and presents no objects of curiosity except the tomb-stone, which has a fine inscription in Cufic characters, containing a passage of the Koran from the chapter entitled, Souret el Kursy. As the character is not the ancient Cufic, I suspect that the stone was not intended originally to cover this grave: there is no date in the inscription. The Sherif Serour, predecessor of Ghaleb, had the vanity, on his death-bed, to order his family to bury his body close to the tomb of Khadidje, in the same enclosure where it still remains. At a short distance from hence, the tomb of Umna, the mother of Mohammed, is shown. It was covered with a slab of fine marble, bearing a Cufic inscription, in an older character than the former. The Wahabys broke it, and removed the two pieces, to show their indignation at the visits paid to the receptacles of the bones of mortals, which was, in their estimation, a species of idolatry. Even at these tombs I found women, to whom permission was granted to spread their handkerchiefs, and ask alms of every visitor.

In walking about these extensive cemeteries, I found many other tomb-stones with Cufic inscriptions, but not in a very ancient character. I could decipher no date prior to the sixth century of the Hedjra (the twelfth of our era); but the greater part of them contain mere prayers, without either the name of the deceased, or a date. The tombs, in general, are formed of four large stones placed in an oblong square, with a broad stone set upright at one end, bearing the inscription. I saw no massive tomb or turban cut in stone, or any such ornament as is used in other parts of Asia. A few small buildings have been raised by the first families of Mekka, to enclose the tombs of their relations; they are paved inside, but have no roof, and are of the most simple construction. In two or three of them I found trees planted, which are irrigated from cisterns built within the enclosure for the reception of rain-water: here, the families to whom they belong sometimes pass the day. Of several buildings, surmounted with domes, in which men celebrated for their learning had been interred, the domes were invariably broken down by the Wahabys: these fanatics, however, never touched the tombs themselves, and every where respected the remains of the dead. Among the tombs are those of several Pashas of Syria and of Egypt, constructed with little ornament.

At the extremity of almost every tomb, opposite to the epitaph, I found the low shrub saber, a species of aloe, planted in the ground: it is an evergreen, and requires very little water, as its Arabic name, *saber*, (patience) implies: it is chosen for this purpose from an allusion to the patience necessary in waiting for the resurrection. On the whole, this burial-ground is in a state of ruin, caused, it is said, by the devastations of the Wahabys; but, I believe, still more by the little care which the Mekkawys take of the graves containing the bodies of their relations and friends.

The places visited out of the town are:—

Djebel Abou Kobeys. This mountain is one of the highest in the immediate neighbourhood of the town, and commands it from the east. Muselman tradition says that it was the first mountain created upon earth; its name is found in almost every Arabic historian and poet. Two different spots upon its summit are visited by the pilgrims. The one is called Mekan el Hedjar (the spot of the stone), where Omar, who afterwards succeeded to the Khalifat, used to call the people to prayers, in the first years of Islam, when the Koreysh or inhabitants of Mekka were, for the greater part, idolaters. Here is shown a cavity cut in the rock, resembling a small tomb, in which it is said that God, at the deluge, ordered the guardian angels to place the black stone, revered by them long before Abraham built the Kaaba, and to make the rock unite over it, that the waters might not touch it; and that, after the deluge, the angel Gabriel split the rock, and conveyed the stone back to the site of the Kaaba. The other place of visit, or Zyara, is across a narrow valley, at a short distance from the former, on the summit of the mountain; it is called Mekan Shak el Kamr, or place where the moon was split—one of Mohammed's greatest miracles. The story, however, is now differently related by the Mekkawys, who say that, when he was praying here at mid-day, the first people among the incredulous Koreysh came and desired him to convince them at once, by some miracles,* that he was really the prophet of the Almighty. "What shall I do," he replied, "to make you true believers?" "Let the sun retire," said they, "and the moon and stars appear; let the moon descend upon earth, come to this mountain, enter into one of the sleeves of your gown, issue by the other, return to the firmament, and then let day-light shine again upon us." Mohammed retired, addressed a short prayer to the Deity, and the whole miracle was forth-

* It is recorded by historians, that at the desire of some unbelieving Koreysh, he caused the full moon to appear as if cleft asunder, so that one half was visible behind Djebel Abou Kobeys, and the other at the opposite side of the hemisphere, above Djebel Kaykaan.

with performed; after which the Koreysh were converted. These and similar tales, applied to different places by the Mekkawys, for the purpose of extorting money from the pilgrims, are quite unsupported by the authenticated traditions of the prophet. To this spot the people of Mekka resort, that they may enjoy a view of the new moon of Ramadhan, and of the month following it. Between these two places, and a little to the east of them, are the ruins of a solid building, some walls only remaining. It is said to have formerly been a state prison of the sherifs of Mekka. In it are several dungeon-like towers, and it was probably a castle built upon Djebel Kobeys by Mekether el Hashemy, a chief of Mekka, about the year 530 or 540 of the Hedjra; or it may have been a mosque called Mesdjid Ibrahim, which, according to Azraky, stood here in the seventh century of our era. It is vulgarly believed at Mekka that whoever eats a roasted sheep's head upon Djebel Kobeys, will be for ever cured of all head-aches.

Djebel Nour, the mountain of light. This lies to the north of the town. Passing the Sherif's garden-house on the road towards Arafat, a little further on, we enter a valley, which extends in a direction N. E. by N. and is terminated by the mountain, which is conical. Steps were formerly cut in the steep ascent, but they are now ruined; and it required three quarters of an hour, and much fatiguing exertion, to reach the top. In the rocky floor of a small building, ruined by the Wahabys, a cleft is shown, about the size of a man in length and breadth. It is said that Mohammed, wearied, and grieved at the assertions of his enemies and dubious adherents at Mekka, who had given out that God had entirely abandoned him, retired to this mountain, and stretched himself out in the cleft, imploring help from above. The angel Gabriel was despatched to him with that short chapter of the Koran, which we call the ninety-fourth, beginning with the words " Have we not gladdened thy breast ?"—the previous chapter alludes also to his state of grief. A little below this place is a small cavern in the red granite rock, which forms the upper stratum of this mountain; it is called Mogharat el Hira.* Here several other passages

* In the time of the Pagan Arabs this mountain was called Djebel Hira. I may here

of the Koran are said to have been revealed to the prophet, who often repaired to this elevated spot; but none of those present could tell me what those passages were. The guardians of these two places are Bedouins of the tribe of Lahyan (or Laha-yn).

I had left Mekka on foot, at night, with a large party of hadjys, to visit this place, which is usually done on Saturdays. We were on the summit before dawn; and when the sun rose, a very extensive view presented itself to the north and west, the other points being bounded by mountains. The country before us had a dreary aspect, not a single green spot being visible: barren black and grey hills, and white sandy valleys, were the only objects in sight. On the declivity of the mountain, a little way from the top, is a small stone reservoir, built to supply the visitors with water. It was dry when I saw it, and in bad repair.

Djebel Thor. About an hour and a half south of Mekka, to the left of the road to the village of Hosseynye, is a lofty mountain of this name, higher, it is said, than Djebel Nour. On the summit of it is a cavern in which Mohammed and his friend Abou Beker took refuge from the Mekkawys before he fled to Medina. A spider had spun its web before the entrance, and his pursuers seeing this, supposed, of course, that the fugitives could not be within. To this circumstance an allusion is made in the Koran (chap. ix.) I did not visit the spot.

El Omra. Of this building I have already spoken: it is a small chapel with a single row of columns, on the road to Wady Fatme. Every pilgrim is required to visit it; but he is left to his own discretion respecting the places before mentioned. The Omra is surrounded by ruins of several habitations: there is a copious well near it, and traces of cultivation are seen in the valley. I believe the well to be that called by the historians of Mekka "Bir Tenaym." According to Fasy, a mosque, called Mesdjed Ahlyledje, stood here in the earliest times of Islam. I shall conclude my description of Mekka with that of

add, that a great many mountains and valleys in the Hedjaz have lost their ancient names. This is amply proved by the topographical notices of Azraky, of the historians of Medina, and of Zamakhshary, in his valuable work entitled El Myat o' el djebal.

the opening of the Kaaba, which I deferred, that the description of the mosque might not be interrupted.

The Kaaba is opened only three times in the year : on the 20th of the month of Ramadhan, on the 15th of Zulkade, and on the 10th of Moharram (or Ashour, as the Arabs call it). The opening takes place one hour after sun-rise, when the steps are wheeled up to the gate of the building: as soon as they touch the wall, immense crowds rush upon them, and in a moment fill the whole interior of the Kaaba. The steps are lined by the eunuchs of the mosque, who endeavour in vain to keep order, and whose sticks fall heavy upon those who do not drop a fee into their hands; many of the crowd, however, are often unmercifully crushed. In the interior every visitor is to pray eight rikats, or make sixteen prostrations; in every corner of it two rikats: but it may easily be conceived how these prayers are performed, and that while one is bowing down, another walks over him. After the prayers are finished, the visitor is to lean with extended arms against any part of the wall, with his face pressed against it, and thus to recite two pious ejaculations. Sobbing and moaning fill the room; and I thought I perceived most heartfelt emotions and sincere repentance in many of the visitors: the following, and other similar ejaculations, are heard, and many faces are bedewed with tears: " O God of the house, O God forgive me, and forgive my parents, and my children ! O God, admit me into paradise ! O God, deliver our necks from hell-fire, O thou God of the old house !" I could not stay longer than five minutes; the heat was so great that I almost fainted, and several persons were carried out with great difficulty, quite senseless.

At the entrance sits a Sherif, holding the silver key of the Kaaba in his hand, which he presents to be kissed by the pilgrim, who for this pays a fee, on coming out; money is also given to a eunuch, who sits by that Sherif. Some eunuchs on the steps, and several menial officers and servants on the pavement below, which surrounds the Kaaba, expect also to be paid. I heard many hadjys animadvert severely upon this shameful practice, saying that the most holy spot upon earth should not be made the scene of human avarice and greediness; but the Mekkawys are invulnerable to such reproaches.

The Kaaba remains open till about eleven o'clock. On the following day it is opened exclusively for women. After visiting the Kaaba it is thought necessary to perform the towaf round it.

The interior of the Kaaba consists of a single room, the roof of which is supported by two columns, and it has no other light than what is received by the door. The ceiling, the upper half of the two columns, and the side walls, to within about five feet of the floor, are hung with a thick stuff of red silk, richly interwoven with flowers and inscriptions in large characters of silver; the lower part of each column is lined with carved aloe-wood; and that part of the walls below the silk hangings is lined with fine white marble, ornamented with inscriptions cut in relief, and with elegant arabesques; the whole being of exquisite workmanship. The floor, which is upon a level with the door, and therefore about seven feet above the level of the area of the mosque, is laid with marble of different colours. Between the pillars numerous lamps are suspended, donations of the faithful, and said to be of solid gold; they were not touched by the Wahabys.* In the north-west corner of the chamber is a small gate, which leads up to the flat roof of the building. I observed nothing else worthy of remark; but the room is so dark, that it requires some time before any thing can be seen in it. The interior ornaments are coeval with the restoration of the Kaaba, which took place A. D. 1627. I am unacquainted with any holy ceremony observed in washing the floor of the Kaaba, as mentioned in the Travels of Aly Bey el Abasy: I have seen the Towasheys perform that duty, in the same manner as on the pavement around it; although it appears from the history of Asamy, that the floor of the Kaaba is sometimes washed by great personages.

The visit to the interior of the Kaaba forms no part of the religious duty of the pilgrim, and many of them quit Mekka without seeing it. I saw it twice; on the 15th of Zulkade, and the 10th of Moharram. At the latter period the new hangings, brought from Cairo by Mohammed Aly, had been put up: they were of very rich stuff, much finer and

* Kotobeddyn relates, that the Sheikhs of Mekka stole the golden lamps suspended in the Kaaba, and conveyed them away in the wide sleeves of their gowns. Many golden lamps were sent here by Sultan Soleyman.

closer in texture than the black exterior cover. The old hangings, which had been up for more than twenty years, were now publicly sold to devotees at the rate of about one dollar for a piece of six inches square. The right of offering these hangings was in the person who gave the exterior kessoua, though exceptions sometimes occurred, as in A. H. 865, when Shah Rokh, king of Persia, sent a magnificent covering for the interior.*

Before the gate called Bab-es-Salam is a shop where pieces both of the exterior and interior coverings are constantly for sale: those of the latter are most esteemed. I have seen waistcoats made of them, which, of course, are reckoned the safest coat of mail that one of the faithful can wear. In the same shop are sold drawings of Mekka and Medina, done in a coarse and most gaudy style upon paper or linen, and small impressions of prayers, &c. from engravings on wood. I bought some of these, for the same purpose as the Zemzem bottles which I took from hence.

* See Kotobeddyn.

REMARKS ON THE INHABITANTS OF MEKKA AND DJIDDA.

MEKKA and Djidda are inhabited by the same class of people; and their character and customs are the same. I have already remarked that all the rich Mekkawys have houses at Djidda, and that the commercial employments of the two cities are alike.

The inhabitants of Mekka may be all styled foreigners, or the offspring of foreigners, except a few Hedjaz Bedouins, or their descendants, who have settled here. The ancient tribe of Koreysh, which was divided into a wandering and a settled branch, is almost extinct. There are some Bedouins of Koreysh still in the neighbourhood; but the settled Koreysh, who were the inhabitants of Mekka in the time of Mohammed, have either been destroyed, or have migrated, in consequence of the frequent intestine wars. At this moment three Koreysh families only, descendants of the ancient tribe of that name, are found at Mekka, the head of one of which is the Nayb, or keeper of the mosque; and the two others are poor people, also attached to its service. The neighbourhood of the great mart of Djidda, the yearly arrival of immense caravans, and the holy house, have attracted, however, a sufficient number of strangers to supply the place of the Koreysh. In every hadj some of the pilgrims remain behind: the Mohammedan, whenever resident for any time in a town, takes a wife, and is thus often induced to settle permanently on the spot. Hence most of the Mekkawys are descendants of foreigners from distant parts of the globe, who have adopted Arabian manners, and, by intermarrying, have produced a race which can no longer be distinguished from the indigenous Arabians. On questioning shopkeepers, merchants, olemas, metowafs, and indeed people of every description, they are found to be the sons, grandsons, or descendants of foreigners. The most numerous are those whose fathers came from Yemen and Hadramaut; next to them in numbers are the descendants of Indians, Egyptians, Syrians, Mogrebyns, and Turks. There are also Mekkawys of Persian origin; Tatars, Bokhars, Kurds, Afghans; in short, of almost every Mohammedan country in the world. The Mekkawy is careful in preserving, by tradition, the knowledge of his original country. My metowaf or guide traced his descent to an Usbek Tatar, from the neighbourhood of Bokhara, and whenever any hadjys arrived from that quarter, he never failed to recommend himself as their guide, though entirely ignorant of their language.

There is, however, one branch of the ancient Arabians remaining in Mekka; these are the native Sherifs, (as distinguished from the descendants of foreign Sherifs who have settled here :) they derive their pedigree from Hassan and Hosseyn, the sons of Fatme, the daughter of Mohammed; a descent claimed equally by the other Sherifs, but whose genealogies are supposed to be less authentic. The Mekka Sherifs form a large class, into which no foreigners are admitted, and it is spreading over many other parts of Arabia. I am not thoroughly acquainted with their history, or the period at which they began to branch out into particular tribes; and I can only state that they acknowledge many, but not all Sherifs of Yemen, and other parts of the Hedjaz, as their distant relations: at present they are divided into several tribes, out of one of which the reigning Sherif must be chosen, as I shall mention below. At Mekka a difference is observed in the name given to the Sherifs, according to their profession. Those who are employed in study and the law, and occupied more or less about the temple and its dependencies are called Seyd, while those who become soldiers, and mix in state affairs, are known exclusively by the term Sherif. The Seyds are followers of religion (say the Mekkawys), the Sherifs are soldiers. The son usually follows the vocation of the father. These native Sherifs are the head men of the town, or at least were so before their pride was broken by the Turkish conquest.

Though a mixed population, the inhabitants of Mekka wear the same sort of dress, and have the same customs; and although of different origin, they seem to be much less tenacious of their national costume and manners in this holy city than any where else. In Syria and Egypt, strangers from all parts of Asia retain with the greatest strictness the dress and mode of living of their native countries, though established for life in their new abodes; a circumstance which renders the view of an eastern bazar infinitely more interesting than any large assemblage of people in Europe. In the Hedjaz, on the contrary, most of the foreign visitors change their native costume for that of the people of the country; and their children born there are brought up and clothed in the fashion of the Mekkawys. The Indians, as I have already remarked in speaking of Djidda, offer an exception to this general rule; they form a distinct colony, and retain their native language, which the children of other strangers usually forget, their mothers being in many instances Arabs, natives of Mekka.

The colour of the Mekkawy and Djiddawy is a yellowish sickly brown, lighter or darker according to the origin of the mother, who is very often an Abyssinian slave. Their features approach much nearer to those of Bedouins than I have observed in any townsmen of the East; this is particularly observable in the Sherifs, who are gifted with very handsome countenances; they have the eye, face, and aquiline nose of the Bedouin, but are more fleshy. The lower class of Mekkawys are generally stout, with muscular limbs, while the higher orders are distinguishable by their meagre emaciated forms, as are also all those inhabitants who draw their origin from India or Yemen. The Bedouins who surround Mekka, though poor, are much stronger-bodied than the wealthier Bedouins of the interior of the Desert, probably because their habits are less roving, and because they are less exposed to the hardships of long journies. The Mekkawy, it may be generally said, is inferior in strength and size to the Syrian or Egyptian, but far exceeds him in expressive features, and especially in the vivacity and brilliancy of the eye.

All the male natives of Mekka and Djidda are tattooed with a particular mark, which is performed by their parents when they are forty days of age. It consists of three long cuts down both cheeks, and two on the right temple, the scars of which, sometimes three or four lines in breadth, remain through life. It is called Meshále. The Bedouins do not follow this practice; but the Mekkawys pride themselves in the distinction, which precludes the other inhabitants of the Hedjaz from claiming, in foreign countries, the honour of being born in the holy cities. This tattooing is sometimes, though very seldom, applied to female children. The people of Bornou, in the interior of Africa, have a similar, though much slighter, mark on both cheeks.

The dress of the higher classes, in winter, is a cloth *benish*, or upper cloak; and a *djubbe*, or under cloak, likewise of cloth, and such as is worn in all parts of Turkey. A showy silk gown, tied with a thin cashmere sash, a white muslin turban, and yellow slippers, constitute the rest of the dress. In summer, instead of the cloth benish, they wear one of very slight silk stuff, of Indian manufacture, called Moktar khána.

The highest classes, who affect the Turkish fashion in their dress, wear red Barbary caps under the turban; those of the other classes are of linen richly embroidered with silk, the work of the women of Mekka, and a common present from a woman to her lover: on the top sometimes are embroidered in large characters sentences of the Koran.

The gowns of well-dressed people of the middle class are generally of white India muslin, without any lining; they are called *beden*, and differ from the common Levantine *antery*, in being very short, and without sleeves, and in being of course much cooler: over the beden a djubbe of light cloth, or Indian silk stuff, is worn, which, in time of great heat, a man throws over his shoulders; the gown and under-shirt are then his only covering. The shirts are of Indian silk or Egyptian or Anatolian linen, and as fine as the wearer can afford to purchase.

The lower classes usually wear, at least in summer, nothing but a shirt, and instead of trowsers a piece of yellow Indian nankin, or striped Egyptian linen round their loins; over this, in winter, they have a beden of striped Indian calico, but without a belt to tie it round the body. The lower and middle classes wear sandals instead of shoes, a custom very agreeable in this hot climate, as it contributes to the coolness of the feet. The best sandals come from Yemen, where all kinds of leather manufacture seem to flourish. In summer, many people, and all the lower Indians, wear the cap only, without the turban. The usual turban is of Indian cambric, or muslin, which each class ties round the head in a particular kind of fold. Those who style themselves Olemas, or learned doctors, allow the extremity to fall down in a narrow stripe to the middle of their back. The Mekkawys are cleaner in their dress than any Eastern people I have seen. As white muslin, or white cambric, forms the principal part of their clothing, it requires frequent washing; and this is regularly done, so that even the poorest orders endeavour to change their linen at least once a week. With the higher and middle classes, the change is, of course, more frequent. The rich wear every day a different dress; and it is no uncommon thing with many to possess thirty or forty suits. The people of the Hedjaz delight in dress much more than the northern Mohammedans; and the earnings of the lower classes are mostly spent in clothes. When a Mekkawy returns home from his shop, or even after a short walk into the town, he immediately undresses, hangs up his clothes over a cord tied across his sitting-room, takes off his turban, changes his shirt, and then seats himself upon his carpet, with a thin under-cap upon his head. In this dishabille they receive visitors; and to delineate a Mekkawy, he should be represented sitting in his undress, near a projecting latticed window, having in one hand a sort of fan, generally of this form,

made of chippings of date-leaves, with which he drives away the flies; and in the other, the long snake of his Persian pipe.

On feast-days they display their love of dress in a still higher degree; from the richest to the poorest, every one must then be dressed in a new suit of clothes; and if he cannot afford to buy, he hires one from the dealers for two or three days. On these occasions, as much as one hundred piastres are sometimes given for the hire of a dress, worth altogether, perhaps, fifteen hundred or two thousand piastres. No one is then content with a dress suited to his station in life, but assumes that of the class above him. The common shopkeeper, who walks about the whole year in his short gown, with a napkin round his loins, appears in a pink-coloured benish, lined with satin, a gold-embroidered turban, a rich silk sash, worked with silver thread, and a djombye, or crooked knife, stuck in his sash, the scabbard of which is covered with coins of silver and gold. The children are dressed out in the same expensive manner; and a person would submit to be called a thief, rather than allow those of equal rank to exceed him in finery. In general, the most gaudy colours are preferred; and the upper cloak must always be a contrast in colour to the garment worn beneath it. During festivals, cashmere shawls are also worn, though seldom seen at other times, except on women, and the warlike Sherifs; but every Mekkawy in easy circumstances has an assortment of them in his wardrobe. After the feast, the fine suit is laid aside, and every one returns to his wonted station. Every grown-up Mekkawy carries a long stick; among the lower orders, they may rather be called bludgeons. An olema is never seen without his stick. Few persons go armed, except among the lower classes, or the Sherifs, who carry crooked knives in their belts.

The women of Mekka and Djidda dress in Indian silk gowns, and very large blue striped trowsers, reaching down to the ankles, and embroidered below with silver thread; over these they wear the wide gown called *habra*, of black silk stuff, used in Egypt and Syria; or a blue and white striped silk *mellaye* of Indian manufacture. The face is concealed by a white, or light blue *borko;* on the head, covered by the mellaye, they wear a cap like the men's, around which a piece of coloured muslin is tightly twisted in folds. The head-dress is said to be less ornamented with gold coins, pearls, and jewels, than that of the ladies of Egypt and Syria; but they have, at least, one string of sequins tied round it: many have gold necklaces, bracelets, and silver ankle-rings. The poorer women wear the blue Egyptian shirt, and large trowsers, like those already mentioned; and bracelets of horn, glass, or amber.

The children of Mekka are not so spoiled by their parents as they are in other countries of the East; as soon as they can walk freely, they are allowed to play in the street before the house, clad in very light clothes, or rather half-naked. On this account, probably, they are stouter and healthier than the bandaged children of Syria and Egypt; of whom it may be truly said that they are often nursed to death.

There are few families at Mekka, in moderate circumstances, that do not keep slaves. Mohammed found the African slave-trade so firmly established in Arabia, that he made no effort to abolish it; and thus he has confirmed, and extended throughout Northern Africa, this traffic, with all its attendant cruelties, besides those which have followed the propagation of Islam. The male and female servants are negroes, or *noubas*, usually brought from Sowakin: the concubines are always Abyssinian slaves. No wealthy Mekkawy prefers domestic peace to the gratification of his passions; they all keep mistresses in common with their lawful wives: but if a slave gives birth to a child, the master generally marries her, or, if he fails to do so, is censured by the community. The keeping of Abyssinian concubines is still more prevalent at Djidda. Many Mekkawys have no other than Abyssinian wives, finding the Arabians more expensive, and less disposed to yield to the will of the husband. The same practice is adopted by many foreigners, who reside in the Hedjaz for a short time. Upon their arrival, they buy a female companion, with the design of selling her at their departure; but sometimes their stay is protracted; the slave bears a child; they marry her, and become stationary in the town. There are very few men unmarried, or without a slave. This, indeed, is general in the East, and no where more so than at Mekka. The mixture of Abyssinian blood has, no doubt, given to the Mekkawys that yellow tinge of the skin which distinguishes them from the natives of the Desert. Among the richer classes, it is considered shameful to sell a concubine slave. If she bears a child, and the master has not already four legally married wives, he takes her in matrimony; if not, she remains in his house for life; and in some instances the number of concubines is increased to several dozen, old and young. The middling and lower classes in Mekka are not so scrupulous as their superiors: they buy up young Abyssinians on speculation; educate them in the family; teach them cooking, sewing, &c.; and then sell them at a profit to foreigners, at least such as prove barren. I have been informed by physicians, barbers, and druggists, that the practice of causing abortion is frequent here. The seed of the tree which produces the balsam of Mekka, is the drug commonly used for this purpose. The Mekkawys make no distinction whatever between sons born of Abyssinian slaves and those of free Arabian women.

The inhabitants of Mekka have but two kinds of employment,—trade, and the service of the Beitullah, or Temple; but the former has the preference, and there are very few olemas, or persons employed in the mosque, who are not engaged in some commercial affairs, though they are too proud to pursue them openly. The reader has probably remarked, in the foregoing description of Mekka, how few artisans inhabit its streets; such as masons, carpenters, tailors, shoemakers, smiths, &c., and these are far inferior, in skill, to the same class in Egypt. With the exception of a few potteries and dying-houses, the Mekkawys have not a single manufactory; but, like the people of Djidda, are dependent upon other countries for a supply of their wants. Mekka, therefore, has necessarily a considerable degree of foreign commerce, which is chiefly carried on, during the pilgrimage, and some months preceding it, by the wealthy hadjys, who bring from every Muselman country its native productions to Djidda, either by sea or across the Desert from Damascus, exchanging them amongst each other; or receiving from the merchants of Mekka the goods of India and Arabia, which the latter have accumulated the whole year in their warehouses. At this period, Mekka becomes one of the largest fairs of the East, and certainly the most interesting, from the variety of nations which frequent it. The value of the exports from Mekka is, however, greatly superior to that of the imports, and a considerable sum of money, in dollars and sequins, required to balance them. Of these, some part finds its way to Yemen and India; and about one-fourth remains in the hands of the Mekkawys. So profitable is this trade, that the goods bought at Djidda from the merchants, who purchase them out of the ships which arrive there from India, yield, when sold wholesale at Mekka, during the Hadj, a clear gain of twenty to thirty per cent., and of fifty per cent. when sold in retail. It is not surprising, therefore, that all the people of Mekka are merchants. Whoever can make up a sum of a few hundred dollars, repairs to Djidda, and lays it out on goods, which he exposes for sale during the pilgrimage. Much profit is also fraudulently made: great numbers of hadjys are ignorant of the Arabic language, and are consequently placed in the hands of brokers or interpreters, who never fail to make them pay dearly for their services; indeed, all Mekka seems united in the design of cheating the pilgrims.

Formerly, when the caravans enjoyed perfect security on the road, goods were chiefly transported by land to Mekka: at present, few merchants trust their property to the hazards of a passage across the Desert; they rather forego the advantage of importing them into Mekka duty-free, the great privilege possessed by the caravans, and carry them by sea to Djidda, on which road all the hadjys of Africa and Turkey pay a double duty; once in Egypt, and again at Djidda: both duties are received by Mohammed Aly. At present, therefore, the smaller traffic only is carried on by the caravans, which remain but a few days at Mekka. The shopkeepers and retail dealers of the city derive greater profits from them than the wholesale merchants. The principal business of the latter occurs during the months previous to the pilgrimage, when foreign merchants arrive by the way of Djidda, and have full leisure to settle their affairs before the Hadj takes place.

In time of peace with the interior, there is a considerable trade with the Bedouins, and especially with the inhabitants of the towns of Nedjed, who are in want of India goods, drugs, and articles of dress, which they procure either from Medina, or at a cheaper rate from Mekka. Coffee, so much used in the Desert, is imported by the people of Nedjed themselves, who send their own caravans to the coffee country of Yemen.

The Mekkawys, especially those who are not sufficiently opulent to trade in India goods, (which require a good deal of ready cash, and lie sometimes long on hand,) employ their capital during the interval of the Hadj, in the traffic of corn and provisions. This was much more profitable formerly than it is at present; for Mohammed Aly having made these articles a monopoly, the people are now obliged to purchase the grain in Djidda, at the Pasha's own price, and to be contented with a moderate gain on re-selling it at Mekka. After paying freight, however, it still leaves a profit of fifteen or twenty per cent.; and it is a species of traffic peculiarly attractive to the smaller capitals, as, the prices being very variable, it is a lottery by which money may sometimes be doubled in a short time.

At the approach of the pilgrimage, every kind of provision rises in value; and, in a smaller proportion, every other article of trade. Those who have warehouses filled with corn, rice, and biscuits, are sure to obtain considerable profits. To provide food, during their stay, for an influx of population amounting to sixty thousand human beings, and for twenty thousand camels, together with provisions for their return homewards, is a matter of no small moment, and Mohammed Aly has not yet ventured to take the whole of it into his hands. Every Mekkawy possessing a few dollars, lays them out in the purchase of some kind of provision, which, when the Hadj approaches, he transports upon his ass from Djidda to Mekka.

Whenever the interior of Arabia is open to caravans, Bedouins from all the surrounding parts purchase their yearly provision of corn at Mekka; which itself also, in time of peace, receives a considerable quantity of corn from Yemen, especially Mokhowa, a town which is ten days' journey distant, at the western foot of the great chain, and the mart of the Arabs who cultivate those mountains. I heard that the imports from Mokhowa amounted to half the demand of Mekka; but this seems doubtful, though I have no means of forming a correct estimate, as the route is at present unfrequented, and Mekka receives its provisions wholly from Djidda. The consumption of grain, it may be observed, is much greater in Arabia than in any of the surrounding countries; the great mass of the population living almost entirely upon wheat, barley, lentils, or rice; using no vegetables, but a great deal of butter.

Unless a person is himself engaged in commercial concerns, or has an intelligent friend among the wholesale merchants, it is difficult, if not impossible, for him to obtain any accurate details of so extensive a trade as that carried on by Mekka. I shall, therefore, abstain from making any partial, and, on that account, probably erroneous remarks, on its different branches, with which I am not well acquainted, and which I could find no one at Mekka to explain to me.

It will naturally be supposed that Mekka is a rich town: it would be still more so, if the lower classes did not so rapidly spend their gains in personal indulgences. The wholesale merchants are rich; and as the whole of their business is carried on with ready money, they are less exposed to losses than other Eastern merchants. Most of them have an establishment at Djidda, and the trade of both towns is closely connected. During the time of the Wahabys, the interior of Arabia was opened to Mekka; but the foreign imports, by sea and land, were reduced to what was wanted for the use of the inhabitants. The great fair of the pilgrimage no longer took place; and although some foreign hadjys still visited the holy city, they did not trust their goods to the chance of being seized by the Wahabys. Under these circumstances, the principal inducement with the Mekkawys to remain in the town, namely, their unceasing gains, no longer existed. The rich waited for a renewal of the Hadj caravans; but many of the poor, unable longer to find subsistence, retired from Mekka, and settled at Djidda, or other harbours on the Red Sea; whither they have been followed by many of the more respectable traders.

Trade is carried on by means of brokers, many of whom are Indians: in general, the community of Indians is the wealthiest in

Mekka. They are in direct intercourse with all the harbours of Hindostan, and can often afford to undersell their competitors. Many of them, as has been already observed, are stationary here, while others are constantly travelling backward and forward between India and the Hedjaz. They all retain their native language, which they teach their children, and also many merchants of Mekka superficially, so that most of the latter understand, at least, the Hindostanee numerals, and the most ordinary phrases employed in buying and selling. The Indians labour under great difficulties in learning Arabic; I never heard any of them, however long resident in the Hedjaz, speak it with a tolerable accent: in this respect they are inferior to the Turks, whose pronunciation of Arabic so often affords subject of ridicule to the Arabian mob. The children of Indians, born at Mekka, of course speak Arabic as their native language. The Indians have the custom of writing Arabic with Hindostanee characters.

They are said to be extremely parsimonious; and, from what I saw of them in the houses of some of their first merchants, they seem to deserve the character. They are shrewd traders, and an overmatch, sometimes, even for the Arabians. They are despicable, from their want of charity; but they display among themselves a spirited manner, which makes them respected, and even sometimes dreaded, at Mekka. Many of them have partners in India; consequently they receive their goods cheaper than they can be bought from the Indian ships at Djidda: hence the inferior dealers and shopkeepers at Mekka often find it more convenient to purchase from them at short credit, than to go to Djidda, where every thing must be paid for in ready money. With the exception of one or two houses, no Arabian merchants of Mekka receive their goods direct from India, but purchase them from the India fleet. Of all the people at Mekka none are more strict in the performance of their religious rites than the Indians.

Dealers, when bargaining in the presence of others from whom they wish to conceal their business, join their right hands under the corner of the gown or sleeve of one of the parties; by touching the different joints of the fingers they note the numerals, and thus silently conclude their bargain.

The Mekkawys who do not ostensibly follow commerce, are attached to the government, or to the establishment of the mosque; but as I have already said, they all engage, more or less, in some branch of traffic, and the whole population looks forward to the period of the Hadj as the source of their income.

The persons attached to the mosque have regular salaries, partake in the general presents made to it, expect many private donations from charitable devotees, and share in the stipends which are brought by the Syrian and Egyptian caravans. These stipends, called Surra, (of which I have already given an account,) derive their origin principally from the Sultans of Constantinople, who, upon their accession to the throne, generally fix a certain yearly sum for the maintenance of the poor, and the worthiest individuals of Mekka and Medina. They are distributed in both towns by the Kadhy, as he thinks proper; but if a person has been once presented with a stipend, he enjoys it for life, and it descends to his children. He receives a ticket signed by the Kadhy, the Sherif, and the Surra-writer, and his name is entered in a register at Mekka, of which a duplicate is sent annually by the returning Hadj to Constantinople, where the name is enrolled in the general Surra-book. The Surra is made up at Constantinople in a great number of small packets, each containing the stipulated sum, and indorsed with the name of the individual to whom it is destined. If any fresh sum is sent to be distributed, the Kadhy divides it, informs the inspector of the Surra at Constantinople to whom the money has been given, and in the following year the additional packages, addressed to the new pensioners, are added to the former number. Some of the Surras are brought from Egypt, but the far greater part from Constantinople, by way of Syria: this part is very regularly received. Each caravan has its own Surra-writer, whose duty also it is to distribute all the other money or tribute which the caravan pays to Bedouins and Arabs, on its road to Mekka.

The Surra for Mekka is distributed in the mosque, under the windows of the Kadhy's house, after the departure of the Hadj. There are persons who receive so small a sum as one piastre; the greater number from ten to twenty piastres; but there are a few families who receive as much as two thousand piastres annually. Although not always given to the most worthy, many poor families derive support from this allowance. The tickets are transferable; the Kadhy and the Sherif must sign the transfer; and the new name, a small compliment being given to the Kadhy's scribe, is registered and sent to Constantinople. In former times a Mekkawy could scarcely be induced to sell his Surra, which he considered an honour as well as the most certain provision for his family. The value, however, of the Surra has much changed. During the time of the Wahabys the tickets had almost entirely lost their value, as for eight years their holders had received no pay. They have now recovered a little; but some were lately sold at two years and a half purchase, which may afford an idea of the opinion current at Mekka as to the stability of the Turkish government, or the probability of the return of the Wahabys.

The idlest, most impudent, and vilest individuals of Mekka adopt the profession of guides (*metowaf* or *delyl*); and as there is no want of those qualities, and a sufficient demand for guides during the Hadj, they are very numerous. Besides the places which I have described in the town, the metowafs accompany the hadjys to all the other places of resort in the sacred district, and are ready to perform every kind of service in the city. But their utility is more than counterbalanced by their importunity and knavery. They besiege the room of the hadjy from sun-rise to sun-set; and will not allow him to do any thing without obtruding their advice: they sit down with him to breakfast, dinner, and supper; lead him into all possible expenses, that they may pocket a share of them; suffer no opportunity to pass of asking him for money; and woe to the poor ignorant Turk who employs them as his interpreter in any mercantile concern. My first delyl was the man of Medina at whose house I lodged during the last days of Ramadhan. On returning to Mekka a second time, I unfortunately met him in the street; and though I was far from giving him a hearty welcome, having sufficient reason to suspect his honesty, he eagerly embraced me, and forthwith made my new lodgings his home. At first he accompanied me every day in my walks round the Kaaba, to recite the prayers used on that occasion: these, however, I soon learned by heart, and therefore dispensed with his services on the occasion. He sat down regularly at dinner with me, and often brought a small basket, which he ordered my slave to fill with biscuits, meat, vegetables, or fruit, and carried away with him. Every third or fourth day he asked for money: "It is not you who give it," he said; "it is God who sends it to me." Finding there was no polite mode of getting rid of him, I told him plainly, that I no longer wanted his services; language to which a Mekka delyl is not accustomed. After three days, however, he returned, as if nothing had happened, and asked me for a dollar. "God does not move me to give you any thing," I replied; "if he judged it right, he would soften my heart, and cause me to give you my whole purse." "Pull my beard," he exclaimed, "if God does not send you ten times more hereafter than what I beg at present." "Pull out every hair of mine," I replied, "if I give you one para, until I am convinced that God will consider it a meritorious act." On hearing this he jumped up, and walked away, saying, "We fly for refuge to God, from the hearts of the proud and the hands of the avaricious." These people never speak ten words without pronouncing the name of God or Mohammed; they are constantly seen with the rosary in their hands, and mumble prayers even during conversation. This character of the metowafs is so applicable to the people of Mekka in general, that at Cairo they use the following proverb, to repress the importunity of an insolent beggar: "Thou art like the Mekkawy, thou sayest 'Give me,' and 'I am thy master.'"

As I was obliged to have a delyl, I next engaged an old man of Tatar origin, with whom having made a sort of treaty at the outset, I had reason to be tolerably satisfied. What I paid at Mekka to the delyls, and at the places of holy visit, amounted, perhaps, altogether to three hundred and fifty piastres, or thirty dollars; but I gave no presents, either to the mosque, or to any of its officers, which is done only by great hadjys, or by those who wish to be publicly noticed. Some of the delyls are constantly stationed near the Kaaba, waiting to be hired for the walks round it; and if they see a pilgrim walking alone, they often, unasked, take hold of his hand, and begin to recite the prayers. The charge for this service is about half a piastre; and I have observed them bargaining with the hadjy at the very gate of the Kaaba, in the hearing of every body. The poorer delyls are contented with the fourth of a piastre. Many shopkeepers, and people of the third class, send their sons who know the prayers by heart, to this station, to learn the profession of delyl. Those who understand the Turkish language earn great wages. As the Turkish hadjys usually arrive by way of Djidda, in parties of from eight to twelve, who have quitted their homes in company, and live together at Mekka, one delyl generally takes charge of the whole party, and expects a fee in proportion to their number. It often happens that the hadjys, on returning home, recommend him to some other party of their countrymen, who, on reaching Djidda, send him orders to provide lodgings for them in Mekka, to meet them at Djidda, to superintend their short journey to the holy city, and to guide them in the prayers that must be recited on first entering it. Some of these delyls are constantly found at Djidda during the three months immediately preceding the Hadj: I have seen them on the road to Mekka, riding at the head of their party, and treated by them with great respect and politeness. A Turk from Europe, or Asia Minor, who knows not a word of Arabic, is overjoyed to find a smooth-tongued Arab who speaks his language, and who promises all kinds of comforts in Mekka, which he had been taught to consider as a place where nothing awaited him but danger and fatigue. A delyl who has twelve Turkish hadjys under his care for a month, generally gains as much as suffices for the expenses of his house during the whole year, besides new clothing for himself and all his children.

Some of these delyls have a very singular office. The Mohammedan law prescribes that no unmarried woman shall perform the pilgrimage; and that even every married woman must be accompanied by her husband, or at least a very near relation (the Shafay sect does not even allow the latter). Female hadjys sometimes arrive from Turkey for the Hadj; rich old widows, who wish to see Mekka before they die; or women who set out with their husbands, and lose them on the road by disease. In such cases, the female finds at Djidda, delyls (or, as this class is called, Muhallil) ready to facilitate their progress through the sacred territory in the character of husbands.

The marriage contract is written out before the Kadhy; and the lady, accompanied by her delyl, performs the pilgrimage to Mekka, Arafat, and all the sacred places. This, however, is understood to be merely a nominal marriage; and the delyl must divorce the woman on his return to Djidda: if he were to refuse a divorce, the law cannot compel him to it, and the marriage would be considered binding; but he could no longer exercise the lucrative profession of delyl; and my informant could only recollect two examples of the delyl continuing to be the woman's husband. I believe there is not any exaggeration of the number, in stating that there are eight hundred full-grown delyls, besides boys who are learning the profession. Whenever a shopkeeper loses his customers, or a poor man of letters wishes to gain as much money as will purchase an Abyssinian slave, he turns delyl. The profession is one of little repute; but many a prosperous Mekkawy has, at some period of his life, been a member of it.

From trade, stipends, and the profits afforded by hadjys, the riches which annually flow into Mekka are very considerable, and might have rendered it one of the richest cities in the East, were it not for the dissolute habits of its inhabitants. With the exception of the first class of merchants, who, though they keep splendid establishments, generally live below their income, and a great part of the second class, who hoard up money with the view of attaining the first rank, the generality of Mekkawys, of all descriptions and professions, are loose and disorderly spendthrifts. The great gains which they make during three or four months, are squandered in good living, dress, and the grossest gratifications; and in proportion as they feel assured of the profits of the following year, they care little about saving any part of those of the present. In the month of Moharram, as soon as the Hadj is over, and the greater part of the pilgrims have departed, it is customary to celebrate marriage and circumcision feasts. These are celebrated at Mekka in a very splendid style; and a man that has not more than three hundred dollars to spend in the year, will then throw away half that sum in the marriage or the circumcision of his child. Neither the sanctity of the holy city, nor the solemn injunctions of the Koran, are able to deter the inhabitants of Mekka from the using of spirituous liquors, and indulging in all the excesses which are the usual consequences of drunkenness. The Indian fleet imports large quantities of *raky* in barrels. This spirit, mixed with sugar, and an extract of cinnamon, is sold under the name of cinnamon-water. The Sherifs in Mekka and Djidda, great merchants, olemas, and all the chief people are in the habit of drinking this liquor, which they persuade themselves is neither wine nor brandy, and therefore not prohibited by the law. The less wealthy inhabitants cannot purchase so dear a commodity; but they use a fermented liquor made from raisins, and imported from Tayf, while the lower classes drink *bouza*. During my stay at Tayf, a Turk belonging to the suite of Mohammed Aly Pasha distilled brandy from grapes, and publicly sold it at forty piastres the bottle.

The Mekkawys are very expensive in their houses: the rooms are embellished with fine carpets, and an abundance of cushions and sofas covered with brocade: amidst the furniture is seen much beautiful china-ware, and several nargiles adorned with silver. A petty shopkeeper would be ashamed to receive his acquaintances in a house less splendidly fitted up. Their tables also are better supplied than in any other country of the East, where even respectable families live economically in this respect. A Mekkawy, even of the lower class, must have daily on his table meat which costs from one and a half to two piastres the pound; his coffee-pot is never removed from the fire; and himself, his women and children are almost constantly using the nargile, and the tobacco which supplies it cannot be a very trifling expense.

The women have introduced the fashion, not uncommon in Turkey, of visiting each other at least once a week with all their children; the visit lasts the whole day, and an abundant entertainment is provided on the occasion: the vanity of each mistress of a house makes her endeavour to surpass her acquaintances in show and magnificence; thus a continual expense is entailed on every family. Among the sources of expenditure must be enumerated the purchasing of Abyssinian female slaves who are kept by the men, or money bestowed on the public women whom several of them frequent. Considerable sums are also lavished in sensual gratification still more vicious and degrading, but unfortunately as prevalent in the towns of the Hedjaz as in some other parts of Asia, or in Egypt under the Mamelouks. It has been already observed that the temple of Mekka itself, the very sanctuary of the Mohammedan religion, is almost publicly and daily contaminated by practices of the grossest depravity: to these no disgrace is here attached; the young of all classes are encouraged in them by the old, and even parents have been so base as to connive at them for the sake of money. From such pollution, however, the encampments of the Arabian Bedouins are exempt; although their ancestors were not, in this respect, immaculate, if we may credit some scandalous anecdotes recorded by Eastern historians.

But my account of the public women (who are very numerous) must here be resumed. I have already observed that the quarter called Shab Aamer was the residence of the poorer class; those of the higher order are dispersed over the town. Their outward behaviour is more decent than that of any public women in the East, and it requires the experienced eye of a Mekkawy to ascertain by a particular movement in her gait, that the veiled female passing before him belongs to the venal tribe. I shall not venture to speak of the married women of the Hedjaz: I have heard anecdotes related, little to their credit; but in the East, as in other countries, the young men sometimes boast of favours which they never have enjoyed. The exterior demeanour of the women of Djidda and Mekka is very decorous: few of them are ever seen walking or riding in the street; a practice so common at Cairo, though contrary to Oriental ideas of propriety: and I lived in three different houses at Mekka without having seen the unveiled faces of the female inmates.

The great merchants of Mekka live very splendidly: in the houses of Djeylany, Sakkat, Ageyl, and El Nour, are establishments of fifty or sixty persons. These merchants obtained their riches principally during the reign of Ghaleb, to whom Djeylany and Sakkat served as spies upon the other merchants. Their tables are furnished daily in abundance with every native delicacy, as well as with those which India and Egypt afford. About twenty persons sit down to dinner with them; the favourite Abyssinian slaves, who serve often as writers or cashiers, are admitted to the table of their master; but the inferior slaves and the servants are fed only upon flour and butter. The china and glass ware, in which the dishes are served up, is of the best quality; rosewater is sprinkled on the beards of the guests after dinner, and the room is filled with the odours of aloe-wood, burnt upon the nargiles. There is great politeness without formality; and no men appear in a more amiable light, than the great Mekkawys dispensing hospitality to their guests. Whoever happens to be sitting in the outer hall, when dinner is served up, is requested to join at table, which he does without conceiving himself at all obliged by the invitation, while the host, on his part, appears to think compliance a favour conferred upon him.

The rich Mekkawys make two meals daily, one before mid-day, the other after sun-set; the lower classes breakfast at sun-rise, and eat nothing more till near sun-set. As in the negro countries, it is very indecorous for a man to be seen eating in the streets: the Turkish soldiers, who retain their native manners, are daily reprehended by the people of Mekka for their ill-breeding in this respect.

Before the Turkish conquest, and the wars of the Sherif with the Wahabys which preceded it, the merchants of Mekka led a very happy life. During the months of May and June they went to attend the sale of India goods at Djidda. In July and August (unless the Hadj happened in these months) they retired to their houses at Tayf, where they passed the hottest season, leaving their acting partners or writers at Djidda and Mekka. During the months of the pilgrimage, they were of course always at Mekka; and every wealthy Mekkawy family followed the Hadj to Arafat as a tour of pleasure, and encamped for three days at Wady Muna.

In the month of Radjeb, which is the seventh after the month of the Hadj, a caravan used always to set out from Mekka for Medina, composed of several hundred merchants, mounted upon dromedaries. At that time a large fair was held at Medina, and frequented by many of the surrounding Bedouins, and people of the Hedjaz and Nedjed.

The merchandize for its supply was sent from Mekka by a heavy caravan of camels, which set out immediately after the merchants, and was called *Rukub el Medina.** They remained about twenty days at Medina, and then returned to Mekka. This frequent, yet regular change of abode, must have been very agreeable to the merchants, particularly in those times, when they could calculate with certainty that the next pilgrimage would be a source of new riches to them. Tayf and Medina being now half-ruined, the merchants of Mekka resort to Djidda, as their only place of recreation: but even those who have wives and houses there, talk of their establishments at Mekka as their only real homes, and in it they spend the greater part of the year.

The inhabitants of Mekka, Djidda, and (in a less degree) of Medina, are generally of a more lively disposition than either the Syrians or Egyptians. None of those silent, grave automatons are seen here, so common in other parts of the Levant, whose insensibility or stupidity is commonly regarded among themselves as a proof of feeling, shrewdness, and wisdom.

The character of the Mekkawy resembles, in this respect, that of the Bedouin; and did not greediness of gain often distort their features, the smile of mirth would always be on their lips. In the streets and bazars, in the house, and even in the mosque, the Mekkawy loves to laugh and joke. In dealing with each other, or in talking on grave subjects, a proverb, a pun, or some witty allusion, is often introduced, and produces laughter. As the Mekkawys possess, with this vivacity of temper, much intellect, sagacity, and great suavity of manners, which they well know how to reconcile with their innate pride, their conversation is very agreeable; and whoever cultivates a mere superficial acquaintance with them, seldom fails to be delighted with their character. They are more polite towards each other, as well as towards strangers, than the inhabitants of Syria and Egypt, and retain something of the good-natured disposition of the Bedouins, from whom they derive their origin. When they accost each other in

---

* In general, the Arabs of the Hedjaz call the caravans *Rukub;* speaking of the Baghdad caravan, they say *Rukub es' Shám,* or *Rukub el Erak.*

the streets for the first time in the course of the day, the young man kisses the elder's hand, or the inferior that of his superior in rank, while the latter returns the salute by a kiss upon the forehead. Individuals of equal rank and age, not of the first class, mutually kiss each other's hands.* They say to a stranger, " O faithful," or " brother;" and the saying of the prophet, " that all faithful are brethren," is constantly upon their lips. " Welcome, a thousand times welcome," says a shopkeeper to his foreign customer; " you are the stranger of God, the guest of the holy city; my whole property is at your disposal." When the service of any one is wanted, the applicant says, " Our whole subsistence, after God, is owing to you pilgrims; can we do less than be grateful?" If in the mosque a foreigner is exposed to the sun, the Mekkawy will make room for him in a shady place; if he passes a coffee-shop, he will hear voices calling him to enter and take a cup of coffee; if a Mekkawy takes a jar to drink from any public water-seller, he will offer it, before he sets it to his mouth, to any passenger; and upon the slightest acquaintance, he will say to his new friend, " When will you honour me at home, and take your supper with me?" When they quarrel among themselves, none of those scurrilous names or vile language is heard, so frequently used in Egypt and Syria; blows are only given on very extraordinary occasions, and the arrival of a respectable person puts an immediate stop to any dispute, on his recommending peace: " God has made us great sinners," they will then say, " but he has bestowed upon us, likewise, the virtue of easy repentance."

To these amiable qualities the Mekkawys add another, for which they must also be commended: they are a proud race, and though their pride is not founded upon innate worth, it is infinitely preferable to the cringing servility of the other Levantines, who redeem their slavish deference to superiors by the most overbearing haughtiness towards those below them. The Mekkawys are proud of being

* In shaking hands, the people of the Hedjaz lay hold of each other's thumbs with the whole hand, pressing it, and again opening the hand three or four times. This is called Mesáfeha, and is said to have been a habit of Mohammed.

natives of the holy city, of being the countrymen of their prophet; of having preserved, in some degree, his manners; of speaking his pure language; of enjoying, in expectation, all the honours in the next world, which are promised to the neighbours of the Kaaba; and of being much freer men than any of the foreigners whom they see crowding to their city. They exhibit this pride to their own superiors, whom they have taught to treat them with great forbearance and circumspection; and they look upon all other Mohammedan nations as people of an inferior order, to whom their kindness and politeness are the effect of their condescension. Many good consequences might result from this pride, without which a people cannot expect to sustain its rank among nations. It has prevented the people of Mekka from sinking so deep into slavery as some of their neighbours; but it excites them to nothing laudable, while its more immediate effects are seen in the contempt which they entertain for foreigners. This contempt, as I have already remarked, in speaking of Djidda, is chiefly displayed towards the Turks, whose ignorance of the Arabic language, whose dress and manners, the meanness of their conduct whenever they cannot talk as masters; their cowardice exhibited whenever the Hadj has been assailed in its route across the Desert, and the little respect that was shown to them by the Governors of Mekka, as long as the Sherif's power was unbroken, have lowered them so much in the estimation of the Arabians, that they are held in the Hedjaz as little better than infidels; and although many of the Mekkawys are of Turkish origin, they heartily join the rest of their townsmen in vilifying the stock from which they sprang. The word *Turky* has become a term of insult towards each other among the children. *Noszrany* (Christians), or *Yahoudy* (Jews), are often applied to the Turks by the people of Mekka; and their manners and language afford a perpetual source of ridicule or reproach. The Syrians and Egyptians experience similar effects from the pride of the people of the Hedjaz, but especially the former, as the Egyptians, of all foreigners, approach nearest to the people of Arabia in customs and language, and keep up the most intimate intercourse with them. But the haughty Syrian Moslim, who calls Aleppo or Damascus " Om el Donia," (the mother of the world,) and believes no race of men equal to his own, nor any language so pure as the Syrian, though it is undoubtedly the worst dialect of the Arabic next to the Moggrebyn, is obliged to behave here with great modesty and circumspection, and at least to affect politeness. Although an Arab, he is reproached with dressing and living like a Turk; and to the epithet Shámy (Syrian) the idea is attached of a heavy, untutored clown. If the Arabians were to see the Turks in the countries where they are masters, their dislike towards them would be still greater; for it must be said, that their behaviour in the holy city is, in general, much more decent and conformable to the precepts of their religion, than in the countries from which they come.

The Mekkawys believe that their city, with all the inhabitants, is under the especial care of Providence, and that they are so far favoured above all other nations. " This is Mekka! this is the city of God!" they exclaim, when any surprise is expressed at the greater part of them having remained in the town during the stagnation of trade and the absence of pilgrims: " None ever wants his daily bread ere; none fears here the incursion of enemies." That Saoud saved the town from pillage; that no plundering took place when the Turkish cavalry, under Mostafa Bey, recaptured it from the Wahabys; that the capture of Sherif Ghaleb led to no massacres within the precincts of Mekka, are to them so many visible miracles of the Almighty, to prove the truth of that passage of the Koran, (chap. 106.) in which it is said, " Let them adore the God of the house (the Kaaba), who feeds them in hunger, and secures them from all fear." But they forget to look back to their own history, which mentions many terrible famines and sanguinary battles, that have happened in this sacred asylum. Indeed, the Hedjaz has suffered more from famine than, perhaps, any other Eastern country. The historians abound with descriptions of such lamentable events: I shall only mention one that happened in 1664, when, as Asamy relates, many people sold their own children at Mekka for a single measure of corn; and when, at Djidda, the populace fed publicly on human flesh.

A Mekkawy related to me, that having once resolved to abandon the city, in consequence of the non-arrival of Turkish hadjys, who supplied his means of subsistence, an angel appeared to him in his sleep on the night previous to his intended departure. The angel had a flaming sword in his hand, and stood upon the gate of Mekka, through which the dreamer was about to leave the town, and exclaimed, " Unbeliever, remain! the Mekkawys shall eat honey, while all the other people of the earth shall be content with barley bread!" In consequence of this vision he abandoned his project, and continued to live in the town.

The exterior politeness of the people of Mekka is in the same proportion to their sincerity, as are their professions of zealous faith and adherence to their religion, with the observance of its precepts. Many of them, especially those who have no particular interest in imposing upon the hadjys by an appearance of extreme strictness, are very relaxed in observing the forms of their religion, thinking it quite sufficient to be Mekkawys and to utter pious ejaculations in public, or supposing that the rigid practice of its precepts is more particularly incumbent upon foreign visitors, who see Mekka only once in their life. Like the Bedouins, many of them are either very irregular in their prayers, or do not pray at all. During the Friday's prayers, which every Moslim resident in a town is bound to attend, the mosque is filled chiefly with strangers, while many of the people of Mekka are seen smoking in their shops. After the pilgrims have left the town, the service in the mosque is very thinly attended. They never distribute alms, excusing themselves by saying that they were placed by Providence in this town to receive charity, and not to bestow it. They ape the manners recorded of Mohammed, but in his most trifling habits only: their mustachios are cut short, and their beard kept regularly under the scissors, because it was the prophet's custom to do so. In like manner they allow the end of the turban to fall loosely over the cap; every other day they put kohhel or antimony on their eye-lids, and have always in their hands a messouak or tooth-brush made of a thin branch of the shrub Arak, or one imported by the Persian hadjys. They know by heart many passages of the Koran and Hadyth, (or sacred traditions,) and allude to, or quote them every moment; but they forget that these precepts were given for rules of conduct, and not for mere repetition. Intoxicating liquors are sold at the very gates of the mosque: the delyls themselves act in direct contradiction of the law by loudly reciting prayers in the mosque to their pupils the hadjys, in order to allure by their sonorous voices other pilgrims to their guidance, carrying at the same time the common large stick of the Mekkawys. It is also a transgression against the law, when the intoxicating hashysh is openly smoked: cards are played in almost every Arab coffee-house, (they use small Chinese cards,) though the Koran directly forbids games of hazard. The open protection afforded by the government to persons both male and female of the most profligate character, is a further encouragement to daily transgressions against the rigid principles of the Mohammedan law. Cheating and false swearing have ceased to be crimes among them. They are fully conscious of the scandal of these vices: every delyl exclaims against the corruption of manners, but none set an example of reformation; and while acting constantly on principles quite opposite to those which they profess, they unanimously declare that times are such, as to justify the saying, " In el Haram fi belád el Harameyn," " that the cities forbidden to infidels abound with forbidden things."

In a place where there is no variety of creeds, persecution cannot show itself; but it is probable that the Mekkawys might easily be incited to excesses against those whom they call infidels: for I have always remarked in the East, that the Muselmáns most negligent in performing the duties of their religion are the most violent in urging its precepts against unbelievers; and that the grossest superstition is generally found among those who trifle with their duties, or who, like many Osmanlys, even deride them, and lay claim to free-thinking. There is no class of Turks more inveterate in their hatred against Christians than those who, coming frequently into intercourse with them, find it convenient to throw off for a while the appearance of their prejudices. In all the European harbours of the Mediterranean, the Moggrebyns live like unbelievers; but when at home, nothing but fear can induce them to set bounds to their fanaticism. It is the same with the Turks in the Archipelago, and I might adduce many examples from Syria and Egypt in corroboration of this assertion. If fanaticism has somewhat decreased within the last twenty years throughout the

Turkish empire, the circumstance, I think, may be ascribed solely to the decreasing energy of the inhabitants, and the growing indifference for their own religion, and certainly not to a diffusion of more philanthropic or charitable principles. The text of the Mohammedan law is precise in inciting its followers to unceasing hatred and contempt of all those who profess a different creed. This contempt has not decreased; but animosity gives way to an exterior politeness, whenever the interest of the Mohammedan is concerned. The degree of toleration enjoyed by the Christians, depends upon the interest of the provincial government under which they live: and if they happen to be favoured by it, the Turkish subject bows to the Christian. In all the eastern countries which I have visited, more privileges are allowed to Christians in general than the Moslim code prescribes; but their condition depends upon the fiat of the governor of the town or district; as they experienced about seven years since at Damascus, under Yousef Pasha, when they were suddenly reduced to their former abject state. Twenty years ago, a Copt of Egypt was in much the same situation as a Jew is now in Barbary; but at present, when the free-thinking, though certainly not liberal, Mohammed Aly finds it his interest to conciliate the Christians, a Greek beats a Turk without much fear of consequences from the mob; and I know an instance of an Armenian having murdered his own Muselmán servant, and escaped punishment, on paying a fine to government, although the fact was publicly known. Convinced as the Turks must now be, in many parts of the East, of the superiority of these Europeans, whom they cannot but consider as the brethren of their Christian subjects, their behaviour towards the latter will, nevertheless, be strictly regulated by the avowed sentiments of their governors; and it would be as easy for Mohammed Aly by a single word to degrade the Christians in Egypt, as he found it to raise them to their present consideration, superior, I believe, to what they enjoy in any other part of Turkey.

The hatred against Christians is nearly equal in every part of the Ottoman empire; and if the Moslims sacrifice that feeling, it is not to the principles of charity or humanity, but to the frown of those who happen to be in power; and their baseness is such, that they will kiss to-day the hands of him whom they have trodden under foot yesterday. In examining into the fanatical riots, many of which are recorded in the chanceries of the European consuls in the Levant, it will generally be found that government had a share in the affrays, and easily succeeded in quelling them. The late Sultan Selim, in his regenerating system, which led him to favour the Christians, found no opposition from the mass of his people, but from the jealous Janissaries; and when the latter had prevailed, the demi-Gallicized grandees of Constantinople easily sunk again into *Sunnys*. Sometimes, indeed, a rash devotee, or mad Sheikh or Dervish at the head of a few partisans, affords an exception to these general statements; and will insult a Christian placed in the highest favour with the public authorities, as happened at Damascus in 1811, to the Greek Patriarch, after Yousef Pasha had been repulsed: but his countrymen, although cherishing the same principles, and full of the same uncharitableness, seldom have the courage to give vent to their feelings, and to follow the example of the Saint. None of those genuine popular commotions, which were once so frequent in Europe, when the members of the reigning church saw individuals of a rival persuasion extending their influence, are now witnessed in the East. Whatever may be thought of it in a moral point of view, we must respect the energy of a man who enters headlong into a contention, of at least uncertain issue, and generally detrimental to his own worldly interests, merely because he fancies or believes that his religious duty commands his exertions. The Moslim of the Turkish empire, as far as I have had an opportunity of remarking, easily suppresses his feelings, his passions, the dictates of his conscience, and what he supposes agreeable to the will of the Almighty, at the dictates of his interest, or according to the wish or example of the ruling power.

In the time of the Sherif, Christians were often ill treated at Djidda; they could not wear the European dress, or approach the quarter of the town situated towards the gate of Mekka. But since the arrival of Mohammed Aly's army, they walk about, and dress as they like. In December 1814, when two Englishmen passed the gate of Mekka on a walk round the town, (the first persons, probably, in a

European dress, who had ever passed the holy boundary,) a woman was heard to exclaim, "Truly the world must be near its end, if Kafirs (or infidels) dare to tread upon this ground!" Even now, if a Christian dies there, it is not permitted that he should be interred on shore; the body is carried to a small desert island in the harbour. When, in 1815, the plague raged in the Hedjaz, an event which had never before been known, the Kadhy of Djidda, with the whole body of olemas, waited upon the Turkish governor of the city, to desire him to demolish a windmill which some Greek Christians from Cairo had built withoutside one of the gates, by order of Mohammed Aly. They were certain, they said, that the hand of God had visited them on account of this violation of the sacred territory by Christians. Some years ago an English ship was wrecked near Djidda, and among various spoils obtained from the wreck by Sherif Ghaleb was a large hog, an animal probably never before seen at Djidda: this hog, turned loose in the town with two ostriches, became the terror of all the sellers of bread and vegetables; for the mere touching of so unclean an animal as the hog, even with the edge of the gown, renders the Moslim impure, and unable to perform his prayers without previous ablution. The animal was kept for six months, when it was offered by the Sherif to an American captain for fifty dollars; but such a price being of course refused, it soon after died of a surfeit, to the great satisfaction of the inhabitants.

The Mekkawys, however, tolerate within their walls notorious heretics. I have already mentioned the Ismaylys, an idolatrous sect from India, who appear here in the garb of Moslims. The Persian hadjys, well known as sectaries of Aly, and revilers of Mohammed and his immediate followers, are not subjected to any particular inconveniences. The Sherif tolerated them, but levied a capitation-tax on each. The Sherifs, however, themselves, as I shall presently explain, are mostly of the sect of Zyoud, Muselmans who dispute with the orthodox Sunnyes (the great opponents of the Persian sectaries,) several of their principal dogmas.

Whenever the word Christian or European is mentioned by the

Mekkawys, it is coupled with the most opprobrious and contemptuous epithets. They include them all in the appellation of Káfer, without having any clear ideas of the different nations of which they are composed. The English, however, being more in contact with them, from their Indian possessions, are often called exclusively "El Kafer," or "the Infidels;" and whenever this appellation is so used, the English are to be understood. Thus, they say "El Kafer fy'l Hind," the Kafer in India; or "Merkeb el Kafer fy Djidda," the Kafer's ship at Djidda, always meaning the English.

When the French invaded Egypt, a Moggrebyn saint at Mekka, called Sheikh el Djeylany, a distant relation of a wealthy merchant at Mekka, and who had for some time been in the habit of delivering lectures in the great mosque, mounted the pulpit, and preached a crusade against the infidels, who had seized upon the gate of the Kaaba, as Egypt is styled. Being a very eloquent speaker, and held in much veneration, many Arabs flocked to his standard, others gave him money; and it is said that even many women brought him their gold and silver trinkets, to assist him in his holy enterprise. He embarked at Djidda with his zealous followers, on board a small fleet, and landed at Cosseir. The governments of Mekka and Djidda seem to have had little share in the enterprise, though they threw no obstacles in its way. The fate of these Arabs (many of whom were of the same Wahaby tribes who afterwards offered so much resistance to Mohammed Aly), and the fury with which they encountered the French in Upper Egypt, are already known to the reader by Denon's animated description. Sheikh Djeylany was killed, and very few of his followers returned. I believe their number is rather over-rated by Denon; for I never heard it stated at more than fifteen hundred.

The Mekkawys, like the inhabitants of Turkey, are in general free from the vices of pilfering and thieving; and robberies are seldom heard of, although, during the Hadj, and in the months which precede and follow it, Mekka abounds with rogues, who are tempted by the facility of opening the locks of this country.

Formerly the slaves of the Sherif were noted for their disorderly behaviour; Ghaleb, however, established good order among them; and during his reign, a burglary was never committed without the discovery and punishment of the perpetrator.

The streets of Mekka abound with beggars and poor hadjys, who are supported by the charity of strangers; for the Mekkawys think themselves privileged to dispense with this duty. Of them, however, many adopt mendicity as a profession, especially during the Hadj, when the pilgrims are bound to exercise that virtue which is so particularly enjoined by the precepts of Mohammed. The greater part of the beggars are Indians, others Syrians, Moggrebyns, and Egyptians: the Negroes are but few, as these generally prefer labour to begging; but a large proportion comes from Yemen. It is generally said in the East, that Mekka is the paradise of beggars: some perhaps may save a little money, but the wretched aspect of others plainly shows how much their expectations must have been disappointed. The Indians are the most modest among them; they accost the passenger with the words " Ya allah'ya kerim!" " O God, O bounteous God!" and if alms are refused, they walk away, without a word except the repetition of " Ya allah, ya kerim." Not so the Yemeny or Mekkawy; " Think of your duty as a pilgrim," he cries; " God does not like the cold-hearted; will you reject the blessings of the faithful? Give, and it shall be given unto thee;" and with these and many other pious sentences they address the passenger, and when they have the alms safe in their hand, they often say, as my delyl did, " It is God, and not you, who gives it to me." Some of these beggars are extremely importunate, and seem to ask for alms as if they were legally entitled to it. While I was at Djidda, a Yemen beggar mounted the minaret daily, after mid-day prayer, and exclaimed loud enough to be heard through the whole bazar, " I ask from God fifty dollars, a suit of clothes, and a copy of the Koran; O faithful, hear me, I ask of you fifty dollars," &c. &c. This he repeated for several weeks, when at last a Turkish pilgrim, struck by the singularity of the beggar's appeal, desired him to take thirty dollars, and discontinue his cries, which reflected shame upon the charity of all the hadjys present. " No," said the beggar, " I will not take them, because I am convinced that God will send me the whole of what I beg of him so earnestly." After repeating his public supplication for some days more, the same hadjy gave him the whole sum that he asked for; but without being thanked. I have heard people exclaim in the mosques at Mekka, immediately after prayers, "O brethren, O faithful, hear me! I ask twenty dollars from God, to pay for my passage home; twenty dollars only. You know that God is all-bountiful, and may send me a hundred dollars; but it is twenty dollars only that I ask. Remember that charity is the sure road to paradise." There can be no doubt that this practice is sometimes attended with success.

But learning and science cannot be expected to flourish in a place where every mind is occupied in the search of gain, or of paradise; and I think I have sufficient reason for affirming that Mekka is at present much inferior even in Mohammedan learning to any town of equal population in Syria or Egypt. It probably was not so when the many public schools or Medreses were built, which are now converted into private lodgings for pilgrims. El Fasy says, that in his time there were eleven medreses in Mekka, besides a number of *rebats*, or less richly endowed schools, which contained also lodgings for poor hadjys; many of the Rebats in the vicinity of the mosque still remain, but are used only as lodging-houses. There is not a single public school in the town where lectures are given, as in other parts of Turkey; and the great mosque is the only place where teachers of Eastern learning are found. The schools in which boys are taught to read and write, are, as I have already mentioned, held in the mosque, where, after prayers, chiefly in the afternoon, some learned olemas explain a few religious books to a very thin audience, consisting principally of Indians, Malays, Negroes, and a few natives of Hadramaut and Yemen, who, attracted by the great name of Mekka, remain here a few years, until they think themselves sufficiently instructed to pass at home for learned men. The Mekkawys themselves, who wish to improve in science, go to Damascus or to Cairo. At the latter many of them are constantly found, studying in the mosque El Azhar.

The lectures delivered in the mosque at Mekka resemble those of other Eastern towns. They are delivered *gratis*; each lecture occupies one hour or two; and any person may lecture who thinks himself competent to the task, whether he belongs to the mosque or not. This happens also in the Azhar at Cairo, where I have seen more than forty different persons occupied at the same time in delivering their lectures. The subjects of the lectures in the Beitullah of Mekka, are, as usual, dissertations on the law, commentaries on the Koran, and traditions of the Prophet. There were none, during my residence, on grammar, logic, rhetoric, or the sciences, nor even on the *Towhyd*, or explanation of the essence or unity of God, which forms a principal branch of the learning of Moslim divines. I understood, however, that sometimes the Arabic syntax is explained, and the Elfye Ibn Malek on grammar. But the Mekkawys who have acquired an intimate knowledge of the whole structure of their language, owe it to their residence at Cairo.

There is no public library attached to the mosque; the ancient libraries, of which I have already spoken, have all disappeared. The Nayb el Haram has a small collection of books which belonged originally to the mosque; but it is now considered as his private property, and the books cannot be hired without difficulty. The Azhar at Cairo is on a very different footing. To each of the Rowak, or private establishments for the different Mohammedan nations, which it contains, (and which are now twenty-six in number,) a large library is annexed, and all the members of the Rowak are at liberty to take books from it to assist them in their studies. Mekka is equally destitute of private libraries, with the exception of those of the rich merchants, who exhibit a few books to distinguish them from the vulgar; or of the olemas, of whom some possess such as are necessary for their daily reference in matters of law.

The Wahabys, according to report, carried off many loads of books; but they were also said to have paid for every thing they took : it is not likely that they carried away all the libraries of Mekka, and I endeavoured in vain to discover even a single collection of books. Not a book-shop or a book-binder is found in Mekka. After the return of the Hadj from Arafat, a few of the poorer olemas expose some books for sale in the mosque, near Bab-es'-Salam : all those which I saw were on the law, korans with commentaries, and similar works, together with a few on grammar. No work on history, or on any other branch of knowledge, could be found; and, notwithstanding all my pains, I could never obtain a sight of any history of Mekka, although the names of the authors were not unknown to the Mekkawys. They told me that book-dealers used formerly to come here with the Hadj from Yemen, and sell valuable books, brought principally from Szanaa and Loheya. The only good work I saw at Mekka was a fine copy of the Arabic Dictionary called Kamous; it was purchased by a Malay for six hundred and twenty piastres; at Cairo it might be worth half that sum. Many pilgrims inquired for books, and were inclined to pay good prices for them; and it was matter of surprise to me that the speculating Mekkawys did not avail themselves of this branch of trade, not so lucrative certainly as that of coffee and India goods. I much regretted my total want of books, and especially the copies of the historians of Mekka, which I had left at Cairo; they would have led me to many inquiries on topography, which by Azraky in particular is treated with great industry.

The Persian hadjys and the Malays are those who chiefly search for books: the Wahabys, it is said, were particularly inquisitive after historical works; a remark I heard repeated at Medina. During my stay at Damascus, which is the richest book-market in the East, and the cheapest, from being very little frequented by Europeans, I heard that several Arabs of Baghdad, secretly commissioned for that purpose by Saoud, the Wahaby chief, had purchased there many historical works. When Abou Nokta plundered the harbours of Yemen, he carried off a great number of books, and sent them to Derayeh.

The scarcity of valuable books at Mekka may, perhaps, be ascribed to the continual purchases made by pilgrims; for there are no copyists at Mekka to replace the books which have been exported.* The want of copyists is, indeed, a general complaint also in Syria and Egypt, and must, in the end, lead to a total deficiency of books in those countries, if the exportation to Europe continues. There are at Cairo, at this time, not more than three professed copyists, who write a good hand, or who possess sufficient knowledge to enable them to avoid the grossest

---

* At Cairo, I saw many books in the Hedjaz character, some of which I purchased.

errors. At Mekka, there was a man of Lahor, who wrote Arabic most beautifully, though he spoke it very indifferently. He sat in a shop near Bab-es'-Salam, and copied for the hadjys such prayers as it was necessary to recite during the pilgrimage. The hand-writing of the Hedjaz is different from that used in Egypt or Syria; but a little practice makes it easily read. In general, not only every country, but every province, even, of the East, has its peculiar mode of writing, which practice alone can enable one to distinguish. There are shades of difference in the writing of the Aleppines, of the people of Damascus, and of Acre; and, in Egypt, the writing of a Cahirein is easily distinguished from that of a native of Upper Egypt. That of the Moslims is different every where from that of the Christians, who are taught to write by their priests, and not by Turkish schoolmasters. The Copts of Egypt have also a character differing from that of the other Christians established in the country. An experienced person knows, from the address of a letter, the province and the race to which the writer belongs. The dialects, and the style of letter-writing are not less distinguishable than the hand-writing; and this remark is particularly applicable to the complimentary expressions with which the letters always abound. The style of Syria is the most flowery; yet even in letters of mere business we find it used. That of Egypt is less complimentary; that of the Hedjaz is simple and manly, and approaches to Bedouin frankness, containing, before the immediate purport of the letter, only a few words of inquiry after the health and welfare of the person addressed. Each country has also its peculiar manner of folding a letter. In the Hedjaz, letters are sealed with gum-arabic; and a small vessel full of the diluted gum is suspended near the gate of every large house or khan.

Whatever may be the indifference of the Mekkawys for learning,*

---

* I may mention, as a strong proof of the neglect of learning at Mekka, that of a dozen persons, respectable from their situations in life, of whom I inquired respecting the place Okath, not one of them knew where it was, or if it still existed. The Okath was the place where the ancient Arabian poets, as late even as the time of Mohammed, used to recite their works to crowds assembled there at a great fair. The prize poems were afterwards suspended at the Kaaba. It is to this custom that we owe the celebrated poems called the

the language of their city is still more pure and elegant, both in phraseology and pronunciation, than that of any other town where Arabic is spoken. It approaches more nearly than any other dialect to the old written Arabic, and is free from those affectations and perversions of the original sense, which abound in other provinces. I do not consider the Arabic language as on the decline : it is true, there are no longer any poets who write like Motanebbi, Abol' Ola, or Ibn el Faredh; and a fine flowing prose the Arabs never possessed. The modern poets content themselves with imitating their ancient masters, humbly borrowing the sublime metaphors and exalted sentiments produced from nobler and freer breasts than those of the olemas of the present day. But even now, the language is deeply studied by all the learned men; it is the only science with which the orthodox Moslim can beguile his leisure hours, after he has explored the labyrinth of the law; and every where in the East it is thought an indispensable requisite of a good education, not only to write the language with purity, but to have read and studied the classic poets, and to know their finest passages by heart. The admiration with which Arabic scholars regard their best writers, is the same as that esteem in which Europeans hold their own classics. The far greater part of the Eastern population, it is true, neither write nor read ; but of those who have been instructed in letters, a much larger proportion write elegantly, and are well read in the native authors, than among the same class in Europe.

The Mekkawys study little besides the language and the law. Some boys learn at least as much Turkish as will enable them to cheat the Osmanly pilgrims to whom their knowledge of that tongue may recommend them as guides. The astronomer of the mosque learns to know the exact time of the Sun's passing the meridian, and occupies himself occasionally with astrology and horoscopes. A Persian doctor, the only avowed medical professor I saw at Mekka, deals in nothing

---

Seba Moallakat. A Bedouin of Hodheyl told me that the Okath was now a ruined place in the country of Beni Naszera, between two and three days' journey south of Tayf. But in El Fasy's history, I find it stated to be one day's journey from Tayf; and that it ceased to be frequented as a fair in A. H. 129. El Azraky says that it was at that distance from Tayf, on the road to Szanaa in Yemen, and belonged to the tribe of Beni Kanane.

but miraculous balsams and infallible elixirs; his potions are all sweet and agreeable; and the musk and aloe-wood which he burns, diffuse through his shop a delicious odour, which has contributed to establish his reputation. Music, in general so passionately loved among the Arabs, is less practised at Mekka than in Syria and Egypt. Of instruments they possess only the *rababa*, (a kind of guitar,) the *nay*, (a species of clarinet,) and the *tambour*, or *tambourine*. Few songs are heard in the evenings, except among the Bedouins in the skirts of the town. The choral song called Djok, is sometimes sung by the young men at night in the coffee-houses, its measure being accompanied with the clapping of hands. In general, the voices of the Hedjazys are harsh, and not clear: I heard none of those sonorous and harmonious voices which are so remarkable in Egypt, and still more in Syria, whether giving utterance to love songs, or chanting the praises of Mohammed from the minarets, which in the depth of night has a peculiarly grand effect. Even the Imams of the mosque, and those who chant the anthems, in repeating the last words of the introductory prayers of the Imam, men who in other places are chosen for their fine voices, can here be distinguished only by their hoarseness and dissonance.

The Sherif has a band of martial music, similar to that kept by Pashas, composed of kettle-drums, trumpets, fifes, &c.: it plays twice a day before his door, and for about an hour on every evening of the new moon.

Weddings are attended by professional females, who sing and dance: they have, it is said, good voices, and are not of that dissolute class to which the public singers and dancers belong in Syria and Egypt. The Mekkawys say, that before the Wahaby invasion, singers might be heard during the evening in every street, but that the austerity of the Wahabys, who, though passionately fond of their own Bedouin songs, disapproved of the public singing of females, occasioned the ruin of all musical pursuits:—this, however, may be only an idle notion, to be ranked with that which is as prevalent in the East as it is in Europe, that old times were always better in every respect than the present.

The *sakas* or water-carriers of Mekka, many of whom are foreigners, having a song which is very affecting from its simplicity and the purpose for which it is used, the wealthier pilgrims frequently purchase the whole contents of a saka's water-skin, on quitting the mosque, especially at night, and order him to distribute it gratis among the poor. While pouring out the water into the wooden bowls, with which every beggar is provided, they exclaim "Sebyl Allah, ya atshan, Sebyl!" "hasten, O thirsty, to the ways of God!" and then break out in the following short song of three notes only, which I never heard without emotion.

Lento.

Ed - djene wa el moy fe za ta ly Saheb es sa byl

Ed-djene wa el moy fezata ly Saheb es-Sabyl. "Paradise and forgiveness be the lot of him who gave you this water!"

I cannot describe the marriage-feasts as celebrated at Mekka, not having attended any; but I have seen the bride carried to the house of her husband, accompanied by all her female friends. No canopy is used on this occasion, as in Egypt, nor any music; but rich clothes and furniture are displayed, and the feasting is sumptuous, and often lasts for three or four days. On settling a marriage, the money to be paid for the bride is carried in procession from the house of the bridegroom to that of the girl's father; it is borne through the streets upon two tabourets, wrapped up in a rich handkerchief, and covered again with an embroidered satin stuff. Before the two persons who hold these tabourets, two others walk, with a flask of rose-water in one hand, and a censer in the other, upon which all sorts of perfumes and odours are burning. Behind them follow, in a long train, all the kindred and friends of the bridegroom, dressed in their best clothes. The price paid for virgins among the respectable classes, varies at Mekka from forty to three hundred dollars, and from ten to twenty dollars among the poor classes. Half the sum only is usually paid down; the other half is left in possession of the husband, who pays it in case he should divorce his wife.

The circumcision feasts are similar to those at Cairo: the child, after the operation, is dressed in the richest stuffs, set upon a fine horse highly adorned, and is thus carried in procession through the town with drums beating before him.

Funerals differ in nothing from those in Egypt and Syria.

The people of Mekka, in general, have very few horses; I believe that there are not more than sixty kept by private individuals. The Sherif has about twenty or thirty in his stables; but Sherif Ghaleb had a larger stud. The military Sherifs keep mares, but the greater part of these were absent with the army. The Bedouins, who are settled in the suburb Moabede, and in some other parts of the town, as being concerned with public affairs, have also their horses; but none of the merchants or other classes keep any. They are afraid of being deprived by the Sherif of any fine animal they might possess, and therefore content themselves with mules or gedishes (geldings of a low breed). Asses are very common, but no person of quality ever rides upon them. The few horses kept at Mekka are of noble breed, and purchased from the Bedouins: in the spring they are usually sent to some Bedouin encampment, to feed upon the fine nutritious herbage of the Desert. Sherif Yahya has a gray mare, from the stud of Ghaleb, which was valued at twenty purses; she was as beautiful a creature as I ever saw, and the only one perfectly fine that I met with in the Hedjaz. The Bedouins of that country, and those especially around Mekka, are very poor in horses; a few Sheikhs only having any, pasture being scarce, and the expense of a horse's keep being three piastres a day.

In the Eastern plain, behind Tayf, horses are more numerous, although much less so than in Nedjed and the deserts of Syria, in consequence of the comparative scarcity of corn, and the uncertainty of the rain; a deficiency of which often leaves the Bedouin a whole year without vegetation; a circumstance that rarely happens in the more northern deserts, where the rains seldom fail in the proper seasons.

GOVERNMENT OF MEKKA.

The territories of Mekka, Tayf, Gonfade, (which stretches southwards as far as Haly, on the coast,) and of Yembo, were, previous to the Wahaby and Egyptian conquests, under the command of the Sherif of Mekka, who had extended his authority over Djidda also, though this town was nominally separated from his dominions, and governed by a Pasha, sent thither by the Porte, to be sole master of the town, and to divide its revenue with the Sherif. The Sherif, raised to his station by force or by personal influence, and the consent of the powerful Sherif families of Mekka, held his authority from the Grand Signor, who invariably confirmed the individual that had possessed himself of it.* He was invested annually with a pelisse, brought from Constantinople by the Kaftandji Bashy; and, in the Turkish ceremonial, he was ranked among the first Pashas of the empire. When the power of the Pashas of Djidda became merely nominal, and the Porte was no longer able to send large armies with the Hadj caravans of the Hedjaz, to secure its command over that country, the Sherifs of Mekka became independent, and disregarded all the orders of the Porte, although

---

* The government of the Hedjaz has often been a subject of dispute between the Khalifes of Baghdad, the Sultans of Egypt, and the Imams of Yemen. The honour attached, even to a nominal authority over the holy cities, was the only object they had in view, although that authority, instead of increasing their income, obliged them to incur great expenses. The right of clothing the Kaaba, and of having their name inserted in the Friday's prayers in the mosque, was the sole benefit they derived. The supremacy of Egypt over Mekka, so firmly established from the beginning of the fifteenth century, was transferred, after the conquest of that country by Selim I., to the Sultans of Constantinople.

they still called themselves the servants of the Sultan, received the annual investiture of the pelisse, acknowledged the Kadhi sent from Constantinople, and prayed for the Sultan in the great mosque. Mohammed Aly has restored the authority of the Osmanlys in the Hedjaz, and usurps all the power of the Sherif; allowing to the present Sherif Yahya a merely nominal sway.

The Sherif of Mekka was chosen from one of the many tribes of Sherifs, or descendants of the Prophet, who settled in the Hedjaz; these were once numerous, but are now reduced to a few families of Mekka. Till the last century, the right of succession was in the Dwy* Barakat, so called after Barakat, the son of Seyd Hassan Adjelan, who succeeded his father in A. H. 829; he belonged to the sherif tribe of Katade, which was originally settled in the valley of Alkamye, forming part of Yembo el Nakhel, and was related, by the female side, to the Beni Hashem, whom they had dispossessed of the government of Mekka in A. H. 600, after the death of the last Hashemy, called Mekether. During the last century, the Dwy Barakat had to sustain many wars with their rival tribes, and finally yielded to the most numerous, that of Dwy Zeyd, to whom the present Sherifs belong, and which, together with all the Ketade, form part of the great tribe of Abou Nema. Most of the Barakat emigrated; many of them settling in the fertile valleys of the Hedjaz, and others in Yemen. Of the Sherifs still existing in and about Mekka, besides the tribes above mentioned, the following five were named to me: Abadele, Ahl Serour, Herazy, Dwy Hamoud, Sowamele.†

The succession to the government of Mekka, like that of the Bedouin Sheikhs, was not hereditary; though it remained in the same tribe as long as the power of that tribe preponderated. After the

---

* *Dwy* means *Ahl*, or family.

† In addition to these, I find several others mentioned by Asamy, as Dwy Masoud, Dwy Shambar, Dwy el Hareth, Dwy Thokaba, Dwy Djazan, Dwy Baz. It would demand more leisure than I enjoy, to compile a history of Mekka from the above-mentioned sources. D'Ohsson has given an historical notice on the Sherifs of Mekka, in which are several errors. The long pedigrees that must be traced, to acquire a clear notion of the rulers of any part of Arabia, render the history of that country extremely intricate.

death of a Sherif, his relative, whether son, brother, or cousin, &c. who had the strongest party, or the public voice in his favour, became the successor. There were no ceremonies of installation or oaths of allegiance. The new Sherif received the complimentary visits of the Mekkawys; his band played before the door, which seems to be the sign of royalty here, as it is in the black country; and his name was henceforth inserted in the public prayers. Though a succession seldom took place without some contest, there was little bloodshed in general; and though instances of cruelty sometimes occurred, the principles of honour and good faith which distinguish the wars of the Desert tribes, were generally observed. The rivals submitted, and usually remained in the town, neither attending the levees of their victorious relative, nor dreading his resentment, after peace had once been settled. During the war, the rights of hospitality were held as sacred as they are in the Desert; the dakhyl, or refugee, was always respected: for the blood shed on both sides, atonement was made by fines paid to the relations of the slain, and the same laws of retaliation were observed, which prevail among the Bedouins. There was always a strong party in opposition to the reigning power; but this opposition was evinced more in the protection afforded to individuals persecuted by the chief, than in open attempts against his authority. Wars, however, frequently happened; each party had its adherents among the neighbouring Bedouins; but these were carried on according to the system in Bedouin feuds, and were seldom of long duration.

Though such customs might have a tendency to crush the power of the reigning Sherif, they were attended with bad consequences to the community: every individual was obliged to attach himself to one or other of the parties, and to some protector, who treated his adherents with the same tyranny and injustice that he experienced from his superior; laws were little respected; every thing was decided by personal influence. The power of the Sherifs was considerably diminished by Serour, who reigned from 1773 to 1786; but even, in later times, Ghaleb, although possessed of more authority than any of his predecessors, had often to fight with his own relations.

This continued prevalence of intestine broils, the wars and contentions of the prevailing parties, the vicissitudes of fortune which attended them, and the arts of popularity which the chiefs were obliged to employ, gave to the government of the Hedjaz a character different from that of most of the other governments in the East, and which it retained, in outward appearance, even after Ghaleb had almost succeeded in reigning as a despot. None of that ceremony was observed, which draws a line of distinction between the Eastern sovereigns, or their vicegerents, and the people. The court of the Sherif was small, and almost entirely devoid of pomp. His title is neither Sultan, nor Sultan Sherif, nor "Sire," as Aly Bey Abbas asserts. "Sydna," "our Lord," was the title which his subjects used in conversing with him; or that of "Sádetkum," or "your Highness," which is given to all Pashas. The distance between the subject and the chief was not thought so great as to prevent the latter, in cases of need, from representing his griefs personally, and respectfully but boldly demanding redress.

The reigning Sherif did not keep a large body of regular troops; but he summoned his partisans among the Sherifs, with their adherents, whenever war was determined upon. These Sherifs he attached to his person by respecting their rank and influence, and they were accustomed to consider him in no other light than as the first among equals.

To give a history of the events which have occurred at Mekka since the period at which the Arabian historians conclude, (about the middle, I believe, of the seventeenth century,) would be a work of some labour, as it must be drawn from verbal communications; for nobody, in this country, thinks of committing to paper the events of his own times. The circumstances under which I visited the place would have prevented me from obtaining any very extensive and accurate information on the political state of the country, even if I had had leisure, as such inquiries would have obliged me to mix with people of rank, and those holding offices; a class of society which, for obvious reasons, it was my constant endeavour to shun. The following is the amount of what information I was able to collect concerning the recent history of Mekka.

1750. Sherif Mesaad was appointed to the government of Mekka, which he held for twenty years. The power of the Sherifs involved him in frequent wars with them; as he seldom succeeded, their influence remained undiminished. Having betrayed symptoms of enmity towards Aly Beg, then governor of Egypt, the latter sent his favourite slave, Abou Dahab, whom he had made Beg, with a strong body of soldiers, as chief of the Hadj caravan, to Mekka, in order to expel Mesaad; but the Sherif died a few days before his arrival.

1769, or 1770. After Mesaad's death, Hosseyn, who, although of the same tribe, had been his opponent on every occasion, was raised by his own party to the government, and confirmed therein by the assistance of Abou Dahab. He continued to rule till the year

1773 or 4, when he was slain in a war with Serour, the son of Mesaad. The name of Serour, who reigned thirteen or fourteen years, is still venerated by the Mekkawys: he was the first who humbled the pride and power of the Sherifs, and established rigid justice in the town. Previous to his reign, every Sherif had in his house at Mekka an establishment of thirty or forty armed slaves, servants, and relations, besides having powerful friends among the Bedouins. Ignorant of every occupation but that of arms, they lived upon the cattle which they kept among the Bedouins, and in different parts of the Hedjaz; the surra which they were entitled to receive from the Hadj; and the presents which they exacted from the pilgrims, and from their dependents in the town. Some of them, in addition to these general sources of income, had extorted from former chief Sherifs lucrative sinecures, such as duties on ships, or on certain articles of merchandize; tolls collected at one of the gates of Djidda; the capitation-tax levied upon the Persian pilgrims, &c. &c. Their behaviour in the town was wild and disorderly; the orders of the chief Sherif were disregarded; every one made use of his personal authority to increase his wealth; family quarrels frequently occurred; and, in the time of the Hadj, they often waylaid small parties of pilgrims in their route from Medina or Djidda to Mekka, plundering those who made no defence, and killing those who resisted.

After a long struggle, Serour succeeded at length in reducing the Sherifs to obedience, chiefly by cultivating the goodwill of the common class of Mekkawys, and of the Bedouins, by his great simplicity of manners, personal frugality, and generosity towards his friends, together with a reputation for excessive bravery and sagacity. He had often made peace with his enemies; but fresh wars as repeatedly broke forth. It is said that he once discovered a conspiracy to murder him in one of his nightly walks round the Kaaba; and that he generously spared the lives of the conspirators, and only banished them. He strengthened the great castle of Mekka; kept a large body of armed slaves and Bedouins constantly in his service, the expenses of which he defrayed by his commercial profits, being an active trader with Yemen; and, finally, he obliged the most powerful Sherif families to expatriate themselves, and seek for refuge in Yemen, while many Sherifs were killed in battle, and others fell by the hands of the executioner. After this, Serour applied himself to re-establish the administration of justice; and numerous acts are related of him, which reflect equal honour upon his love of equity and his sagacity. He drove the Jews from Djidda, where they had acquired considerable riches by their brokerage and fraudulent dealings; protected the pilgrims in their progress through the Hedjaz; and regulated the receipt of customs and taxes, which had previously been levied in a very arbitrary manner. When he died, the whole population of Mekka followed his remains to the grave. He is still considered by the Mekkawys as a kind of saint, and his name is venerated even by the Wahabys.

1785, or 86. After the death of Serour, Abd el Mayn, one of his brothers, succeeded for four or five days, when his younger brother Ghaleb, by his superior skill in intrigue, and by the great popularity which his valour, understanding, and engaging address had acquired for him in the time of Serour, dispossessed Abd el Mayn, and suffered him quietly to retire. During the first years of his reign, Ghaleb was the tool of Serour's powerful slaves and eunuchs, who were completely masters of the town, and indulged in the same disorderly behaviour, injustice, and oppression which had formerly characterized the Sherifs. Ghaleb, however, soon freed himself from their influence, and acquired at length a firmer authority over the Hedjaz than any of his predecessors had possessed, and which he retained till the wars of the Wahabys, and the treachery of Mohammed Aly put an end to his reign. Ghaleb's government was milder than that of Serour, though far from being so just. Very few individuals were put to death by his orders; but he became avaricious, and culprits were often permitted to purchase their lives by large fines. To accomplish this extortion, he filled his prisons with the refractory; but blood only flowed in his transactions with the Wahabys. During his wars with these invaders, the younger sons of Serour Abdulla ibn Serour, and Seyd ibn Serour, attempted to wrest the government from their uncle, but without success; when reconciled with Ghaleb, they were permitted to return quietly to Mekka, and here they resided when Mohammed Aly arrived. He sent Abdulla to Cairo together with Ghaleb, but was ordered by the Porte to set the former at liberty. Abdulla had been once at Constantinople to obtain the Sultan's assistance against Ghaleb. The great temerity of Abdulla has gained him more admirers than friends at Mekka; but it seems probable that, should the Turks be again obliged to abandon the Hedjaz, he would replace his brother Yahia, the present chief, who received the appointment from Mohammed Aly in 1813, and whose reputation and influence at Mekka are only suited to this honorary situation. The Pasha having seized the revenues of the government of Mekka, has assigned to the Sherif a monthly allowance of only fifty purses, or about eight hundred pounds, to support both his troops and his household. The latter is nominally the same it was before the Turkish conquest, and consists of a few Sherifs, some Mekkawys, and Abyssinian or black slaves, who are indiscriminately appointed to the several employments about his person, the pompous titles of which are borrowed from the red book of the Turkish court. At Yembo, Tayf, Mekka, and Djidda, Ghaleb kept his vizier, who was called El Hakem at Mekka and Tayf. He had, besides, his khasnadar, or treasurer; his selahdar, or sword-bearer; moherdar, or keeper of the seal; and a few other officers, who, however, were far from keeping up so strict an etiquette, or being persons of as much consequence, as those officers are in the Turkish court. The whole of the private establishment of Ghaleb consisted of fifty or sixty servants and officers, and as many slaves and eunuchs. Besides his wives, he kept about two dozen of Abyssinian slaves, and double that number of females to attend upon them and to nurse his children. In his stables were from thirty to forty horses of the best Arabian breed; half a dozen mules, upon which he sometimes rode; and as many dromedaries. I learned from one of his old servants, that an erdeb (about fifteen bushels) was issued daily from the store for the use of the household; this, with perhaps half a hundred weight of butter, and two sheep, formed the principal expenditure of provision. It was partly consumed by the Bedouins, who came to Mekka upon business, and who were in the habit of repairing to the Sherif's house, to claim his hospitality, just as they would alight at the tent of a Sheikh in an encampment in the Desert. When they departed, their sacks were filled with provisions for the road, such being the Arab custom, and the Sherifs of Mekka having always shown an anxious desire to treat the Bedouins with kindness and liberality.

The dress of the Sherif is the same as that of all the heads of Sherif families at Mekka; consisting, usually, of an Indian silk gown, over which is thrown a white *abba*, of the finest manufacture of El Ahsa, in the Persian Gulf; a Cashmere shawl, for the head; and yellow slippers, or sometimes sandals, for the feet. I saw no Mekkawy Sherifs with green turbans. Such of them as enter into the service of government, or are brought up to arms, and who are called by the Mekkawys exclusively "Sherifs," generally wear coloured Cashmere shawls; the others, who lead a private life, or are employed in the law and the mosque, tie a small white muslin shawl round their caps. The Sherifs, however, possess one distinguishing mark of dress—a high woollen cap of a green colour, round which they tie the white muslin or the Cashmere shawl; beyond which the cap projects, so as to screen the wearer's face from the rays of the sun: for its convenience in this respect, it is sometimes used also by elderly persons; but this is far from being a common fashion.

When the Sherif rides out, he carries in his hand a short, slender stick, called *metrek*, such as the Bedouins sometimes use in driving their camels; a horseman, who rides close by him, carries in his hand an umbrella or canopy, of Chinese design, adorned with silk tassels, which he holds over the Sherif's head when the sun incommodes him. This is the only sign of royalty by which the Sherif is distinguished when he appears in public; and even this is not used when he walks in the street. The Wahabys compelled him to lay aside the canopy, and to go on foot to the mosque, alleging as a reason, that it was inconsistent with the requisite humility, to come into the presence of the Kaaba on horseback. But when Ghaleb was in full power at Mekka, he obliged the Pashas who accompanied the pilgrim caravan, to acknowledge his right of precedency on all occasions; and he disseminated throughout the Hedjaz a belief that his rank was superior to that of any officer of the Porte; and that even at Constantinople the Sultan himself ought, in strictness of etiquette, to rise and salute him. I have already mentioned the annual investiture of the Sherif by the Kaftandjy Bashy. According to the ceremonial practised on the arrival of the caravan, the Sherif pays the first visit to the Pasha, or Emir el Hadj. The latter, on returning the visit, receives a horse, richly caparisoned, from the Sherif. After the return of the Hadj from Wady Muna, the Pasha presents him, on the first day, with a similar horse; and they both exchange visits in their tents at Muna. When the caravan is ready to leave Mekka, on its return home, the Sherif visits the Pasha a second time, in his camp outside the town, and is there presented with another horse.

The Sherif is supposed to have under his jurisdiction all the Bedouin tribes of the Hedjaz; at least they are named in his own and the Porte's registers, as the dutiful subjects of the Sultan and of the Sherif. When in the full enjoyment of his power, Ghaleb possessed a considerable influence over these tribes, but without any direct authority. They looked upon the Sherif, with his soldiers and friends, in the same light as one of their own Sheikhs, with his adherents; and all the laws of war current in the Desert, were strictly observed by the Sherif. In his late expeditions against the Wahabys, he was accompanied by six or eight thousand Bedouins, who joined him, as they would have joined another Sheikh, without receiving any regular pay for their services, but following their own chiefs, whose interest and attachment Ghaleb purchased by presents.

To those who are unacquainted with the politics of the Desert, the government of Mekka will present some singularities; but every thing is easily explained, if the Sherif be considered as a Bedouin chief, whom wealth and power have led to assume arbitrary sway; who has adopted the exterior form of an Osmanly governor, but who strictly adheres to all the ancient usages of his nation. In former times, the heads of the Sherif families at Mekka exercised the same influence as the fathers of families in the Bedouin encampments; the authority of the great chief afterwards prevailed, and the others were obliged to submit; but they still retain, in many cases, the rights of their forefathers. The rest of the Mekkawys were considered by the contending parties, not as their equals, but as settlers under their domination; in the same way as Bedouin tribes fight for villages which pay to them certain assessments, and whose inhabitants are considered to be on a much lower level than themselves. The Mekkawys, however, were not to be dealt with like inhabitants of the towns in the northern provinces of Turkey; they took a part in the feuds of the Sherifs, and shared in the influence and power obtained by their respective patrons. When Serour and Ghaleb successively possessed themselves of a more uncontrolled authority than any of their predecessors had enjoyed, the remaining Sherifs united more closely with the Mekkawys, and, till the most recent period, formed with them a body respectable for its warlike character, as was evinced in frequent quarrels among themselves; and a resistance against the government, when its measures affected their lives, although they were so far reduced as never to revolt when their purses only were assailed.

The government of Ghaleb, notwithstanding his pecuniary extortion, was lenient and cautious: he respected the pride of the Mekkawys, and seldom made any attempts against the personal safety or even fortunes of individuals, although they smarted under those regulations which affected them collectively. He permitted his avowed enemies to live peaceably in the bosom of their families, and the people to indulge in bloody affrays among themselves, which frequently happened either in consequence of blood-revenge, or the jealousies which the inhabitants of different quarters of the town entertained against each other; sometimes fighting for weeks together, but generally with sticks, lances, and daggers, and not with fire-arms.

The Sherifs, or descendants of Mohammed, resident at Mekka and in the neighbourhood, who delight in arms, and are so often engaged in civil broils, have a practice of sending every male child, eight days after its birth, to some tent of the neighbouring Bedouins, where it is brought up with the children of the tent, and educated like a true Bedouin for eight or ten years, or till the boy is able to mount a mare, when his father takes him back to his home. During the whole of the above period, the boy never visits his parents, nor enters the town, except when in his sixth month; his foster-mother then carries him on a short visit to his family, and immediately returns with him to her tribe. The child is, in no instance, left longer than thirty days after his birth in the hands of his mother; and his stay among the Bedouins is sometimes protracted till his thirteenth or fifteenth year. By this means, he becomes familiar with all the perils and vicissitudes of a Bedouin life; his body is inured to fatigue and privation; and he acquires a knowledge of the pure language of the Bedouins, and an influence among them that becomes afterwards of much importance to him. There is no sherif, from the chief down to the poorest among them, who has not been brought up among the Bedouins; and many of them are also married to Bedouin girls. The sons of the reigning Sherif family were usually educated among the tribe of Adouan, celebrated for the prowess and hospitality of its members; but it has been so much reduced by the intestine wars of the Sherifs, in which they always took part, and by the late invasion of Mohammed Aly, that they found it expedient to abandon the territory of the Hedjaz, and seek refuge in the encampments of the tribes of the Eastern plain. Othman el Medhayfe, the famous Wahaby chief, a principal instrument employed by Saoud in the subjugation of the Hedjaz, was himself a Sheikh of Adouan; and Sherif Ghaleb had married his sister. The other Sherifs sent their children to the encampments of Hodheyl, Thekyf, Beni Sad, and others; some few to the Koreysh, or Harb.

The Bedouins in whose tent a Sherif has been educated, were ever after treated by him with the same respect as his own parents and brethren; he called them respectively, father, mother, brother; and received from them corresponding appellations. Whenever they came to Mekka, they lodged at the house of their pupil, and never left it without receiving presents. During his pupilage, the Sherif gave the name of Erham to the more distant relatives of the Bedouin family, who were also entitled to his friendship and attention; and he considered himself, during his life, as belonging to the encampment in which he had passed his early years: he termed its inhabitants "our people," or, "our family;" took the liveliest interest in their various fortunes; and, when at leisure, often paid them a visit during the spring months, and sometimes accompanied them in their wanderings and their wars.

Sherif Ghaleb always showed himself extremely attentive to his Bedouin foster-parents; whenever they visited him, he used to rise from his seat, and embrace them, though in no way distinguished from any meanly-dressed inhabitant of the Desert. Of course, it often happened that Sherif boys could not easily be induced to acknowledge their real parents at home; and they sometimes escaped, and rejoined the friends of their infancy, the Bedouins in the Desert.

The custom which I have just described is very ancient in Arabia. Mohammed was educated among foreigners, in the tribe of Beni Sad; and his example is continually quoted by the Mekkawys, when speaking of the practice still usual among the Sherifs. But they are almost the only people in Arabia by whom it is now followed. The Bedouins called Mowalys,[*] once a potent tribe, but now reduced to a small number, and pasturing their flocks in the vicinity of Aleppo, are the only Arabs among whom I met with any thing similar. With them it is an esta-

---

[*] This tribe is originally from the Hedjaz: it lived in the neighbourhood of Medina, and is often mentioned by the historians of that town, during the first century after Mohammed.

blished usage, that the son of the chief of that tribe should be educated in the family of another individual of the same tribe, but generally of a different encampment, until he is sufficiently old to be able to shift for himself. The pupil calls his tutor Morabby, and displays the greatest regard for him during the rest of his life.

The Sherifs derive considerable advantages from their Bedouin education; acquiring not only strength and activity of body, but some part of that energy, freedom of manners, and boldness, which characterize the inhabitant of the Desert; together with a greater regard to the virtues of good faith and hospitality, than if they had been brought up in Mekka.

I did not see many Sherifs. Of the small number now remaining, some were employed, during my residence at Mekka, either as guides with the army of Mohammed Aly, or were incorporated by him in a small corps of Bedouins, commanded by Sherif Radjeh, one of their most distinguished members; or in the service of Sherif Yahya, who sent them on duty to the advanced posts towards Yemen. Some of them had retired, after Ghaleb was taken, to the Wahabys, or to Yemen, where a few of them still remained. Those whom I had an opportunity of seeing, were distinguished by fine manly countenances, strongly expressive of noble extraction; and they had all the exterior manners of Bedouins; free, bold, frank, warm friends; bitter enemies; seeking for popularity, and endowed with an innate pride, which, in their own estimation, sets them far above the Sultan of Constantinople. I never beheld a handsomer man than Sherif Radjeh, whose heroism I have mentioned in my history of Mohammed Aly's campaign, and the dignity of whose deportment would make him remarked among thousands; nor can a more spirited and intelligent face be easily imagined, than was that of Sherif Ghaleb. Yahya, the present Sherif, is of a very dark complexion, like that of his father; his mother was a dark brown Abyssinian slave.

The Mekkawys give the Sherifs little credit for honesty, and they have constantly shown great versatility of character and conduct; but this could hardly be otherwise, considering the sphere and the times in which they moved: their Bedouin education has certainly made them preferable, in many respects, to the common class of Mekkawys.

It is a rule among the Sherifs, that the daughters of the reigning chief can never marry; and while their brothers are often playing in the streets with their comrades, from whom they are in no way distinguished, either in dress or dignity of appearance, the unfortunate girls remain shut up in the father's house. I have seen a son of Sherif Ghaleb, whose father was then in exile at Salonica, play before the door of his house. But I have heard that, when the boys of the reigning Sherif return from the Desert, and are not yet sufficiently grown up to appear with a manly air in public, they are kept within their father's house or court-yard, and seen only by the inmates of the family, appearing for the first time in public, on horseback, by the side of their father; from which period they are considered to be of age, soon after marry, and take a share in public affairs.

The greater part of the Sherifs of Mekka, and those especially of the reigning tribe of Dwy Zeyd, are strongly suspected to be Muselman sectaries, belonging to the Zyoud, or followers of Zeyd, a sect which has numerous proselytes in Yemen, and especially in the mountains about Sada. This, however, the Sherifs do not acknowledge, but comply with the doctrines of the orthodox sect of Shafeÿs, to which most of the Mekkawys belong; but the Sherifs residing abroad do not deny it; and whenever points of law are discussing upon which the Zyoud are at variance with the Sunnys, the Sherifs always decline taking an active part in the discussion.

I believe that the Zeyds are divided into different sects. Those of Yemen and Mekka acknowledge as the founder of their creed El Imam el Hady ill el Hak Yahyn ibn el Hosseyn, who traces his pedigree to Hassan, the son of Aly. He was born at Rass, in the province of Kasym, in A. H. 245, and first rose as a sectary at Sada, in Yemen, in 280. He fought with the Abassides, took Sana, out of which he was driven, afterwards attacked the Karmates, and died of poison at Sada in A. H. 298. Others trace the origin of this sect higher, to Zeyd ibn Aly Zeyn el Aabedyn ibn el Hosseyn ibn Aly ibn Aby Taleb, who was killed at Koufa in A. H. 121, by the party of the Khalif Hesham. The

Zeydites appear, generally, to entertain a great veneration for Aly; at the same time that they do not, as the Persians, curse Abou Beker and Omar. They entertain notions different from those of the Sunnys respecting the succession of the twelve Imams, but agree, in other respects, much more with them than with the Persians. The Zeydites of Yemen, to whom the Imam of Sana himself belongs, designate their creeds as the fifth of the orthodox Mohammedan creeds, next to the Hanefys, Shafeys, Malekys, and Hanbalys, and for that reason they are called Ahl el Khams Mezaheb. In Yemen they publicly avow their doctrines; at Mekka they conceal them. I heard that one of their principal tenets is, that in praying, whether in the mosque, or at home, no other expressions should be used than those contained in the Koran, or such as are formed from passages of that book.

The Mekkawys regard the Zyoud as heretics; and assert that, like Persians, they hold in disrespect the immediate successors of Mohammed. Stories are related of the Zyoud in Yemen writing the name of Mawya over the most unclean part of their houses, to show their contempt of him; but such tenets are not avowed, and the Sherifs agree outwardly in every point with the Sunnys, whatever may be their private opinions.

I have already stated that the Kadhy of Mekka is sent annually from Constantinople, according to the usual practice of the Turkish government with respect to the great cities of the empire. This system began with the early emperors, who thought that, by depriving the provincial governors of the administration of justice, and placing it in the hands of a learned man sent periodically from Constantinople, and quite independent of the governors, they might prevent the latter from exercising any undue influence over the courts of law, at the same time that the consequences likely to result from the same judge remaining in office for any length of time were avoided. But manners are very different throughout the empire from what they were three hundred years ago. In every town the Kadhy is now under the immediate influence of the governor, who is left to tyrannize at pleasure, provided he sends his regular subsidies to the Porte. No person can gain a suit at law unless he enjoys credit with the government, or gives a bribe to the judge, which the governor shares or connives at, in return for the Kadhy's compliance with his interests in other cases. The fees of court are enormous, and generally swallow up one fourth of the sum in litigation; while the court is deaf to the clearest right, if not supported by largesses to the Kadhy and the swarm of officers and servants who surround his seat. These disorders are countenanced by the Porte: the office of Kadhy is there publicly sold to the best bidder, with the understanding that he is to remunerate himself by the perquisites of his administration.

In those countries where Arabs flock to his court, the Kadhy, who generally knows but little of the Arabic language, is in the hands of his interpreter, whose office is usually permanent, and who instructs every new Kadhy in the modes of bribery current in the place, and takes a full share of the harvest. The barefaced acts of injustice and shameless briberies daily occurring in the Mehkames, or halls of justice, would seem almost incredible to an European, and especially an Englishman.

The Kadhy of Mekka has shared the fate of his brother judges in other parts of the empire, and has been for many years so completely under the influence of the Sherif, that all suits were carried directly before his tribunal, and the Kadhy was thus reduced to spend his time in unprofitable leisure. I was informed by the Kadhy himself, that the Grand Signior, in consideration of the trifling emoluments of the situation, had, for some time back, been in the habit of paying to the Kadhy of Mekka one hundred purses per annum out of his treasury. Since the conquest of Mohammed Aly, the Kadhy has recovered his importance, in the same proportion as the influence of the Sherif has been diminished. When I was at Mekka, all law-suits were decided in the Mehkame. Mohammed Aly seldom interposed his authority, as he wished to conciliate the good-will of the Arabs, and the Kadhy himself seems to have received from him very strict orders to act with circumspection; for justice was, at this time, tolerably well administered, at least in comparison with other tribunals; and the inhabitants were not averse to the new order of things. The Kadhy of Mekka appoints to the law-offices of Djidda and Tayf, which are filled by Arabs, not Turks. In law-suits of importance, the Muftis of the four orthodox sects have considerable influence on the decision.

The income of the Sherif is derived principally from the customs paid at Djidda, which, as I have already mentioned, instead of being, according to the intention of the Turkish government, divided between himself and the Pasha of Djidda, were seized wholly by the late Sherifs, and are now in the hands of Mohammed Aly. The customs of Djidda, properly the same as those levied in every other part of the Turkish empire, were much increased by Ghaleb, which was the principal reason why the whole body of merchants opposes him. He had also engrossed too large a share of the commerce to himself. Eight dows belonging to him were constantly employed in the coffee-trade between Yemen, Djidda, and Egypt; and when the sale of that article was slow, he obliged the merchants to purchase his cargoes for ready money at the market-price, in order to send off the sooner his returns of dollars to Yemen. Two of the largest of his vessels (one an English-built ship of three or four hundred tons, purchased at Bombay,) made a voyage annually to the East Indies, and the cargoes which they brought home were either sold to the Hadj at Mekka, or were divided among the merchants of Djidda, who were forced to purchase them.

Besides the port of Djidda, that of Yembo, where the Sherif kept a governor, was subjected to similar duties. He also levied a tax as well upon all cattle and provisions carried from the interior of the country into Djidda, as upon those carried into Mekka, Tayf, and Yembo, except what came with the two great hadj-caravans from the north, which passed every where duty-free. The inhabitants of Mekka and Djidda pay no other taxes than those just mentioned, their houses, persons, and property being free from all other imposts; an advantage which they have never sufficiently acknowledged, though they might have readily drawn a comparison between themselves and their neighbours of Syria and Egypt. The other branches of the Sherif's revenues were the profits derived from the sale of provisions at Mekka, of which, although he did not monopolize them like Mohammed Aly, yet he had always such a considerable stock on hand, as enabled him to influence the daily prices; the capitation-tax on all Persian hadjys, whether coming by land from Baghdad, or by the way of the Red Sea and Yemen; and presents to a considerable amount, either offered to him gratuitously, or extorted from the rich hadjys of all countries.*

Of the money sent from Constantinople to the holy city, temple, &c. a large portion was appropriated by the Sherif to his own treasury; and it is said that he regularly shared in all the presents which were made to the mosque. Ghaleb possessed considerable landed property; many of the gardens round Tayf, and of the plantations in the valley of Hosseynye, Wady Fatme, Wady Lymoun, and Wady Medyk, belonged to him. At Djidda he had many houses and caravansaries, which he let out to foreigners; and so far resembled his successor Mohammed Aly, that the most trifling profit became a matter of consideration with him, his attention being constantly directed towards the acquiring of wealth. The annual revenue of Ghaleb, during the plenitude of his power, may have amounted to about three hundred and fifty thousand pounds sterling; but, since the occupation of the Hedjaz by the Wahabys, it has probably not exceeded half that sum.

As Ghaleb was a merchant and land-owner, and procured all the articles of consumption at the first-hand, the maintenance of his household, with his women and slaves, did not, I should imagine, require above twenty thousand pounds sterling per annum. In time of peace the Sherif kept a small permanent force, not exceeding five hundred men, of whom about one hundred were in garrison at Djidda, fifty at Tayf, as many at Yembo, and the rest at Mekka: of this body about eight hundred were cavalry, in addition to his own mounted household. Many of the soldiers were his domestic slaves; but the greater part were Bedouins from different parts of Arabia; those from Yemen, the mountains of Asyr, and Nedjed, being the most numerous. Their pay was from eight to twelve dollars per month;

* Formerly, when the Sherifs of Mekka were more powerful, they levied a tribute upon the two great pilgrim-caravans, similar to that exacted by the Bedouins on the road. Abou Nima, in A. H. 654, took from every camel of the Yemen caravan thirty dirhems, and fifty upon every one in the Egyptian caravan.

and they were commanded by Sherifs, whom they obeyed as Bedouins obey their leader during war, that is to say, that, trained to no regular exercise, they accompanied the Sherif whenever he took a ride out of the town, and on returning fired off their guns, according to the Arabian custom, in leaping wildly about. The arms of the infantry were a matchlock and crooked knife; the horsemen had a lance.

When Ghaleb engaged in war, this force was increased by the accession of many Sherifs and their retinues, who received no pay, but occasional presents, and a share in the booty acquired; these wars being generally directed against some Bedouin tribes, whose cattle was the sole object of invasion. Upon these occasions, the Sherif was joined also by other Bedouins, who returned with their Sheikhs to their homes, as soon as the expedition was terminated. On the breaking out of the Wahaby war, and when the Wahabys began to make successful attacks upon the Hedjaz, Ghaleb found it necessary to increase his standing force; he therefore added to it a number of black slaves, thereby augmenting it to eight hundred, following, in this respect, the practice of his predecessors, who always considered their own purchased slaves as the most faithful men under their command;[*] he also enlisted additional numbers of Bedouins, and had, during the whole of the contest, generally from two to three thousand men; a number thought fully sufficient to guard his cities. Whenever he planned an attack on the Wahabys, he collected his allies among the Bedouins, and advanced several times towards Nedjed with an united force of ten thousand men. When those allies were obliged, successively, to yield to the invaders, and the southern Bedouins, on whom Ghaleb always principally depended, were conquered by the great exertions and activity of Othman el Medhayfe, Ghaleb found himself alone, with his few troops, unable to prolong the contest, and was soon driven to extremities and obliged to submit, though he still kept a corps of troops in his pay, after Saoud had obtained firm possession of the Hedjaz, and conducted his affairs with such consummate

---

[*] During the last century, the Sherifs of Mekka constantly kept a small corps of Georgian Mamelouks as their body-guard.

skill, as to maintain his authority, and command the respect of the Wahabys.

The expenses attending the increased forces of the Sherif during the Wahaby war, were considerable; it was necessary to make donations to the Sherif and the Bedouins, to keep them in his interest; but it happened, for once, that his interests were equally their own; and Bedouins, though never tired of asking for presents, are generally content with small sums. It may hence be easily conceived that Ghaleb never, during any period of his reign, lived up to the amount of his income; and it was a general, and, I believe, well-founded opinion in the Hedjaz, that during the twenty-seven years of his official life, he had amassed a large treasure in money. When Mohammed Aly seized his person, the amount of the whole of his disposable property found at Mekka and Djidda, was calculated at about two hundred thousand or two hundred and fifty thousand pounds sterling; and it was presumed that he had either secreted his treasure in the castle of Mekka, or sent it to his friends in India, while Mohammed Aly was making preparations for his attack. It is most probable that he employed both modes of secreting his wealth, and thus made another addition to the large sums daily buried in the East, by persons in authority, as well as by private individuals. But such is the bad use to which Eastern rulers apply their riches, that the public prosperity of the country suffers little by the loss.*

* The prevalence of the practice of concealing riches in Turkey, and the cause of it, will at once appear from the following account of a circumstance which happened in 1813, at Cairo. Mohammed Aly having demanded 15,000 purses from the Copts employed in the finances of Egypt, they divided the sum among themselves; and Moallem Felteos, an old man, who had been in former times a chief financier, was assessed at twelve hundred purses, or about 18,000*l.* sterling: this he refused to pay, alleging his poverty; but, after long parleys, at last offered to give two hundred purses. The Pasha sent for him, threatened, and, seeing him obstinate, ordered him to be beaten: after receiving five hundred strokes with the stick, and being nearly half dead, he swore that he could pay no more than two hundred purses. Mohammed Aly thought he was telling the truth; but his son, Ibrahim Pasha, who happened to be present, said that he was sure the man had more money. Felteos, therefore, received three hundred additional strokes, after which he confessed that he was possessed of the sum demanded, and promised to pay it. He was then permitted to

return home; and at the end of a fortnight, being so much recovered from the effects of his beating that he could walk about, commissioners were sent to his house from the Pasha, labourers were called, and Felteos descended with them into the privy of his house, at the bottom of which they removed a large stone which closed up a small passage containing a vaulted niche, where two iron chests were deposited. On opening these, two thousand purses in sequins were found, twelve hundred of which the Pasha took, and left the remainder to the owner, who died three months after, not in consequence of the blows he had received, but of grief for the loss of his money. Had he been able secretly to remove the treasure, he would probably have done so, had not a guard been posted in his house immediately on his promising to pay; the Pasha suspecting that the money was concealed in some secret spot, according to a practice general in the East.

CLIMATE AND DISEASES OF MEKKA AND DJIDDA.

THE climate of Mekka is sultry and unwholesome; the rocks which enclose its narrow valley, intercept the wind, especially that from the north, and reflect the rays of the sun with redoubled heat. In the months of August, September, and October, the heat is excessive: during my residence at Mekka a suffocating hot wind pervaded the atmosphere for five successive days in September. The rainy season usually begins in December; but the rains are not uninterrupted, as in other tropical countries falling only at intervals of five or six days but then with great violence. Showers are not unfrequent, even in summer: the Mekkawys say that the clouds coming from the sea-side are those which copiously irrigate the ground; while those which come from the East, or the high mountains, produce only mere showers, or gushes. The want of rain is very frequently felt here: I was told that four successive years of copious rains are seldom experienced; which is, probably, the main reason why all the Bedouins in this neighbourhood are poor, the greater part of their cattle dying in years of drought, from want of pasturage.

The air of Mekka is generally very dry. Dews begin to fall in the month of January, after a few heavy showers of rain: the contrary is the case at Djidda, where the atmosphere, even during the greatest heat, is damp, arising from the sea vapours, and the numerous marshes on that low coast. The dampness of the air is there so great, that in the month of September, in a hot and perfectly clear day, I found my upper gown wet completely through, from being two hours in the open air. There are heavy dews also by night, during that month and in October; thick fogs appeared on the coast, in the evening and morning. During the summer months, the wind blows generally between east and south, seldom veering to the west, but sometimes to the north. In September, the regular northerly winds set in, and continue during the whole winter. In the Hedjaz, as on the sea-coast of Egypt, the northeast wind is more damp than any other; and during its prevalence, the stone pavement in the interior of the houses always appeared as if covered with moisture.

The diseases prevalent in both towns are much the same; and the coast of the Hedjaz is perhaps among the most unhealthy countries of the East. Intermittent fevers are extremely common, as are likewise dysenteries, which usually terminate in swellings of the abdomen, and often prove fatal. Few persons pass a whole year without a slight attack of these disorders; and no stranger settles at Mekka or Djidda, without being obliged to submit, during the first months of his residence, to one of these distempers; a fact, of which ample proof was afforded in the Turkish army, under Mohammed Aly Pacha. Inflammatory fevers are less frequent at Djidda than at Mekka; but the former place is often visited with a putrid fever, which, as the inhabitants told me, sometimes appeared to be contagious; fifty persons having been known to die of it in one day. Asamy and Fasy mention frequent epidemical diseases at Mekka: in A. H. 671, a pestilence broke out, which carried off fifty persons a day; and in 749, 793, and 829, others also infected the town: in the latter year two thousand persons died. These authors, however, never mention the plague; nor had it made its appearance in the Hedjaz within the memory of the oldest inhabitants; whence a belief was entertained,· that the Almighty protected this holy province from its ravages; but, in the spring of 1815, it broke out with great violence, as I shall mention in another place, and Mekka and Djidda lost, perhaps, one-sixth of their population.

Ophthalmia is very little known in the Hedjaz. I saw a single instance of leprosy, in a Bedouin at Tayf. The elephantiasis and Guinea-worm are not uncommon, especially the former, of which I have seen many frightful cases. It is said that stone in the bladder is frequent at Mekka, caused, perhaps, by the peculiar quality of the water; to the badness of which many other diseases also may be ascribed in this hot country, where such quantities of it are daily drunk. I heard that the only surgeons who knew how to perform the operation of extracting the stone from the bladder, are Bedouins of the tribe of Beni Sad, who live in the mountains, about thirty miles south of Tayf. In time of peace, some of them repair annually to Mekka, to perform this operation, the knowledge of which they consider as a secret hereditary in some families of their tribe. They are said to use a common razor, and, in general, with success.

Sores on the legs, especially on the shin-bone, are extremely common both at Mekka and Djidda; but more so at the latter place, where the dampness of the atmosphere renders their cure much more difficult; indeed, in that damp climate, the smallest scratch, or bite of any insect, if neglected, becomes a sore, and soon after an open wound: nothing is more common than to see persons walking in the streets, having on their legs sores of this kind, which, if neglected, often corrode the bone. As their cure demands patience, and, above all, repose, the lower classes seldom apply the proper remedies in time; and when they have increased to such a state as to render their application indispensably necessary, no good surgeons are to be found; fever ensues, and many of the patients die. I believe that one-fourth of the population of Djidda is constantly afflicted with ulcers on their legs; the bad nature of these sores is further aggravated by the use of seawater for ablutions.

During my stay at Mekka, I seldom enjoyed perfect good health. I was twice attacked by fever; and, after the departure of the Syrian Hadj, by a violent diarrhœa, from which I had scarcely recovered when I set out for Medina. In those days, even when I was free from disease, I felt great lassitude, a depression of spirits, and a total want of appetite. During the five days of the Hadj, I was luckily in good health, though I was under great apprehensions from the consequences of taking the ihram. My strength was greatly diminished, and it required much effort, whenever I left my room, to walk about.

I attributed my illness chiefly to bad water, previous experience having taught me that my constitution is very susceptible of the want of good light water, that prime article of life in eastern countries. Brackish water in the Desert is perhaps salutary to travellers: heated as they are by the journey, and often labouring under obstructions from the quality of their food on the road, it acts as a gentle aperient, and thus supplies the place of medicinal draughts; but the contrary is the case when the same water is used during a continued sedentary residence, when long habit only can accustom the stomach to receive it. Had I found myself in better health and spirits, I should probably have visited some of the neighbouring valleys to the south, or passed a few months among the Bedouins of the Hedjaz; but the worst effect of ill health upon a traveller, is the pusillanimity which accompanies it, and the apprehensions with which it fills the mind, of fatigues and dangers, that, under other circumstances, would be thought undeserving of notice.

The current price of provisions at Mekka in December, 1814, was as follows:—

	Piastres.	Paras.
1 lb. of beef	2	10
1 lb. of mutton	2	0
1 lb. of camel's flesh	1	0
1 lb. of butter	5	0
1 lb. of fresh unsalted cheese	3	0
A fowl	6	0
An egg	0	8
1 lb. of milk	2	0
1 lb. of vegetables, viz. leek, spinach, turnips, radishes, calabashes, egg-plants, green onions, petrosiles, &c. &c.	0	30

	Piastres.	Paras.
A small, round, flat loaf of bread	0	20
1 lb. of dry biscuits	0	32
1 lb. of raisins from Tayf	1	20
1 lb. of dates	0	25
1 lb. of sugar (Indian)	2	10
1 lb. of coffee	2	20
A pomegranate	0	15
An orange	0	15
A lemon, (the size of a walnut, the same species as the Egyptian lemon)	0	10
1 lb. of good Syrian tobacco	6	0
1 lb. of common tobacco	1	30
1 lb. of tombac, or tobacco for the Persian pipe	3	0
1 keyle of wheat	3	0
1 do. of flour	3	20
1 do. of Indian rice	3	0
1 do. of lentils from Egypt	2	30
1 do. of dried locusts	1	0
A skin of water	1	20
As much wood as will cook two dishes	0	20
A labourer for the day	3	0
A porter for going in town the distance of half a mile	1	0
Common wages of servants,* besides clothes and food, per month	30	0
Wages of craftsmen, as smiths, carpenters, &c. per day, besides food	5	0

N.B. The Spanish dollar was worth from nine to twelve piastres during my residence at Mekka, changing its value almost daily.

* The Mekkawys have only slaves; but many Egyptians are ready to enter into the service of hadjys. The most common servants in the families of Mekka are the younger sons or some poor relations.

One piastre equal to forty paras or diwanys, as they are called in the Hedjaz. The pound, or rotolo, of Mekka, has a hundred and forty-four drams. The Egyptian erdeb, equivalent to about fifteen English bushels, is divided here into fifty keyles or measures. At Medina the erdeb is divided into ninety-six keyles. The pound of Djidda is nearly double that of Mekka.

THE HADJ, OR PILGRIMAGE.

THE time has passed (and, probably for ever,) when hadjys or pilgrims, from all regions of the Muselman world, came every year in multitudes, that they might visit devotionally the sacred places of the Hedjaz. An increasing indifference to their religion, and an increase of expense attending the journey, now deter the greater part of the Mohammedans from complying with that law of the Koran, which enjoins to every Moslim who can afford it, the performance of a pilgrimage to Mekka, once at least in his life. To those whom indispensable occupations confine to their homes, the law permits a substitution of prayers; but even with this injunction few people now comply, or it is evaded by giving a few dollars to some hadjy, who, taking from several persons commissions of the same kind, includes all their names in the addition consequently made to the prayers recited by him at the places of holy visit. When Muselman zeal was more ardent, the difficulties of the journey being held to increase the merit of it, became with many an additional incitement to join the caravans, and to perform the whole journey by land; but at present, most of the pilgrims do not join any regular Hadj caravan, but reach Djidda by sea from Egypt, or the Persian Gulf; commercial and lucrative speculations being the chief inducements to this journey.

In 1814, many hadjys had arrived at Mekka, three or four months previous to the prescribed time of the pilgrimage. To pass the Ramadhan in this holy city, is a great inducement with such as can afford the expense, to hasten their arrival, and prolong their residence in it.

THE HADJ, OR PILGRIMAGE. 247

About the time when the regular caravans were expected, at least four thousand pilgrims from Turkey, who had come by sea, were already assembled at Mekka, and perhaps half that number from other distant quarters of the Mohammedan world. Of the five or six regular caravans which, formerly, always arrived at Mekka a few days before the Hadj, two only made their appearance this year; these were from Syria and Egypt; the latter composed entirely of people belonging to the retinue of the commander of the Hadj, and his troops; no pilgrims having come by land from Cairo, though the road was safe.

The Syrian caravan has always been the strongest, since the time when the Khalifes, in person, accompanied the pilgrims from Baghdad. It sets out from Constantinople, and collects the pilgrims of Northern Asia in its passage through Anatolia and Syria, until it reaches Damascus, where it remains for several weeks. During the whole of the route from Constantinople to Damascus, every care is taken for the safety and convenience of the caravan; it is accompanied from town to town by the armed forces of the governors; at every station caravan-saries and public fountains have been constructed by former Sultans, to accommodate it on its passage, which is attended so far with continual festivities and rejoicings. At Damascus, it is necessary to prepare for a journey of thirty days, across the Desert to Medina; and the camels which had transported it thus far, must be changed, the Anatolian camel not being able to bear the fatigues of such a journey. Almost every town in the eastern part of Syria furnishes its beasts for the purpose; and the great Bedouin Sheikhs of the frontiers of that country contract largely for camels with the government of Damascus. Their number must be supposed very great, even if the caravan be but thinly attended, when it is considered that besides those carrying water and provisions for the hadjys and soldiers, their horses, and the spare camels brought to supply such as may fail on the road, daily food for the camels themselves must be similarly transported; as well as provisions, which are deposited in castles on the Hadj route, to form a supply for the return. The Bedouins take good care that the camels shall not be overloaded, that the numbers wanted may thus be increased. In 1814, though the caravan consisted of not more than four or five thousand persons, including soldiers and servants, it had fifteen thousand camels.*

The Syrian caravan is very well regulated, though, as in all matters of oriental government, the abuses and exceptions are numerous. The Pasha of Damascus, or one of his principal officers, always accompanies this caravan, and gives the signal for encamping and starting, by firing a musket. On the route, a troop of horsemen ride in front, and another in the rear, to bring up the stragglers. The different parties of hadjys, distinguished by their provinces or towns, keep close together; and each knows its never-varying station in the caravan, which is determined by the geographical proximity of the place from whence it comes. When they encamp, the same order is constantly observed; thus the people from Aleppo always encamp close by those of Homs, &c. This regulation is very necessary to prevent disorder in night-marches.†

The hadjys usually contract for the journey with a Mekowem, one who speculates in the furnishing of camels and provisions to the Hadj.

---

* El Fasy relates that, when the mother of Motasem b'Illah, the last of the Abassides, performed the pilgrimage in A. H. 631, her caravan was composed of one hundred and twenty thousand camels. When Solyman Ibn Abd el Malek performed the pilgrimage in A. H. 97, nine hundred camels were employed in the transport of his wardrobe only. It is observable that none of the Othman Emperors of Constantinople ever performed the pilgrimage in person. The Khalife El Mohdy Abou Abdallah Mohammed expended on his pilgrimage in A. H. 160, thirty millions of dirhems. He carried with him an immense number of gowns to distribute as presents. He built fine houses at every station from Baghdad to Mekka, and caused them to be splendidly furnished; he also erected mile-stones along the whole route, and was the first Khalife who carried snow with him, to cool sherbet on the road, in which he was imitated by many of his successors. Haroun el Rasheid, who performed the pilgrimage nine times, spent, in one of his visits, one million and fifty thousand dynars in presents to the Mekkawys and the poor hadjys. El Melek Nasir eddyn Abou el Maaly, Sultan of Egypt, carried with him, on his pilgrimage in A. H. 719, five hundred camels, for the transport of sweetmeats and confectionary only; and two hundred and eighty for pomegranates, almonds, and other fruits: in his travelling larder were one thousand geese, and three thousand fowls. Vide Makrisi's Treatise *Man Hadj myn el Kholafa.*

† In our author's Syrian Travels, (p. 242.) the reader will find some further remarks on this Hadj-caravan, and in the Appendix to that volume (No. 3.) an account of the route between Damascus and Mekka.—ED.

THE HADJ, OR PILGRIMAGE. 249

From twenty to thirty pilgrims are under the care of the same Mekowem, who has his tents and servants, and saves the hadjys from all fatigue and trouble on the road: their tent, coffee, water, breakfast, and dinner are prepared for them, and they need not take the slightest trouble about packing and loading. If a camel should die, the Mekowem must find another; and, however great may be the want of provisions on the road, he must furnish his passengers with their daily meals. In 1814, the hire of one Mekowem, and the boarding at his table, was one hundred and fifty dollars from Damascus to Medina, and fifty dollars more from Medina to Mekka. Out of these two hundred dollars, sixty were given by the Mekowem to a man who led the camel by the halter during the night-marches; a precaution necessary in so great a caravan, when the rider usually sleeps, and the animal might otherwise easily wander from the path. In addition to the stipulated hire, the Mekowem always receives some presents from his pilgrims. On the return to Syria, the sum is something less, as many camels then go unloaded.

Few travellers choose to perform the journey at their own risk, or upon their own camels; for if they are not particularly protected by the soldiery, or the chief of the caravan, they find it difficult to escape the ill-treatment of the Mekowem at watering-places, as well as on the march; the latter endeavouring to check, by every means in their power, the practice of travelling independent of them, so that it is rarely done except by rich hadjys, who have the means of forming a party of their own amounting to forty or fifty individuals.

At night, torches are lighted, and the daily distance is usually performed between three o'clock in the afternoon, and an hour or two after sun-rise on the following day. The Bedouins who carry provisions for the troops, travel by day only, and in advance of the caravan, the encampment of which they pass in the morning, and are overtaken in turn, and passed by the caravan on the following night, at their own resting-place. The journey with these Bedouins is less fatiguing than with the great body of the caravan, as a regular night's rest is obtained; but their bad character deters most pilgrims from joining them.

At every watering-place on the route are a small castle and a large tank, at which the camels water. The castles are garrisoned by a few persons, who remain during the whole year to guard the provisions deposited there. It is at these watering-places, which belong to the Bedouins, that the Sheikhs of the tribes meet the caravan, and receive the accustomed tribute. Water is plentiful on the route: the stations are no where more distant than eleven or twelve hours' march; and in winter, pools of rain-water are frequently found. Those pilgrims who can travel with a litter, or on commodious camel-saddles, may sleep at night, and perform the journey with little inconvenience; but of those whom poverty, or the desire of soon acquiring a large sum of money, induces to follow the caravan on foot, or to hire themselves as servants, many die on the road from fatigue.

The Egyptian caravan, which starts from Cairo, is under the same regulations as the Syrian, but seldom equals the latter in numbers, being composed of Egyptians only, besides the military escort. Its route is more dangerous and fatiguing than that of the Syrian caravan; the road along the shore of the Red Sea leading through the territories of wild and warlike tribes of Bedouins, who frequently endeavour to cut off a part of the caravan by open force. The watering-places too are much fewer on this route than on the other; three days frequently intervening between the wells, which are, besides, seldom copious, and, with the exception of two or three, are of bad brackish water. In 1814, this caravan was composed of soldiers only with the retinue of the sacred camel, and some public officers; all the Egyptian pilgrims having preferred taking the route by Suez. In 1816, several grandees of Cairo joined the Hadj, one of whom had one hundred and ten camels for the transport of his baggage and retinue, and eight tents: his travelling expenses in going and coming must have amounted to ten thousand pounds. There were also about five hundred peasants, with their women, from upper and lower Egypt, who were less afraid of the fatigues and dangers of the Desert than of the Sea. I saw with them a party of public women and dancing-girls, whose tents and equipage were among the most splendid in the caravan. Female hadjys of a similar class accompany the Syrian caravan also.

The Persian Hadj, which used to set out from Baghdad, and come through Nedjed to Mekka, was discontinued about the time when the Wahabys stopped the Syrian Hadj. After Abdullah ibn Saoud had made peace with Tousoun Pasha in 1815, it ventured to cross the Desert, and passed by Derayeh unmolested; but within four days' journey of Mekka, it was attacked by the Beni Shammar, a tribe which had remained neuter during the war between Tousoun and the Wahabys. The caravan then returned to Derayeh; through the intercession of Saoud, the goods of which it had been plundered were restored; and he sent a party of his own people to escort it to the holy city.

The Persian caravan is usually escorted by the Ageyl Arabs, of Baghdad. As its pilgrims are known to be sectaries, they are exposed to great extortions on the road: Saoud exacted a heavy capitation-tax from them, as did Sherif Ghaleb at Mekka, amounting in latter times to thirty sequins per head. Persian hadjys are all persons of property, and no pilgrims suffer so much imposition as they during the whole route. Great numbers of them come by sea: they embark at Bassora for Mokha, and if they fall in with the trade-wind, run straight to Djidda; if not, they form themselves into a caravan, and come by land along the coast of Yemen. In 1814, when I was present at the Hadj, the few Persians who came by land, had passed through Baghdad to Syria, and had followed the Syrian caravan, accompanied by Baghdad camel-drivers.

It deserves notice here, that the Persians were not always permitted to come to the holy city; being notorious heretics, who conceal their doctrines only during the Hadj, that they may not give offence to the Sunnys. In 1634, a few years after the temple of Mekka had been rebuilt, Sultan Murad IV. commanded that no Persian of the sect of Aly should be allowed to perform the pilgrimage, or enter the Beittullah. This prohibition was complied with for several years; but the money expended by the Persians soon re-opened the way to Arafat and the Kaaba. We learn from Asamy, that, in 1625, a sectary of Aly was impaled alive at Mekka, because he would not abjure his creed.

The Moggrebyn Hadj caravan has for many years ceased to be regular. It is usually accompanied by a relative of the King of Morocco, and proceeds from his residence by slow marches towards Tunis and Tripoly, collecting additional pilgrims in every district through which it passes. Its route from Tripoly is along the shores of the Syrtis to Derne, and from thence along the coast of Egypt, passing either by Alexandria, or taking the direction of the Natron lakes straight for Cairo, from whence it follows the common pilgrim-route. This caravan returning from Mekka always visits Medina, which the Egyptian Hadj never does, and sometimes extends its route by land as far as Jerusalem. Few troops accompany it; but its pilgrims are well armed, and ready to defend themselves: of the two other great caravans, no body fights but the escort.

The last Moggrebyn caravan passed through Egypt in 1811; the Wahabys permitted them to visit Mekka, as they saw that they were free from those scandalous practices with which they upbraided the Egyptians and Syrians; but the caravan experienced many misfortunes on its return, from enemies, and from a want of guides, and provisions, in consequence of which many of its people died. The pilgrims from Barbary arrive now usually by sea at Alexandria, and re-embark at Suez, in parties of fifty or a hundred at a time. Although poorly dressed, they have generally sufficient money to defray their expenses, and few of them are beggars; of this class, however, I saw a small party, Arabs from Draa, on the S. E. side of Mount Atlas, who had set out with the Egyptian caravan by land in September, 1816. They told me that they had obtained a free passage by sea from Tunis to Alexandria. One of them was a Bedouin of the Shilouh nation, whose encampment, when he left it, was at twenty days' journey from Tombuctou.

In the Moggrebyn caravan also are generally found some natives of the island of Djerba, or Girba, who are strongly suspected of being sectaries of Aly; and some of whom are often stationary at Cairo, inhabiting the quarter called Teyloun, and keeping themselves wholly separate from all other Moggrebyns established in the town. But the far greater part of the caravan is from the kingdom of Marocco. I believe that two thousand is the largest yearly number of Barbary pilgrims. The last caravans comprised altogether from six to eight thousand men.

Two Yemen pilgrim caravans used to arrive at Mekka, in former times, by land. The one called Hadj el Kebsy, started from Sada, in Yemen, and took its course along the mountains to Tayf and to Mekka. Two itineraries of this caravan, with some notices on it, will be found in the Appendix. The other, which was formed of natives of Yemen, and of Persians and Indians who had arrived in the harbours of that country, came along the coast. This caravan was discontinued about 1803, and has not yet been re-established. It was once considerable, and rich in merchandize and coffee; and sometimes enjoyed the honour of being accompanied by the Imáms of Yemen. Like the Syrian and Egyptian caravans, it had a particular place assigned for its camp near Mekka, where a large stone tank was built to supply it with water.

I have seen the route of an Indian pilgrim caravan, laid down in several maps as starting from Maskat, and coming by Nedjed to Mekka; but I could obtain no information respecting it; that such, however, existed formerly, appears from the frequent mention of it made by the historian Asamy. Those persons whom I questioned assured me that no such caravan had arrived within their memory; but I believe that, in the time of peace, Indian, Persian, and Arab beggars, in small parties, sometimes arrive in the Hedjaz by the above route.

Before the power of the Sherifs was broken by the chief Sherif Serour, the former extorted from every caravan that came to Mekka considerable sums, besides the surra to which they were entitled. As soon as they heard of the near approach of a caravan, they issued from Mekka with all their armed retinue and their Bedouin friends, and often disputed with the leaders of the caravan for several days before the amount of the tribute was settled.

To the regular caravans above mentioned, must be added large bodies of Bedouins, which resort to Mekka, during peace, from every part of the Desert; for even among the least religious Bedouins, the title of hadjy is respected: Nedjed sends its pilgrims, as do also the Southern Bedouins. When the Wahabys were in possession of Mekka, hosts of these sectaries came to Arafat, as much, perhaps, for the purpose of paying their court to the chief, who, it was known, liked to see his Arabs collected there, as from religious motives. The last time the Wahabys performed the Hadj was in 1811, shortly after the first defeat of Tousoun Pasha at Djedeyde: they were accompanied by large bodies of Bedouins of Kahtan, Asyr, with others from the most interior part of the Desert. The plunder taken from the Turkish army was sold to the Mekkawys in the market at Arafat. I shall here observe that Aly Bey el Abassy has made a strange mistake with respect to the host of Wahabys, whom he saw entering Mekka at the time of the pilgrimage; for he fancied that they came to take possession of the town, and flattered himself that he was present at the first conquest of Mekka by the Wahabys, while every child in the place could have informed him that this event happened three years before his arrival in the Hedjaz.

At present, as I have already mentioned, most of the hadjys arrive by sea at Djidda: those who come from the north embark at Suez or Cosseir, and among them are a large proportion of the Barbary pilgrims, many Turks from Anatolia and European Turkey, Syrians, and numerous dervishes from Persia, Tartary, and the realms watered by the Indus. The want of shipping on the Red Sea, occasioned by the increased demand for ships to accommodate the Turkish army of the Hedjaz, renders the passage precarious; and they sometimes lose the opportunity, and arrive too late for the pilgrimage, as happened to a party in 1814, who reached Mekka three days after the Hadj, having been long detained at Suez. From the bad quality of the vessels, and their crowded state, the passage is very disagreeable, and often dangerous. Nothing has yet been done by Mohammed Aly Pasha to make this voyage more commodious to the pilgrims; but, on the contrary, he has laid a tax upon them, by forcing a contract for their passage to Djidda at a high price, (it was eighteen dollars a head in 1814), with his governor at Suez, who distributed them on board the Arab ships, and paid to the masters of the vessels only six dollars per head. Formerly hadjys were permitted to carry with them from Suez as great a quantity of provisions as they chose, part of which they afterwards sold in the Hedjaz to some profit; but at present none can embark with more than what is barely sufficient for his own consumption during the pilgrimage. The advantage of carrying along with them their provisions, chiefly butter, flour, biscuits, and dried flesh, purchased at cheap prices in Egypt, for the whole journey, was a principal reason for preferring a sea voyage; for those who go by land must purchase all their provisions at Mekka, where the prices are high.

If the foreign pilgrims, on their arrival at Cairo, cannot hear of any ships lying in the harbour of Suez, they often pursue their way up the Nile as far as Genne, and from thence cross the Desert to Cosseir, from whence it is but a short voyage to Djidda. In returning from the Hedjaz, this Cosseir route is preferred by the greater part of the Turkish hadjys. The natives of Upper Egypt go by Cosseir; likewise many negro pilgrims, after having followed the banks of the Nile from Sennar down to Genne. The usual fare for hadjys from Cosseir to Djidda, is from six to eight dollars.

In the last days of the Mamelouks, when they held possession of Upper Egypt, while the lower was conquered by Mohammed Aly, many Turkish hadjys who repaired to the Hedjaz in small parties, though it was then in the hands of the Wahabys, suffered much ill-treatment from the Mamelouks, on their return to Egypt; many of them were stripped and slain in their passage down the Nile. The sanguinary Greek, Hassan Beg el Yahoudy, boasted of having himself killed five hundred of them. These massacres of inoffensive pilgrims furnished Mohammed Aly with an excuse for his treachery in putting the Mamelouks to death at the castle of Cairo.

Other pilgrims arrive by sea from Yemen and the East Indies, namely, Mohammedan Hindous, and Malays; Cashmerians, and people from Guzerat; Persians, from the Persian Gulf; Arabians, from Bassora, Maskat, Oman, Hadramaut; and those from the coasts of Melinda and Mombaza, who are comprised under the generic name of the people of the Sowahel, i. e. the level coast; Abyssinian Moslims, and many negro pilgrims, who come by the same route. All Moslims dwelling on the coasts of the ocean are certain of finding, towards the period of the Hadj, some ship departing from a neighbouring harbour for the Red Sea; but the greater number arrive with the regular Indian fleet in May, and remain at Mekka or Medina till the time of the Hadj; soon after which, they embark on board country ships at Djidda for Yemen, where they wait till the period of the trade-winds to pass the Bab el Mandeb. Multitudes of beggars come to Mekka from the above-mentioned countries; they get a free passage from charitable individuals in their own country, or the cost of it is defrayed by those who employ them as their proxies in performing the Hadj; but when they land, they are thrown entirely upon the charity of other hadjys; and the alms they collect, must serve to carry them back to their homes.

Few pilgrims, except the mendicants, arrive without bringing some productions of their respective countries for sale; and this remark is applicable as well to the merchants, with whom commercial pursuits are the main object, as to those who are actuated by religious zeal; for to the latter, the profits derived from selling a few native articles at Mekka, diminish, in some degree, the heavy expenses of the journey. The Moggrebyns, for example, bring their red bonnets and woollen cloaks; the European Turks, shoes and slippers, hardware, embroidered stuffs, sweetmeats, amber, trinkets of European manufacture, knit silk purses, &c.; the Turks of Anatolia bring carpets, silks, and Angora shawls; the Persians, cashmere shawls and large silk handkerchiefs; the Afghans, tooth-brushes, called Mesouak Kattary, made of the spongy boughs of a tree growing in Bokhara, beads of a yellow soap-stone, and plain, coarse shawls, manufactured in their own country; the Indians, the numerous productions of their rich and extensive region; the people of Yemen, snakes for the Persian pipes, sandals, and various other works in leather; and the Africans bring various articles adapted to the slave-trade. The hadjys are, however, often disappointed in their expectations of gain; want of money makes them hastily sell their little adventures at the public auctions, and often obliges them to accept very low prices.

Of all the poor pilgrims who arrive in the Hedjaz, none bear a more respectable character for industry than the Negroes, or *Tekrourys*, as they are called here. All the poorer class of Indians turn beggars as soon as they are landed at Djidda. Many Syrians and Egyptians follow the same trade; but not so the Negroes. I have already stated in a former journal, that the latter reach the Hedjaz by the three harbours of Massouah, Souakin, and Cosseir. Those who come by Sennar and Abyssinia to Massoua, are all paupers. The small sum of one dollar carries them from Massoua to the opposite coast of Yemen; and they usually land at Hodeyda. Here they wait for the arrival of a sufficient number of their countrymen, to form a small caravan, and then ascend the mountains of Yemen, along the fertile valleys of which, inhabited by hospitable Arabs, they beg their way to Djidda or to Mekka.* If rich enough to spare two dollars, they obtain, perhaps, a passage from Massoua direct to Djidda, where they meet with such of their countrymen as may have landed there from Souakin or Cosseir. Immediately on their arrival at Djidda or Mekka, they apply themselves to labour: some serve as porters, for the transport of goods and corn from the ships to the warehouses; others hire themselves to clean the court-yards, fetch wood from the neighbouring mountains, for the supply of which the inhabitants of Djidda and Mekka are exclusively indebted to them, as none of their own lazy poor will undertake that labour, although four piastres a day may be gained by it. At Mekka, they make small hearths of clay, (kánoun,) which they paint with yellow and red; these are bought by the hadjys, who boil their coffee-pots upon them. Some manufacture small baskets and mats of date-leaves, or prepare the intoxicating drink called *bouza*; and others serve as water-carriers: in short, when any occasion requires manual

* In 1813, a party of Tekrourys, about sixty in number, having taken that road, the Arabs of those mountains, who are Wahabys, and who had often seen black slaves among the Turkish soldiers, conceived that the negro hadjys were in the habit of entering into the service of the Turks. To prevent the party then passing from being ever opposed to them, they waylaid the poor Tekrourys on the road, and killed many of them.

labour, a Tekroury from the market is always employed. If any of them is attacked by disease, his companions attend upon him, and defray his expenses. I have seen very few of them ask for charity, except on the first days after their arrival, before they have been able to obtain employment. From Mekka, they either travel by land, or sometimes make a sea voyage by way of Yembo to Medina, where they again supply the town with fire-wood. Indeed, the hadjys would be much at a loss in the Hedjaz, if they could not command the laborious services of these blacks. During the Wahaby conquest, they continued to perform the pilgrimage; and it is said that Saoud expressed a particular esteem for them.*

When these negroes have completed the Hadj, and the visit to Mekka, they repair to Djidda, where they continue to work till an opportunity offers of sailing to Souakin; for very few, if any, return by way of Abyssinia. On leaving the Hedjaz, they all possess a sufficient sum of money, saved from the profits of their industry, to purchase some small adventure, or, at least, to provide, on their reaching Souakin, for a more comfortable passage through the Desert than that which they experienced on their outward journey, and then proceed homewards by Shendy and Cordofan. Many of them, however, instead of returning on the completion of the pilgrimage, disperse over Arabia, visit the mosque at Jerusalem, or Ibrahim's (Abraham's) tomb at Hebron, and thus remain absent from their home for many years, subsisting always upon the product of their own labour.

The benefactors to the Kaaba have enriched the temple of Mekka, and the idle persons employed in it; but no one has thought of forming any establishment for facilitating the pilgrimage of the poor negroes and Indians, or of procuring for them a free passage across the gulf to the Hedjaz; the expense of which, amounting to a dollar or two, is that which they feel most heavily. They often arrive in the harbours of the African side of the gulf, after having spent the

* Makrisi states, in his treatise on the Khalifes who performed the Hadj, that in A. H. 724, a negro king called Mousa arrived at Cairo on his way to Mekka, and was splendidly entertained by Kalaoun, then Sultan of Egypt. He had with him, according to Makrisi, fourteen thousand chosen female slaves.

little they had taken with them from home, or having been robbed of it on the journey; and finding, perhaps, no means there of earning as much as will pay their passage across the Red Sea, are obliged to wait till the return of their richer companions from the Hedjaz, who charitably pay for their passage.

The poor Indians afford a complete contrast, both in appearance and character, to the negroes: more wretched countenances can hardly be imagined; they seem to have lost not only all energy, but even hope. With bodies which appear scarcely capable of withstanding a gust of wind, and voices equally feeble, they would be worthy objects of commiseration, did not daily experience prove that they delight to appear in this plight, because it secures to them the alms of the charitable, and exempts them from labour. The streets of Mekka are crowded with them; the most decrepid make their doleful appeals to the passenger, lying at full length on their backs in the middle of the street; the gates of the mosque are always beset with them; every coffee-house and water-stand is a station for some of them; and no hadjy can purchase provisions in the markets, without being importuned by Indians soliciting a portion of them. I saw among them one of those devotees who are so common in the north of India and in Persia: one of his arms was held up straight over his head, and so fixed by long habit, that it could not be placed in any other situation. From the curiosity which he excited, I was led to suppose that such characters seldom find their way to the Hedjaz.

Dervishes of every sect and order in the Turkish empire are found among the pilgrims; many of them madmen, or at least assuming the appearance of insanity, which causes them to be much respected by the hadjys, and fills their pockets with money. The behaviour of some of them is so violent, and at the same time so cunning, that even the least charitably disposed hadjys give willingly something to escape from them. They mostly come from other countries; for among the Arabians themselves there are fewer crazy of these people than in other parts of the east. Egypt chiefly abounds with them; and almost every village in the valley of the Nile furnishes some *Masloub*, or reputed madman, whom the inhabitants regard as an inspired being, and a blessing sent to them from heaven.*

The arrival of strangers from all parts of the Mohammedan world, from Tombuctou to Samarkand, and from Georgia to Borneo, would render Djidda a most desirable residence for an inquisitive European traveller, who, by affording assistance to poor hadjys, and spending a small sum in provisions for them, would attract large numbers to his house, and might thus collect much information respecting the most distant and unknown parts of Africa and Asia. All, except the higher classes of Mekkawys, let out their houses during the Hadj, and demand from their under-tenants as much for a few weeks or months as they pay to the proprietor for a whole year. I paid for one room with a small kitchen and a by-place for my slave, fifteen dollars for six weeks, which equalled the annual rent of the whole house received by the landlord; and I should have been obliged to pay the same price if I had taken it only during the fortnight preceding and following the Hadj. The house in which I hired these rooms was divided into several lodgings, and was let altogether to different hadjys at one hundred and twenty dollars, the owners having retired into apartments so mean that strangers would not occupy them.

Of the numerous pilgrims who arrive at Mekka before the caravan, some are professed merchants; many others bring a few articles for sale, which they dispose of without trouble. They then pass the interval of time before the Hadj very pleasantly; free from cares and apprehensions, and enjoying that supreme happiness of an Asiatic, the *dolce far niente*. Except those of a very high rank, the pilgrims live together in a state of freedom and equality. They keep but few servants: many, indeed, have none, and divide among themselves the various duties of house-keeping, such as bringing the provisions from market and cooking them, although accustomed at home to the

---

* In 1813, the Christian community of Gous, in Upper Egypt, had the honour of possessing an insane youth, who walked about the bazars quite naked. But the Moslims of the place growing jealous, seized him one night, and converted him by circumcision into a Mohammedan saint.

services of an attendant. The freedom and oblivion of care which accompany travelling, render it a period of enjoyment among the people of the East as among Europeans; and the same kind of happiness results from their residence at Mekka, where reading the Koran, smoking in the streets or coffee-houses, praying or conversing in the mosque, are added to the indulgence of their pride in being near the holy house, and to the anticipation of the honours attached to the title of hadjy for the remainder of their lives; besides the gratification of religious feelings, and the hopes of futurity, which influence many of the pilgrims. The hadjys who come by the caravans pass their time very differently. As soon as they have finished their tedious journey, they must undergo the fatiguing ceremonies of visiting the Kaaba and Omra; immediately after which, they are hurried away to Arafat and Mekka, and, still heated from the effects of the journey, are exposed to the keen air of the Hedjaz mountains under the slight and inadequate covering of the ihram: then returning to Mekka, they have only a few days left to recruit their strength, and to make their repeated visits to the Beitullah, when the caravan sets off on its return; and thus the whole pilgrimage is a severe trial of bodily strength, and a continual series of fatigues and privations. This mode of visiting the holy city is, however, in accordance with the opinions of many most learned Moslim divines, who thought that a long residence in the Hedjaz, however meritorious the intention, is little conducive to true belief, since the daily sight of the holy places weakened the first impressions made by them. Notwithstanding the general decline of Muselmán zeal, there are still found Mohammedans whose devotion induces them to visit repeatedly the holy places. I knew Turks established at Cairo, who, even while the Wahaby faith predominated in the Hedjaz, went every year by way of Cosseir to Mekka; and there are a few individuals who reside constantly in that city, that they may pass the remainder of their days in pious duties and abstraction from the world. During my stay, a Turkish grandee arrived from Constantinople; he had been Kahwadjy Bashy to Sultan Selym; and the present Grand Signior had permitted him to go, that he might die in the sacred territory, where his arrival was announced by princely donations to the mosque.

The Syrian and Egyptian caravans always arrive at fixed periods; generally a day or two before the departure of the Hadj for Arafat. Both caravans usually pass by Beder, on the same day, or with an interval of one day only. The Syrian caravan coming from Medina, and the Egyptian from Yembo el Nakhel, prosecute their route from Beder to Mekka, at a short distance from each other. On the 5th of the month of Zul Hadj, A. H. 1229, or the 21st of November, 1814, the approach of the Syrian caravan was announced by one of its Mekowem, who came galloping into the town, to win the prize which is always awarded to the Sabbák, or him who brings the first tidings of the safe arrival of that caravan. The loud acclamations of the mob followed him to the governor's house, where his horse expired the moment he dismounted. The news was the more important, as nothing had been heard of this Hadj, and rumours had even been circulated of the Bedouins having plundered it on the road to the north of Medina. Two hours after, many other persons belonging to it arrived; and in the night the whole body came up, and encamped, with the Pasha of Damascus at their head, in the plain of Sheikh Mahmoud.

Early the next morning, the Egyptian caravan also arrived. The heavy baggage and the camels were sent to the usual place of encampment of the Egyptian Hadj, in the Moabede; but the Mahmal, or holy camel, remained at Sheikh Mahmoud, that it might pass from thence in procession next day through the town. Mohammed Aly Pasha arrived unexpectedly this morning from Tayf, to be present at the Hadj, and to inspect the cavalry which had come with the Egyptian caravan, a reinforcement that strongly excited his hopes of success against the Wahabys. He was dressed in a very handsome ihram, having two large entirely white cashmirene shawls wrapped round his loins and shoulders: his head was bare; but an officer held over it an umbrella to protect him from the sun, while riding through the streets. On the same morning, all the hadjys resident at Mekka took the ihram at their own lodgings, with the usual ceremonies, preparatory to their setting out for Arafat; and at mid-day they assembled in the mosque, where a short sermon was preached on the occasion. The hadjys who had come with the caravan had already taken the ihram at Asfan, two stations in advance of Mekka; but a great number of them, especially the servants and camel-drivers, did not throw off their ordinary dresses, and even appeared in them at Arafat, without causing either surprise or indignation. There is no religious police or inquisition here; and every body is left to the dictates of his conscience, either to observe or neglect the precepts of the canonical law.

Great bustle prevailed this evening in the town. Every body was preparing for his journey to Arafat; Syrian hadjys came to engage lodgings, to inquire about the state of the markets, and to pay their first visits to the Kaaba. A number of pedlars and petty shopkeepers left the town to establish themselves at Arafat, and to be ready there for the accommodation of the pilgrims. A number of camel-drivers from Syria and Egypt led their unloaded camels through the streets, offering to let them out to the hadjys going to Arafat. The rate of hire this year was very moderate, on account of the great number of beasts of burden: I engaged two of these camels, for the journey of four days to Arafat and back again, for three dollars.

On the 8th of Zul Hadj, early in the morning, the Syrian Hadj passed in procession through the town, accompanied by all its soldiers, and carrying the Mahmal in front. All its baggage was left at Sheikh Mahmoud, excepting the tents that were to be pitched at Arafat. Most of the hadjys were mounted in the Shebrye, a sort of palankeen placed upon the camel. The great people, and the Pasha of Damascus himself, rode in *takhtrouans*, a kind of closed litter or box carried by two camels, one before and the other behind, and forming a very commodious conveyance, except that it is necessary always to have a ladder, by means of which one may mount or descend. The camels' heads were decorated with feathers, tassels, and bells; but their heads, bent down towards the ground, showed how much they were fatigued by their journey. While these passed, the streets were lined by people of all classes, who greeted the caravan with loud acclamations and praise. The martial music of the Pasha of Damascus, a dozen of fine caparisoned horses led in front of his litter, and the rich *takhtrouans* in which his women rode, particularly attracted attention.

Soon after the Syrians had passed, the Egyptian procession followed, consisting of its Mahmal or sacred camel, (for each of the caravans carries one,) and the Shebryes of the public officers, who always accompany the Hadj; but not a single private pilgrim was to be seen in its suite. The good appearance of the soldiers who were with them, the splendour of the Mahmal, and of the equipage of the Emir el Hadj, who was a commander of the Turkish horsemen called Delhis, drew from the Mekkawys many signs of approbation, such as had been given to those who immediately preceded them. Both caravans continued their route to Arafat without stopping.

Before mid-day, all the hadjys who had resided for some time at Mekka, likewise mounted their camels, and crowded the streets as they pressed forward to follow the Hadj. They were joined by the far greater part of the population of Mekka, who make it a rule to go every year to Arafat; and by a similar portion of the population of Djidda, who had been assembled here for some time. During five or six days, the gates of Djidda, thus deserted by so many people, remain shut.

I left my lodgings on foot, after mid-day, with a companion and a slave-boy mounted on two camels, which I had hired from a Syrian driver, a native of Homs. It is thought meritorious to make the six hours' journey to Arafat on foot, particularly if the pilgrim goes barefooted. Many hadjys did so; and I preferred this mode, because I had led a very sedentary life for some months. We were several hours before we could reach the outskirts of the town beyond the Moabede, so great was the crowd of camels; and many accidents happened. Of the half-naked hadjys, all dressed in the white ihram, some sat reading the Koran upon their camels; some ejaculated loud prayers; whilst others cursed their drivers, and quarrelled with those near them, who were choking up the passage. Beyond the town the road widens, and we passed on through the valleys, at a very slow march, for two hours, to Wady Muna, in the narrow entrance of which great confusion again occurred. The law enjoins that the hadjys shall recite five prayers at Muna, Mohammed having always done so; that is to say, that they shall arrive there at noon, in time for the mid-day prayer, and remaining until the next morning, shall perform the prayers of the Aszer, of Mogreb, and of Ashe, and that of the dawn on the ensuing day. The inconvenience, however, arising from a delay on the route has led to the neglect of this precept for some time past; and the Hadj now passes Muna, on its way to Arafat, without halting.

In advance of Muna, we had the mosque of Mozdelife to our right, whither many pilgrims went to recite the Salat el Aszer and Salat el Mogreb; but the caravan continued its march. Beyond Mozdelife, we again entered the mountains by the pass called El Mazoumeyn, on the eastern side of which we issued towards the plain of Arafat. Here the pilgrims passed between the two pillars called Alameyn, and, on approaching the vicinity of Djebel Arafat, dispersed over the plain in search of their place of encampment. I reached the camp about three hours after sun-set; but the last stragglers did not arrive till midnight. Numberless fires were seen lighted on an extent of ground of three or four miles in length; and high and brilliant clusters of lamps marked the different places of encampment of Mohammed Aly, Soleyman Pasha, and the Emir el Hadj of the Egyptian caravan. Hadjys were seen in every direction wandering among the tents in search of their companions, whom they had lost in the confusion on the road; and it was several hours before the noise and clamour had subsided. Few persons slept during that night: the devotees sat up praying, and their loud chants were particularly distinguished on the side of the Syrian encampment; the merry Mekkawys formed themselves into parties, singing the jovial songs called *djok*, accompanied by clapping of hands; and the coffee-houses scattered over the plain were crowded the whole night with customers.

The night was dark and cold, and a few drops of rain fell. I had formed a resting-place for myself by means of a large carpet tied to the back part of a Mekkawy's tent; and having walked about for the greater part of the night, I had just disposed myself to sleep, when two guns, fired by the Syrian and Egyptian Hadj, announced the approaching dawn of the day of pilgrimage, and summoned the faithful to prepare for their morning prayers.

To illustrate the following account, a plan of Arafat is annexed;

and the figures and marks of reference which it contains are explained below.*

At sun-rise on the 9th of Zul Hadj, every pilgrim issued from his tent, to walk over the plains, and take a view of the busy crowds assembled there. Long streets of tents, fitted up as bazars, furnished all kinds of provisions. The Syrian and Egyptian cavalry were exercised by their chiefs early in the morning, while thousands of camels were seen feeding upon the dry shrubs of the plain all round the camp. I walked to Mount Arafat, to enjoy from its summit a more distinct view of the whole. This granite hill, which is also called *Djebel er' Rahme*, or the Mountain of Mercy, rises on the north-east side of the plain, close to the mountains which encompass it, but separated from them by a rocky valley; it is about a mile, or a mile and a half in circuit; its sides are sloping, and its summit is nearly two hundred feet above the level of the plain. On the eastern side broad stone steps lead up to the top, and a broad unpaved path, on the western, over rude masses of granite, with which its declivity is covered. After mounting about forty steps, we find a spot a little on the left, called Modaa Seydna Adam, or the place of prayer of our Lord Adam, where, it is related, that the father of mankind used to stand while praying; for here it was, according to Mohammedan tradition, that the angel Gabriel first instructed Adam how to adore his Creator. A marble slab, bearing an inscription in modern characters, is fixed in the side of the mountain. On reaching about the sixtieth step, we come to a

1. Mount Arafat.
2. Mohammed's place of prayer on its summit.
3. Platform of the preacher.
4. Modaa Seydna Adam.
5. Djama es' Szakhra.
6. Wady Arna.
7. Tent of the lady of Mohammed Aly Pasha.
8. The Egyptian caravan.
9. Tent of Mohammed Aly.
10. Camp of the cavalry of Mohammed Aly.
11. The Syrian caravan.
12. Tent of Solyman Pasha of Damascus.
13. Camp of the cavalry of Solyman Pasha.
14. Tent of the family of Djeylany.
15. Camp of the chief persons of Mekka and Turkish hadjys who had not come with the caravans.
16. Camp of Indians and lower class of Mekka, where also I myself halted.
17. The market.
18. The house of the Sherif.
19. Tent of Sherif Yahya.
20. Encampment of Bedouins.
21. The mosque called Djama Nimre.
22. El Aalameyn.
23. The well of Basan.

a. a. a. Different reservoirs of water.

The caravans and various parties of hadjys encamp every year exactly on the same spots. The Persian caravan from Baghdad, as soon as it arrives, encamps near the Sherif's house, at the place marked *b*; and the Yemen caravan at *c*. I was myself encamped at *b*.

p. 266.

THE PLAN OF ARAFAT
with the
CAMP OF THE PILGRIMS,
1814.

Canal of Mekka

Road from Muna and Mekka.

Canal of Mekka

Road to Tayf.

London, Published by Henry Colburn, New Burlington St. Feb.y 1829.

Sid.t Hall, sculp.t Bury St.t Bloomsb.y

small paved platform to our right, on a level spot of the hill, where the preacher stands who admonishes the pilgrims on the afternoon of this day, as I shall hereafter mention. Thus high, the steps are so broad and easy that a horse or camel may ascend, but higher up they become more steep and uneven. On the summit the place is shown where Mohammed used to take his station during the Hadj; a small chapel formerly stood over it; but this was destroyed by the Wahabys: here the pilgrims usually pray two rikats, in salutation of Arafat. The steps and the summit are covered with handkerchiefs to receive their pious gifts, and each family of the Mekkawys or Bedouins of the tribe of Koreysh, in whose territory Arafat lies, has its particular spot assigned to it for this purpose. The summit commands a very extensive and singular prospect. I brought my compass to take a circle of bearings; but the crowd was so great, that I could not use it. Towards the western extremity of the plain are seen Bir Bazan and the Aalameyn; somewhat nearer, southwards, the mosque called Djama Nimre, or Djama Seydna Ibrahim; and on the south-east, a small house where the Sherif used to lodge during the pilgrimage. From thence an elevated rocky ground in the plain extends towards Arafat. On the eastern side of the mountain, and close to its foot, are the ruins of a small mosque, built on rocky ground, called Djama el Szakhrat, where Mohammed was accustomed to pray, and where the pilgrims make four prostrations in memory of the prophet. Several large reservoirs lined with stone are dispersed over the plain; two or three are close to the foot of Arafat, and there are some near the house of the Sherifs: they are filled from the same fine aqueduct which supplies Mekka, and the head of which is about one hour and a half distant, in the eastern mountains. The canal is left open here for the convenience of pilgrims, and is conducted round the three sides of the mountains, passing by Modaa Seydna Adam.*

From the summit of Arafat, I counted about three thousand tents dispersed over the plain, of which two thirds belonged to the two

---

* At the close of the sixteenth century, according to Kotobeddyn, the whole plain of Arafat was cultivated.

Hadj caravans, and to the suite and soldiers of Mohammed Aly; the rest to the Arabs of the Sherif, the Bedouin hadjys, and the people of Mekka and Djidda. These assembled multitudes were for the greater number, like myself, without tents. The two caravans were encamped without much order, each party of pilgrims or soldiers having pitched its tents in large circles or *dowars*, in the midst of which many of their camels were reposing. The plain contained, dispersed in different parts, from twenty to twenty-five thousand camels, twelve thousand of which belonged to the Syrian Hadj, and from five to six thousand to the Egyptian; besides about three thousand, purchased by Mohammed Aly from the Bedouins in the Syrian Deserts, and brought to Mekka with the Hadj, to convey the pilgrims to this place, previously to being used for the transport of army-provisions to Tayf.

The Syrian Hadj was encamped on the south and south-west side of the mountain; the Egyptian on the south-east. Around the house of the Sherif, Yahya himself was encamped with his Bedouin troops, and in its neighbourhood were all the Hedjaz people. Here it was that the two Yemen caravans used formerly to take their station. Mohammed Aly, and Soleyman Pasha of Damascus, as well as several of their officers, had very handsome tents; but the most magnificent of all was that of the wife of Mohammed Aly, the mother of Tousoun Pasha, and Ibrahim Pasha, who had lately arrived from Cairo for the Hadj, with a truly royal equipage, five hundred camels being necessary to transport her baggage from Djidda to Mekka. Her tent was in fact an encampment consisting of a dozen tents of different sizes, inhabited by her women; the whole enclosed by a wall of linen cloth, eight hundred paces in circuit, the single entrance to which was guarded by eunuchs in splendid dresses. Around this enclosure were pitched the tents of the men who formed her numerous suite. The beautiful embroidery on the exterior of this linen palace, with the various colours displayed in every part of it, constituted an object which reminded me of some descriptions in the Arabian Tales of the Thousand and One Nights. Among the rich equipages of the other hadjys, or of the Mekka people, none were so conspicuous as that belonging to the family of Djeylany, the merchant, whose tents, pitched in a semicircle, rivalled in beauty those of the two Pashas, and far exceeded those of Sherif Yahya. In other parts of the East, a merchant would as soon think of buying a rope for his own neck, as of displaying his wealth in the presence of a Pasha; but Djeylany has not yet laid aside the customs which the Mekkawys learned under their old government, particularly that of Sherif Ghaleb, who seldom exercised extortion upon single individuals; and they now rely on the promises of Mohammed Aly, that he will respect their property.

During the whole morning, there were repeated discharges of the artillery which both Pashas had brought with them. A few pilgrims had taken up their quarters on Djebel Arafat itself, where some small cavern, or impending block of granite, afforded them shelter from the sun. It is a belief generally entertained in the East, and strengthened by many boasting hadjys on their return home, that all the pilgrims, on this day, encamp upon Mount Arafat; and that the mountain possesses the miraculous property of expansion, so as to admit an indefinite number of the faithful upon its summit. The law ordains that the *wakfe*, or position of the Hadj, should be on Djebel Arafat; but it wisely provides against any impossibility, by declaring that the plain in the immediate neighbourhood of the mountain may be regarded as comprised under the term "mountain," or Djebel Arafat.

I estimated the number of persons assembled here at about seventy thousand. The camp was from three to four miles long, and between one and two in breadth. There is, perhaps, no spot on earth where, in so small a place, such a diversity of languages are heard; I reckoned about forty, and have no doubt that there were many more. It appeared to me as if I were here placed in a holy temple of travellers only; and never did I at any time feel a more ardent wish to be able to penetrate once into the inmost recesses of the countries of many of those persons whom I now saw before me, fondly imagining that I might have no more difficulty in reaching their homes, than what they had experienced in their journey to this spot.

When the attention is engrossed by such a multitude of new objects, time passes rapidly away. I had only descended from Mount

Arafat, and had walked for some time about the camp, here and there entering into conversation with pilgrims; inquiring at the Syrian camp after some of my friends; and among the Syrian Bedouins, for news from their deserts, when mid-day had already passed. The prayers of this period of the day ought to be performed either within, or in the immediate neighbourhood of, the mosque of Nimre, whither the two Pashas had repaired for that purpose. The far greater number of hadjys, however, dispense with this observance, and many of them with the mid-day prayers altogether; for no one concerns himself whether his neighbour is punctual or not in the performance of the prescribed rites. After mid-day, the pilgrims are to wash and purify the body, by means of the entire ablution prescribed by the law, and called Ghossel, for which purpose chiefly, the numerous tents in the plain have been constructed; but the weather was cloudy, and rather cold, which induced nine-tenths of the pilgrims, shivering as they were already under the thin covering of the ihram, to omit the rite also, and to content themselves with the ordinary ablution. The time of Aszer (or about three o'clock, P. M.) approached, when that ceremony of the Hadj takes place, for which the whole assembly had come hither. The pilgrims now pressed forward towards the mountain of Arafat, and covered its sides from top to bottom. At the precise time of Aszer, the preacher took his stand upon the platform on the mountain, and began to address the multitude. This sermon, which lasts till sun-set, constitutes the holy ceremony of the Hadj called Khotbet el Wakfe; and no pilgrim, although he may have visited all the holy places of Mekka, is entitled to the name of hadjy, unless he has been present on this occasion. As Aszer approached, therefore, all the tents were struck, every thing was packed up, the caravans began to load, and the pilgrims belonging to them mounted their camels, and crowded round the mountain, to be within sight of the preacher, which is sufficient, as the greater part of the multitude is necessarily too distant to hear him. The two Pashas, with their whole cavalry drawn up in two squadrons behind them, took their post in the rear of the deep lines of camels of the hadjys, to which those of the people of the Hedjaz were also joined; and here they waited in solemn and respectful silence the conclusion of the sermon. Further removed from the preacher, was the Sherif Yahya, with his small body of soldiers, distinguished by several green standards carried before him. The two Mahmals, or holy camels, which carry on their back the high structure that serves as the banner of their respective caravans, made way with difficulty through the ranks of camels that encircled the southern and eastern sides of the hill, opposite to the preacher, and took their station, surrounded by their guards, directly under the platform in front of him.*

The preacher, or Khatyb, who is usually the Kadhy of Mekka, was mounted upon a finely-caparisoned camel, which had been led up the steps; it being traditionally said that Mohammed was always seated when he here addressed his followers, a practice in which he was imitated by all the Khalifes who came to the Hadj, and who from

---

* The Mahmal (an exact representation of which is given by D'Ohsson,) is a high, hollow, wooden frame, in the form of a cone, with a pyramidal top, covered with a fine silk brocade adorned with ostrich feathers, and having a small book of prayers and charms placed in the midst of it, wrapped up in a piece of silk. (My description is taken from the Egyptian Mahmal.) When on the road, it serves as a holy banner to the caravan; and on the return of the Egyptian caravan, the book of prayers is exposed in the mosque El Hassaneyn, at Cairo, where men and women of the lower classes go to kiss it, and obtain a blessing by rubbing their foreheads upon it. No copy of the Koran, nor any thing but the book of prayers, is placed in the Cairo Mahmal. The Wahabys declared this ceremony of the Hadj to be a vain pomp, of idolatrous origin, and contrary to the spirit of true religion; and its use was one of the principal reasons which they assigned for interdicting the caravans from repairing to Mekka. In the first centuries of Islam, neither the Omeyades nor the Abassides ever had a Mahmal. Makrisi, in his treatise " On those Khalifes and Sultans who performed the pilgrimage in person," says that Dhaher Bybars el Bondokdary, Sultan of Egypt, was the first who introduced the Mahmal, about A. H. 670. Since his time, all the Sultans who sent their caravans to Mekka, have considered it as a privilege to send one with each, as a sign of their own royalty. The first Mahmal from Yemen came in A. H. 960; and in A. H. 1049, El Moayed Billah, king, and Imam of Yemen, who publicly professed the creed of Zeyd, came with one to Arafat; and the caravans of Baghdad, Damascus, and Cairo, have always carried it with them. In A. H. 730, the Baghdad caravan brought it to Arafat upon an elephant (vide Asamy). I believe the custom to have arisen in the battle-banner of the Bedouins, called Merkeb and Otfe, which I have mentioned in my remarks on the Bedouins, and which resemble the Mahmal, inasmuch as they are high wooden frames placed upon camels.

hence addressed their subjects in person. The Turkish gentleman of Constantinople, however, unused to camel-riding, could not keep his seat so well as the hardy Bedouin prophet; and the camel becoming unruly, he was soon obliged to alight from it. He read his sermon from a book in Arabic, which he held in his hands. At intervals of every four or five minutes he paused, and stretched forth his arms to implore blessings from above; while the assembled multitudes around and before him, waved the skirts of their ihrams over their heads, and rent the air with shouts of "Lebeyk, Allahuma Lebeyk," (i. e. Here we are, at thy commands, O God!) During the wavings of the ihrams, the side of the mountain, thickly crowded as it was by the people in their white garments, had the appearance of a cataract of water; while the green umbrellas, with which several thousand hadjys, sitting on their camels below, were provided, bore some resemblance to a verdant plain.

During his sermon, which lasted almost three hours, the Kadhy was seen constantly to wipe his eyes with a handkerchief; for the law enjoins the Khatyb or preacher to be moved with feeling and compunction; and adds that, whenever tears appear on his face, it is a sign that the Almighty enlightens him, and is ready to listen to his prayers. The pilgrims who stood near me, upon the large blocks of granite which cover the sides of Arafat, appeared under various aspects. Some of them, mostly foreigners, were crying loudly and weeping, beating their breasts, and denouncing themselves to be great sinners before the Lord; others (but by far the smaller number,) stood in silent reflexion and adoration, with tears in their eyes. Many natives of the Hedjaz, and many soldiers of the Turkish army, were meanwhile conversing and joking; and whenever the others were waving the ihram, made violent gesticulations, as if to ridicule that ceremony. Behind, on the hill, I observed several parties of Arabs and soldiers, who were quietly smoking their nargyles; and in a cavern just by sat a common woman, who sold coffee, and whose visiters, by their loud laughter and riotous conduct, often interrupted the fervent devotions of the hadjys near them. Numbers of people were present in their ordinary clothes. Towards the conclusion of the sermon, the far greater part of the assembly seemed to be wearied, and many descended the mountain before the preacher had finished his discourse. It must be observed, however, that the crowds assembled on the mountain were, for the greater part, of the lower classes; the pilgrims of respectability being mounted upon their camels or horses in the plain.

At length the sun began to descend behind the western mountains; upon which the Kadhy, having shut his book, received a last greeting of " Lebeyk ;" and the crowds rushed down the mountain, in order to quit Arafat. It is thought meritorious to accelerate the pace on this occasion; and many persons make it a complete race, called by the Arabs, *Ad'dafa min Arafat*. In former times, when the strength of the Syrian and Egyptian caravans happened to be nearly balanced, bloody affrays took place here almost every year between them, each party endeavouring to out-run and to carry its *mahmal* in advance of the other. The same happened when the *mahmals* approached the platform at the commencement of the sermon; and two hundred lives have on some occasions been lost in supporting what was thought the honour of the respective caravans. At present the power of Mohammed Aly preponderates, and the Syrian hadjys display great humility.

The united caravans and the whole mass of pilgrims now moved forward over the plain; every tent had been previously packed up, to be ready for the occasion. The pilgrims pressed through the Aalameyn, which they must repass on their return; and night came on before they reached the defile called El Mazoumeyn. Innumerable torches were now lighted, twenty-four being carried before each Pasha; and the sparks of fire from them flew far over the plain. There were continual discharges of artillery; the soldiers fired their muskets; the martial bands of both the Pashas played; sky-rockets were thrown as well by the Pashas' officers, as by many private pilgrims; while the Hadj passed at a quick pace in the greatest disorder, amidst a deafening clamour, through the pass of Mazoumeyn, leading towards Mezdelfe, where all alighted, after a two hours' march. No order was observed here in encamping; and every one lay down on the spot that first presented itself, no tents being pitched except those of the Pashas and their suites; before which was an illumination of lamps in the form of high arches, which continued to blaze the whole night, while the firing of the artillery was kept up without intermission.

In the indescribable confusion attending the departure of the Hadj from Arafat, many pilgrims had lost their camels, and were now heard calling loudly for their drivers, as they sought them over the plain : I myself was among their number. When I went to the mountain of Arafat, I ordered my camel-driver and my slave to remain in readiness upon the spot where they then were, till I should return to them after sun-set; but seeing, soon after I quitted them, that the other loaded camels pressed forward towards the mountain, they followed the example; and when I returned to the place where I left them, they were not to be found. I was therefore obliged to walk to Mezdelfe, where I slept on the sand, covered only by my ihram, after having searched for my people during several hours

On the 10th of the month of Zul Hadj, or the day of the feast called Nehar el Dhahye, or Nehar el Nahher, the morning gun awoke the pilgrims before dawn. At the first appearance of day-break, the Kadhy took his station upon the elevated platform which encloses the mosque of Mezdelfe, usually called Moshar el Harám, and began a sermon similar to that which he had preached the day before. The Hadj surrounded the mosque on all sides with lighted torches, and accompanied the sermon with the same exclamations of "Lebeyk Allah huma Lebeyk;" but though this sermon forms one of the principal duties of the pilgrimage, by far the greater number of the hadjys remained with their baggage, and did not attend it. The sermon is not very long, lasting only from the first dawn till sun-rise; a space of time much shorter of course in this latitude, than in our northern countries. The Salat el Ayd, or the prayer of the feast, is performed at the same time by the whole community according to its rites. When the first rays of the sun shot athwart the cloudy sky, the pilgrims moved on at a slow march towards Wady Muna, one hour distant from hence.

On arriving at Wady Muna, each nation encamped upon the spot which custom has assigned to it, at every returning Hadj. After disposing of the baggage, the hadjys hastened to the ceremony of throwing stones at the devil. It is said that, when Abraham or Ibrahim returned from the pilgrimage to Arafat, and arrived at Wady Muna, the devil Eblys presented himself before him at the entrance of the valley, to obstruct his passage; when the angel Gabriel, who accompanied the Patriarch, advised him to throw stones at him, which he did, and after pelting him seven times, Eblys retired. When Abraham reached the middle of the valley, he again appeared before him, and, for the last time, at its western extremity, and was both times repulsed by the same number of stones. According to Azraky, the Pagan Arabs, in commemoration of this tradition, used to cast stones in this valley as they returned from the pilgrimage; and set up seven idols at Muna, of which there was one in each of the three spots where the devil appeared, at each of which they cast three stones. Mohammed, who made this ceremony one of the chief duties of the hadjys, increased the number of stones to seven. At the entrance of the valley, towards Mezdelfe, stands a rude stone pillar, or rather altar, between six and seven feet high, in the midst of the street, against which the first seven stones are thrown, as the place where the devil made his first stand: towards the middle of the valley is a similar pillar, and at its western end a wall of stones, which is made to serve the same purpose. The hadjys crowded in rapid succession round the first pillar, called "Djamrat el Awla;" and every one threw seven small stones successively upon it: they then passed to the second and third spots, (called "Djamrat el Owsat," and "Djamrat el Sofaly," or "el Akaba," or "el Aksa,") where the same ceremony was repeated. In throwing the stones, they are to exclaim, "In the name of God; God is great (we do this) to secure ourselves from the devil and his troops." The stones used for this purpose are to be of the size of a horse-bean, or thereabouts; and the pilgrims are advised to collect them in the plain of Mezdelfe, but they may likewise take them from Muna; and many people, contrary to the law, collect those that have already been thrown.

Having performed the ceremony of casting stones, the pilgrims kill the animals which they bring with them for sacrifice; and all Mohammedans, in whatever part of the world they may be, are bound, at this time, to perform the same rite. Between six and eight thousand sheep and goats, under the care of Bedouins, (who demanded high prices for them,) were ready on this occasion. The act of sacrifice itself is subject to no other ceremonies than that of turning the victim's face towards the Kebly or the Kaaba, and to say, during the act of cutting its throat, "In the name of the most merciful God! O supreme God!" (Bismillah! irrahman irrahhym, Allahou akbar!) Any place may be chosen for these sacrifices, which are performed in every corner of Wady Muna; but the favourite spot is a smooth rock on its western extremity, where several thousand sheep were killed in the space of a quarter of an hour.*

As soon as the sacrifices were completed, the pilgrims sent for barbers, or repaired to their shops, of which a row of thirty or forty had been set up near the favourite place of sacrifice. They had their heads shaved, except those who were of the Shafey sect, who shave only one-fourth of the head here, reserving the other three-fourths till they have visited the Kaaba, after returning to Mekka. They threw off the ihram, and resumed their ordinary clothes; those who could afford it putting on new dresses, this being now the day of the feast. So far the Hadj was completed, and all the pilgrims joined in mutual congratulations, and wishes that the performance of this Hadj might be acceptable to the Deity. "Tekabbel Allah!" was heard on all sides, and everybody appeared contented. But this was not quite the case with myself; for all endeavours to find my camels had hitherto proved vain, such were the immense crowds that filled the valley; and while the other hadjys were dressed in their clothes, I was obliged to walk about in my ihram. Fortunately, my purse, which I had hung about my neck according to the pilgrim custom, (the ihram having no pockets,) enabled me to buy a sheep for sacrifice, and pay a barber. It was not till after sun-set that I found out my people, who had encamped on the northern mountain, and had been all the while under great anxiety about me.

The pilgrims remain two days more at Muna. Exactly at mid-day,

* Kotobeddyn relates that, when the Khalife Mokteder performed the pilgrimage about A. H. 350, he sacrificed on this day forty thousand camels and cows, and fifty thousand sheep. Even now, persons of wealth kill camels. The slaughtering may be performed by proxy.

on the 11th of Zul Hadj, seven small stones are again thrown against each of the three places where the devil appeared; and the same is done on the 12th of Zul Hadj, so that by the three repeated throwings, each time of twenty-one stones, the number of sixty-three is cast during the three days. Many pilgrims are ignorant of the precise tenor of the law in this respect, as they are of several other points in the ceremonies of the pilgrimage, and either throw early in the morning the stones they should throw at mid-day, or do not throw the number enjoined. After the last throwing on the 12th, the Hadj returns to Mekka in the afternoon.

Muna* is a narrow valley, extending in a right line from west to east, about fifteen hundred paces in length, and varying in breadth, enclosed on both sides by steep and barren cliffs of granite. Along the middle, on both sides of the way, is a row of buildings, the far greater part in ruins: they belong to Mekkans or Bedouins of the Koreysh, by whom they are either let out, or occupied during the three days of the Hadj, and left empty the rest of the year, when Muna is never inhabited. Some of these are tolerable stone buildings, two stories high; but not more than a dozen of them are kept in complete repair. On the farthest eastern extremity of the valley, stands a good house, belonging to the reigning Sherif of Mekka, in which he usually lives during those days. It was now occupied by the ladies of Mohammed Aly; Sherif Yahya, after throwing off the ihram, having returned to Mekka, where many hadjys also repair immediately after that ceremony; but it is their duty to revisit Muna at noon on the 11th or 12th of this month, in order to throw the stones, as the neglect of this ceremony would render their pilgrimage imperfect. The remainder of those two days they may spend where they please. In the evening of the day of sacrifice, the merchant hadjys usually go to Mekka, that they may unpack whatever merchandize they have brought there.

* This name is said to be derived from Adam, who, during his stay in the valley, when God told him to ask a favour, replied, "I ask (ytemuna) for paradise;" and this place received its appellation from the answer. Others say it derived its name from the flowing of blood in the day of sacrifice.

278   THE HADJ, OR PILGRIMAGE.

In the open space between the Sherif's house and the habitations of the Mekkans, is situated the mosque called Mesdjed el Kheyf; it is a good solid building, the open square of which is surrounded by a high and strong wall. In the midst of it is a public fountain, with a small dome; and the west side, where the pulpit is placed, is occupied by a colonnade with a triple row of pillars. The mosque is very ancient; it was newly constructed in A. H. 559, by the celebrated Salaheddyn; but it was rebuilt in its present form by Kayd Beg, Sultan of Egypt, in A. H. 874. It is reported, according to Fasy, that at the foot of the mountain behind it, Mohammed received many revelations from heaven, and that Adam was buried in the mosque. Close by it is a reservoir of water, also founded, according to Kotobeddyn, by Kayd Beg; it was now completely dry, as was a similar one where the Syrian Hadj encamped. The want of water at Muna subjected the poorer hadjys to great hardships. Some was brought either from Mezdelife, or from the tank situated beyond Muna, on the road to Mekka, and the skin-full was sold for four piastres. In Fasy's time, there were fifteen wells of brackish water at Muna: it seems that water may be found at a certain depth in all the country round Mekka.

The annexed ground-plan shows whatever is worthy of notice in the town or village of Muna.* The house of Djeylany, the best that it contained, was constantly crowded by visitors, whom he treated

---

* In this plan fig. 1. indicates the house of the Sherif.
2. The tent of Mohammed Aly Pasha.
3. Cavalry of Mohammed Aly Pasha.
4. Egyptian caravan.
5. Tents of Solyman Pasha and his retinue.
6. Tent of Ahmed Bey, commander of the Syrian cavalry.
7. Syrian caravan.
8. Syrian cavalry.
9. The mosque, called Mesdjed el Kheyf.
10. Reservoirs of water, then dry.
11. Camp of poor Indian, Yemen, and Negro pilgrims.
12. Tents serving as coffee-shops.
13. Ruined houses occupied by people of Mekka.
14. The first devil's pillar.
15. The house of Djeylany, the merchant.
16. A row of shops.
17. The second devil's pillar.
18. The house of the Kadhy of Mekka.
19. A vaulted hall, with shops on both sides.
20. A ruined mosque.
21. A large shop, where Abyssinian slaves were exhibited for sale.
22. The house of Sakkat, a rich merchant of Mekka.
23. Camp of Turkish, Hedjaz, and Bedouin pilgrims. (All this ground is uneven and rocky.)
24. The third and last devil's pillar, or wall.
25. A row of barbers' shops.
26. The rock upon which the victims were killed.
27. Paved steps on the road towards Mekka.
28. A small house of the Sherif, where he throws off the ihram, and dresses.
29. The spot where Abraham prepared to sacrifice his son, and close by the birth-place of Ismayl.
30. The mountain called Djebel Thebeyr.

sumptuously. The houses of the Kadhy and the rich families of Sakkat, were next to it; and, on the same side of the way, a long, narrow hall had been lately repaired and fitted up, where about fifty Mekkan and Turkish shopkeepers exhibited their wares. The houses of the northern row are almost totally in ruins: the row of shops (No. 16.) on that side were open without any doors. There were, besides, many sheds constructed in the midst of the street, where victuals might be purchased in great abundance, but at exorbitant prices.

On the declivity of the mountain to the north, called Djebel Thebeyr, a place is visited by the hadjys, where Abraham, as some accounts inform us, requested permission to offer up his son as a sacrifice. A granite block, cleft in two, is shown here, upon which the knife of Abraham fell, at the moment when the angel Gabriel showed him the ram close by. At the touch of the knife the stone separated in two. It is in commemoration of this sacrifice that the faithful, after the Hadj is completed, slaughter their victims. The commentators on the law, however, do not agree about the person whom Abraham intended to sacrifice. Some state him to have been Yakoub (Jacob), but the far greater number Ismayl. In the immediate neighbourhood of the block is a small cavern, capable of holding four or five persons, where Hadjer (or Hagar) is said to have given birth to Ismayl; this, however, directly contradicts even Mohammedan tradition, which says that Ismayl was born in Syria, and that his mother Hadjer carried him into the Hedjaz, when an infant at her breast; but the small cavern offering itself so conveniently, justified the substitution of Muna for Syria, as a fit birth-place for the father of the Bedouins, more especially as it attracts so many pious donations to the Mekkans, who sit around with outspread handkerchiefs. Where the valley terminates towards Mekka, is a small house of the Sherif, in which he makes his sacrifice, and throws off the ihram. It was mentioned, that in a side-valley leading from this place towards Djebel Nour, stands a mosque called Mesdjed el Ashra, where the followers of Mohammed used to pray; but I did not visit it. According to Azraky, another mosque, called Mesdjed el Kabsh, stood near the cavern; and Fasy says there was one between the first and second of the devil's pillars, which is probably that marked 20 in the plan.

To every division of the hadjys, its place of encampment is appointed in Wady Muna, or at Arafat; but the space is here much narrower. The Egyptian Hadj alights near the house of the Sherif, where Mohammed Aly had pitched his tent, in the vicinity of his cavalry. Two large leathern vessels, constantly kept filled with water, were placed in front of his tent, for the use of the hadjys. At a short distance from it, towards the Mesdjed el Kheyf, stood the tent of Soleyman Pasha of Damascus, whose caravan was encamped on the opposite side of the way; before his tent was placed a row of ten field-pieces, which he had brought with him from Damascus. His ammunition had exploded on the way, while the caravan halted at Beder, and fifty people had been killed by the accident; but Mohammed Aly had furnished him with a fresh supply; and the guns were frequently discharged, as were twelve others which stood near Mohammed Aly's tent. The greatest number of hadjys had encamped without any order, on the rocky and uneven plain behind the village to the north. The tents of the Mekkans were very neatly fitted up; and this being now the feast, men, women, and children were dressed in their best apparel. At night, few people ventured to sleep, on account of thieves, who abound at Muna. A hadjy had been robbed, on the preceding night, of three hundred dollars; and at Arafat several dozen of camels were stolen by the Bedouins: two of the thieves had been pursued and seized, and carried before Mohammed Aly at Muna, who ordered them to be beheaded. Their mutilated bodies lay before his tent the whole of the three days, with a guard, to prevent their friends from taking them away. Such exhibitions create neither horror nor disgust in the breast of an Osmanly; their continual recurrence hardens his feelings, and renders him insensible to the emotions of pity. I heard a Bedouin, probably a friend of the slain, who stood near the bodies, exclaim, "God have mercy upon *them;* but no mercy upon him who killed them!"

The street, which extends the whole length of Muna, was now converted into a market and fair: every inch of ground not built upon, was occupied by sheds or booths, made of mats; or by small tents, fitted up as shops. Provisions, and merchandize of every kind, had been brought here from Mekka; and, contrary to the custom in other Mohammedan countries, where all commerce is laid aside during the feast-days, all the merchants, shopkeepers, and brokers, were busily employed in traffic. The merchants who had arrived with the Syrian caravan, began their bargains for Indian goods, and exhibited samples of the articles which they had themselves brought, and which were lying in the warehouses at Mekka. A number of poor hadjys were crying their small adventures, which they carried along the street on their heads; and as all business was confined to this single street, the mixture of nations, costumes, and merchandize, was still more striking than at Mekka.*

In the afternoon of the first day of Muna, the two Pashas paid mutual visits; and their cavalry manœuvred before their tents. Among the troops of Soleyman Pasha, about sixty Sambarek (Zembourek) attracted notice: these are artillerymen, mounted on camels, having a small swivel before them, which turned on a pivot fixed to the pommel of the camel's saddle. They fire while at a trot, and the animal bears the shock of the discharge with great tranquillity. The Syrian cavalry consisted of about fifteen hundred men, principally delhys; no infantry whatever being with the caravan. Soleyman Pasha appeared to-day with a very brilliant equipage; all his body-guards were dressed in richly-embroidered stuffs glittering with gold, and were well mounted, though the Pasha's own stud was very indifferent. After the two

---

* This pilgrimage among the Pagan Arabs was, at all times, connected with a large fair held at Mekka. In the month before the pilgrimage, they visited some other neighbouring fairs, namely, those of Okath, the market of the tribe of Kenane; of Medjna and Zou el Medjaz; the markets of the tribe of Hodeyl; and of Hasha, that of the Beni Lazed. After having spent their time in amusements at those fairs, they repaired to the Hadj at Arafat, and then returned to Mekka, where another large fair was held (see Azraky). At Arafat and Muna, on the contrary, they scrupulously abstained from any traffic during the days of their sojourning there, and the performance of the holy rites; but the Koran abrogated this observance, and by a passage in chap. ii. permitted trafficking even in the days of the Hadj; at least it has been so explained. (See El Fasy.)

Pashas had interchanged visits, their officers followed the example, and were admitted to kiss the hands of the Pashas, when each of them received presents in money, according to his rank. The Kadhy, the rich merchants of Mekka, and the grandees among the hadjys, likewise paid their respects to the Pashas, and each of their visits lasted about five minutes. An immense crowd was, at the same time, assembled in a wide semicircle round their open tents, to witness this brilliant sight. In the afternoon, a body of negro pilgrims, under a leader, made their way through this crowd, and, walking up to Soleyman Pasha, (who sat quite alone, smoking upon a sofa in the recess of his tent,) boldly saluted him, and wished him joy on the accomplishment of the pilgrimage; in return they received some gold coins. They afterwards tried the same experiment with Mohammed Aly Pasha; but received only blows on the back from his officers, in return for their compliments. Among the curiosities which attracted the notice of the crowd, was a curricle belonging to the wife of Mohammed Aly, which stood in the gateway of the Sherif's house. This lady had carried it on board her ship to Djidda, from whence she rode in it to Mekka and Arafat, her person being, of course, completely concealed; it was drawn by two fine horses, and was seen frequently afterwards parading the streets of Mekka.

At night, the whole valley blazed; every house and tent was lighted up; before the tents of the Pashas were fine illuminations; and the Bedouins made large bonfires upon the summits of the mountains. The noise of guns continued throughout the night; fire-works were exhibited; and several of the Mekkans let off rockets.

The second day of the feast at Muna was passed in the same manner as the first; but the putrefying carcases of the sheep became excessively offensive in some parts of the valley, as very few of the richer hadjys can consume the victims which they kill. The Hanefys are not even allowed by the laws of their sect to eat more than one-eighth of a sheep. The greater part of the flesh falls to the lot of the poorer hadjys, and the entrails are thrown about the valley and the street. The negroes and Indians were employed in cutting some of the meat into slices, and drying it for their travelling provision.*

To-day many hadjys performed their prayers in the Mesdjed el Kheyf, which I found crowded with poor Indians, who had taken up their quarters in it. The pavement was thickly spread with carrion; and on cords extended between the columns were suspended slices of meat, for the purpose of being dried. The sight and smell were very disgusting; and many hadjys seemed surprised that such indecencies should be allowed. In general, foreign hadjys see many practices at Mekka, which are not calculated to inspire them with great veneration for the holy places of their religion; and although some may, nevertheless, retain all their religious zeal undiminished, others, we may be assured, lose much of it in consequence of what they witness during the Hadj. It is to this loss of respect for religion, and to the nefarious and shameful practices in some measure legitimatised by their frequent occurrence in the holy city, that we must attribute those proverbs which reflect upon the hadjys as less religious and less trustworthy than any other persons. But our Christian holy-land is liable to some censure, for practices of the same kind. The most devout and rigid Mohammedans acknowledge and deplore the existence of this evil; and prove that they are either more clear-sighted or more sincere than the Christian pilgrim Chateaubriand.†

---

* Until the sixteenth century, it was an established rule with the Sultans of Egypt, and afterwards with those of Constantinople, to furnish, at Muna, all the poor hadjys with food at the expense of the royal treasury. The Pagan Arabs distinguished themselves more particularly during the Hadj for their hospitality; and such of them as went on the pilgrimage, were gratuitously entertained by all those whose tents they passed on the road; they having previously prepared for that purpose large supplies of food. (See Kotobeddyn.)—Among the wonders which distinguish Muna from other valleys, El Fasy relates that it occasionally extends its dimensions to accommodate any number of pilgrims; that on the day of sacrifice, no vultures ever carry off the slaughtered lambs, thus leaving them for the poor hadjys; and that, notwithstanding the quantity of raw flesh, no flies ever molest the visiters at this place. That the last remark is false, I can declare from my own experience.

† Mons. C. may have had very statesman-like motives for giving in his Itinerary so highly coloured a picture of Palestine and its priesthood; but, as a traveller, he cannot

At mid-day on the 12th of Zul Hadj, immediately after having thrown the last twenty-one stones, the hadjys left Muna, and returned along the valley to Mekka, evincing their high spirits by songs, loud talking, and laughter; a contrast to the gloom which affected every body in proceeding here four days ago. On arriving at Mekka, the pilgrims must visit the Kaaba, which in the mean time has been covered with the new black clothing brought from Cairo, walk seven times round it, and perform the ceremony of the Say: this is called the Towaf el Ifadhe. He then takes the ihram once more, in order to visit the Omra; and on returning from the Omra, again performs the Towaf and Say, and with this the ceremony of the Hadj is finally terminated.

The principal duties incumbent upon the hadjy are, therefore:—
1. that he should take the ihram; 2. be present, on the 9th of Zul Hadj, from afternoon till sun-set, at the sermon preached at Arafat; 3. attend a similar sermon at Mezdelfe, at sun-rise of the 10th of Zul Hadj; 4. on the 10th, 11th, and 12th of Zul Hadj, throw on each day twenty-one stones against the devil's pillars at Muna; 5. perform the sacrifice at Muna; or, if he is too poor, substitute for it a fast at some future time; and, 6. upon his return to Mekka, visit the Kaaba and the Omra. The law makes so many nice distinctions, and increases so greatly the number of rules which are to guide the pilgrim at every step, that very few can flatter themselves with being quite regular hadjys; but as no ritual police is kept up during the ceremony, every one is completely his own master, and assumes the title of hadjy, whether he has strictly performed all the duties or not. It is enough for such that they have been at Arafat on the proper day—this is the least distinction: but a mere visit to Mekka does not authorise a man to style himself hadjy; and the assumption of this title without some further pretensions, exposes him to ridicule. There is not any formal certificate given to hadjys at Mekka, as at Jerusalem; but many of the great people purchase a few drawings of the town, &c.; annexed to which is an attestation of four witnesses, that the purchasers were

escape blame for having departed from the truth, and often totally misrepresented the facts that fell under his observation.

regular hadjys. If the 9th of Zul Hadj, or the day of El Wakfe, falls upon a Friday, it is held to be particularly fortunate.

Some hadjys are anxious to acquire the title of "Khadem el Mesdjed," or servant of the mosque, which may be obtained at the expense of about thirty dollars; for this sum, a paper, bestowing that appellation upon him, is delivered to the purchaser, signed by the Sherif and Kadhy. It is not uncommon to permit even Christians to obtain the privilege of calling themselves servants of the Mesdjed, and the honour is particularly sought for by the Greek inhabitants of the islands and shores of the Archipelago; as, in case of their being captured by the Barbary pirates, such a certificate is often respected by the most rigid Moggrebyns. I saw a Greek captain who obtained one for two hundred dollars; he had commanded one of Mohammed Aly's dows, and was now on his way home; and he felt satisfied that, whatever ship he might hereafter take under his charge in the Archipelago, would be secured by this certificate from the pirates. In former times, this title of Khadem appears to have been of more importance than it is now; for I find, in the historians of Mekka, many great people mentioned, who annexed it to their names.

After the return of the Hadj from Muna, the principal street of Mekka becomes almost impassable from the crowds assembled there. The Syrian hadjy merchants hire shops, and make the best use of the short time which is granted to them for their commercial transactions. Every body purchases provisions for his journey home; and the pursuit of gain now engrosses all minds, from the highest to the lowest. The two caravans usually leave Mekka about the 23d of Zul Hadj, after ten days' stay in the town. Sometimes the leaders of them are prevailed upon by the merchants, who pay highly for the favour, to grant a respite of a few days; but this year they did not require it, as the caravan was detained by Mohammed Aly, who, preparing to open his campaign against the Wahabys, thought proper to employ about twelve thousand camels of the Syrian Hadj in two journies to Djidda, and one to Tayf, for the transport of provisions. As to the Egyptian caravan, which, as I have already mentioned, contained no private hadjys, it was wholly detained by Mohammed Aly, who ordered all the horsemen and camels that had accompanied it, to assist him in his campaign. The Mahmal, or sacred camel, was sent back by sea to Suez, a circumstance which had never before occurred. The Syrian caravan did not leave Mekka till the 29th of Zul Hadj; and the incessant labour to which its camels had been subjected, weakened them so much, that numbers of them died on their return through the Desert. The caravans of unloaded camels which were hourly leaving Mekka for Djidda, to take up provisions there, facilitated the short journey to that place of those hadjys who wished to return home by sea.

Having heard that the supply of money for which I had written to Cairo on my first reaching Djidda, had been received there, I rode over in the night of the 1st of December, and remained in that town six or seven days. The hadjys who had, in the mean while, daily flocked into it on their return from Mekka, were seen encamped in every quarter, and thus it soon became as crowded as Mekka had just been. Among the ships in the harbour, ready to take hadjy passengers on board, was a merchant-vessel lately arrived from Bombay, belonging to a Persian house at that presidency, and commanded by an English captain, who had beat up to Djidda against the trade-winds, at this late season. I passed many agreeable hours in the company of Captain Boag, on board his ship, and regretted that my pursuits should call me away so soon. Two other Europeans had arrived at Djidda about the same time, by way of Cairo; the one an Englishman, who was going to India; the other a German physician. This gentleman was a Hanoverian by birth, and a baron: misfortunes of a very distressing nature had driven him from his home, and he had thought of practising his profession at Djidda, or of proceeding to Mokha; but his mind was too unsettled to determine upon any thing; and he was of too independent a character to receive either counsel or assistance. I left him at Djidda when I returned to Mekka, and learnt afterwards that he died there in the month of March, of the plague, and that he was buried by the Greeks of Djidda upon an island in the harbour.

When I returned to Mekka, about the 8th or 9th of December, I found no longer the same multitudes of people; but the beggars had become so numerous and troublesome, that many of the hadjys preferred staying all day at home, to escape at once the importunities, the expense of acceding to them, or the scandal of wanting charity. These beggars were soliciting alms to carry them home; and their numbers were increased by many pilgrims of respectable appearance, whose money had been spent during the Hadj. It was my intention, in returning to Mekka, to join the Syrian caravan, and travel with it as far as Medina; I therefore, in imitation of some other Syrian pilgrims who had arrived at Mekka before the caravan, engaged with a Bedouin of the Harb tribe for two of his camels; although most of the hadjys, who, after the pilgrimage, visit Mohammed's tomb at Medina, accompany the Syrian caravan, agreeing with some Mekowem to defray all expenses on the road; but it is better, for many reasons, to travel with Bedouins than with towns-people, especially on a route across the Bedouin territory. An accident, however, prevented me from availing myself of this opportunity.

The caravan being ready for departure on the 15th of December, I packed up my effects in the morning, and at noon a gun was fired, to announce that Soleyman Pasha had quitted the plain of Sheikh Mahmoud, where the caravan had been encamped; but still my Bedouin had not arrived. I ran out towards Sheikh Mahmoud, when I understood that a rumour, whether false or true, having been spread, that Mohammed Aly was only waiting to see the camels all assembled in the morning upon the plain, that he might seize and send them to Tayf, several Bedouins had made their escape during the night: it was evident that those with whom I had bargained were among the number. In the hurry and bustle of departure no other camels could possibly be found; and I was therefore obliged to return to the town, together with several Mekkans, who had been disappointed in the same manner.

At the moment of starting, the leader of the Damascus caravan always distributes a certain quantity of provision to the poor. Soleyman Pasha had, for this purpose, heaped up two hundred camel-loads near his tent; and when he mounted his horse, at a given signal it was seized upon by those who were waiting, in the most outrageous and disorderly manner: a party of about forty negro pilgrims, armed with sticks, secured a considerable part of the heap to themselves.

It is usual for the Syrian Hadj to stop two or three days, on its return, in Wady Fatme, the first station from Mekka, to allow the camels some fine pasturage in that neighbourhood; but Soleyman Pasha, who entertained a great distrust of Mohammed Aly, and was particularly fearful lest he should make some further demand upon his caravan for camels, performed an uninterrupted march for two stations, and passed Wady Fatme; thus disappointing many Mekkan shopkeepers, who had repaired thither in hopes of establishing a market for the time. The Pasha became delirious during the journey, and, before he reached Damascus, was put under restraint by his own officers: he recovered his senses at Damascus, but died there soon after.

I was obliged to remain at Mekka a whole month after the departure of the Hadj, waiting for another opportunity of proceeding to Medina. I might have easily gone from Djidda, by sea, to Yembo; but I preferred the journey by land. At this time the people of the Hedjaz were kept in anxious suspense, on account of Mohammed Aly, who was preparing to set out from Mekka, in person, against the Wahabys. They knew that, if his expedition should fail, the Bedouins of the Hedjaz would immediately resort to their wonted practices, and cut off the route to the interior from all travellers; and experience had also taught them, that if the Wahabys obtained possession of the country a second time, the town of Mekka alone could indulge in any hope of escaping from being plundered. These considerations retarded the departure of caravans for Medina. A strong caravan usually leaves Mekka on the 11th of Moharrem, (corresponding this year with the 2nd of January, 1815,) the day after the opening of the Kaaba, which always takes place on the 10th of Moharrem, or the day called Ashour. Towards the end of December, the inhabitants were alarmed by a false report of the arrival of a Wahaby force, by the way of the seacoast, from the south: soon after, in the first days of January, 1815, Mohammed Aly set out from Mekka. He met the Wahaby army, four days after, at Byssel, in the neighbourhood of Tayf, where he gained the complete victory of which I have elsewhere given the details; this was no sooner known at Mekka, than the caravan for Medina, which had long been prepared, set out, on the 15th of January.

After the Syrian Hadj had departed, and the greater part of the other pilgrims retired to Djidda, waiting for an opportunity to embark, Mekka appeared like a deserted town. Of its brilliant shops, one-fourth only remained; and in the streets, where a few weeks before it was necessary to force one's way through the crowd, not a single hadjy was seen, except solitary beggars, who raised their plaintive voices towards the windows of the houses which they supposed to be still inhabited. Rubbish and filth covered all the streets, and nobody appeared disposed to remove it. The skirts of the town were crowded with the dead carcases of camels, the smell from which rendered the air, even in the midst of the town, offensive, and certainly contributed to the many diseases now prevalent. Several hundreds of these carcases lay near the reservoirs of the Hadj, and the Arabs inhabiting that part of Mekka never walked out without stuffing into their nostrils small pieces of cotton, which they carried suspended by a thread round the neck.* But this was not all. At this time the Mekkans are in the habit of emptying the privies of their houses; and, too lazy to carry the contents beyond the precincts of the town, they merely dig a hole in the street, before the door of the dwelling, and there deposit them, covering the spot only with a layer of earth. The consequences of such a practice may easily be imagined.

The feasts of nuptials and circumcision now take place, being always celebrated immediately after the Hadj, as soon as the Mekkans are left to themselves, and before the people have had time to spend the sums gained during the residence of the pilgrims; but I saw many

---

* The Arabs in general, even the Bedouins, are much more sensitive than the Europeans concerning the slightest offensive smell. This is one of the principal reasons why the Bedouins never enter a town without repugnance. They entertain a belief that bad smells affect the health by entering through the nostrils into the lungs; and it is for this reason, more than for the disagreeable sensation itself arising from the smell, that Arabs and Bedouins are often seen covering their noses with the skirts of their turbans, in walking through the streets.

more funerals than nuptial processions. Numbers of hadjys, already ill from the fatigues of the road, or from cold caught while wearing the ihram, are unable to proceed on their journey homewards; they remain in the hope of recovering strength, but often terminate their existence here. If they have some companion or relative with them, he carries off the dead man's property, on paying a fee to the Kadhy; if he is alone, the Kadhy and Sherif are his heirs, and these inheritances are no inconsiderable source of income. When I quitted Mekka, there were still remaining there perhaps a thousand hadjys, many of whom intended to pass a whole year in the holy city, and to be present at another Hadj; others to protract their residence only for a few months.

On the day of quitting Mekka, it is thought becoming to pay a parting visit to the Kaaba, called Towaf el Wodaa, and to perform the Towaf and Say. The hadjys generally do it when every thing is ready for departure, and mount their camels the moment they have finished the ceremony.

JOURNEY FROM MEKKA TO MEDINA.

On the 15th of January, 1815, I left Mekka with a small caravan of hadjys, who were going to visit the tomb of the prophet: it consisted of about fifty camels, the property of some Bedouins of the Ryshye and Zebeyde tribes, who either accompanied their beasts themselves, or had sent slaves with them. I had hired two camels, to carry myself and my slave and baggage; and, as is customary in the Hedjaz, I had paid the money in advance, at the rate of one hundred and eighty piastres per camel. My late cicerone, with whom I had every reason to be satisfied, though not quite free from those professional vices already mentioned, accompanied me out of town, as far as the plain of Sheikh Mahmoud, where the camels had assembled, and from whence the caravan started at nine o'clock in the evening. The journey to Medina, like that between Mekka and Djidda, is performed by night, which renders it much less profitable to the traveller, and, in winter time, much less comfortable than it would be by day.

Having proceeded an hour and a quarter,[*] we passed the Omra: thus far the road is paved in several parts with large stones, particularly on the ascents. We passed through valleys of firm sand, between irregular chains of low hills, where some shrubs and stunted acacia-trees grow. The road, with few exceptions, was perfectly level.

---

[*] I had bought a watch at Mekka, and had obtained a good compass from the English ship at Djidda.

At five hours from Mekka, we passed a ruined building called El Meymounye, with the tomb of a saint, the dome of which was demolished by the Wahabys. Near it is a well of sweet water, and a small birket, or reservoir, built of stone: a little building annexed to the tomb serves as a sort of khan for travellers. For the first six hours from Mekka our road lay N.W., when we turned a steep hill, which caravans cannot cross, and proceeded N.N.W. to Wady Fatme, which we reached at the end of eight hours from Mekka, just at the first appearance of dawn.

January 16th. We alighted on the spot where the pilgrim caravans repose on the day before they reach Mekka, in a part of the valley of Fatme, called Wady Djemmoum. Wady Fatme is low ground, abounding in springs and wells; it extends in an E.N.E. direction to the distance of four or five hours, until it nearly joins Wady Lymoun. To the west of our resting-place, it terminates at about an hour and a half's distance, being about six hours in its whole length. The most western point is called Medoua. On the western side are the principal plantations; to the east it is cultivated in a few spots only. It presented to the view on that side a plain of several miles in breadth, covered with shrubs, and flanked on both sides by low barren hills or elevated ground; but towards its eastern extremity it is said to be very well cultivated. Wady Fatme has different appellations in different parts; but the whole is commonly known to the people of Djidda and Mekka by the name of *El Wady*, or the valley. By the Arabian historians it is usually called Wady Merr. Between Wady Fatme and Hadda, (the station so named on the Djidda road,) are the two places, called Serouat and Rekany. (See Asamy.)

The cultivated grounds in Wady Fatme contain principally date-trees, which supply the markets of the two neighbouring towns; and vegetables, which are carried every night, on small droves of asses, to Mekka and Djidda. Wheat and barley are also cultivated in small quantities. The Wady being well supplied with water, might easily be rendered more productive than it now is; but the Hedjaz people are generally averse to all manual labour. Near the place where we alighted, runs a small rivulet, coming from the eastward, about three feet broad, and two feet deep, and flowing in a subterranean channel cased with stone, which is uncovered for a short space where the caravans take their supply of water, which is much more tepid than that of the Zemzem at Mekka, and is much better tasted. Close by are several ruined Saracen buildings and a large khan; and here also, according to Fasy, stood formerly a Mesdjed called El Fath. Among the date-groves are some Arab huts belonging to the cultivators of the soil, chiefly of the Lahyan tribe; the more wealthy of them belong to the tribe of the Sherifs of Mekka, called Dwy Barakat, who live here like Bedouins, in tents and huts. They have a few cattle; their cows, like all those of the Hedjaz, are small, and have a hump on their shoulders. Wady Fatme is also distinguished for its numerous henna-trees, with the odoriferous flowers of which, reduced to powder, the people of the East dye the palms of the hands, the soles of the feet, or the nails of both. The henna of this valley is sold at Mekka to the hadjys in small red leathern bags; and many of them carry some of it home, as a present to their female relations. I think it probable that the Oaditæ of Ptolemy were the inhabitants of this valley, (Wady, Oadi).

We found at our halting-place a party of about twenty servants and camel-drivers belonging to the Turkish army at Mekka, who had left that place secretly to escape the embargo laid by Mohammed Aly upon all persons of their description. They were without any provisions, and had very little money; but hearing that there was a caravan to start for Medina, they thought they should be able to accompany it thither. Some of them, who were Egyptians, intended to go to Yembo; others, who were Syrians, had formed the plan of returning home through the Desert by the Hedjaz route, and of begging their way along the Bedouin encampments, not having money enough to pay for their passage by sea to Suez.

We left our resting-place at three o'clock P. M., and were one hour in crossing the Wady to its northern side; from whence the Hadj road, on which we travelled, rises gently between hills, through valleys full of acacia-trees, in a direction N. 40 W. The rock is all granite of the gray and red species. At the end of two hours, the country opens, the trees diminish, and the course changes to N. 55 W. Towards sun-set I had walked a little way in front of the caravan, and being tired, sat down under a tree to wait its approach; when five Bedouins crept along the bushes towards me, and suddenly snatched up my stick, the only weapon which was lying on the ground behind me. Their leader said that I I had, was, no doubt, a deserter from the Turkish army, and therefore their lawful prize. I offered no resistance; but seeing them much less determined than Bedouin robbers generally are, I concluded that they were not free from fear. I told them, therefore, that I was a hadjy, and belonged to a large caravan escorted by Harb Bedouins; that they might wait a little before they stopped me, to assure themselves of this fact by the arrival of the caravan; and that they had better not offer me any violence, as our guides would no doubt know the perpetrators, and would report it to those who had the power to punish them. I felt assured that they had no intention of doing me any bodily harm, and was under no apprehension, especially as I had only a travelling dress and a few dollars to lose, should the worst happen. One of them, an old man, advised his comrades to wait a little; for that it would not be well to incur the consequences of robbing a hadjy. During our parley, I looked impatiently for the caravan coming in sight; but it had stopped behind for a quarter of an hour, to allow the travellers time to perform the evening prayers, a daily practice among them, of which I was yet ignorant. This delay was very much against me, and I expected every moment to be stripped, when, the tread of the camels being at last heard, the Bedouins retreated as suddenly as they had approached.

Although the road from Mekka to Medina was considered safe even for caravans unarmed like ours, yet stragglers are always exposed; and had it not been for the terror with which, a few days before, Mohammed Aly's victory over the Wahabys had inspired all the neighbouring Bedouins, I should probably have been punished for my imprudence in walking on alone. We rode the greater part of the night, over a plain more gravelly than sandy, where some ashour trees grow among the acacias, the same species (*Asclepia gigantea*) which I have so often mentioned in my Nubian Travels. This ground is called El Barka. After a seven hours' march, we stopped at El Kara.

January 17th. We slept a few hours during the night, a circumstance that seldom occurred on this journey. El Kara is a black, flinty plain, with low hills at a great distance to the east: it bears a few thorny trees, but affords no water. I was struck by its great resemblance to the Nubian Desert, south of Shigre. Although in the midst of winter, the heat was intense the whole morning of our stay at Kara. Nobody in the caravan had a tent, and I was more exposed than any person; all the others being mounted on a *shebrye*, or *shekdof*, a sort of covered camel-saddle, which affords some shelter from the sun, both while on the camel, and when placed on the ground: the shebrye serves for one person, and the shekdof for two—one sitting on each side of the camel. But I had always preferred the open seat upon a loaded camel, as more commodious, besides being more Arab-like, and affording the advantage of mounting or dismounting without the aid of the driver, and without stopping the animal; which it is very difficult to effect with those machines on their back, especially the shekdof, where both riders must keep continually balancing each other.

I formed to-day a closer acquaintance with my fellow-travellers; for, in small caravans, every one endeavours to be upon friendly terms with his companions. They were Malays, or, as they are called in the Levant, Jawas; and, with the exception of a few of them, who came from the coast of Malacca, all British subjects, natives of Sumatra, Java, and the coast of Malabar. The Malays come regularly to the Hadj, and often bring their women with them, three of whom were in our caravan. Many remain for years at Mekka, to study the Koran and the law, and are known among the Indians in the Hedjaz as scrupulous adherents to the precepts, or at least to the rites, of their religion. Few of them talk Arabic fluently; but they all read the Koran, and, even when travelling, are engaged in studying it. They defray the expenses of their journey by selling aloe-wood, the best kind of which, called Ma Wardy, they told me, cost, in their country, between three and four dollars per pound, and sells at Mekka at between twenty and twenty-five dollars. Their broad, long features, and prominent forehead, their short but stout stature, and their decayed teeth, which present a striking contrast to the pearly teeth of the Arabs, every where distinguish them, although they wear the common Indian dress. Their women, who all went unveiled, wore robes and handkerchiefs of striped silk stuff, of Chinese manufacture. They appeared to be people of very sober habits and quiet demeanour, but avaricious in the extreme; and their want of charity was sufficiently proved by their treatment of the destitute fugitives who had joined the caravan at Wady Fatme. They lived, during the whole journey, upon rice and salted fish: they boiled the rice in water, without any butter, a dear article in the Hedjaz, but which they did not dislike; for several of them begged my slave to give them secretly some of mine, for seasoning their dish. As they were people of property, avarice alone could be the motive for this abstemious diet; but they were sufficiently punished by the curses of the Bedouins, who had, of course, expected to partake of their dinners, and could not be prevailed upon to swallow the watery rice. Their copper vessels were all of Chinese manufacture, and instead of the *abrik*, or pot, which the Levantines use in washing and making their ablutions, they carried with them Chinese tea-pots.

During this journey, I had frequent opportunities of learning the opinion entertained by these Malays of the government and manners of the English, their present masters; they discovered a determined rancour and hostile spirit towards them, and greatly reviled their manners, of which, however, the worst they knew was, that they indulged too freely in wine, and that the sexes mixed together in social intercourse; none, however, impeached the justice of the government, which they contrasted with the oppression of their native princes; and although they bestowed upon the British the same opprobrious epithets with which the fanatic Moslims every where revile Europeans, they never failed to add, "but their government is good." I have overheard many similar conversations among the Indians at Djidda and Mekka, and also among the Arabian sailors who trade to Bombay and Surat; the spirit of all which was, that the Moslims of India hate the English, though they love their government.

We left our resting-place at ten o'clock P.M., and proceeded over the plain of Kara, in a direction N. 40 W. At the end of three hours we passed a ruined building called Sebyl el Kara, where a well, now filled up, formerly supplied the passengers with water. I saw no hills to the west, as far as my eyes could reach. The plain is here overgrown with some trees and thick shrubs. We continued to cross it till six hours, where it closes; and the road begins to ascend slightly through a broad woody valley: here is situated Bir Asfán, a large, deep well, lined with stone, with a spring of good water in the bottom. This is a station of the Hadj. There is another way from Wady Fatme to Asfan, four miles to the eastward of our route. We passed the well without stopping. Samhoudy, the historian of Medina, mentions a village at Asfan, with a spring called Owla; there is now no village here. At seven hours begins a very narrow ascending passage between rocks, affording room for only one camel. The torrents which rush down through this passage in winter have entirely destroyed the road, and filled it with large, sharp blocks of stone; the Hadj route seemed, in several places, to be cut out of the rock, but the night was too dark for seeing any thing distinctly. At the end of eight hours we reached the top of this defile, where a small building stands, perhaps the tomb of a Sheikh. From hence we rode over a wide plain, sometimes sandy, and in other parts a mixture of sand and clay, where trees and shrubs grow. At fourteen hours, near the break of dawn, we passed a small Bedouin encampment, and alighted, at the end of fifteen hours, in the neighbourhood of a village called Kholeys. We had made several short halts during the night, and kindled fires to warm ourselves.

Kholeys stands upon a wide plain, in several parts of which date-groves are seen, with fields, where *dhourra*, *bemye*, and *dokken* are cultivated. Several hamlets appear scattered about, which are comprised in the general name of Kholeys; the largest is called Es-Souk, or the market-place, near which the Hadj encamps. A small rivulet, tepid, like that in Wady Fatme, rises near the Souk, and is collected on the outside of the village in a small birket, now ruined, and then waters the plain. Near the birket there are also the ruins of a sebyl.* According to Kotobeddyn, the birket and sebyl were built by Kayd Beg, Sultan of Egypt, about A. H. 885. At that time, Kholeys had its own Emir, who was a very powerful person in the Hedjaz. I saw plenty of cattle, cows, and sheep; but the Arabs complained that their plantations suffered from drought, no rain having yet fallen, though the season was far advanced. The water from the rivulet did not appear sufficient to irrigate all the cultivated grounds, and the supply was even less than it might have been, as half of the water was suffered, through negligence, to escape from the narrow channels.

The village Es-Souk contains about fifty houses, all built of mud, and very low: its main street is lined with shops, kept by the people of Kholeys, and frequented by all the neighbouring Bedouins. The principal article for sale was dates, with which most of the shops were filled; in the others were sold dhourra, barley, lentils and onions, (both from Egypt,) rice, and some other articles of provision; but no wheat, that grain being little used by the Bedouins of this country: there were also spices, a few drugs, the bark of a tree for tanning the water-skins, and some butter. Milk was not to be found, for no one likes to be called a milk-seller. A tolerably well-built mosque stands by the rivulet, near some gigantic sycamore trees. I found in it two negro hadjys from Darfour; they had, the night before, been stripped on the road of a few piastres, earned at Mekka: one of them having attempted to defend himself, had been severely beaten; and they now intended to go back to Djidda, and endeavour to retrieve their loss by a few months' labour. One of the Bedouins who had stripped them, was smoking his pipe in the village; but they had not the means of proving the robbery against him, nor of obtaining justice. Kholeys is the chief seat of the Arab tribe of Zebeyd, a branch of Beni Harb, and the residence of their Sheikh. The greater part of them are Bedouins; and many even of those who cultivate the ground, pass some part of the

* A sebyl is a small, open building, often found by the side of fountains; in these sebyls travellers pray, and take their repose.

year under tents in the Desert, for the purpose of pasturing their cattle upon the wild herbage. A few families of Beni Amer, (or *Aamer*,*) another branch of Harb, are mixed with this tribe at Kholeys. Before the Turkish conquest, the usual currency at this market was dhourra; at present, piastres and paras are taken. Kholeys often sends small caravans to Djidda, which is two long days' journeys, or three caravan journeys distant. I was told that the neighbouring mountains were well peopled with Bedouins. About three hours distant, in a N. E. direction, is a fertile valley called Wady Khowar, known for its numerous plantations of bananas, by which the fruit-markets of Mekka and Djidda are supplied.

January 18th. Having filled our water-skins, we set out at three o'clock, P. M. Our road lay N. 20 E. over the plain. In two hours we came to a high hill, called Thenyet Kholeys, the steep side of which was deeply covered with sand, through which our camels ascended with difficulty. Some ancient ruins of a large building stand on its top, and the road on both sides of the hill is lined with walls, to prevent too great an accumulation of the sand. It was covered with carcases of camels, the relics of the late Hadj caravans. On descending the other side, a plain extended before us to the north and east, as far as the eye could reach. To the E. N. E. high mountains were visible, distant between twenty and thirty miles. Descending into the plain, we took the direction N. 10 W. At three hours and a half the plain, which thus far had been firm gravel, changed into deep sand, with tarfa (or tamarisk) trees, which delight particularly in sand, and in the driest season, when all vegetation around them is withered, never lose their verdure. It is one of the most common productions of the Arabian Desert, from the Euphrates to Mekka, and is also frequent in the Nubian deserts: its young leaves form an excellent food for camels. At four hours and a quarter, we found the road covered with a saline crust, indicating the neighbourhood of the sea ; from hence, our course was in various directions.

According to the usual practice in the Hedjaz, the camels walk in

---

* The *Beni Aamer* must not be confounded with *Amer*, another tribe of Harb.

a single row—those behind tied to the tails of those that precede them. The Arab, riding foremost, was to lead the troop; but he frequently fell asleep, as well as his companions behind; and his camel then took its own course, and often led the whole caravan astray. After a twelve hours' march, we alighted at the Hadj station called Kolleya, and also Kobeyba. Every spot in the plains of Arabia is known by a particular name; and it requires the eye and experience of a Bedouin to distinguish one small district from another: for this purpose, the different species of shrubs and pasturage produced in them by the rains, are of great assistance; and whenever they wish to mention a certain spot to their companions, which happens to have no name, they always designate it by the herbs that grow there; as, for instance, *Abou Shyh, Abou Agál*, &c.

About two hours distant from the spot where we rested, to the north-east, is water, with a small date-grove. I heard that the sea was from six to eight hours distant. The mountains continued to be seen between twenty and thirty miles on the east; their summits sharp, and presenting steep and insulated peaks. They are inhabited by the tribe of Ateybe, which in the seventeenth century, according to Asamy, also inhabited Wady Fatme. In the morning some Bedouin women appeared, with a few starved herds of sheep and goats, which were searching for the scanty herbage. No rain had fallen in the plain, and every shrub was withered; yet these Bedouins did not dare to seek for better pasturage in the neighbouring mountains, which did not belong to the territory of their tribe; for, whenever there is a drought, the limits of each territory are rigorously watched by the shepherds. I went out with several of the Malays to meet the women, and to ask them for some milk; the Malays had taken money with them to buy it; and I had filled my pockets with biscuit, for the same purpose. They refused to take the money, saying they were not accustomed to sell milk; but when I made them a present of the biscuits, they filled my wooden bowl in return. During the passage of the Hadj, these poor Bedouins fly in all directions, knowing the predatory habits of the soldiers who escort the caravan.

January 19th. We left Kolleya at half-past one o'clock P. M., and proceeded over the plain. In three hours, we came to low hills of moving sand; at four hours, to a stony plain, with masses of rock lying across the road: direction N. 25 W. At the end of nine hours, we halted during the night near the village of Rabegh, our road having been constantly level. Three or four hamlets, little distant from each other, are all comprised under this appellation; the principal of which, like that of Kholeys, is distinguished by the additional name of Es-Souk, or the market-place. The neighbouring plain is cultivated, and thick plantations of palm-trees render Rabegh a place of note on this route. Amongst the palm-trees grow a few tamarinds, or Thamr Hindy, the green fruit of which was now sufficiently ripe and pleasant. A few of these trees likewise grow at Mekka. Some rain had fallen here lately, and the ground was, in many parts, tilled. The ploughs of those Arabs, which are drawn by oxen or camels, resemble those delineated by Niebuhr, and which are, I believe, generally used in the Hedjaz and Yemen.* Rabegh possesses the advantage of a number of wells, the water of which is, however, but indifferent: its vicinity to the sea, which, as I heard, was six or seven miles distant, though the view of it was hid by palm-groves, causes the coast of Rabegh to be visited by many country ships that are in want of water. The Bedouins of this coast are active fishermen, and bring hither from the more distant ports their salted fish; a quantity of which may always be found in the market, where it is bought up by the Arab ships' crews, who consume a great part of it, and carry the rest to Egypt or Djidda. The inhabitants of Rabegh are of the above-mentioned Harb tribes of Aamer and Zebeyd, principally the latter. In the opposite mountains, to the east, live the Beni Owf, another tribe of Harb. The hadjys passing by sea from Egypt to Djidda, are obliged to take the ihram opposite to Rabegh, which they may do either on shore, or on board ship.

An accident occurred here, which showed in the strongest light the total want of charity in our companions the Malays. There were several poorer Malays, who, unable to pay for the hire of a camel, fol-

---

* I cannot conceive what could have led Ptolemy to place a river in the direction between Mekka and Yembo, as certainly no river empties itself into the sea any where in the Hedjaz. In winter time, many torrents rush down from the mountains.

lowed their comrades on foot; but as our night journeys were long, these men came in sometimes an hour or two after we had alighted in the morning. To-day one of them was brought in under an escort of two Bedouins of the tribe of Owf, who told us that they had found him straying in the Desert, and that he had promised them twenty piastres if they would guide him to the caravan, and that they expected his friends would make up this sum, the man, as they saw, being himself quite destitute of money. When they found that none of our party showed any inclination to pay even the smallest part of this sum, and that all of them disclaimed any knowledge or acquaintance with the man, who, they said had joined the caravan at starting from Mekka without his person being in the least known to them, the Bedouins declared that they should take the little clothing he had upon him, and keep him a prisoner in their tents till some other Malays should pass, who might release him. When the caravan was preparing to start, they seized him, and carried him off a short distance towards the wood. He was so terrified that he had lost the power of speech, and permitted himself to be led away, without making the slightest resistance. Our own guides were no match for the Owf, a tribe much dreaded for its warlike and savage character; there was no judge in the village of Rabegh, to whose authority an appeal might be made; and the two Bedouins had a legitimate claim upon their prisoner. I should have performed no great act of generosity in paying his ransom myself; but I thought that this was a duty incumbent upon his countrymen the Malays, and therefore used all my endeavours to persuade them to do it. I really never met with such hard-hearted, unfeeling wretches; they unanimously declared that they did not know the man, and were not bound to incur any expense on his account. The camels were loaded; they had all mounted, and the leader was on the point of starting, when the miserable object of the dispute broke out in loud lamentations. I had waited for this moment. Relying on the respect I enjoyed in the caravan from being supposed a hadjy in some measure attached to Mohammed Aly's army, and the good-will of our guides, which I had cultivated by distributing victuals liberally amongst them ever since we left Mekka, I seized the leader's camel, made it couch down, and exclaimed, that the caravan should not proceed till the man was released. I then went from load to load, and partly by imprecating curses on the Malays and their women, and partly by collaring some of them, I took from every one of their camels twenty paras, (about three pence,) and, after a long contest, made up the twenty piastres. This sum I carried to the Bedouins who had remained at a distance with their prisoner, and representing to them his forlorn state, and appealing to the honour of their tribe, induced them to take ten piastres. According to true Turkish maxims, I should have pocketed the other ten, as a compensation for my trouble; I, however, gave them to the poor Malay, to the infinite mortification of his countrymen. The consequence was, that, during the rest of the journey, they entirely discarded him from their party, and he was thrown upon my hands, till we arrived at Medina, and during his residence there. I intended to have provided him with the means of returning to Yembo, but I fell dangerously ill soon after my arrival at Medina, and know not what afterwards became of him.

Several pilgrims were begging for charity in the market of Rabegh. These poor people, in starting from Mekka for Medina with the great caravan, fancy that they are sufficiently strong to bear the fatigues of that journey, and know that, in travelling with the caravan, charitable hadjys are to be found who will supply them with food and water; but the long night-marches soon exhaust their strength, they linger behind on the road, and, after great privations and delays, are obliged to proceed on their journey by other opportunities. An Afghan pilgrim here joined our party; he was an old man, of very extraordinary strength, and had come the whole way from Kaboul to Mekka on foot, and intended to return in the same manner. I regretted his slight acquaintance with Arabic, as he seemed an intelligent man, and could no doubt have given me some interesting information respecting his country.

January 20th. We left Rabegh at four P. M. Our road lay N. 8 W., in most parts of black flint, interspersed with some hills of sand, upon which were a few trees. Having enjoyed no repose whatever for the last two days, I fell asleep upon my camel, and can only say, that after a ride of eleven hours, over hilly and sandy ground, we alighted at

Mastoura, a station of the Hadj. Two large and deep wells, cased with stone, afford here a copious supply of good water. Near them stood the tomb of a saint called Sheikh Madely, which had been demolished by the Wahabys. About ten miles east of this is a high mountain, called *Djebel Ayoub*, "Job's Mountain," overtopping the other summits of the chain of which it forms a part, and covered in many spots with trees. It is inhabited by the Owf tribe. The whole road from Kolleya to this place is dangerous on account of the robberies of these Bedouins; and the caravan never passes without losing some of its loads or camels. In the time of the Wahabys it was completely secure; the Sheikhs of the Harb, and the whole tribe being made responsible for all depredations committed in their territory. The Wahabys, however, had not been able to subdue the Owf in their own mountains; and a proof of their independence appeared in the long hair which this tribe wore, contrary to the Wahaby precept, which had established it as a universal law to shave the head bare.

We found, at the wells of Mastoura, several flocks of camels and sheep, which the Owf shepherds and shepherdesses were watering. I bought from them a lamb for a few piastres and some tobacco, and divided it among our guides and those who accompanied us on foot. The Malays came to ask me for their share, giving me to understand that their compliance with my entreaties in favour of their poor countryman, was deserving of reward; but the Bedouins who were with us, saved me, by their taunting reprimands, the trouble of answering them. Several tombs of hadjys were seen near the wells, which the Wahabys had respected; for they seldom injured any tombs that pride or bigotry had left unadorned.

January 21st. We set out at three o'clock P.M. The plain we crossed is either flinty, or presents spots of cultivable clay. The direction was north. After proceeding over a sandy plain, covered with low brush-wood, for two hours and a half, we had Djebel Ayoub about six miles distant: then begins a lower ridge of mountains, running parallel to the road. Here we quitted the great Hadj route, which turns off in a more westerly direction, and we proceeded towards the mountains N. 15 E. to reach Szafra by the nearest route. After a march of thirteen hours, over uneven ground and low hills, we halted near day-break, in a sandy plain, by the well called Bir-es'-Sheikh. It will have been observed, that our night marches were always very long; but the rate of the camel's walk was very slow, scarcely more than two miles an hour, or two and a quarter. Bir-es'-Sheikh is a well between thirty and forty feet deep, and fifteen feet in diameter, solidly cased with stone; the work of men who felt more anxiety for the convenience of travellers to the holy cities, than the present chiefs of the faithful evince. If pressed for time, the Hadj sometimes takes this route; but it goes usually by Beder, where the Egyptian and Syrian caravans, on their road to Mekka, follow each other, at the interval of one day or two, their time of setting out upon the journey invariably taking place on fixed days. We were now close to the great chain, which, since we left Kholeys, had been on our right: a ridge of it, a few miles north of Bir-es'-Sheikh, takes a westerly direction towards the sea, and at its extremity lies Beder. We met Bedouins at this well also; they were of the tribe of Beni Salem, or Sowaleme: our guides bought a sheep of them, and roasted it in the *Medjba*, a hole dug in the sand, and lined with small stones, which are heated; the flesh is laid upon them, and then covered by cinders and the wet skin of the animal, and closely shut up with sand and clay. In an hour and a half the meat is cooked, and, as it loses none of its juices, has an excellent flavour.

January 22nd. We left the well at half-past three P.M. Route N. 10 W. ascending over uneven ground. In an hour and a half we entered the mountains, at the angle formed by the great chain on one side, and the above-mentioned branch, which extends towards Beder, on the other. From hence we continued N.N.E. in valleys of sandy soil, full of detached rocks. High mountains with sharp-pointed summits, and entirely barren, enclosed the road on both sides. The Eastern mountain, which here runs parallel with it, is called Djebel Sobh; the territory of the powerful tribe of Beni Sobh, a branch of the Beni Harb. Their mountains contain many fertile valleys, where date-trees grow, and some dhourra is sown. It is here that the Mekka balsam-tree is principally found, and the Senna Mekka, or Arabian senna, which the Syrian caravan exports, is collected exclusively in this district. The passage into the interior parts of this mountain is described as very difficult, and could never be forced by the Wahabys. Numerous families of the other tribes of Harb had retreated thither, with all their goods and cattle, from the arms of Saoud; and while all the Hedjaz Bedouins submitted to the Wahaby dominion, the Sobh was the only tribe which successfully defended their territory, and boldly asserted their independence.

After a march of six hours and a half, the road began to ascend among low rocky hills. At seven hours and a half we entered Wady Zogág, a narrow valley of gentle ascent, full of loose stones, and overgrown with acacia-trees. In proceeding up, it grew narrower, the path became steeper, and more difficult for the camels. At the end of thirteen hours, we came to level ground at its top, and there entered the valley of Es' Szafra, close by the village of the same name, at which we alighted.

January 23d. Our camels being tired, having found very little food on the road, though they always had the whole morning to pasture, and several of them threatening to break down, the drivers stopped here the whole day. Like the before-mentioned Bedouin villages, Szafra is a market-place for all the surrounding tribes: its houses are built on the declivity of the mountain, and in the valley, which is narrow, leaving scarcely room enough for the date-groves which line both sides of it. A copious rivulet flows down the valley, the water of which is dispersed among the date-trees, and irrigates some cultivated fields in the wider parts of the windings of this valley. Wheat, dhourra, barley, and dokhen are sown here; of vegetables the Badendján, or egg-plant, Meloukhye onions and radishes are cultivated; and vines, lemon, and banana-trees abound. The soil is every where sandy, but rendered fertile by irrigation: copious rains had fallen three days since in the mountains, and a torrent twenty feet broad, and three or four feet deep, was still flowing. The date-groves extend about four miles; they belong to the inhabitants of Szafra, as well as of neighbouring Bedouins, who keep some of their own people, or Arab labourers, employed in irrigating the grounds, and repair hither themselves when the dates are ripe. The date-trees pass from one person to another in the course of trade, and are sold by the single tree; the price paid to a girl's father on marrying her, consists often in date-trees. They all stand in deep sand, which is collected from the middle parts of the valley, and heaped up round their root, and must be renewed annually, as the torrents usually wash it away. Every small grove is enclosed by a mud or stone wall; the cultivators inhabit several hamlets, or insulated houses, scattered among the trees. The houses are low, and generally have only two rooms, and there is a small courtyard for the cattle. Several springs of running water, and many wells, are found in the gardens; the principal rivulet has its source in a grove close to the market; a small Mesdjed or mosque is built beside it, and it is overshadowed by a few large wild chesnut-trees. I saw no others of that species in the Hedjaz. Here, too, the water of the spring was tepid, but in a less degree than at Rabegh and Kholeys.

The inhabitants of this valley, the name of which is celebrated in the Hedjaz for the abundance of its dates, are of the Beni Salem tribe, the most numerous branch of Harb, and, like most other tribes of the Hedjaz, partly Bedouins and partly settled inhabitants; the latter remaining in their houses and gardens the whole year round, though they dress and live in the same manner as their brethren under tents. The Wahaby chief had been aware of the importance of this station; and having succeeded, after a long resistance, in overpowering the Beni Harb, who held the key of the Northern Hedjaz,* thought it necessary to keep a watchful eye over this valley, and there built several strong blockhouses or towers, in which the collectors of his revenues resided, and where they deposited the taxes collected from the valley. All these Bedouins were decidedly hostile to the Wahaby system: even now, though free from their yoke, they load them with as many reproaches,

---

* In this enterprise he was assisted by Medheyan, formerly a chief of Harb, who had been deprived of his post by Djezy, a fortunate rival. Medheyan was afterwards treacherously seized by the Turks at Medina, and beheaded at Constantinople; and Djezy, a friend of Mohammed Aly, was killed by the Turkish governor of Medina, for having spoken too highly of his services.

as the Mekkans bestow praises on them. Before the Wahaby invasion, the Beni Harb had never known a master, nor had the produce of their fields ever been taxed. The Sherif of Mekka certainly assumed a nominal supremacy over them; but they were in fact completely independent, and their Sheikhs seconded the Sherif's views so far only as they were thought beneficial, or of pecuniary advantage to their own people. The latter now complained greatly of the heavy taxation imposed by the Wahabys, and said that, besides the money they were obliged to pay into Saoud's treasury, the chief of all the Wahaby Sheikhs of the Hedjaz, Othman el Medheyfe, had extorted from them many additional sums. I thought the accuracy of this information doubtful; for I knew that the Wahaby chief had always shown particular care in preventing such acts of injustice in his officers, and punished those who were guilty. They also told me that not only had their gardens and plantations been taxed, but the very water with which they irrigated them had been assessed at a yearly sum.

The dress of the people of Szafra consists of a shirt, and a short gown of coarse Indian coloured calico, over which they wear a white *abba* of light texture, the same as that worn by the Bedouins of the Euphrates, near Aleppo, and which is similar to the dress of all the Beni Harb who have become settlers; while the Bedouins of the tribe wear the brown and white striped abba. The profits which they derive from the passage of caravans, and their petty dealings, seem to have had a baneful influence upon their character, for they cheat as much as they can: they are, however, not destitute of commiseration and hospitality towards the poor hadjys, who, in their passage, contrive to collect from the shops as much as is necessary for their daily food. We here met several poor pilgrims on their way to Medina, who had nothing to subsist upon but what they obtained from the generosity of the Bedouins on the road. This was not the first time that I reflected how ill had been applied the splendid liberality of many Khalifes and Sultans, who, while they enriched Mekka and Medina, and spent enormous sums to provide for the sumptuous passage of the great Hadj caravans through the holy land, yet entirely neglected to provide for the comfort and security of the immense number of poor pilgrims who are continually travelling through that country. Half-a-dozen houses of charity, established between Mekka and Medina, with an annual endowment of a few thousand dollars, would be of more real service to the cause of their religion, than all the sums spent in feeding the idle, or keeping up a vain show. On the whole of this route between Mekka and Medina, there is not a public khan, nor has any thing been done for the benefit of travellers, beyond keeping the wells in repair. The only instance of a truly charitable act in any of the sovereigns who enriched Mekka, recorded by the historians, is the building of an hospital at Mekka, in A. H. 816, by order of Moayed, Sultan of Egypt. No traces of it now remain.

In the market-street of Szafra, which is called Souk-es'-Szafra, dates are the principal article for sale. The pound, which costs twenty-five paras at Mekka, was sold here for ten. Honey, preserved in sheep-skins, forms another article of trade here. The neighbouring mountains are full of bee-hives. In those districts which are known to be frequented by bees, the Bedouins place wooden hives upon the ground, and the bees never fail to take possession of them. The honey is of the best quality; I saw one sort of it as white, and almost as clear, as water. Drugs and spices, and some perfumes, of which the Bedouins of those countries are very fond, may here also be purchased.

Szafra and Beder are the only places in the Hedjaz where the balsam of Mekka, or Balesan, can be procured in a pure state. The tree from which it is collected grows in the neighbouring mountains, but principally upon Djebel Sobh, and is called by the Arabs *Beshem*. I was informed that it is from ten to fifteen feet high, with a smooth trunk, and thin bark. In the middle of summer, small incisions are made in the bark; and the juice, which immediately issues, is taken off with the thumb-nail, and put into a vessel. The gum appears to be of two kinds; one of a white, and the other of a yellowish-white colour: the first is the most esteemed. I saw here some of the latter sort, in a small sheep-skin, which the Bedouins use in bringing it to market: it had a strong, turpentine smell, and its taste was bitter. The people of Szafra usually adulterate it with sesamum oil, and tar. When they try its purity, they dip their finger into it and then set fire to it; if it burn without hurting or leaving a mark on the finger, they judge it to be of good quality; but if it burn the finger as soon as it is set on fire, they consider it to be adulterated. I remember to have read, in Bruce's Travels, an account of the mode of trying it, by letting a drop fall into a cup filled with water; the good Balesan falling coagulated to the bottom, and the bad dissolving, and swimming on the surface. I tried this experiment, which was unknown to the people here, and found the drop swim upon the water; I tried also their test by fire upon the finger of a Bedouin, who had to regret his temerity: I therefore regarded the balsam sold here as adulterated; it was of less density than honey. I wished to purchase some; but neither my own baggage, nor any of the shops of Szafra, could furnish any thing like a bottle to hold it: the whole skin was too dear. The Bedouins, who bring it here, usually demand two or three dollars per pound for it, when quite pure; and the Szafra Arabs re-sell it to the hadjys of the great caravan, at between eight and twelve dollars per pound in an adulterated state. It is bought up principally by Persians.

The Balesan for sale at Djidda and Mekka, from whence it comes to Cairo, always undergoes several adulterations; and if a hadjy does not casually meet with some Bedouins, from whom he may purchase it at first hand, no hopes can be entertained of getting it in a pure state. The richer classes of the hadjys put a drop of Balesan into the first cup of coffee they drink in the morning, from a notion that it acts as a tonic. The seeds of the tree from which it is obtained, are employed in the Hedjaz to procure abortion.

I must notice here, as a peculiarity in the customs of the Beni Salem tribe, that, in case of the *Dye*, or the fine for a man slain, (amounting here to eight hundred dollars,) being accepted by the deceased's family, the sum is made up by the murderer and his family, and by his relations; the former paying one-third, and the kindred two-thirds; a practice which, as far as my knowledge extends, does not prevail in any other part of the Desert.

Our Bedouin guides had here a long quarrel with the Malays. The guides had bargained in the market for two camels, to replace two that were unfit to continue the journey; but not having money enough to pay for them, they required the assistance of the Malays, and begged them to lend ten dollars, to be repaid at Medina. The Malays refused, and being hardly pressed, endeavoured to engage my interposition in their behalf; but the Bedouins forced the money from them by the same means which I had employed on a former occasion: the purse of a Malay, which had been concealed in a bag of rice, now came to light; it probably contained three hundred dollars. The owner was so much frightened by this discovery, and the apprehension that the Arabs would murder him on the road for the sake of his money, that by way of punishment for his avarice, they contrived to keep him in a constant state of alarm till we arrived at Medina.

January 24th. We left the Souk-Es'-Szafra* at 3 p.m., and rode along the valley, which widens a little beyond the market-place. The brilliant verdure of the date-trees and plantations form a singular contrast with the barren mountains on each side. Our direction was N. 10 E. I found the rock here composed throughout of red Thon stone, with transverse strata of the same substance, but of a green colour; beyond Djedeyde, a little higher up, I found, in my return from Medina, feldspar rocks. At one hour from the Souk, we passed a similar village in the valley, called El Kharma, which is comprised within the Wady Szafra. At the end of two hours, we came to a public fountain in ruins, on the road, near a well half choked up. The valley here divides; one branch turns towards the N.W.; the other, which we followed, N.N.E. Two hours and a half, we passed a hamlet called Dar el Hamra, with gardens of date-trees, and plantations, inhabited by the tribe of Howaseb, another branch of Harb. Several small watch-towers had been built here on the summits of the neighbouring mountains, on both sides of the valleys, by Othman el Medhayfe, to secure this passage. Plenty of bananas were offered us for sale, as we passed this place. At the end of two hours and three quarters, the road begins to ascend, and the soil of the valley, which thus far from Szafra is gravel intermixed with sand, now becomes stony.

* During the night, a Kurd courier, mounted upon a dromedary, escorted by several Bedouins, passed through Szafra; he came from the head-quarters of Mohammed Aly, and was the bearer of the intelligence of the capture of Tarabe to Tousoun Pasha, at Medina.

In four hours and a quarter we passed the village called Mokad, which also produces dates.

We stopped here for a quarter of an hour; where we were surrounded by many of the inhabitants; and on remounting my camel, I found that several trifling articles had been pilfered from my baggage. This defile is particularly dreaded by the Hadj caravans; and stories are related of daring robberies committed by the Arabs which appear almost incredible. They dress sometimes like Turkish soldiers, and introduce themselves into the caravan while on their march during the night; and in this manner they carried off, the year before, one of the finest led horses of the Pasha of Damascus, the chief of the Syrian caravan. They jump from behind upon the camel of the sleeping hadjy, stop his mouth with their abbas, and throw down to their companions whatever valuables they find upon him. If discovered, they draw their daggers and cut their way through; for, if taken, they can expect no mercy. The usual mode of punishment on such occasions, is to impale them at the moment the caravan starts from the next station, leaving them to perish on the stake, or be devoured by wild beasts. The horrors of such a punishment, however, do not deter others from committing the same crimes; and individuals among the Bedouins pride themselves in being reckoned expert Hadj-robbers, because great courage and dexterity are necessary to such a character. From hence our road lay N. 20 E. A barren valley about three hundred yards across begins here, which, at the end of six hours and a half, conducted us with many windings to Djedeyde, situated in a spot where the road becomes straight and has a steep ascent. I saw a great many date-trees on both sides of the valley, which takes the general name of Djedeyde, and is divided into several villages. Near the southern entrance is the market-place, or Es'-Souk Djedeyde, which appeared to be of greater extent than that of Szafra; but it is now almost in ruins. From thence the valley becomes still narrower, running between steep rocks for about one hour. It was in this spot that Mohammed Aly's first expedition against the Wahabys, under the command of his son Tousoun Beg, was defeated in autumn 1811. They had possession of both mountains, and the discharges of musketry from each side reached across the valley, where the Turkish army attempted in vain to pass. Most of the Sheikhs of the tribe of Harb, and the two great southern Wahaby chiefs, Othman el Medheyfe and Tamy, were present, with two of the sons of Saoud.

At seven hours and a half, we passed El Kheyf, the last village in the valley of Djedeyde; several insulated groups of houses are also scattered along the valley. About eighty tents of Turkish soldiers were pitched here, to guard this pass; one of the most important positions in the Hedjaz, because it is the only way by which caravans can proceed from Mekka or Yembo to Medina. The Harb tribe are well fitted, by their warlike temper, to defend this post. Even before the Wahaby conquest, they had repeatedly been at war with the Syrian caravan, and Djezzar Pasha himself had been several times repulsed here, and obliged to take the eastern Hadj route, at the back of the great chain, rather than submit to the exorbitant demands of the Beni Harb for permitting the Hadj to pass through their territories. Abdullah Pasha of Damascus, who conducted the Hadj eighteen times in person to Mekka, was compelled to do the same. Whenever the Harb are in amity with the caravan, they have a right to a considerable passage duty, which is paid at Djedeyde.

Szafra appeared to me better peopled, and to contain more houses, than are now in Djedeyde. In speaking of this pass, the Arabs generally join the two names, and say, " the valley of Szafra and Djedeyde." Beyond El Kheyf the valley widens, and forms many windings. Our caravan was here in constant fear of robbers, which kept us awake, though the severe cold during the night would not have suffered us to sleep. Our main direction from Kheyf was N. 40 E. At twelve hours, gently ascending through the valley, we entered a plain, situated in the midst of the mountains, about ten miles in length, called El Nazye, where we alighted.

January 25th. We remained encamped here the whole day, some passengers having acquainted us that disturbances had broken out on the road before us, which we did not discover to be a false report till the next day. The rocks surrounding this plain are partly of granite, and partly of lime-stone. The plain is thickly covered with acacia-trees.

Good water is found on the side of the mountains, but not in the plain itself. Some Bedouins of Beni Salem, to which tribe the inhabitants of Djedeyde also belong, pastured their flocks here: they were chiefly occupied in collecting food for their camels from the acacia-trees; for this purpose, they spread a straw mat under the tree, and beat its boughs with long sticks, when the youngest and freshest leaves, from the extremities of the twigs, fall down: these are esteemed the best food for camels. I saw them sold in measures, in the market at Szafra. We exchanged some biscuits for milk with these Bedouins; and one, to whom I had given a small dose of rhubarb, brought me some fresh butter in return.

January 26th. We started at two P. M., and an hour and a half's march over the plain brought us to the mountain. The whole breadth of this plain is about six miles. We then entered the mountain in the direction N. 50 E. The mixed rocks of granite and lime-stone present no regular strata. We next passed through a short defile, and, at the end of two hours and a half, entered a small plain called Shab el Hál, between the mountains, where were several encampments of Bedouins. At five hours, we entered a broad valley, running in a straight line, and covered with white sand. The night was cold, and the moon shone beautifully; I therefore walked in front of the caravan, whose pace being slow, I soon advanced, without perceiving it, to a considerable distance a-head. Finding that it did not come up, I sat down under a tree, and was going to light a fire, when I heard the tread of horses advancing towards me. I kept hidden behind the trees, and presently saw some Bedouins of very suspicious appearance pass by. After waiting a long time for the caravan, and unable to account for its delay, I retraced my steps, and found the camels standing at rest, and taking breath, and every soul upon them fast asleep, the foot-passengers being still behind. This happened to us several times during our journey. When the camel hears no voices about it, and is not urged by the leader, it slackens its pace, and at last stands still to rest; and if the leading camel once stops, all the rest do the same. I roused the Arabs, and we proceeded. The next day, we learnt that some travellers had been plundered this night on the road—no doubt by the horsemen who passed me, and who probably dispersed when they saw a large caravan approaching.

The valley in which we were travelling is called *Wady es' Shohada*, or the "Valley of Martyrs," where many followers of Mohammed are said to have been killed in battle: their remains are covered by rude heaps of stones in different parts of the valley. Here also are seen several tombs of hadjys; and I observed some walls, much ruined, where a small chapel or mosque appeared to have stood: no water is found here. This is a station of the Hadj caravan. At the end of nine hours, we issued from this *wady*, which is on a very slight ascent; and then taking a direction E. N. E. we crossed a rocky ground, and entered a wide plain called El Fereysh, where two small caravans from Medina bound to Yembo passed us. At the end of eleven hours and a half we alighted.

The plain of Fereysh, according to the historian Asamy, was the scene of a sanguinary battle, between the Sherif of Mekka and the Bedouin tribes of Dhofyr and Aeneze, in A. H. 1063. The Dhofyr, who are now settled in Mesopotamia, towards Baghdad, were at that time pasturing their herds in the neighbourhood of Medina.

January 27th. The rocks here are all of red granite. A party of Bedouins, with their women, children, and tents passed us; they belonged to the tribe of Harb, called El Hamede, and had left the upper country, where no rain had yet fallen, to seek better pasturage in the lower mountains. While we were encamped, a heavy storm, with thunder and lightning, overtook us, and the rain poured down: as it threatened to be of long duration, and we had no tents, it was thought advisable to proceed. We started in the afternoon; and it continued to rain during the rest of the day and the whole night, which, joined to the cold climate in these elevated regions, was severely felt by all of us. Our road ascended through rocky valleys full of thorny trees; it was crossed by several torrents that had rapidly swollen, and which we passed with difficulty. After seven hours' march we reached the summit of this chain of mountains, when the immense eastern plain lay stretched before us: we passed several insulated hills. The ground is covered with black and brown flints. In nine hours we passed at some distance to the west of the date-plantations, and the few houses built round the well called Bir Aly. At the end of ten hours, in the middle of the night, just as the weather had cleared up, and a severe frost succeeded the rain, we arrived before the gate of Medina. It was shut, and we had to wait till day-light before it could be opened. Being unable to light a fire on the wet ground with wet fuel, and being all completely soaked with the rain, the sharp frost of the morning became distressing to us, and was probably the cause of the fever which confined me so long in this town; for I had enjoyed perfect health during the whole journey.

We entered Medina at sun-rise on the 28th of January, the thirteenth day after our leaving Mekka, having halted two days on the road. The Hadj caravan usually performs the journey in eleven days, and, if pressed for time, in ten.

The Bedouins apply to the whole country between Mekka and Medina, west of the mountains, the name of El Djohfe, which, however, is sometimes understood to mean the country from Mekka to Beder only.

MEDINA.

The caravan alighted in a large court-yard in the suburb, where the loads were deposited; and all the travellers who had come with it immediately dispersed in quest of lodgings. With the help of a Mezowar, a professional class of men, similar to the delyls at Mekka, I procured, after some trouble, a good apartment in the principal market-street of the town, about fifty yards from the great mosque. I transported my baggage to those lodgings, where I was called upon by the Mezowar to visit the mosque and the holy tomb of Mohammed; it being a law here, as at Mekka, that a traveller arriving in the town must fulfil this duty, before he undertakes the most trifling business.

The ceremonies are here much easier and shorter than at Mekka, as will be presently seen. In a quarter of an hour I had gone through them, when I was at liberty to return home to arrange my domestic affairs. My Mezowar assisted me in the purchase of all necessary provisions, which were not obtained without difficulty; Tousoun Pasha, the governor of the town, having, by his inconsiderate measures, frightened away the Bedouins and camel-drivers, who used to bring in provisions. Flour and butter, however, those prime articles in an Eastern kitchen, were to be had before sun-set, though not found in the public market; but it was three days before I could procure any coal, the want of which was sensibly felt at this cold season of the year. Hearing that Yahya Effendi, the physician of Tousoun Pasha, the same person who in July last had taken my bill upon Djidda, was here. I paid him a visit next day, and showed him a letter received at Mekka, before I had left that town, from my Cairo banker, mentioning the payment of the bill, no news of which had yet reached Yahya himself. Much as this gentleman's acquaintance had been of service to me on that occasion, a good deal took place now to detract from it. At a visit which he paid me soon after, he happened to see my small stock of medicines, the same that I had in my Nubian journey, during which it never was touched, some emetics and purges only having been used whilst I staid at Djidda and Mekka; I had therefore half a pound of good bark in my medicine sack, untouched. Several persons of the Pasha's court were at this time ill of fevers; Tousoun Pasha himself was in an indifferent state of health, and his physician had few medicines fit for such cases. He begged of me the bark, which I gave him, as I was then in good health, and thought myself already in the vicinity of Egypt, where I hoped to arrive in about two months. I owed him, moreover, some obligations, and was glad to testify my gratitude. Two days after I had cause to repent of my liberality; for I was attacked by a fever, which soon took a very serious turn. As it was intermittent, I wished to take bark; but when I asked the physician for some of it, he assured me that he had already distributed the last dram, and he brought me, instead of it, some of the powder of the Gentiana, which had lost all its virtue from age. My fever thus increased, accompanied by daily and repeated vomiting, and profuse sweats, being for the whole first month quotidian. The emetics I took proved of no service; and after having from want of bark gone through the course of medicines I thought applicable to the case, and being very seldom favoured with a visit from my friend Yahya Effendi, I left my disease to nature. After the first month, there was an interval of a week's repose, of which had I been able to profit by taking bark, my disorder would, no doubt, have been overcome; but it had abated only to return with greater violence, and now became a tertian fever, while the vomiting still continued, accompanied by occasional faintings, and ended in a total prostration of strength. I was now unable to rise from my carpet, without the assistance of my slave, a poor fellow, who by habit and nature was more fitted to take care of a camel, than to nurse his drooping master.

I had by this time lost all hope of returning to Egypt, and had prepared myself for dying here. Despondency had seized me, from an apprehension that, if the news of my death should arrive in England, my whole Hedjaz journey would, perhaps, be condemned as the unauthorised act of an imprudent, or at least over-zealous missionary; and I had neither books, nor any society, to divert my mind from such reflections: one book only was in my possession, a pocket edition of Milton, which Captain Boag, at Djidda, had kindly permitted me to take from his cabin-library, and this I must admit was now worth a whole shelf full of others. The mistress of my lodgings, an old infirm woman, by birth an Egyptian, who during my stay took up her quarters in an upper story, from which she could speak to me without being seen, as it opened into my own room below, used to converse with me for half an hour every evening; and my cicerone, or Mezowar, paid me occasional visits, in order, as I strongly suspected, to seize upon part of my baggage in case of my death. Yahya Effendi left the town in the month of March, with the army of Tousoun Pasha, which marched against the Wahabys.

About the beginning of April, the returning warmth of the spring put a stop to my illness; but it was nearly a fortnight before I could venture to walk out, and every breeze made me dread a return of the fever. The bad climate of the town, its detestable water, and the great number of diseases now prevalent, made me extremely desirous to leave Medina. My original intention was, to remain here, at most, one month, then to take some Bedouin guides, and with them to cross the Desert to Akaba, at the extremity of the Red Sea, in a straight direction, from whence I might easily have found my way to Cairo. In this route I wished to visit Hedjer, on the Syrian Hadj road, where I expected to find some remains of the remotest antiquity, that had not been described by any other traveller, while the interior of the country might have offered many other objects of research and curiosity. It was, however, utterly impossible for me to perform this journey in my convalescent state; nor had I any hopes of recovering, in two months, strength sufficient for a journey of such fatigue. To wait so long, continually exposed to suffer again from the climate, was highly unadvisable; and I panted for a change of air, being convinced that, without it, my fever would soon return. With these feelings I abandoned the long-projected design of my journey, and now determined on going to Yembo, on the sea-coast, and from thence to embark for Egypt; a decision in some degree rendered necessary by the state of my purse, which a long stay at Medina had greatly reduced. When I found myself strong enough to mount a camel, I looked out for some conveyance to Yembo, and contracted with a Bedouin, who, together with his companions, forming a small caravan, started for that place on the 21st of April, within six days of three months after my arrival at Medina, eight weeks of which time I had been confined to my couch.

My remarks on Medina are but scanty; with good health, I should have added to them: but as this town is totally unknown to Europeans, they may contain some acceptable information. The plan of the town was made by me during the first days of my stay, and I can vouch for the correctness of its outlines; but I had not the same leisure to trace it in all its details, as I had that of Mekka.

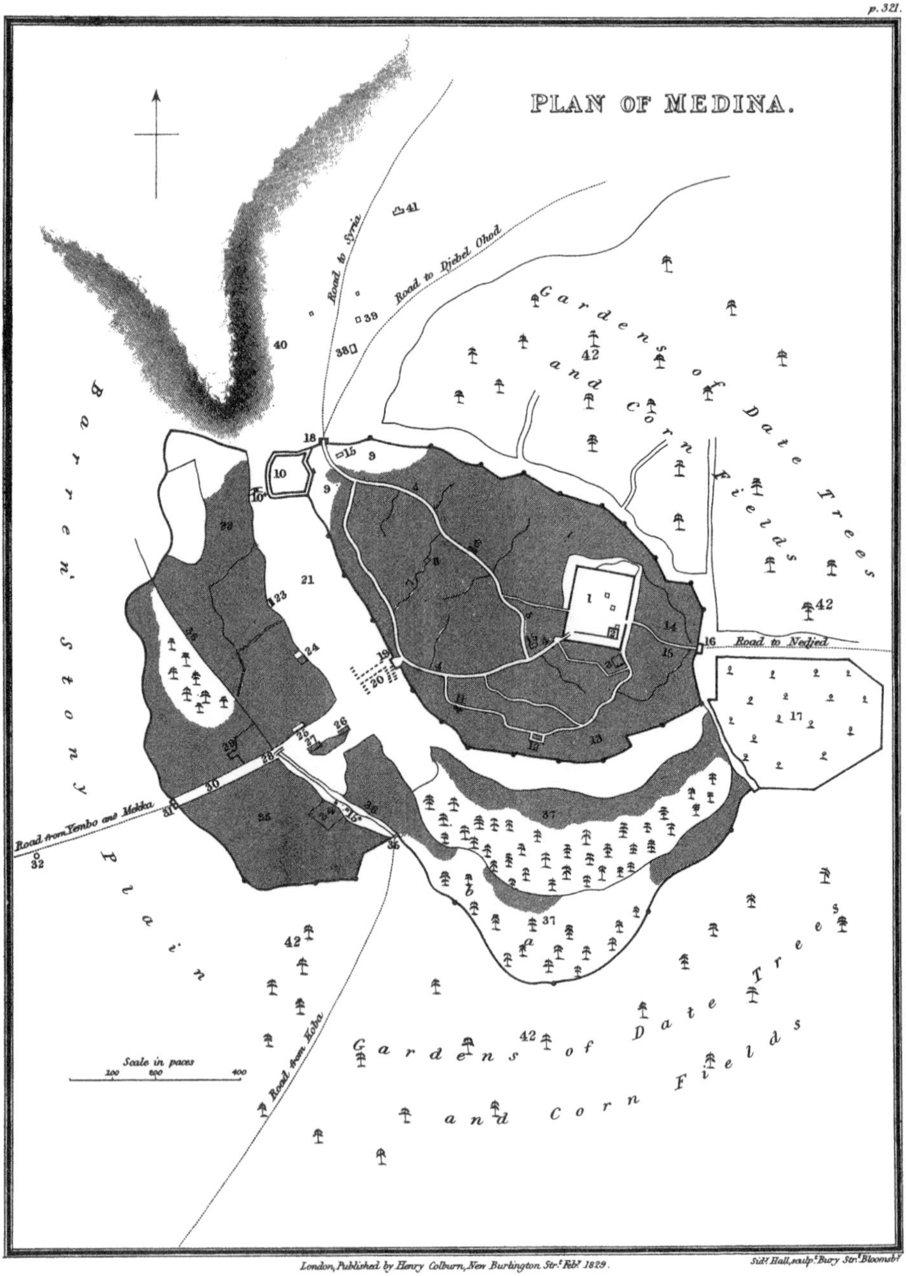

London, Published by Henry Colburn, New Burlington Str.t Feb.y 1829.
Sid.y Hall, sculp.t Bury Str.t Bloomsb.y

DESCRIPTION OF MEDINA.*

MEDINA is situated on the edge of the great Arabian Desert, close to the chain of mountains which traverses that country from north to south, and is a continuation of Libanon. I have already stated in my Journal through Arabia Petræa, that the chain on the east of the Dead Sea runs down towards Akaba. From thence, it extends along the shore of the Red Sea as far as Yemen, sometimes close to the sea,

* EXPLANATION OF THE PLAN OF MEDINA.

1. The great Mosque, called El Haram.
2. The Prophet Mohammed's tomb, called El Hejra.
3. House of the Sheikh el Haram.
4. Principal Market-street.
5. Street called El Belát.
6. Public School, called Medrese el Hamdye.
7. Street called Zogag el Towal.
8. House of the Kadhy.
9. Ruined quarters.
10. The Castle.
10.* A small gate.
11. A public bath.
12. A corn magazine.
13. Quarter of Beni Hosseyn.
14. Quarter of El Agowat.
15. Steps leading down to the canal, in different parts of the town.
15.* Wells, at the bottom of which the canal water flows.
16. The gate called Báb el Djoma.
17. Burial-ground, called El Bekya.
18. Gate called Bab el Shámy.
19. Gate called Bab el Masry.
20. Shops and huts.
21. The open space called El Monákh, the halting-place of Bedouins and soldiers.
22. A quarter of the suburbs called El Wadjeha, with fields and ruined houses.
23. House of the Turkish Governor.
24. A basin filled with canal water.
25. The best private building of the town, where the Pasha's women reside.
26. The mosque called Mesdjed Omar.
27. Another mosque.
28. A bridge on the bed of the torrent.
29. The Pasha's house, with a large garden.
30. Street and quarter called El Ambarye.
31. The gate called Báb el Ambarye.
32. A small tower, built of the skulls of Wahabys killed when the Turks took the town.
33. Quarter of the suburbs called Es' Sahh.
34. A large court-yard where the caravans from Mekka halt.
35. A small gate called Báb Koba.
36. The bed of the Seyl or torrent.
37. Quarters with habitations and gardens.—a. The Quarter called El Shahrye.—b. Quarter called El Hendye.
38. Reservoir of water for the Syrian pilgrims.
39. Different wells of brackish water.
40. Camp of the Syrian pilgrim caravan.
41. A small dome called El Koreyn.
42. Date-groves and fields on three sides of the town.

at others having an intervening plain called by the Arabs *Tahama*, a name which, in Yemen, is also bestowed upon a particular part of it. I have likewise mentioned in that Journal, that the eastern descent of these mountains, all along the Jordan, the Dead Sea, and the valley called Araba, down to Akaba, is much less than the western, and that therefore the great plain of Arabia, which begins eastward of these mountains, is considerably elevated above the level of the sea. I made the same remark in going to Tayf, after having crossed the mountain called Djebel Kora, which forms part of that chain; and the same is to be observed at Medina. The mountain which we had ascended in coming from Mekka, when seen from the coast, presents peaks of considerable height; when we reached the upper plain, in the neighbourhood of Medina, these summits appeared on our left like mere hills, their elevation above the eastern plain being not more than one-third of that from the western sea-shore.

The last undulations of these mountains touch the town on the north side; on its other side, the country is flat, though not always a completely even plain. A branch of the chain, called Djebel Ohod, projects a little into the plain, at one hour's distance from the town, bearing from the latter N.N.E. to N.E.* At eight or ten hours' distance, (E. 6 N.—E. 6 S.) a chain of low hills rises in an eastern direction, across which lies the road to Nedjed. Similar hills, at the same distance, are to the S. E. The country to the south extends on a perfect level as far as can be seen. On the S. W., about an hour, or an hour and a half distant, a branch called Djebel Ayra projects, like Djebel Ohod, from the main chain, into the plain.

The town itself is built on the lowest part of the plain; for it receives the torrents from the western mountains, as well as the currents from the S. and S. E. quarters; and they produce in the rainy season numerous pools of stagnant water, which is left to evaporate gradually; the gardens, trees, and walls, with which the plain abounds, interrupting the free current of air. These gardens, and date-plantations, interspersed with fields, enclose the town on three sides, leaving

* In these bearings the variation of the needle is not computed.

only that part of the plain open to the view, which is on the side of the road towards Mekka, where the rocky nature of the ground renders cultivation impossible. Medina is divided into the interior town, and the suburbs; the interior forms an oval, of about two thousand eight hundred paces in total circuit, ending in a point. The castle is built at the point, upon a small rocky elevation; and the whole is enclosed by a thick stone wall, between thirty-five and forty feet high, flanked by about thirty towers, and surrounded by a ditch, (the work of the Wahabys,) which is in many places nearly filled up. The wall is in complete repair, forming, in Arabia, a very respectable defence; so that Medina has always been considered as the principal fortress of the Hedjaz. The wall was built A. H. 360; and till that time the town was quite open, and daily exposed to the incursions of the neighbouring Bedouins. It was subsequently rebuilt at different times, but principally in A. H. 900, a ditch having been previously carried round it in 751 (v. S.) According to Asamy, it was built as it now stands, with its gates, by order of Solyman ibn Selym, at the close of the sixteenth century of our era. Three fine gates lead into the town: Bab el Masry, on the south side, (which, next to Bab el Fatouh, at Cairo, is the finest town-gate I have seen in the East); Bab es' Shámy, on the north side; and Bab el Djoma, on the east side: a smaller by-gate, called Bab es' Soghyr, in the south wall, had been closed up by the Wahabys. Near the Bab es' Shámy, close to the castle, is a niche in the town-wall, where, it is related, a small chapel once stood, called Mesdjed es' Sabak, from whence the warlike adherents of Mohammed used to start in their exercise of running.

Medina is well built, entirely of stone; its houses are generally two stories high, with flat roofs. As they are not white-washed, and the stone is of a dark colour, the streets have rather a gloomy aspect; and are, for the most part, very narrow, often only two or three paces across: a few of the principal streets are paved with large blocks of stone; a comfort which a traveller little expects to find in Arabia. It is, on the whole, one of the best-built towns I have seen in the East, ranking, in this respect, next to Aleppo. At present, it has a desolate appearance: the houses are suffered to decay; their owners, who formerly derived great profits from the crowd of visiters which arrived here at all times of the year, now find their income diminished, and decline the heavy expense of building, as they know they cannot be reimbursed by the letting out of apartments. Ruined houses, and walls wanting repair, are seen in every part of the town; and Medina presents the same disheartening view as most of the Eastern towns, which now afford but faint images of their ancient splendour.

The principal street of Medina is also the broadest, and leads from the Cairo gate to the great mosque: in this street are most of the shops. Another considerable street, called El Belát, runs from the mosque to the Syrian gate; but many of its houses are in ruins: this contains also a few shops, but none are found in other parts of the town; thus differing from Mekka, which is one continued market. In general, the latter is much more like an Arab town than Medina, which resembles more a Syrian city. I had no time to trace all the different quarters of the town; but I shall here give the names by which they are at present known.

The quarter comprised between the two main streets leading from the Egyptian and Syrian gates to the mosque, are, Es-Saha, Komet Hasheyfe, El Belát, Zogág el Towál, (here is situated the Mekkam, or house of the Kadhy, and several pleasant gardens are attached to the larger buildings;) Zogág el Dhorra, Sakyfet Shakhy, Zogág el Bakar.

The quarters lying to the north of the street El Belát, extending to the north of the mosque, as far as the gate El Djoma, are:—El Hamáta, Zogág el Habs, Zogág Ankyny, Zogág es' Semáhedy, Háret el Meyda, Haret es' Shershoura, Zogág el Bedour, Haret el Agowat, where the eunuchs of the mosque live.

The quarters from the gate El Djoma, along the southern parts of the town, as far as the Egyptian gate, and the great market-street, are: Derwan, Es-Salehye, Zogág Yáhou, Háret Ahmed Heydar, Háret Beni Hosseyn, the tribe of Beni Hosseyn living here; Háret el Besough, Háret Sakyfet, Er-Resás, Zogág el Zerendy, Zogág el Kibreit,

Zogág el Hadjamyn, Háret Sydy Málek, where Málek ibn Anes, the founder of the Malekite sect, had his house, and Háret el Kamáshyn. Very few large buildings, or public edifices, are found in the precincts of the town. The great mosque, containing the tomb of Mohammed, is the only temple. A fine public school, called Medrese el Hamdye, in the street El Belát; a similar one, near the mosque, where the Sheikh el Haram, or its guardian, lives; a large corn-magazine, enclosing a wide yard, in the southern quarter of the town; a bath, (the only one,) not far distant from it, built in A. H. 973, by Mohammed Pasha, vizier of Sultan Soleyman, are all the public buildings which fell under my observation.* This want of splendid monuments was likewise remarked by me at Mekka. The Arabians, in general, have little taste for architecture; and even their chiefs content themselves in their mansions with what is merely necessary. Whatever public edifices are still found in Mekka and Medina, are the work of the Sultans of Egypt or of Constantinople; and the necessary expenses incurred annually by these distant sovereigns, for the sake of the two holy cities, were too great to allow of any augmentation for mere show. For the want of public buildings, however, in the town, a compensation is made by the number of pretty private habitations, having small gardens, with wells, the water of which is used in irrigation, and fills marble basins, round which, in summer-time, the owners pass the hours of noon under lofty sheds.

The castle, which I have mentioned above, is surrounded by very strong walls, and several high and solid towers. I was not permitted to enter it, on applying at the gate. It contains sufficient space for six or eight hundred men; has many arched rooms, bomb-proof; and, if well garrisoned, and furnished with provisions, may be deemed impregnable by an Arabian force, as it is built upon a rock, and therefore cannot be undermined. To European artillery, however, it would appear an insignificant fort. It contains a deep well of good water.

* The historian of Medina mentions several Okals, or public khans, in this town; but I saw none, nor do I believe that they now exist.

Two or three guns only are at present mounted on its towers; nor were there more than a dozen serviceable guns to defend the whole town.

On the west and south of the town extend the suburbs, which cover more ground than the town itself. They are separated from it by an open space, narrow on the south side, but widening on the west, before the Cairo gate, where it forms a large public place, called Monákh; a name implying that caravans alight there, which is really the case, as it is always crowded with camels and Bedouins. Several rows of small huts and sheds are erected here, in which provisions are sold, principally corn, dates, vegetables, and butter; and a number of coffee-huts, which are beset the whole day with visiters. The side of the suburbs fronting the Monákh has no walls; but on the outside, to the west and south, they are enclosed by a wall, of inferior size and strength to the interior town wall. In several parts it is completely ruined; on the south side only it is defended by small towers. Four gates lead from the suburbs into the open country; they are small wooden doors, of no strength, except that leading from the Cairo gate, which is larger and better built than the rest.

The greater part of the suburbs consists in large court-yards, with low apartments built round them, on the ground-floor, and separated from each other by gardens and plantations. These are called *Hosh*, (plur. *Hyshan*,) and are inhabited by all the lower classes of the town, many Bedouins who have become settlers here, and all those who are engaged in agriculture. Each hosh contains thirty or forty families; thus forming so many small separate hamlets, which, in times of unsettled government, are frequently engaged in desperate feuds with each other. The cattle is kept in the midst of the court-yard, in each of which is a large well; and the only gate of entrance is regularly shut at night. On the S. and N. W. sides of the town, within the precincts of the wall, the suburbs consist entirely of similar court-yards, with extensive gardens between and behind them. On the west side, directly opposite the Cairo gate and the Monákh, the suburb consists of regular and well-built streets, with houses resembling those of the interior of the town. The broad street, called El Ambarye, crosses this part of the suburb, and has good buildings on both sides. In this neighbourhood lived Tousoun Pasha, in a private dwelling; and near it, in the best house of the town, belonging to the rich merchant Abd el Shekour, lived the Pasha's mother, the wife of Mohammed Aly, and his own women, who had lately come on a visit.

The principal quarters of the suburbs are Háret el Ambarye, Háret el Wádjeha, Háret es' Sahh, Háret Abou Aysa, Háret Masr, Háret el Teyar, Háret Nefýse, Háret el Hamdye, Háret el Shahrye, Háret el Kheybarye, Háret el Djafar. Many people of the interior town have their summer houses in these quarters, where they pass a month in the date-harvest. Every garden is enclosed by mud walls, and several narrow by-lanes, just broad enough for a loaded camel to cross the suburbs in every direction.

There are two mosques in the Monákh: the one, called Mesdjed Aly, or the mosque of the Prophet's cousin, is said to be as old as the time of Mohammed; but the building, as it stands, was rebuilt in A. H. 876. Mohammed is said to have often prayed here; and, for the convenience of the inhabitants of the suburbs who are at a distance from the great mosque, the *Khotbe*, or Friday's prayer, is likewise performed in it. The other mosque, called Mesdjed Omar, to which a public medrese, or school, was attached, serves at present as a magazine, and quarters for many soldiers. To both these mosques the historian of Mekka applies the name of Mesdjed el Fath: he calls the one Mesdjed el Aala, from standing on the highest part of the town. Two other mosques, the one called Mesdjed Aly Beker, and the other Mesdjed Zobáb, stood in this neighbourhood in the sixteenth century; and the Monákh at that time bore the name of Djebel Sola, the Arabians applying the name of Djebel (or mountain) to any slightly elevated spot of ground. In the same author's time there were fifteen mosques in this town and its neighbourhood, all now ruined; and he gives the names and history of thirty-seven that were erected in the former ages of Islám.

I was told, that in the quarter El Ambarye the house where Mohammed lived is still shown; but many doubt this tradition, and the spot is not visited as one of the holy places. Here, as in Mekka, no ancient buildings are found. The winter rains, the nitrous, damp atmosphere during the rainy season, and the intense heat which follows it, are destructive to buildings; and the cement employed in their construction being of a very indifferent quality, the stones soon become loosened and the walls decay.

The town is supplied with sweet water by a fine subterraneous canal, carried hither from the village of Koba, about three quarters of an hour distant, in a southern direction, at the expense of Sultan Solyman, the son of Selym I. The water is abundant, and, in several parts of the town, steps are made down to the canal, where the inhabitants supply themselves with water, but are not, like the people of Mekka, obliged to pay for it. On the skirts of the Monákh, a large reservoir, cased with stone, has also been made, on a level with the canal, which is constantly kept full. The water in the canal runs at the depth of between twenty and twenty-five feet below the surface; it is derived from several springs at Koba, and, though not disagreeable to the taste, is nevertheless of bad quality. If left for half an hour in a vessel, it covers the sides of it with a white nitrous crust; and all foreigners, who are not accustomed to it from their earliest youth, complain of its producing indigestion. It is tepid at its source in Koba, and even at Medina slightly preserves its temperature. There are also many wells scattered over the town; every garden has one, by which it is irrigated; and wherever the ground is bored to the depth of twenty-five or thirty feet, water is found in plenty. Of some wells the water is sweet enough for drinking; of others quite brackish. The fertility of the fields and gardens is in proportion to the quality of the well-water; those irrigated with brackish water, repay badly the labour of their owners; the date-trees alone thriving equally well in any place.

In addition to the water of the wells and the aqueduct, the town in winter time receives a supply from the considerable torrent called Seyl el Medina, or Seyl Bathán, which flows from S. to N. passing across the suburbs, and losing itself in a stony valley to the N. W.* A heavy rain for one night will fill its bed, though it usually decreases as fast

---

* All the neighbouring torrents lose themselves in a low ground in the western mountains, called El Ghába, and also El Zaghába. See Samhoudy.

as it swells. In that part of the suburb, called El Ambarye, we find a good arched stone bridge thrown across its banks, where it is about forty feet in breadth. The neighbouring country abounds with similar torrents, which fill many ponds and low grounds, where the water often remains till the summer months: these, together with the wells, contribute to render the environs of this town celebrated for the abundance of water, surpassing, in this respect, perhaps, any other spot in northern Arabia, and which had made this a considerable settlement of Arabs, long before it became sacred among the Moslims, by the flight, residence, and death of Mohammed, to which it owes its name of Medina, or Medinet el Neby.

The great abundance of water has made cisterns of little use in the town; and I do not believe that more than two or three houses have them; though it would be very desirable to collect the rain-water for drinking, from the torrents, in preference to the nitrous water of Koba. During heavy rains the Monakh, between the suburbs and the town, becomes a complete lake, and the S. and S.E. environs are covered with a sheet of water. The inhabitants hail these inundations as a sure promise of plenty, because they not only copiously irrigate their date-trees, but likewise cause verdure to spread over the more distant plains inhabited by Bedouins, on whose imports of cattle and butter Medina depends for its consumption.

The precious jewel of Medina, which sets the town almost upon a level with Mekka, and has even caused it to be preferred to the latter, by many Arabic writers,* is the great mosque, containing the tomb of Mohammed. Like the mosque of Mekka, it bears the name of El Haram, on account of its inviolability; a name which is constantly given to it by the people of Medina, while, in foreign parts, it is more generally known under the appellation of Mesdjed en' Neby, the mosque or temple of the Prophet, who was its original founder. The ground-plan will show that this mosque is situated towards the eastern extremity of the town, and not in the midst of it, as the Arabian his-

---

* This is particularly the case with the sect of the Malekites, who pretend that Medina is more to be honoured than Mekka.

torians and geographers often state. Its dimensions are much smaller than those of the mosque at Mekka, being a hundred and sixty-five paces in length, and a hundred and thirty in breadth; but it is built much upon the same plan, forming an open square, surrounded on all sides by covered colonnades, with a small building in the centre of the square.* These colonnades are much less regular than those at Mekka, where the rows of pillars stand at much the same depth on all sides. On the south side of this mosque, the colonnade is composed of ten rows of pillars behind each other; and on the west side are four rows; on the north, and part of the east side, only three rows. The columns themselves are of different sizes. On the south side, which contains the Prophet's tomb, and which forms the most holy part of the building, they are of larger dimensions than in the other parts, and about two feet and a half in diameter. They have no pediments, the shafts touching the ground; and the same diversity and bad taste are as conspicuous in the capitals here as in the mosque at Mekka, no two being alike. The columns are of stone, but, being all plastered white, it is difficult to decide of what species. To the height of about six feet from the ground they are painted with flowers and arabesques, in a coarse and gaudy style; by which means, probably, it was intended to remedy the want of pediments. Those standing nearest to that part of the southern colonnade called El Rodha, are cased for half their height with bright glazed green tiles or slates, decorated with arabesques of various colours: the tiles seem to be of Venetian pottery, and are of the same kind as those used to cover stoves in Germany and Switzerland.

* The representations of this mosque, given both by Niebuhr and D'Ohhson, are very incorrect, being copied, probably, from old Arab drawings. I had intended to make a correct plan of it, but was prevented by my illness; and I should not wish to add one from mere recollection. Samhoudy states its dimensions as quite different, and says that it is two hundred and forty pikes in length, one hundred and sixty-five pikes in breadth on the S. side, and one hundred and thirty on the N. side. He adds that there are two hundred and ninety-six columns. I am not quite sure whether the building has been materially changed since his time, and after the fire in A. H. 886; but 1 believe not, and regard his account as much exaggerated.

The roof of the colonnade consists of a number of small domes, white-washed on the outside, in the same manner as those of Mekka. The interior walls are also white-washed all round, except the southern one, and part of the S. E. corner, which are cased with slabs of marble, nearly up to the top. Several rows of inscriptions, in large gilt letters, are conducted along this wall, one above the other, and have a very brilliant effect upon the white marble. The floor under the colonnades, on the west and east sides, and part of the north, is laid out with a coarse pavement; the other part of the N. side being unpaved, and merely covered with sand; as is likewise the whole open yard. On the south side, where the builder of the mosque has lavished all this ornament, the floor is paved with fine marble across the whole colonnade; and in those parts nearest to the tomb of Mohammed, this pavement is in mosaic, of excellent workmanship, forming one of the best specimens of that kind to be seen in the East. Large and high windows, with glass panes, (of which I know not any other instance in the Hedjaz,) admit the light through the southern wall: some of them are of fine painted glass. On the other sides, smaller windows are dispersed along the walls, but not with glass panes.*

Near the S. E. corner stands the famous tomb, so detached from the walls of the mosque, as to leave between it and the S. wall a space of about twenty-five feet, and fifteen between it and the E. wall. The enclosure, which defends the tomb from the too near approach of visitors, forms an irregular square of about twenty paces, in the midst of the colonnade, several of its pillars being included within it: it is an iron railing, painted green, about two-thirds the height of the columns, filling up the intervals between them, so as to leave their upper part projecting above it, and entirely open. The railing is of good workmanship, in imitation of filligree, and is interwoven with open-worked inscriptions of yellow bronze, supposed by the vulgar to be of gold, and of so close a texture, that no view can be gained into

* The art of painting glass with durable colours seems never to have been lost in the East.

the interior, except by several small windows, about six inches square, which are placed in the four sides of the railing, about five feet above the ground. On the south side of the railing, where are the two principal of these windows, before which the visiters stand when praying, the railing is thinly plated over with silver, and the often-repeated inscription of " La Illaha il Allah al hak al Mobyn," (" There is no God but God, the evident Truth,") is carried in silver letters across the railing all round these windows. This enclosure is entered by four gates, three of which are constantly kept shut, and one only is opened, every morning and evening, to admit the eunuchs, whose office it is to clean the floor and light the lamps. Each of these gates has its particular name: Báb en' Neby, Báb Errahme, Báb et Touba, Báb Setna Fatme. The permission to enter into this enclosure, which is called El Hedjra, is granted gratis to people of rank, as Pashas, or chiefs of the Hadj caravans, and may be purchased by other people from the principal eunuchs, at the price of about twelve or fifteen dollars, distributed in presents among them: but few visiters avail themselves of this privilege, because they well know that, on entering the enclosure, nothing more is to be seen than what falls under their observation when peeping in at the windows of the railing, which are constantly kept open; and I was myself not inclined to attract general notice, by thus satisfying my curiosity. What appears of the interior is a curtain carried round, which takes up almost the whole space, having between it and the railing an open walk, of a few paces only in breadth. The curtain is equal in height to the railing; but I could not distinguish from below, whether, like the latter, it is open at the top. There is a covering, (as the eunuchs affirm,) of the same stuff of which the curtain is made; this is a rich silk brocade, of various colours, interwoven with silver flowers and arabesques, with a band of inscriptions in golden characters, running across the midst of it, like that of the covering of the Kaaba. This curtain is at least thirty feet high: it has a small gate to the north, which is always shut; no person whatever being permitted to enter within its holy precincts, except the chief eunuchs, who take care of it, and who put on, during the night, the new curtain sent from

DESCRIPTION OF MEDINA.   333

Constantinople, whenever the old one is decayed, or when a new Sultan ascends the throne. The old curtains are sent to Constantinople, and serve to cover the tombs of the sultans and princes.*

According to the historian of Medina, the curtain covers a square building of black stones, supported by two pillars, in the interior of which are the tombs of Mohammed, and his two earliest friends and immediate successors, Abou Beker and Omar. As far as I could learn here, these tombs are also covered with precious stuffs, and in the shape of catafalques, like that of Ibrahim in the great mosque of Mekka. They are said to be placed in the following order:

```
       ▢
    ▢
 ▢
```

The largest being that of Mohammed, and the one above it Abou Beker's. The historian says, that these tombs are deep holes; and that the coffin which contains the dust of Mohammed, is cased with silver, and has on the top a marble slab, inscribed, "Bismillahi Allahuma Sally aley." ("In the name of God, bestow thy mercy upon him.") They did not always stand in their present position: Samhoudy places them at different times thus:

```
 ▢ ▢      ▢ ▢        ▢
  ▢         ▢         ▢
                      ▢
```

The stories once prevalent in Europe, of the prophet's tomb being suspended in the air, are unknown in the Hedjaz; nor have I ever heard them in other parts of the East, though the most exaggerated accounts of the wonders and the riches of this tomb are propagated by those who have visited Medina, and wish to add to their own importance by relating fabulous stories of what they pretend to have

---

* See D'Ohsson. The historian of Medina says, that in his time it was changed every six years, and that the income from several villages in Egypt was set apart at Cairo for the manufacturing of those curtains.

seen. Round these tombs the treasures of the Hedjaz were formerly kept, either suspended on silken ropes, drawn across the interior of the building, or placed in chests on the ground. Among these, may be particularly mentioned a copy of the Koran, in Cufic characters, kept there as a precious relic, from having belonged to Othman ibn Affan. It is said still to exist in Medina; but we may doubt whether it escaped the conflagration which destroyed the mosque. I have related, in my history of the Wahabys, that during the siege of Medina considerable portions of the treasures, more particularly all the golden vessels, were seized by the chiefs of the town, ostensibly for the purpose of being distributed among the poor, but that they were, finally, divided among themselves. When Saoud took the town, he entered the Hedjra himself, and penetrated behind the curtain, where he seized upon every thing valuable he found; of this he sold a part to the Sherif of Mekka, and the rest he carried with him to Derayeh. Among the precious articles which he took, the most valuable is said to have been a brilliant star set in diamonds and pearls, which was suspended directly over the Prophet's tomb. It is often spoken of by the Arabs, who call it Kokab ed'durry. Here were deposited all sorts of vessels, set with jewels, ear-rings, bracelets, necklaces, and other ornaments, sent as presents from all parts of the empire, but brought principally by great hadjys who passed through Medina. There is no doubt that the whole formed a collection of considerable value, but far from being inestimable, as the people are inclined to fancy. Sherif Ghaleb estimated that part of it which he bought, at one hundred thousand dollars. The chiefs of the town are said to have carried off about one hundred weight of golden vessels, at most worth forty or fifty thousand dollars; and what Saoud took with him is said to have consisted chiefly in pearls and corals, and was certainly not worth more than Ghaleb's purchase. The total value, therefore, might have amounted to about three hundred thousand dollars. Money never appears to have been deposited here; for whatever presents were made to the mosque in cash, were immediately distributed among its attendants. There is good reason for supposing, however, that the donations of the faithful, which accumulated here for ages, amounted to a much greater sum than what is stated above; but it would be strange if the governors of Medina, who were often independent, or the guardians of the tomb themselves, should not have made occasional draughts upon this treasure, in the same manner as the olemas of Mekka, about three hundred years since, stole the golden lamps of the Kaaba, and carried them out of the temple, hid under their wide sleeves, according to Kotobeddyn the historian.

Tousoun Pasha, on his arrival at Medina, made search for the golden vessels, which had been re-sold by the chiefs of the town to some other of the inhabitants, and not yet melted. He found several of them, which he bought from the owners for about ten thousand dollars, and replaced them in their original situation.

The floor between the curtain and the railing, and of all this part of the mosque, is laid with various coloured marbles in mosaic: here glass lamps are suspended all round the curtains, which are lighted every evening, and remain burning all night. The whole of this enclosure, or Hedjra, is covered with a fine lofty dome, rising far above the domes which form the roof of the colonnades, and visible at a great distance from the town; and the visiters coming to Medina, as soon as they catch the sight of it, repeat certain prayers. The covering is of lead surmounted with a globe of considerable size, and a crescent, both glittering with gold.[*]

It is reported that they are of massy gold; which can scarcely be believed, if we consider the little inclination that even the richest and most powerful of the Sultans have shown, to ornament with splendour either the mosque of Mekka or Medina. The Wahabys, allured by the appearance of the globe, and acting upon their invariable practice of destroying all domes or cupolas erected over the tombs of mortals, among whom Mohammed was to be reckoned, attempted to destroy the dome, and throw down the globe and crescent; but their solid construction, and the lead covering, rendered this a difficult undertaking: two of the workmen slipped from the smooth roof, and were preci-

---

[*] The globe was gilt, and the crescent sent from Constantinople, by the Sultan Soleyman ibn Selym. (See Asamy.) The cupola, and the whole of the temple as it now stands, was built by Kait Beg, Sultan of Egypt, from A. H. 881 to 892.

pitated below, after which the work of destruction was abandoned; a circumstance which is now cited as a visible miracle worked by the Prophet in favour of his monument.

Near the curtain of the Hedjra, but separated from it, though within the precincts of the railing, which here, to admit it, deviates a little from its square shape, is the tomb of Setna Fatme, the daughter of Mohammed, and wife of Aly: it consists of a catafalque forming a cube, covered with a rich embroidered black brocade, and without any other ornament. But some difference of opinion exists, whether her remains actually rest here or in the burial-ground called Bakya, beyond the town. Till this dispute, however, be settled, the pilgrims are conducted to both places, and made to pay double fees. On the E. wall of the mosque, nearly opposite to this tomb, a small window is shown, at the place where the archangel Gabriel is said to have repeatedly descended from heaven, with messages to Mohammed. It is called Mahbat Djybrail.

Mohammedan tradition says, that when the last trumpet shall sound, Aysa (Jesus Christ) is to descend from heaven to earth, and to announce to its inhabitants the great day of judgment: after which he is to die, and will be buried in this Hedjra, by the side of Mohammed: that, when the dead shall rise from their graves, they will both rise together, ascend to heaven, and Aysa, on that day, will be ordered by the Almighty to separate the faithful from the infidels. In conformity with this tradition, the spot is pointed at through the curtain of the Hedjra, where the tomb of Aysa will be placed.

Outside the railing on the north, close by the tomb of Fatme, is a square bench in the mosque, elevated above the ground about four feet, and fifteen paces square, called El Meyda, or the table. Here the eunuch guardians of the mosque sit; and the councils of the primates of the town, or their principal assemblies, are often held here.

A wooden partition about eight feet high, and richly painted with arabesques, runs from the western side of the railing across the mosque, parallel with the south wall, and about twenty-five feet distant from it, and terminating near the gate called Báb-es-Salám, thus extending from the Hedjra nearly across the whole breadth of the mosque. It has several small doors, and is made to separate the holy place called El Rodha from the common passage of the visitors, who, on entering through Báb-es'-Salam, pass forward towards the Hedjra, along the columns standing between this partition and the south wall. Next to the Hedjra, that part of the southern colonnade north of the partition is considered the most holy place in the mosque, and called Rodha, i. e. a garden, or the Garden of the Faithful; a name bestowed upon it by Mohammed, who said: " Between my tomb and my pulpit is a garden of the gardens of Paradise." The pulpit of the mosque stands close to this partition, about midway between the Hedjra and the west wall of the mosque, and the name Rodha strictly belongs to that space only which is between the pulpit and the Hedjra, though the whole southern colonnade of the temple to the north of the partition is often comprised under that appellation. It is on account of this name of Rodha, or garden, that the columns within its limits are painted to the height of five or six feet with flowers and arabesques, to assist the imagination, which otherwise might not readily discover any resemblance between this place and the Garden of Eden. Two *mahrabs*, or niches, towards which the people turn when praying, as they indicate the exact bearing of the Kaaba,* are placed on both sides of the pulpit, and are, together with it, of exquisite workmanship, being the finest mosaic. One niche was sent from Egypt as a present to the mosque, by Kait Beg, and the other from Constantinople by Sultan Soleyman ibn Selym. The floor of the Rodha is covered with a number of handsome carpets, sent hither from Constantinople; and, as at Mekka, they are the only articles of real value that I saw in the mosque, and may be worth, altogether, about a thousand pounds. The upper part of the colonnades is covered with mats.

The congregation assembles upon the carpets of the Rodha, this being the favourite spot for prayers. No ceremony is observed in the seats; every one may place himself where he likes: it is however understood, that the first row nearest to the partition, and those espe-

* The Mahrab was turned S. 11 W. (variation not computed), which is therefore taken here as the exact bearing of Mekka.

cially in the immediate neighbourhood of the Imám, are destined for people of rank, and no one who does not belong to that class intrudes himself there. The entrance to the Rodha, near Báb-es'-Salám, has a splendid appearance: the gaudy colours displayed on every side, the glazed columns, fine carpets, rich pavement, the gilt inscriptions on the wall to the south, and the glittering railing of the Hedjra in the back-ground, dazzle the sight at first; but, after a short pause, it becomes evident that this is a display of tinsel decoration, and not of real riches. When we recollect that this spot is one of the holiest of the Mohammedan world, and celebrated for its splendour, magnificence, and costly ornaments, and that it is decorated with the united pious donations of all the devotees of that religion, we are still more forcibly struck with its paltry appearance. It will bear no comparison with the shrine of the most insignificant saint in any Catholic church in Europe, and may serve as a convincing proof, that in pious gifts the Mohammedan have at no period equalled the Catholic devotees; without noticing many other circumstances, which help to strengthen the belief, that, whatever may be their superstition and fanaticism, Mohammedans are never inclined to make as many pecuniary sacrifices for their religious establishments, as Catholic, and even Protestant Christians do for theirs.

The ceremonies on visiting the mosque are the following:—At first the pilgrim, before he enters the town, is to purify himself by a total ablution, and, if possible, to perfume his body with sweet odours. When he arrives in sight of the dome, he is to utter some pious ejaculations. When he intends to visit the temple, the cicerone, or, as he is here called, Mezowar, leads him into the gate called Báb-es'-Salám, passing his right foot first over the threshold, which is the general custom in all mosques, and particularly insisted upon here. While reciting some prayers, he steps forward into the Rodha, where he performs a short prayer, with four prostrations, as a salutation to the mosque, during which he is enjoined to recite the two short chapters (109th and 112th) of the Koran. He then passes through one of the small doors of the partition of the Rodha, and walks slowly towards the railing of the Hedjra, before the western window of which, on its south side, he takes his stand; with arms half raised he addresses his invocations to Mohammed, in the words "Salam aleyka ya Mohammed, Salam ya Rasoul illah," &c. recapitulating about twenty of the different surnames or honorable titles of Mohammed, and prefixing to each of them " Salam aleyk." He next invokes his intercession in heaven, and distinctly mentions the names of all those of his relations and friends whom he is desirous to include in his prayers: it is for this reason, that an inhabitant of Medina never receives a letter from abroad, without being entreated, at the end of it, to mention the writer's name at the tomb of the Prophet. If the pilgrim is delegated on the pilgrimage for another, he is bound here to mention the name of his principal. In this prayer an expression is used, as at all the places visited for their sanctity about the town, but which appeared to me little calculated to inspire the visiter with humane or charitable feelings; among other favours supplicated in prayer to the Deity, the following request is made: " Destroy our enemies, and may the torments of hell-fire be their lot."

After these prayers are said, the visiter is desired to remain a few minutes with his head pressed close against the window, in silent adoration; he then steps back, and performs a prayer of four prostrations, under the neighbouring colonnade, opposite the railing; after which he approaches the second window, on this same side, said to face the tomb of Abou Beker, and goes through prayers similar to those said at the former window, (called *Shobák-en'-Neby,*) which are recited in honour of Abou Beker. Stepping back a second time to the colonnade, he again performs a short prayer, and then advances to the third window on this side of the railing, which is opposite that part of the curtain behind which the tomb of Omar is said to lie: similar prayers are said here. When this ceremony is finished, the visiter walks round the S.E. corner of the Hedjra, and presents himself before the tomb of Setna Fatme, where, after four prostrations, a prayer is addressed to *Fatme-e'-Zohera,* or the bright blooming Fatme, as she is called. He then returns to the Rodha, where a prayer is said as a salutation to the Deity on leaving the mosque, which completes this ceremony, the performance of which occupies at most twenty minutes.

On every spot where prayers are to be said, people sit with handkerchiefs spread out to receive the gifts of the visiters, which appear to be considered less as alms, than as a sort of toll; at least, a well-dressed visiter would find it difficult to make his way without paying these taxes. Before the window of Setna Fatme sits a party of women, (Fatme being herself a female saint,) who likewise receive gifts in their handkerchiefs. In the Rodha stand the eunuchs, or the guardians of the temple, waiting till the visiter has finished his last prayer of salutation, to wish him joy on having successfully completed the *zyara* or visit, and to receive their fees; and the great gate of Báb-es'-Salám is constantly crowded with poor, who closely beset the visiter, on his leaving the mosque: the porter also expects his compliment, as a matter of right. The whole visit cost me about fifteen piastres, and I gave ten piastres to my cicerone; but I might, perhaps, have got through for half that sum.

The ceremonies may be repeated as often as the visiter wishes: but few perform them all, except on arriving at Medina, and when on the point of departing. It is a general practice, however, to go every day, at least once, to the window opposite Mohammed's tomb, and recite there a short prayer: many persons do it whenever they enter the mosque. It is also a rule never to sit down in the mosque, for any of the usual daily prayers, without having previously addressed an invocation to the Prophet, with uplifted hands, and the face turned towards his tomb. A similar practice is prevalent in many other mosques in the East, which contain the tomb of a saint. The Moslim divines affirm, that prayers recited in the mosque of Medina are peculiarly acceptable to the Deity; and invite the faithful to perform this pilgrimage, by telling them that one prayer said in sight of the Hedjra is as efficacious as a thousand said in any other mosque except that of Mekka.

I have already stated, that the north and east sides, and part of the west side, of the mosque are by no means so well built as the south side, where are the Hedjra and Rodha. The columns in those parts are more slender, and less carefully painted; the pavement is coarse, and no kind of ornament is seen on the white plastered walls, except on the east side, where the coarsely painted representations of the mosque of St. Sophia, of Sultan Ahmed, of Bayazed Waly, and of Scutari, celebrated temples in the capital, attract some notice: they are painted in water-colours, upon the white wall, without the smallest attention to perspective. The whole north side was at present under repair; and the old pavement had been removed, to be replaced by a better one.

The open court enclosed between the colonnades is unpaved, and covered with sand and gravel. In the midst of it stands a small building, with a vaulted roof, where the lamps of the mosque are kept. Near it is a small enclosure of low wooden railing, which contains some palm-trees, held sacred by the Moslims, because they are said to have been planted by Fatme, and another tree, of which the stem only now remains, and which I believe to have been a nebek, or lotus-tree. By it is a well, called Bir-en-Neby, the water of which is brackish, and for this reason, probably, enjoys no reputation for holiness. Samhoudy says that it is called Es-Sháme.

In the evening lamps are lighted round the colonnades; but principally on the south side, where they are in greater numbers than on the others; they are suspended from iron bars, extending from column to column. The eunuchs and the servants of the mosque are employed in lighting them; for a small donation to the latter, the visiters to the tomb are permitted to assist, and many foreign hadjys are anxious to perform that office, which is thought meritorious, and for which they are particularly praised by the eunuchs: but they are never allowed to light the lamps in the interior of the Hedjra. On the sides of the Mambar, or the pulpit, and of both the Mahrabs, large wax candles are placed, as thick as a man's body, and twelve feet high, which are lighted in the evening by means of a ladder placed near them. They are sent from Constantinople. The lady of Mohammed Aly, who was now at Medina, had brought several of these candles as a present to the mosque, which had been transported with great difficulty from Yembo to this place.

The mosque has four gates: 1. Báb-es-Salam, formerly called Báb Merouán, (according to Samhoudy), on the south-west corner, is the principal one, by which the pilgrim is obliged to enter the mosque at his first visit. It is a beautiful arched gateway, much superior to any of those of the great mosque at Mekka, though inferior in size to several of them, and handsomer than any gate of a mosque I had before seen in the East. Its sides are inlaid with marble and glazed tiles of various colours; and a number of inscriptions in relief, in large gilt characters, above and on the sides of the arch, give it a very dazzling appearance. Just before this gate is a small fountain, filled by the water of the canal, where people usually perform their ablutions, if they do not choose to do it in the mosque itself, where jars are kept for the purpose.

2. Báb Errhame, formerly called Báb Atake, in the west wall, by which the dead are carried into the mosque, when prayers are to be read over them.

3. Báb Ed' Djeber, called often likewise Báb Djybrail; and

4. Báb el Nesa, on the east wall, the first close to the tomb of Setna Fatme, the other a little farther on.

A few steps lead from the neighbouring streets up to the gates, the area of the mosque being on a somewhat higher level, contrary to what is seen at Mekka. About three hours after sun-set the gates are regularly shut, by means of folding-doors coated with iron, and not opened till about an hour before dawn; but those who wish to pray all night in the mosque, can easily obtain permission from the eunuch in guard, who sleeps near the Hedjra. During Ramadhan, the mosque is kept open the whole night.

On the north-west and north sides are several small doors opening into the mosque, belonging to public schools or medreses originally annexed to it, but which have now forfeited their ancient distinction. On this side the schoolmasters sit with the boys in a circle round them, and teach them the rudiments of reading.

The police of the mosque, the office of washing the Hedjra and the whole of the building, of lighting the lamps, &c. &c. is entrusted to the care of forty or fifty eunuchs, who have an establishment similar to that of the eunuchs of the Beitullah at Mekka; but they are persons of greater consequence here; they are more richly dressed, though in the same costume; usually wear fine Cashmere shawls, and gowns of the best Indian silk stuffs, and assume airs of great importance. When they pass through the Bazar, every body hastens to kiss their hands; and they exercise considerable influence in the internal affairs of the town. They have large stipends, which are sent annually from Constantinople by the Syrian Hadj caravan; they share also in all donations made to the mosque, and they expect presents from every rich hadjy, besides what they take as fees from the visiters of the Hedjra. They live together in one of the best quarters of Medina, to the eastward of the mosque, and their houses are said to be furnished in a more costly manner than any others in the town. The adults are all married to black or Abyssinian slaves.

The black eunuchs, unlike those of Europe, become emaciated; their features are extremely coarse, nothing but the bones being distinguishable; their hands are those of a skeleton, and their whole appearance is extremely disgusting. By the help of thick clothing they hide their leanness; but their bony features are so prominent, that they can be distinguished at first sight. Their voice, however, undergoes little, if any change, and is far from being reduced to that fine feminine tone so much admired in the Italian singers.

The chief of the eunuchs is called Sheikh el Haram; he is also the chief of the mosque, and the principal person in the town; being consequently of much higher rank than the Aga, or chief of the eunuchs at Mekka. He is himself a eunuch, sent from Constantinople, and usually belonging to the court of the Grand Signor, who sends him hither by way of punishment or exile, in the same manner as Pashas are sent to Djidda. The present Sheikh el Haram had been formerly Kislar Agassi, or prefect of the women of the Emperor Selym, which is one of the first charges in the court. Whether it was the dignity of his former employ, of which the eastern grandees usually retain the rank through life, even if they are dispossessed of it, or his new dignity of Sheikh el Haram, that gave him his importance, I am unable to say; but he took, on every occasion, precedence of Tousoun Pasha, whose rank was that of Pasha of Djidda, and of three tails; and the latter, whenever they met, kissed the Sheikh's hands, which I have seen him do in the mosque. He has a court composed in a manner similar to that of a Pasha, but much less numerous. His dress is given with the most minute accuracy in D'Ohhson's work: it consists of a fine pelisse, over a rich embroidered silk gown, made in the fashion of the capital; a khandjar, or dagger, set with diamonds, stuck in his belt; and a kaouk, or high bonnet, on his head. The present Sheikh kept about a dozen horses: whenever he walked out, a number of servants, or Ferráshyn of the mosque, armed with large sticks, walked before him.

The person of the Sheikh el Haram was respected by the Wahabys: when Saoud took Medina, he permitted the Sheikh, with several other eunuchs, to retire to Yembo, with his wives, and all his baggage and valuables; but would not receive another into the town; and the eunuchs themselves then appointed one of their number to preside over them, till after an interval of eight years, when the present chief was sent from Constantinople; but his influence over the affairs of the town is reduced to a mere shadow of what it was.

A eunuch of the mosque would be highly affronted if he were so termed by any person. Their usual title is Aga. Their chief takes the title of Highness, or Sadetkom, like a Pasha, or the Sherif of Mekka.

Besides those eunuchs, the mosque reckons among its servants a number of the inhabitants of the town; these are called Ferráshyn, a name implying that their duty consists in keeping the mosque clean, and spreading the carpets. Some of them attend at the mosque to light the lamps, and to clean the floor, together with the eunuchs; with others it is a mere sinecure, and some of the first people of the town belong to this body. I am unacquainted how the office is obtained, but believe that it is purchased from the Sheikh el Haram. The name of each Ferrásh is put down in the lists which are yearly sent to Constantinople, and they all share in the stipends which the town receives from that capital, and the whole Turkish empire, in which there is always a considerable portion for the Ferráshyn. It would appear that the office is hereditary; at least often transmitted from father to son. The number is fixed at five hundred; but to increase it, an expedient has, according to D'Ohhson, been adopted, of dividing each number into half, and third, and eighth shares; and any fractional part may be bestowed upon an individual, who thus becomes an inferior member of the corps. Many of these Ferráshyn are *in partibus*, the title having been given to great foreign hadjys, dispersed over the whole empire, who think themselves honoured in possessing it.

Many of these Ferráshyn are, at the same time ciceroni, or Mezowars, and exercise also, the very lucrative profession of saying prayers for the absent. Most hadjys of any consequence who pass here, form an acquaintance with some of these men, their guides over the holy places. On their return home, they often make it a pious rule to send annually some money, one or two zecchins, to their ancient cicerone, who is thus bound in honour to recite some prayers, in the name of the donor, before the window of the Hedjra. These remittances, wrapped up in small sealed papers, with the address upon them, are collected in every province or principal town of Anatolia, or Turkey in Europe, from whence they are principally sent, and brought to Medina by the Surra writer of Constantinople, who accompanies the pilgrim caravan, and is at the head of its financial department. Some of the principal Ferráshyns have monopolized whole towns and provinces; the natives of those parts, who pass through Medina, being introduced to them by their countrymen. The correspondents of others are dispersed over the whole empire. The profits which they derive from this profession, which resemble those accruing to Roman Catholic priests for the reading of masses, are very considerable: I have heard that some of the principal Ferráshyn have from four to five hundred correspondents dispersed over Turkey, from each of whom they receive yearly stipends, the smallest of which is one Venetian zecchin.

The number of Ferráshyn, as well as of Mezowars, is very great. The duties of their office can be so easily performed, that they are for the greater part a very idle class. During the time of the Wahabys, however, their perquisites ceased; and, as few pilgrims then arrived, they were reduced to great extremities, from which they are now beginning slowly to recover. They complain, that the long cessation of the yearly stipends has accustomed so many original correspondents to withhold their gifts, that, although the caravan intercourse is reestablished, little inclination appears to renew them.

The Wahabys are forbidden by their law to visit the tomb of the Prophet, or to stand before the Hedjra and pray for his intercession in heaven. As Mohammed is considered by them a mere mortal, his tomb is thought unworthy of any particular notice. It was as much a strict religious principle, as a love of plunder, that induced Saoud to carry off the treasures of the Hedjra, which were thought little adapted in decency and humility to adorn a grave. The tomb itself he left untouched; and, for once, gave way to the national feelings of the Arabians, and perhaps to the compunctions of his own conscience, which could not entirely divest itself of earlier impressions; he neither removed the brocade from the tomb, nor the curtain which encloses it. Dreams, it is said, terrified him, or withheld his sacrilegious hand; and he in like manner respected that of Fatme: but, on the other hand, he ruined, without exception, all the buildings of the public burial-ground, where many great saints repose, and destroyed even the sculptured and ornamented stones of those tombs, a simple block being thought by him quite sufficient to cover the remains of the dead.

In prohibiting any visit to the tomb, the Wahabys never entertained the idea of discontinuing the visit to the mosque. That edifice having been built by the Prophet, at the remarkable epoch of his flight from Mekka, which laid the first foundations of Islám, it is considered by them as the most holy spot upon earth, next to the Beitullah of Mekka. Saoud had indeed once given orders, that none of these Turkish pilgrims, who still flocked from Yembo to this tomb, even after the interruption of the regular pilgrim-caravans, should any more be permitted to enter Medina: and this he did to prevent what he called their idolatrous praying; a practice which it was impossible to abolish without excluding them at once from the mosque; this prohibition Saoud did not think proper to enforce: he therefore preferred keeping them from the city, under pretence that their improper behaviour rendered such a proceeding necessary. He himself, with all his adherents, often paid a devout visit to the holy mosque; and in the treaty of peace which his son Abdallah, concluded with

DESCRIPTION OF MEDINA. 347

Tousoun Pasha in 1815, it is expressly stipulated that the Wahabys should be permitted to visit the Mesdjed-e'-Neby, or the mosque of the Prophet, (not his tomb,) without molestation.

Even with the orthodox Moslims, the visit to this tomb and mosque is merely a meritorious action, which has nothing to do with the obligations to perform the Hadj, incumbent upon the faithful; but which, like the visit to the mosque at Jerusalem, and the tomb of Abraham at Hebron, is thought to be an act highly acceptable to the Deity, and to expiate many sins, while it entitles the visiter, at the same time, to the pratronage of the Prophet and the Patriarch in heaven: and it is said, that he who recites forty prayers in this mosque, will be delivered from hell-fire and torments after death. As saints, however, are often more venerated than the Deity himself, who it is well known accepts of no other offerings than a pure conscience or sincere repentance, and is therefore not so easily appeased; so the visit to Medina is nearly as much esteemed as that to the house of God, the Beitullah at Mekka; and the visiters crowd with more zeal and eagerness to this shrine, than they do even to the Kaaba. Throughout the year, swarms of pilgrims arrive from all parts of the Mohammedan world, usually by the way of Yembo. The Moggrebyns especially seem the most fervent in their visits: they are, however, brought here by another object, for in this town is situated the tomb of the Imám Málek ibn Anes, the founder of the orthodox sect of the Malekites, to which belong the Moggrebyns.

The mosque at Mekka is visited daily by female hadjys, who have their own station assigned to them. At Medina, on the contrary, it is thought very indecorous in women to enter the mosque. Those who come here from foreign parts, visit the tomb during the night, after the last prayers, while the women resident in the town hardly ever venture to pass the threshold: my old landlady, who had lived close to it for fifty years, assured me that she had been only once in her life within its precincts, and that females of a loose character only are daring enough to perform their prayers there. In general, women are seldom seen in the mosques in the East, although free access is not forbidden: a few are sometimes met in the most holy temples, as that of the Azhar at Cairo, where they offer up their thanks to Providence, for any favour which they may have taken a vow thus to acknowledge. Even in their houses the women seldom pray, except devout old ladies; and it is remarked as an extraordinary accomplishment in a woman, if she knows her prayers well, and has got by heart some chapters of the Koran. Women being considered in the East as inferior creatures, to whom some learned commentators on the Koran deny even the entrance into Paradise, their husbands care little about their strict observance of religious rites, and many of them even dislike it, because it raises them to a nearer level with themselves; and it is remarked, that the woman makes a bad wife, who can once claim the respect to which she is entitled by the regular reading of prayers.

There are no sacred pigeons in this mosque, as in that at Mekka; but the quantity of woollen carpets spread in it, where the most dirty Arabs sit down by the side of the best dressed hadjys, have rendered it the favourite abode of millions of other animals less harmless than pigeons, and a great plague to all visiters, who transfer them to their private lodgings, which thus swarm with vermin.

This mosque being much smaller than that of Mekka, and a strict police kept up in it by the eunuchs, it is less infested with beggars and idle characters than the former. It should seem also, that the tomb of Mohammed inspires the people of Medina with much greater awe, and religious respect, than the Kaaba does those of Mekka; which sentiment deters them from approaching it with idle thoughts, or as a mere pastime: much more decorum is therefore observed within its precincts than within those of the Beitullah.

As at Mekka, a number of Khatybs, Imáms, Mueddins, and other persons belonging to the body of Olemas, are attached to the mosque. The olemas here are said to be more learned than their brethren of Mekka; and those of former days have produced many valuable writings. At present, however, there is less appearance of learning here than at Mekka. During my visits to the mosque I never saw a native Arab teaching knowledge of any kind, and only a few Turkish hadjys explaining some religious books in their own language, to a very few auditors, from whom they collected trifling sums, to defray the expenses of their journey home. Tousoun Pasha, the only one of his family who is not an avowed atheist, frequently attended those lectures, and sat in the same circle with the other persons present. I was told, that in the medrese called El Hamdye some public lectures are delivered; but I had no opportunity of ascertaining the fact. I believe that there is not in the whole Mohammedan empire a town so large as Medina where lectures are not held in the mosques; that this was formerly the case also in this town, is proved by the many pious foundations established exclusively for this purpose, the emoluments of which many olemas still enjoy without performing the duties.

The haram or mosque of Medina, like that at Mekka, possesses considerable property and annuities in every part of the empire. Its yearly income is divided among the eunuchs, the olemas, and the Ferráshyn. The daily expenses of lighting and repairing the building are made to account for the expenditure of the whole. As, excepting the precious articles contained in the Hedjra, no money-treasure has ever been kept in the mosque, a double advantage accrues to the inhabitants of the town, numbers of whom gain a comfortable livelihood, while all are exempted from the danger and the internal broils which would, no doubt, occur, were it known that a large sum of money might be obtained by seizing the mosque. The days are past, in the East, when a public treasure can be deposited in a place sufficiently sacred to guard it from the hands of plunderers. The smallest part of the income of all public foundations is spent in the relief of the poor, or the pious purpose to which it was destined: it serves merely to pamper a swarm of idle hypocrites, who have no other motives for acquiring a smattering of learning, than the hope of sharing in the illegal profits that accrue to the guardians or agents of these institutions.

Like most of the public buildings in the East, the approach to the mosque is choked on all sides by private habitations, so as to leave, in some parts, only an open street between them and the walls of the mosque; while in others the houses are built against the walls, and conceal them. Either three or five minarets (I forget which) are erected on different sides of the building; and one of them is said to stand on the spot where Bellal, the Abyssinian, the Mueddin of Mohammed, and one of his great favourites, used to call the faithful to prayers.

The following brief history of the mosque is taken from Samhoudy, the historian of Medina:

"The mosque of Medina was founded by Mohammed himself, and is therefore called his mosque, or Mesdjed-e'-Neby. When he reached the city, at that time an open settlement of Arabs, called Yathreb, (subsequently Medina,) after his flight from Mekka, and was sure of being now among friends, he erected a small chapel on the spot where his camel had first rested in the town, having bought the ground from the Arabs; and he enclosed it with mud walls, upon which he placed a roof of palm-leaves, supported by the stems of palm-trees for pillars: this edifice he soon after enlarged, having laid the foundations with stone. Instead of the Mahrab, or niche, which is placed in mosques to show the direction in which the faithful ought to turn in their prayers, Mohammed placed a large stone, which was at first turned to the north, towards Jerusalem, and placed in the direction of the Kaaba of Mekka, in the second year of the Hedjra, when the ancient Kebly was changed.

"Omar ibn el Khatab widened the mosque with mud walls and palm-branches, and, instead of the stems of palms, he made pillars of mud. He first carried a wall round the Hedjra, or the place where the body of Mohammed had been deposited at his death, and which was at first enclosed only by palm-branches. The square enclosed by the walls of the mosque was increased to one hundred and forty pikes in length, and one hundred and twenty in breadth, A.H. 17.

"Othman built the walls of hewn stone: in A.H. 29, he renewed the earthen pillars, strengthening the new ones with hoops of iron, and made the roof of the precious Indian wood called Sadj. The square was enlarged to one hundred and sixty pikes by one hundred and fifty; and six gates were opened into it.

"Wolyd, he to whom Damascus owes its beautiful mosque, called Djama el Ammouy, further enlarged the Mesdjed-e'-Neby in A.H. 91.

DESCRIPTION OF MEDINA. 351

Till then, the houses where the wives and daughter and female relations of Mohammed had resided, stood close to the Hedjra, beyond the precincts of the mosque, into which they had private gates. Notwithstanding the great opposition he encountered, Wolyd compelled the women to leave their houses, and to accept a fair price for them; he then razed them, and extended the wall of the mosque on that side. The Greek Emperor, with whom he happened to be at peace, sent him workmen from Constantinople, who assisted in the new building;* several of whom, being Christians, behaved, as it is related, with great indecency; one of them, in particular, when in the act of defiling the very tomb of the Prophet, was killed by a stone which fell from the roof. New stone pillars were now placed in the mosque, with gilt capitals. The walls were cased with marble variously adorned, and parts of them likewise gilt, and the whole building thus completely renewed.

"About A. H. 160, the Khalife El Mohdy still further enlarged the enclosure, and made it two hundred and forty pikes in length; and in this state the mosque remained for several centuries.

"Hakem b'amr Illah, the mad King of Egypt, who sent one of his emissaries to destroy the black stone of the Kaaba, also made an unsuccessful attempt to take from the mosque of Medina Mohammed's tomb, and transport it to Cairo. In A. H. 557, in the time of El Melek el Adel Noureddyn, king of Egypt, two Christians in disguise were discovered at Medina, who had made a subterraneous passage from a neighbouring house into the Hedjra, and stolen from thence articles of great value. Being put to the torture, they confessed having been sent by the King of Spain for that purpose; and they paid for their temerity with their lives. Sultan Noureddyn, after this, carried a trench round the Hedjra, and filled it with lead, to prevent similar attempts.

"In A. H. 654, a few months after the eruption of a volcano near the

---

* Makrisi, in his account of various sovereigns who performed the pilgrimage, says that the Greek Emperor (whom he does not name) sent one hundred workmen to Wolyd, and a present of a hundred thousand *methkal* of gold, together with forty loads of small cut stones, for a mosaic pavement.

town, the mosque caught fire, and was burnt to the ground; but the Korans deposited in the Hedjra were saved. This accident was ascribed to the Persian sectaries of Beni Hosseyn, who were then the guardians of the tomb. In the following year its restoration was undertaken at the expense of the Khalife Mostasem Billah, Ibn el Montaser Billah, and the lord of Yemen, El Mothaffer Shams eddyn Yousef, and completed by El Dhaher Bybars, Sultan of Egypt, in A.H. 657. The dome over the tomb was erected in 678. Several kings of Egypt successively improved and enlarged the building, till A. H. 886, when it was again destroyed by fire occasioned by lightning. The destruction was complete; all the walls of the mosque, and part of those of the Hedjra, the roof, and one hundred and twenty columns fell: all the books in the mosque were destroyed: but the fire appears to have spared the interior of the tomb in the Hedjra. Kayd Beg, then king of Egypt, to whom that country and the Hedjaz owe a number of public works, completely rebuilt the mosque, as it now stands, in A. H. 892. He sent three hundred workmen from Cairo for that purpose. The interior of the Hedjra was cleared, and three deep graves were found in the inside, full of rubbish; but the author of this history, who himself entered it, saw no traces of tombs. The original place of Mohammed's tomb was ascertained with great difficulty. The walls of the Hedjra were then rebuilt, and the iron railing placed round it which is now there. The dome was again raised over it; the gates were distributed as they now are; a new mambar, or pulpit, was sent as a present from Cairo, and the whole mosque assumed its present form. Since the above period, a few immaterial improvements have been made by the Othman Emperors of Constantinople."

GARDENS and plantations, as I have already said, surround the town of Medina, with its suburbs, on three sides, and to the eastward and southward extend to the distance of six or eight miles. They consist principally of date-groves and wheat and barley fields; the latter usually enclosed with mud walls, and containing small habitations for the cultivators. Their houses in the immediate neighbourhood of the town are well built, often with a vestibule supported by columns, and a vaulted sitting-room adjoining, and a tank cased with stone in front of them. They are the summer residence of many families of the town, who make it a custom to pass there a couple of months in the hottest season. Few of the date-groves, unless those dispersed over the fields, are at all enclosed; and most of them are irrigated only by the torrents and winter rains. The gardens themselves are very low, the earth being taken from the middle parts of them, and heaped up round the walls, so as to leave the space destined for agriculture, like a pit, ten or twelve feet below the surface of the plain: this is done to get at a better soil, experience having shown that the upper stratum is much more impregnated with salt, and less fit for cultivation, than the lower. No great industry is any where applied; much ground continues waste; and even where the fields are laid out, no economy whatever is shown in the culture of them. Many spots are wholly barren; and the saline nature of the soil prevents the seed from growing. The ground towards the village of Koba, and beyond it, in a south and east direction, is said to consist of good earth, without any saline mixture; and in value it is consequently much higher than that near the town, which, after rains, I have seen completely covered for several days with a saline crust, partly deposited from the waters, and partly evaporated from the soil itself, in the more elevated spots which the waters do not reach.

Most of the gardens and plantations belong to the people of the town; and the Arabs who cultivate them (called *nowakhele*) are mostly farmers. The property of the gardens is either *mulk* or *wakf;* the former, if they belong to an individual; the latter, if they belong to the mosque, or any of the medreses or pious foundations, from which they are farmed, at very long leases, by the people of Medina themselves, who re-let them on shorter terms to the cultivators. They pay no duties whatever. Not the smallest land-tax, or *miri,* is levied; an immunity which, I believe, all the fertile oases of the Hedjaz enjoyed previous to the invasion by the Wahabys: these, however, had no sooner taken possession of the town, than they taxed the soil, according to their established rule. The fields were assessed, not by their produce in corn, but in dates, the number of date-trees in every field being usually proportionate to the fertility of the soil, and also to its crop of grain. From every erdeb of dates the Wahaby tax-gatherers took their quota either in kind or in money, according to the market-price they then bore. These regulations caused the Wahabys to be disliked here much more than they were at Mekka, where the inhabitants had no fields to be taxed; and where the tax which the Wahabys had imposed was dispensed with, or rather given up to the Sherif, the ancient governor of the town, as I have already remarked. The Mekkans, besides, carried on commerce, from which they could at all times derive some profit, independent of the advantages accruing to them from the foreign hadjys. The people of Medina, on the contrary, are very petty merchants; and their main support depends upon the pilgrims, the yearly stipends from Turkey, or their landed property. As they were obliged entirely to renounce the former, and were curtailed in the profits from the latter; and as the Wahabys showed much less respect for their venerated tomb than they did for the Beitullah at Mekka, we cannot wonder that their name is execrated by the people of Medina, and loaded with the most opprobrious epithets.

The principal produce of the fields* about Medina, is wheat and barley, some clover, and garden-fruits, but chiefly dates. Barley is

---

* They are here called *Beled,* (plur. *Boldan*): the *beled* of such a one.

grown in much larger quantity than wheat; and barley-bread forms a principal article of food with the lower classes. Its harvest is in the middle of March. The crops are very thin; but the produce is of a good quality, and sells in the market of Medina at about fifteen per cent higher than the Egyptian. After harvest, the fields are left fallow till the next year; for though there is sufficient water in the wells* to produce a second irrigation, the soil is too poor to suffer it, without becoming entirely exhausted. No oats are sown here, nor any where else in the Hedjaz. The fruit-trees are found principally on the side of the village of Koba. Pomegranates and grapes are said to be excellent, especially the former: there are likewise some peaches, bananas, and, in the gardens of Koba, a few water-melons, and vegetables, as spinach, turnips, leeks, onions, carrots, and beans, but in very small quantities. The nebek-tree, producing the lotus, is extremely common in the plain of Medina, as well as in the neighbouring mountains; and incredible quantities of its fruit are brought to market in March, when the lower classes make it a prime article of food. But the staple produce of Medina is dates, for the excellence of which fruit this neighbourhood is celebrated throughout Arabia. The date-trees stand either in the enclosed fields, where they are irrigated together with the seeds in the ground, or in the open plain, where they are watered by the rains only: the fruit of the latter, though less abundant, is more esteemed. Numbers of them grow wild on the plain, but every tree has its owner. Their size is, in general, inferior to that of the Egyptian palm-tree, fed by the rich soil of the country, and the waters of the Nile; but their fruit is much sweeter, and has a more fragrant smell.

The many different uses to which almost every part of the date-tree is applied, have already been mentioned by several travellers; they render it as dear to the settled Arab, as the camel is to the Be-

---

* Every garden or field has its well, from whence the water is drawn up by asses, cows, or camels, in large leathern buckets. I believe there are no fields that are not regularly watered, and the seed of none is left merely to the chance of the winter-rains.

douin. Mohammed, in one of the sayings recorded of him, compares the virtuous and generous man to this noble tree. "He stands erect before his Lord; in his every action he follows the impulse received from above, and his whole life is devoted to the welfare of his fellow-creatures."* The people of the Hedjaz, like the Egyptians, make use of the leaves, the outer and inner bark of the trunk, and the fleshy substance at the root of the leaves where they spring from the trunk; and, besides this, they use the kernels of the fruit, as food for their cattle: they soak them for two days in water, when they become softened, and then give them to camels, cows, and sheep, instead of barley; and they are said to be much more nutritive than that grain. There are shops at Medina in which nothing else is sold but date-kernels; and the beggars are continually employed, in all the main streets, in picking up those that are thrown away. In the province of Nedjed the Arabs grind the kernels for the same purpose; but this is not done in the Hedjaz.

Various kinds of dates are found at Medina, as well as in all other fruitful vallies of this country; and every place, almost, has its own species, which grows no where else. I have heard that upwards of one hundred different sorts of dates grow in the immediate neighbourhood of the town; the author of the description of Medina mentions one hundred and thirty. Of the most common sorts are the *Djebely*, the cheapest, and I believe the most universally spread in the Hedjaz; the *Heloua;* the *Heleya*, a very small date, not larger than a mulberry; it has its name from its extraordinary sweetness, in which it does not yield to the finest figs from Smyrna, and like them is covered, when dried, by a saccharine crust. The inhabitants relate, that Mohammed performed a great miracle with this date: he put a stone of it into the earth, which immediately took root, grew up, and within five minutes a full-grown tree, covered with fruit, stood before him. Another miracle is related of the species called *El Syhány*, a tree of

* See also the 1st Psalm, v. 3.—" And he shall be like a tree planted by the rivers of water," &c.

which addressed a loud "Salam Aleykum" to the Prophet, as he passed under it. The *Birny* is esteemed the most wholesome, as it is certainly the easiest of digestion : it was the favourite of Mohammed, who advised the Arabs to eat seven of its fruit every morning before breakfast. The *Djeleby* is the scarcest of them all: it is about three inches in length, and one in breadth, and has a peculiarly agreeable taste, although not so sweet as the *Heleya*. It seems that it grows with great difficulty; for there are, at most, not more than one hundred trees of this species, and they are less fertile than any of the other. They grow in no part of the Hedjaz, but here and in the groves of Yembo el Nakhel. The price of the *Birny* is twenty paras per keile, a measure, containing at least one hundred and twenty dates, while the *Djeleby* is sold at eight dates for twenty paras : they are in great request with the hadjys, who usually carry some of these dates home, to present to their friends, as coming from the city of the Prophet; and small boxes, holding about one hundred of them, are made at Medina, for their conveyance.

Dates form an article of food by far the most essential to the lower classes of Medina : their harvest is expected with as much anxiety, and attended with as much general rejoicings, as the vintage in the south of Europe; and if the crop fails, which often happens, as these trees are seldom known to produce abundantly for three or four successive years, or is eaten up by the locusts, universal gloom overspreads the population, as if a famine were apprehended.

One species of the Medina dates, the name of which I have forgotten, remains perfectly green although ripe, and dried; another retains a bright saffron colour: these dates are threaded on strings, and sold all over the Hedjaz, where they go by the name of *Kalayd es' Sham*, or necklaces of the North; and the young children frequently wear them round the neck. The first dates are eaten in the begining of June, and at that period of their growth are called *Rotab;* but the general date-harvest is at the end of that month. In Egypt it is a month later. Dates are dressed in many different ways by the Arabs; boiled in milk, broiled with butter; or reduced to a thick pulp by boiling in water, over which honey is poured; and the Arabs say that a good housewife will daily furnish her lord, for a month, a dish of dates differently dressed.

In these gardens a very common tree is the *Ithel*, a species of tamarisk, cultivated for its hard wood, of which the Arabs make their camels' saddles, and every utensil that requires strong handles.

In the gardens we seldom find the ground perfectly level, and the cultivation is often interrupted by heaps of rocks. On the N.W. and W. sides of the town, the whole plain is so rocky as to defeat all attempts at improvement. The cultivable soil is clay, mixed with a good deal of chalk and sand, and is of a grayish white colour: in other parts it consists of a yellow loam, and also of a substance very similar to bole-earth; small conical pieces of the latter, about an inch and a half long, and dried in the sun, are sold, suspended on a piece of riband, to the visiters of Medina. It is related that Mohammed cured a Bedouin of Beni Hareth, and several others, of a fever by washing their bodies with water in which this earth had been dissolved; and the pilgrims are eager to carry home a memorial of this miracle. The earth is taken from a ditch at a place called El Medshounye, in the neighbourhood of the town.

All the rocky places, as well as the lower ridge of the northern mountainous chain, are covered by a layer of volcanic rock: it is of a bluish black colour, very porous, yet heavy, and hard, not glazed, like schlacken, and contains frequently small white substances in its pores of the size of a pin's head, which I never found crystallised. The plain has a completely black colour from this rock, and the small pieces with which it is overspread. I met with no lava, although the nature of the ground seemed strongly to indicate the neighbourhood of a volcano. Had I enjoyed better health, I should have made some excursions to the more distant parts of the gardens of Medina, to look for specimens of minerals; but the first days of my stay were taken up in making out a plan of the town, and gaining information on its inhabitants; and I was not afterwards capable of the slightest bodily exertion. It was not till my return to Cairo, that, in reading the description of Medina, which I had purchased at the former place, (and of

DESCRIPTION OF MEDINA.   359

which, and of the descriptions of Mekka, I could never find copies in the Hedjaz, notwithstanding all my endeavours,) I met with the account of an earthquake and a volcanic eruption which took place in the immediate neighbourhood of Medina about the middle of the thirteenth century; and upon inquiry I learnt from a man of Medina, established at Cairo, that the place of the stream of lava is still shown, at about one hour E. of the town. During my stay, I remember to have once made the observation to my cicerone, in going with him to Djebel Ohod, that the country appeared as if all burnt by fire; but I received an unmeaning reply; no hint or information afterwards in the town which could lead me to suppose that I was near so interesting a phenomenon of nature.

Some extracts from the work to which I have alluded, describing this eruption, may be thought worthy of the reader's attention, and are given in the subjoined note.*

From this account the stream of lava must be sought at about one

---

* "On the first of the month Djomad el Akhyr, in A. H. 654, a slight earthquake was felt in the town; on the third, another stronger shock took place, during the day; about two o'clock in the ensuing morning, repeated violent shocks awakened the inhabitants, increasing in force during the rest of the morning, and continuing at intervals till Friday the sixth of the month. Many houses and walls tumbled down. On Friday morning a thundering noise was heard, and at mid-day the fire burst forth. On the spot where it issued from the earth a smoke first arose, which completely darkened the sky. To the eastward of the town, towards the close of day, the flames were visible, a fiery mass of immense size, which bore the appearance of a large town, with walls, battlements, and minarets, ascending to heaven. Out of this flame issued a river of red and blue fire, accompanied with the noise of thunder. The burning waves carried whole rocks before them, and farther on heaped them up like high mounds. The river was approaching nearer to the town, when Providence sent a cool breeze, which arrested its further progress on this side. All the inhabitants of Medina passed that night in the great mosque; and the reflection of the fire changed that night into day-light. The fiery river took a northern direction, and terminated at the mountain called Djebel Wayra, standing in the valley called Wady el Shathat, which is a little to the eastward of Djebel Ohod [two miles and a half from Medina]. For five days the flame was seen ascending, and the river remained burning for three months. Nobody could approach it on account of its heat. It destroyed all rocks; but, (says the historian,) this being the sacred territory of Medina, where Mohammed had

hour distant to the E. of the town. The volcanic productions which cover the immediate neighbourhood of the town and the plain to the west of it, are probably owing to former eruptions of the same volcano; for nothing is said, in the relation, of stones having been cast out of the crater to any considerable distance, and the whole plain to the westward, as far as Wady Akyk, three miles distant, is covered with the above-described volcanic productions. I have little doubt that on many other points of that great chain of mountains, similar volcanoes have existed. The great number of warm springs found at almost every station of the road to Mekka, authorises such a conjecture.

I am here induced, by a passage in the extract contained in the last note, to offer the following remark. According to the strict precept of Mohammed, that part of the territory of Medina which encompassed the town in a circle of twelve miles, having on the S. side Djebel Ayre, and on the N. side Djebel Thor, (a small mountain just behind Djebel Ohod,) as the boundary, should be considered sacred; no person should be slain therein, except aggressors, and enemies, in self-defence, or infidels who polluted it; and neither game should be killed nor trees cut in such a holy territory. This interdiction, however, is at present completely set aside; trees are cut, game is killed, bloody affrays happen in the town itself and

---

ordained that no trees should be cut within a certain space, it spared all the trees it met with in its course. The entire length of the river was four *farsakh*, or twelve miles; the breadth of it four miles; and its depth, eight or nine feet. The valley of Shathat was quite choked up; and the place where it is thus choked, called from this circumstance El Sedd, is still to be seen. The flame was seen at Yembo and at Mekka. An Arab of Teyma (a small town in the N.E. Desert from six to eight days' journey from Medina) wrote a letter during night by the light reflected from it to that distance.

" In the same year, a great inundation of the Tigris happened, by which half the town of Baghdad was destroyed; and at the close of this same year the temple of Medina itself was burnt to the ground.

" The Arabs were prepared to witness such a conflagration; for they remembered the saying of Mohammed, that ' the day of judgment will not happen until a fire shall appear in the Hedjaz, which shall cause the necks of the camels at Basra to shine.' "

in its immediate vicinity; and though an avowed follower of any other religion than the Mohammedan is not permitted to enter the gates of the town, yet several instances occurred, during my stay there, (and while I resided at Yembo,) of Greek Christians employed in the commissariat of the army of Tousoun Pasha encamping within gun-shot of Medina, previous to their departure for the head-quarters of the Pasha, then in the province of Kasym.

ACCOUNT OF SOME PLACES OF ZYARA,

OR OBJECTS OF PIOUS VISITATION IN THE NEIGHBOURHOOD OF MEDINA.

On the day after the pilgrim has performed his first duties at the mosque and the tomb, he usually visits the burial-ground of the town, in memory of the many saints who lie buried there. It is just beyond the town-walls, near the gate of Bab Djoma, and bears the name of El Bekya. A square of several hundred paces is enclosed by a wall which, on the southern side, joins the suburb, and on the others is surrounded with date-groves. Considering the sanctity of the persons whose bodies it contains, it is a very mean place; and perhaps the most dirty and miserable burial-ground in any eastern town of the size of Medina. It does not contain a single good tomb, nor even any large inscribed blocks of stone covering tombs; but instead, mere rude heaps of earth, with low borders of loose stones placed about them. The Wahabys are accused of having defaced the tombs; and in proof of this, the ruins of small domes and buildings are pointed out, which formerly covered the tombs of Othman, Abbas, Setna Fatme, and the aunts of Mohammed, which owed their destruction to those sectaries: but they would certainly not have annihilated every other simple tomb built of stone here, which they did neither at Mekka nor any other place. The miserable state of this cemetery must have existed prior to the Wahaby conquest, and is to be ascribed to the niggardly minds of the towns-people, who are little disposed to incur any expense in honouring the remains of their celebrated countrymen. The whole place is a confused accumulation of heaps of earth, wide pits, rubbish, without a single regular tomb-stone. The pilgrim is made to visit a number of graves, and, while standing before them, to repeat prayers for the dead. Many persons make it their exclusive profession to watch the whole day near each of the principal tombs, with a handkerchief spread out, in expectation of the pilgrims who come to visit them; and this is the exclusive privilege of certain Ferráshyns and their families, who have divided the tombs among themselves, where each takes his post, or sends his servant in his stead.

The most conspicuous personages that lie buried here are Ibrahim, the son of Mohammed, who died in his youth; Fatme, his daughter, according to the opinion of many, who say that she was buried here and not in the mosque; several of the wives of Mohammed; some of his daughters; his foster-mother; Fatme, the daughter of Asad, and mother of Aly; Abbas ibn Abd el Motalleb; Othman ibn Affan, one of the immediate successors of Mohammed, who collected the scattered leaves of the Koran into one volume; the Martyrs, or Shohada, as they are called, who were slain here by the army of the heretics under Yezyd ibn Mawya, whose commander, Moslim, in A. H. 60, (others say 62,) came from Syria and sacked the town, the inhabitants of which had acknowledged the rebel Abdallah ibn Hantala as their chief; Hassan ibn Aly, whose trunk only lies buried here, his head having been sent to Cairo, where it is preserved in the fine mosque called El Hassamya; the Imám Malek ibn Anes, the founder of the sect of the Malekites. Indeed so rich is Medina in the remains of great saints that they have almost lost their individual importance, while the relics of one of the persons just mentioned would be sufficient to render celebrated any other Moslim town. As a formula of the invocation addressed here to the manes of the saint, I shall transcribe that which is said with uplifted hands, after having performed a short prayer of two rikats, over the tomb of Othman ibn Affan: " Peace be with thee, O Othman! Peace be with thee, O friend of the chosen! Peace be with thee, O collector of the Koran! Mayest thou deserve the contentment of God! May God ordain Paradise as thy dwelling, thy resting-place, thy habitation, and thy abode! I deposit on this spot, and near thee, O Othman, the profession everlasting, from this day to the day of judgment, that there is no God but God, and that Mohammed is his servant and his prophet."

The inhabitants of Medina bury all their dead on this ground, in the same homely tombs as those of the saints. Branches of palm-trees are stuck upon the graves, and changed once a year, at the feast of Ramadhan, when the family visits the grave of its relations, where it sometimes remains for several days.

VISIT TO DJEBEL OHOD.—One of the principal Zyara or places of sacred visitation of Medina, is Ohod, with the tomb of Hamze, the uncle of Mohammed. The mountain of Ohod forms part of the great chain, branching out from it into the eastern plain, so as to stand almost insulated. It is three quarters of an hour's walk from the town. In the fourth year of the Hedjra, when Mohammed had fixed his residence at Medina, the idolatrous Koreysh, headed by Abou Sofyan, invaded these parts, and took post at this mountain. Mohammed issued from the town, and there fought, with great disparity of force, the most arduous battle in which he was ever engaged. His uncle Hamze was killed, together with seventy-five of his followers: he himself was wounded, but he killed with his own lance one of the bravest men of the opposite party, and gained at last a complete victory. The tomb of Hamze and of the seventy-five martyrs, as they are called, form the object of the visit to Djebel Ohod.

I started on foot, with my cicerone, by the Syrian gate, in the company of several other visiters; for it was thought unsafe to go there alone, from fear of Bedouin robbers. The visit is generally performed on Thursdays. We passed the place where the Syrian Hadj encamp, and where several wells and half-ruined tanks, cased with stone, supply the pilgrims with water during their three days' stay at this place, in their way to and from Mekka. A little further on is a pretty *kiosk*, with a dome, now likewise half-ruined, called El Goreyn, where the chief of that caravan usually takes up his temporary abode. The road further on is completely level; date-trees stand here and there, and several spots are seen which the people only cultivate when the rains are copious. About one mile from the town stands a ruined edifice of stones and bricks, where a short prayer is recited in remembrance of Mohammed having here put on his coat of mail, when he went to engage the enemy. Farther on is a large stone, upon which it is said that Mohammed leaned for a few minutes on his way to Ohod; the visiter is enjoined to press his back against this stone, and to recite the Fateha, or opening chapter of the Koran.

In approaching the mountain, we passed a torrent, coming from E. or S.E. with water to the depth of two feet, the remains of the rain that had fallen five days ago. It swells sometimes so high as to become impassable, and inundates the whole surrounding country. To the east of this torrent, the ground leading towards the mountain is barren, stony, with a slight ascent, on the slope of which stands a mosque, surrounded by about a dozen ruined houses, once the pleasure villas of wealthy towns-people; near them is a cistern, filled by the torrent-water. The mosque is a square solid-built edifice of small dimensions. Its dome was thrown down by the Wahabys, but they spared the tomb. The mosque encloses the tomb of Hamze, and those of his principal men who were slain in the battle; namely, Mesab ibn Omeyr, Djafar ibn Shemmas, and Abdallah ibn Djahsh. The tombs are in a small open yard, and, like those of the Bekya, mere heaps of earth, with a few loose stones placed around them. Beside them is a small portico, which serves as a mosque: a short prayer is said here, and the pilgrims then advance to the tombs, where they recite the chapter of Yasein (from the Koran), or the short chapter of El Khalas forty times; after which Hamze and his friends are invoked to intercede with the Almighty, and obtain for the pilgrim and all his family, faith, health, wealth, and the utter destruction of all their enemies. Money is given, as usual, at every corner, to the guardians of the mosque, of the tombs, to the Mueddin, Imám, &c. &c.

A little further on, towards the mountain, which is only at a gun-shot distance, a small cupola marks the place where Mohammed was struck in battle by a stone, which knocked out four of his front teeth, and felled him to the ground.* His party thought he was killed; but the angel Gabriel immediately appeared, and exclaimed that he was still alive. At a short distance from this cupola, which like all the rest has been demolished, are the tombs of twelve other partisans of the Prophet, who were killed in the battle. They form together several mounds of rubbish and stones, in which their respective tombs can no longer be distinguished. Prayers are again recited, with that passage of the Koran which says, in speaking of the slain: " Do not think that those who were killed in war with the infidels are dead; no, they are living, and their reward is with their Lord:" a sentence still used to encourage, even in our days, the Turkish soldiers in their battles with Europeans.

The mountain of Ohod consists of different coloured granite; on its sides I likewise found flint, but no lava. The entire mountain is almost four miles in length, from west to east. Having been the scene of the famous battle, which so much contributed to strengthen the party of Mohammed and his new religion, it is not surprising that Djebel Ohod should be the object of peculiar veneration. The people of Medina believe that on the day of resurrection it will be transported into Paradise; and that when mankind shall appear before the Almighty for judgment, they will be assembled upon it, as the most favoured station. The mountain of Ayra, mentioned above as situated to the S. W. of the town, (about the same distance from it as Ohod is, on the other side,) will on that day experience a much less enviable fate. Having denied water to the Prophet, who once lost his way in its valleys, and became thirsty, it will be punished for inhospitality, by being cast at once into hell.

The people of Medina frequently visit Ohod, pitching their tents in the ruined houses, where they remain a few days, especially convalescents, who during their illness had made a vow to slaughter a sheep in honour of Hamze, if they recovered. Once a year, (in July, I

* This story is related here, though the historians of the Prophet do not agree on the subject.

believe,) the inhabitants flock thither in crowds, and remain for three days, as if it were during the feast days of the saint. Regular markets are then kept there: and this visit forms one of the principal public amusements of the town.

KOBA.—In this neighbouring village all the pilgrims visit the spot where Mohammed first alighted on coming from Mekka: it lies to the south of the town, distant about three quarters of an hour. The road to it passes through a plain, overgrown with date-trees, and covered in many spots with white sand. At half an hour from the town begin gardens, which spread over a space of four or five miles in circuit, and form, perhaps, the most fertile and agreeable spot in the Northern Hedjaz. All kinds of fruit-trees (with the exception of apple and pear, none of which I believe grow in Arabia,) are seen in the gardens, which are all enclosed by walls, and irrigated by numerous wells. It is from hence that Medina is supplied with fruits: lemon and orange trees, pomegranates, bananas, vines, peach, apricot, and fig trees, are planted amidst the date and nebek trees, and form as thick groves as in Syria and Egypt, while their shade renders Koba a delightful residence. The *kheroa* (Ricinus, or Palma Christi,) is likewise very common here. The village is frequently visited by the people of Medina ; parties are continually made to spend the day, and many sick people are carried to enjoy the benefits of a cooler atmosphere.

In the midst of these groves stands the Mesdjed of Koba, with about thirty or forty houses. It is a mean building, and much decayed. In the interior of it several holy spots are visited, at each of which a short prayer of two rikats is performed, and some additional invocations recited in honour of the place. We first see here the Mobrak el Naka, the very spot on the floor of the mosque where the she-camel which Mohammed rode, in his flight from Mekka, crouched down, and would not rise again, thus advising her master to stop here, which he did for a few days, previous to his entering Medina. It was to consecrate this spot, that the mosque was founded by Mohammed himself with loose stones, which were changed into a regular building the year after, by Benou Ammer ibn Owf ; but the present building is of modern construction. Further on is shown the spot upon which Mohammed once stood, after his prayers, and distinctly saw from thence Mekka, and all that the Koreysh were doing there; and, thirdly, the spot where the Koranic passage relating to the inhabitants of Koba was revealed to Mohammed : " A temple, from its first day founded in piety ; there thou best standest up to prayers. There men live who like to be purified : and God loves the clean." In this passage an allusion is discovered to the extraordinary personal cleanliness of those who inhabited Koba, more especially in certain acts of ablution.

I saw no inscriptions in this mosque, except those of hadjys who had written their names on the white-washed walls ; a practice in which Eastern travellers indulge as frequently as European tourists, adding often to the names some verses of favourite poets, or sentences of the Koran. The mosque forms a narrow colonnade round a small open courtyard, in which the Mobrak el Naka stands, with a small cupola over it, rising to the height of about six feet. On issuing from the mosque, we were assailed by a crowd of beggars. At a short distance from it, among the cluster of houses, stands a small chapel, called Mesdjed Aly, in honour of Aly, the cousin of Mohammed. Close to it, in a garden, a deep well is shown, called Ayn Ezzerka, with a small chapel, built at its mouth. This was a favourite spot with Mohammed, who used often to sit among the trees with his disciples, enjoying the pleasure of seeing the water issuing in a limpid stream; an object which at the present day powerfully attracts the natives of the East, and, with the addition of a shady tree, is perhaps the only feature of landscape which they admire. When he once was sitting here, the Prophet's seal-ring dropped into the well, and could never be again found ; and the supposition that the ring is still there, renders the well famous. The water is tepid at its source, with a slight sulphureous taste, which it loses in its course. It is collected together with that of several other springs into the canal which supplies Medina, and which is kept constantly flowing by the supply of various channels of well-water. Omar el Khatab first carried the spring to Medina ; but the present canal was built at the expense of the Sultan Soleyman, son of Selim I., about A. H. 973 : it is a very solid subterranean work.

This canal, and that of Mekka, are the greatest architectural curiosities in the Hedjaz. Near to the mosque of Koba stands a building erected by Sultan Morad, for dervishes. A little beyond the village, on the road towards the town, stands a small chapel, called Mesdjed Djoma, in remembrance of the spot where the people of Medina met Mohammed upon his arrival.

EL KEBLETYN.—Towards the N. W. of the town, about one hour distant, a place is visited bearing this name. It is said to consist of two rude pillars (for I did not see it myself,) and was the spot where Mohammed first changed the *Kebly*, or the direction in which prayers are said, in the seventeenth month after the Hedjra, or his flight to Medina. Together with the Jewish Bedouins, his own adherents had till then Jerusalem as their Kebly; but Mohammed now turned it towards the Kaaba, to which that fine passage of the Koran alludes: " Say, to God belong the east and the west ; he directs whomsoever he pleases in the road of piety:"—a sentence written to convince the Moslims, that wherever they turned, in their prayers, God stood before them. Near this spot stands a small ruined chapel.

The above are the only places visited by pilgrims. The country round Koba, and towards the S. E. of the town, presents many spots of nearly equal beauty with Koba, which in summer are places of recreation to the people of Medina ; but I believe there are no villages any where to be seen, only insulated houses, or small groupes of buildings, scattered amongst the date-trees.

ON THE INHABITANTS OF MEDINA.

LIKE the Mekkans, the people of Medina are for the greater part strangers, whom the Prophet's tomb, and the gains which it insures to its neighbours, have drawn to this place. But few original Arabs, descendants of those families who lived at Medina when Mohammed came from Mekka, now remain in the town; on the contrary, we find in it colonies from almost every quarter of the Muselman empire, east and west. I was informed, that of the original Arab residents, to whom the Mohammedan writers apply the name of El Ansar, and who at Mohammed's entrance were principally composed of the tribes of Ows and Khezredj, only about ten families remain who can prove their descent by pedigrees, or well-ascertained traditions: they are poor people, and live as peasants in the suburbs and gardens. The number of Sherifs descended of Hassan, the grandson of Mohammed, is considerable; but most of them are not originally from this place, their ancestors having come hither from Mekka, during the wars waged by the Sherifs for the possession of that town. They almost all belong to the class of olemas, very few military sherifs, like those of Mekka, being found here. Among them is a small tribe of Beni Hosseyn, descended from Hosseyn, the brother of Hassan. They are said to have been formerly very powerful at Medina, and had appropriated to themselves the chief part of the income of the mosque: in the thirteenth century, (according to Samhoudy,) they were the privileged guardians of the Prophet's tomb; but at present they are reduced to about a dozen families, who still rank among the grandees of the town and its most wealthy inhabitants. They occupy a quarter by themselves, and obtain very large profits, particularly from the Persian pilgrims who pass here. They are universally stated to be heretics, of the Persian sect of Aly, and to perform secretly the rites of that creed, although they publicly profess the doctrines of the Sunnys. This report is too general, and confirmed by too many people of respectability, to be doubted: but the Beni Hosseyn have powerful influence in the town, in appearance strictly comply with the orthodox principles, and are therefore not molested.

It is publicly said that the remnants of the Ansars, and great numbers of the peasant Arabs who cultivate the gardens and fields in the neighbourhood of the town, are addicted to the same heresy. The latter, called Nowakhele, (a name implying that they live among date-trees,) are numerous, and very warlike. They had offered determined resistance to the Wahabys, and in civil contests have proved always superior to the town's-people. They are said to be descendants of the partisans of Yezid, the son of Mawya, who took and sacked the town sixty years after the Hedjra. They marry only among themselves; and exhibit on all occasions a great *esprit de corps*. Many of them publicly profess the creed of Aly when in their date-groves, but are Sunnys whenever they come to town. Some of them are established in the suburbs, and they have monopolised the occupation of butchers. In quarrels I have heard individuals among them publicly called sectaries and *rowafedh*, without their ever denying it. In the Eastern Desert, at three or four days' journey from Medina, lives a whole Bedouin tribe, called Beni Aly, who are all of this Persian creed; and it is matter of astonishment to find the two most holy spots of the orthodox Muselman religion surrounded, one by the sectaries of Zeyd, and the other by those of Aly, without an attempt having been made to dislodge them.

Among the ancient families of Medina are likewise reckoned a few descendants of the Abassides, now reduced to great poverty: they go by the name of *Khalifye*, implying that they are descended from the Khalifes.

Most of the inhabitants are of foreign origin, and present as motley a race as those of Mekka. No year passes without some new settlers being added to their number; and no pilgrim caravan crosses the town without leaving here a few of its travellers, who stop at first with the intention of remaining for a year or two only, but generally continue to reside here permanently. Descendants of people from northern Turkey are very numerous; but the greater part trace their origin to settlers of the southern countries of Arabia, Yemen and Hadramaut, and from Syria, and Egypt, and many also from Barbary. My cicerone was called Sheikh Sad-eddyn el Kurdy, because his grandfather was a Kurd who had settled here: the proprietor of the house in which I lived was Seyd Omar, a Sherif of the Yafáÿ tribe of Yemen, whose ancestors had come hither several hundred years since. Indians are likewise found, but in less number than at Mekka. As there, they are druggists, and petty shopkeepers; but I believe that no Indian wholesale dealers in their native products are to be found at Medina. They adhere to their national dress and manners, forming a small colony, and rarely intermarry or mix with the other inhabitants.

The individuals of different nations settled here have in their second and third generations all become Arabs as to features and character; but are, nevertheless, distinguishable from the Mekkans; they are not nearly so brown as the latter, thus forming an intermediate link between the Hedjaz people and the northern Syrians. Their features are somewhat broader, their beards thicker, and their body stouter, than those of the Mekkans; but the Arab face, the expression, and cast of features are in both places the same.

The Medinans in their dress resemble more the Turkish than their southern neighbours: very few of them wear the *beden*, or the national Arab cloak without sleeves; but even the poorer people dress in long gowns, with a cloth *djobbe*, or upper cloak, or, instead of it, an *abba*, of the same brown and white stripe as is common in Syria and all over the Desert. Red Tunis bonnets and Turkish shoes are more used here than at Mekka, where the lower classes wear white bonnets, and sandals. People in easy circumstances dress well, wearing good cloth cloaks, fine gowns, and, in winter, good pelisses, brought from Constantinople by way of Cairo; which I found a very common article of dress in January and February, a season when it is much colder here than Europeans would expect it to be in Arabian deserts. Generally speaking, we may say that the Medinans dress better than the Mekkans, though with much less cleanliness: but no national costume is observed here; and, particularly in the cold of winter, the lower classes cover themselves with whatever articles of dress they can obtain at low prices in the public auctions; so that it is not uncommon to see a man fitted out in the dress of three or four different countries — like an Arab as high as his waist, and like a Turkish soldier over his breast and shoulders. The richer people make a great display of dress, and vie with each other in finery. I saw more new suits of clothes here, even when the yearly feasts were terminated, than I had seen before in any other part of the East. As at Mekka, the Sherifs wear no green, but simple white muslin turbans, excepting those from the northern part of Turkey, who have recently settled here, and who continue to wear the badge of their noble extraction.

Prior to the Wahaby conquest, when the inhabitants were often exposed to bloody affrays among themselves, they always went armed with the *djombye*, or crooked Arabian knife: at present few of these are seen; but every body, from the highest to the lowest, carries in his hand a long heavy stick. The rich have their sticks headed with silver; others fix iron spikes to them; and thus make a formidable weapon, which the Arabs handle with much dexterity. The women dress like those of Mekka; blue gowns being worn by the lower classes, and silk *mellayes* by the higher.

The Bedouins settled in and near the suburbs, use exactly the same costume as those of the Syrian Desert: a shirt, abba, a kessye on the head, a leathern girdle in which the knife is stuck, and sandals on the feet. Even those who have become settlers, form a distinct race, and do not intermix with the rest of the town's-people. They preserve their national dress, language, and customs, and live in their houses as they would under tents in the Desert. Of all Eastern nations, the Arabian Bedouins perhaps are those who abandon their national habits with most reluctance. In Syria, in Egypt, and in the Hedjaz, settlements are seen, the members of which have become cultivators for several centuries back; yet they have adopted only few of the habits of peasants, and still pride themselves on their Bedouin origin and manners.

The Medinans have not the same means of gaining a living, as the Mekkans. Although this town is never free from foreign pilgrims, there is never that immense influx of hadjys which renders Mekka so populous for several months in the year, and which makes it a market for all parts of the East. The hadjys who come to Medina are seldom merchants, or at least do not go there for mercantile pursuits, and therefore leave on the coast their heavy baggage. Even the Syrian merchants who pass with the great caravan seldom engage in trade, unless it be for some camel-loads of tobacco and dried fruits. The Medina trade is therefore merely for home consumption, and to supply the neighbouring Bedouins with articles of dress and provisions. These are received by way of Yembo, and come almost exclusively from Egypt. No great merchants are settled in Medina: the trade is merely retail; and those who possess capital, generally invest it in goods, as usual throughout Syria and Egypt, there not being any public institution like banks, or trading societies, or national funds, from which the capitalist might derive interest for his money. The Turkish law rigorously forbids the taking of interest; and even if it were otherwise, there is not any government nor any class of men to which the people would intrust considerable sums. The investment of capital in landed property is also liable to great risk.* The usual

---

* By a decree of Mohammed Aly in 1813, the purchase of land in Egypt is rendered impracticable; for it orders all the Moltezims (or landed proprietors who shared in the possession of villages and grounds, and who formed a class living on their rents in the country towns,) to receive their yearly revenue from the Pasha's treasury, where they suffered every kind of humiliation and injustice; and the whole of the soil was declared to be the property of government, or in other words of Mohammed Aly himself, who leaves the cultivation of it to the *fellahs* on his own terms. It happened lately that the Fellahs, who

method is to enter into partnership with different petty merchants or retail dealers, and obtain a share of their profits; but it is subject to almost as much anxiety as an active trade, from the necessity of keeping a constant account with the partners, and incessantly watching them. Usury is practised, and an annual interest from thirty to fifty per cent is paid at Cairo for money: but few of the Turkish merchants descend to this practice, which is reckoned dishonorable. Usury is wholly in the hands of Jews, and Christians the outcasts of Europe. There is, perhaps, nothing in the present deplorable state of eastern society that has a more baneful effect upon the minds and happiness of the people, than the necessity of continuing during their whole lives in business full of intrigues and chances. The cheering hopes which animate an European, the prospect of enjoying in old age the profits of early exertions, are unknown to the native of the East, whose retirement would bring nothing but danger, by marking him as wealthy in the eyes of his rapacious governor. The double influence of the Turkish government and Muselman religion have produced such an universal hypocrisy, that there is scarcely a Mohammedan (whose tranquil air, as he smokes his pipe reclining on the sofa, gives one an idea of the most perfect contentment and apathy,) that does not suffer under all the agonies of envy, unsatisfied avarice, ambition, or the fear of losing his ill-gotten property.

Travellers who pass rapidly through the East, without a knowledge of the language, and rarely mixing with any but persons interested in misrepresenting their true character, are continually deceived by the dignified deportment of the Turks, their patriarchal manners and solemn speeches,—although they would ridicule a Frenchman who,

farmed five thousand acres belonging to the village of Damkour near Cairo, were deprived of their leases on the land being declared public property, because the Pasha wished to sow clover for his cavalry upon the soil that the Fellahs had possessed. Landed property in Syria also subjects the owner to great inconveniences: he is oppressed by every governor of a district, and by every soldier who passes; he suffers in his receipts from the extortions of the Pashas, which generally fall more heavily upon the cultivator than upon the monied man: and if he do not constantly watch his peasants, he is most probably cheated out of all his profits.

after a few months' residence in England, and ignorant of the English language, should pretend to a competent knowledge of the British character and constitution; not recollecting that it is much easier for a Frenchman to judge of a neighbouring European nation, than for any European to judge of Oriental nations, whose manners, ideas, and notions are so different from his own. For my own part, a long residence among Turks, Syrians, and Egyptians, justifies me in declaring that they are wholly deficient in virtue, honour, and justice; that they have little true piety, and still less charity or forbearance; and that honesty is only to be found in their paupers or idiots. Like the Athenians of old, a Turk may perhaps know what is right and praiseworthy, but he leaves the practice to others; though, with fine maxims on his lips, he endeavours to persuade himself that he acts as they direct. Thus he believes himself to be a good Muselman, because he does not omit the performance of certain prayers and ablutions, and frequently invokes the forgiveness of God.

At Medina several persons engage in small commercial transactions, chiefly concerning provisions; a lucrative branch of traffic, as the town depends for its support upon the caravans from Yembo, which are seldom regular, and this circumstance causes the prices of provisions continually to fluctuate. The evil consequence of this is, that the richer corn-dealers sometimes succeed in establishing a monopoly, no grain remaining but in their warehouses, the petty traders having been obliged to sell off. Whenever the caravans are delayed for any considerable time, corn rises to an enormous price; and as the chiefs of the town are thus interested, it can scarcely be supposed that the magistrates would interfere.

Next to the provision-trade, that with the neighbouring Bedouins is the most considerable: they provide the town with butter, honey, (a very essential article in Hedjaz cookery,) sheep, and charcoal; for which they take, in return, corn and clothing. Their arrival at Medina is likewise subject to great irregularity; and if two tribes happen to be at war, the town is kept for a month at the mercy of the few substantial merchants who happen to have a stock of those articles in hand. When I first reached Medina, no butter was to be had in the market, and corn was fifty per cent dearer than at Yembo; soon after, it was not to be had at all in the market: at another time salt failed; the same happened with charcoal; and in general the provision-market was very badly regulated. In other eastern towns, as at Mekka and Djidda, a public officer, called *Mohteseb*, is appointed to watch over the sale of provisions; to take care that they do not rise to immoderate prices, and fix a maximum to all the victualling traders, so that they may have a fair but not exorbitant profit. But this is not the case at Medina, because the Mohteseb is there without any authority. Corn is sold twenty per cent dearer in one part of the town than in another, and the same with every other article, so that foreigners unacquainted with the ways of the place are made to suffer materially. During my stay, the communication with Yembo was kept up by a caravan of about one hundred and fifty camels, which arrived at Medina every fortnight, and by small parties of Bedouin traders with from five to ten camels, which arrived every five or six days. The far greater part of the loads was destined for the army of Tousoun Pasha; the rest consisted of merchandize and provisions; but the latter were very inadequate to the wants of the town. I heard from a well-informed person, that the daily consumption of Medina was from thirty to forty erdebs, or twenty-five to thirty-five Hedjaz camel-loads. The produce of the fields which surround the town, is said to be barely sufficient for four months' consumption; for the rest, therefore, it must depend upon Yembo, or imports from Egypt. In time of peace there is plenty: but lately, since the Turkish army has been stationed here, the Bedouins fear to trust their camels in the hands of the Turks, and the supply has fallen much below the wants of the town. The inhabitants were put to great inconvenience on that account, and had greatly reduced their consumption of corn, and eaten up the last of their stock on hand. Tousoun Pasha had very imprudently seized a great number of the Bedouins' camels, and obliged them to accompany his army, which had so terrified them, that, previous to Mohammed Aly's arrival, famine was apprehended from the want of beasts of transport. The Pasha endeavoured to restore confidence, and some of the Bedouins began to return with their beasts.

In time of peace, corn caravans arrive also from Nedjed, principally from that district of it called Kasym; but these were altogether interrupted. I was informed that the transport trade in provisions from Yembo had been shut up for several years after the conquest of Medina by the Wahabys, whose chief, Saoud, wished to favour his own subjects of Nedjed; and that Medina in the mean time drew all its supplies from Nedjed, and its own fields. Provisions were now excessively dear: the lower class lived almost entirely upon dates, and very coarse barley bread; few could afford a little butter, much fewer meat. The fruit of the lotus, or Nebek, which ripened in the beginning of March, induced them to quit the dates, and became almost their sole nourishment for several months; large heaps of it were seen in the market, and a person might procure enough to satisfy himself for a pennyworth of corn, which was usually taken in exchange instead of money, by the Bedouins, who brought the fruit to the town. The vegetables cultivated in the gardens are chiefly for the use of foreigners, and are of very indifferent flavour. Arabs dislike them, and they are only used by those who have acquired the relish in foreign countries. Fresh onions, leeks, and garlic, are the only vegetables of which the Arabs are fond.

The prime article of food at Medina, as I have already stated, is dates. During the two or three months of the date-harvest, (for this fruit is not all ripe at the same time, each species having its season), from July till September, the lower classes feed on nothing else; and during the rest of the year dried dates continue to be their main nourishment. The date-harvest is here of the same importance as that of wheat in Europe, and its failure causes general distress. "What is the price of dates at Mekka or Medina?" is always the first question asked by a Bedouin who meets a passenger on the road. Of these dates a considerable part is brought to Medina from distant quarters, and especially from Fera, a fertile valley in the possession of the Beni Aamer tribe, where there are numerous date-groves: it is three or four days' journey from Medina, and as many from Rabegh in the mountains. The dates are brought from thence in large baskets, in which they are pressed together into a paste, as I have already mentioned.

Although commercial dealings are pretty universal, yet few of the inhabitants ostensibly follow them. Most of the people are either cultivators, or, in the higher classes, landed proprietors, and servants of the mosque. The possession of fields and gardens is much desired; to be a land-owner is considered honorable; and the rents of the fields, if the date-harvest be good, is very considerable. If I may judge from two instances reported to me, the fields are sold at such a rate, as to leave to the owner, in ordinary years, an income of from twelve to sixteen per cent upon his capital, after giving up, as is generally done, half the produce to the actual cultivators. Last year, however, it was calculated that their money yielded forty per cent. The middling classes cannot afford to lay out their small capital in gardens, because to them sixteen or twenty per cent would be an insufficient return; and, in the Hedjaz, no person who trades with a trifling fund is contented with less than fifty per cent annually; and in general they contrive, by cheating foreigners, to double their capital. Those, therefore, only are land-owners, who by trade, or by their income from the mosque, and from hadjys, have already acquired considerable wealth.

The chief support of Medina is from the mosque and the hadjys. I have already mentioned the Ferrashyn, or servants of the mosque, and their profits; to them must be added a vast number of people attached to the temple, whose offices are mere sinecures, and who share in the income of the Haram; a train of ciceroni or mezowars; and almost every householder, who lets out apartments to the pilgrims. Besides the share in the income of the mosque, the servants of every class have their surra or annuity, which is brought from Constantinople and Cairo; and all the inhabitants besides enjoy similar yearly gifts, which also go by the name of surra. These stipends, it is true, are not always regularly distributed, and many of the poorest class, for whom they were originally destined, are now deprived of them; the sums, however, reach the town, and are brought into circulation.* Many

* Kayd Beg, Sultan of Egypt, after having, in A. H. 881, rebuilt the mosque, appropriated a yearly income of seven thousand five hundred erdebs for the inhabitants of the

families are, in this manner, wholly supported by the surra, and receive as much as 100*l.* and 200*l.* sterling per annum, without performing any duty whatever. The Medinans say, that without these surras the town would soon be abandoned to the land-owners and cultivators ; and this consideration was certainly the original motive for establishing them, and the numerous *wakfs,* or pious foundations, which in all parts of the Turkish empire are annexed to the towns or mosques. At present the surra is misapplied, and serves only to feed a swarm of persons in a state of complete idleness, while the poor are left destitute, and not the smallest encouragement is given to industry. As to want of industry, Medina is still more remarkable than Mekka. It wants even the most indispensable mechanics; and the few that live here are foreigners, and only settle for a time. There is a single upholsterer, and only one locksmith in the town ; carpenters and masons are so scarce, that to repair a house, they must be brought from Yembo. Whenever the mosque requires workmen, they are sent from Cairo, or even from Constantinople, as was the case during my stay, when a master-mason from the latter place was occupied in repairing the roof of the building. All the wants of the town, down to the most trifling articles, are supplied by Egypt. When I was here, not even earthen water-jars were made. Some years ago a native of Damascus established a manufacture of this most indispensable article ; but he had left the town, and the inhabitants were reduced to the necessity of drinking out of the half-broken jars yet left, or of importing others, at a great expense, from Mekka No dying, no woollen manufactures, no looms, no tanneries nor works in leather, no iron-works of any kind are seen ; even nails and horse-shoes are brought from Egypt and Yembo. In my account of Mekka, I attributed the general aversion of the people of the Hedjaz from handicrafts, to their indolence and dislike of all manual labour. But the same remark is not applicable to Medina, where the cultivators and gardeners, though not very industrious in improving their land, are nevertheless a hard-working people, and

town, to be sent from Egypt; and Sultan Soleyman ibn Selim allowed five thousand erdebs for the same purpose. (See Kotobeddyn and Samhoudy.)

might apply themselves to occupations in town, without undergoing greater bodily labour than they endure in their fields. I am inclined to think that the want of artisans here is to be attributed to the very low estimation in which they are held by the Arabians, whose pride often proves stronger than their cupidity, and prevents a father from educating his sons in any craft. This aversion they probably inherit from the ancient inhabitants, the Bedouins, who, as I have remarked, exclude, to this day, all handicraftsmen from their tribes, and consider those who settle in their encampment as of an inferior cast, with whom they neither associate nor intermarry. They are differently esteemed in other parts of the East, in Syria, and in Egypt, where the corporations of artisans are almost as much respected as they were in France and Germany during the middle ages. A master craftsman is fully equal in rank and consideration to a merchant of the second class; he can intermarry with the respectable families of the town, and is usually a man of more influence in his quarter, than a merchant who possesses three times more wealth than himself. The first Turkish emperors did every thing in their power to favour industry and the arts; and fifty years ago they still flourished in Syria and Egypt: in the former country they are now upon the decline, except, perhaps, at Damascus; in Egypt they are reduced to the lowest state: for, while Mohammed Aly entices English and Italian workmen into his service, who labour on his sole account, and none of whom prosper, he oppresses native industry, by monopolizing its produce, and by employing the greater part of the workmen himself, at a daily salary thirty per cent less than they might get, if they were permitted to work on their own account, or for private individuals.

The only industrious persons found in Medina are the destitute pilgrims, especially those from Syria, who abound here, and who endeavour by hard labour, during a few months, to earn money sufficient for the expenses of their journey homewards. They work only at intervals, and on their departure the town is often without any artisans for a considerable time. Whilst I resided in Medina, there was but one man who washed linen; when he went away, as the Arabian women will rarely condescend to be so employed, the foreign hadjys were all obliged to wash for themselves. Under these circumstances a traveller cannot expect to find here the most trifling comforts; and even money cannot supply his wants. Here is, however, one class of men, to whom I have already referred in describing Mekka, and who render themselves equally useful at Medina. I mean the black pilgrims from Soudan. Few negroes, or *Tekayrne*, as they are called, come to Mekka, without visiting Medina also, a town even more venerable in their estimation than Mekka. The orthodox sect of Málekites, to which they belong, carry, in general, their respect for Mohammed further than any of the three other sects; and the negroes, little instructed as they usually are, may be said to adore the Prophet, placing him, if not on a level with the Deity, at least very little below him. They approach his tomb with a terrified and appalled conscience, and with more intense feelings than when they visit the Kaaba; and they are fully persuaded, that the prayers which they utter while standing before the window of the Hedjra, will sooner or later obtain their object. A negro hadjy once asked me, after a short conversation with him in the mosque, if I knew what prayers he should recite to make Mohammed appear to him in his sleep, as he wished to ask him a particular question; and when I expressed my ignorance, he told me that the Prophet had here appeared to a great many of his countrymen. These people furnish Medina with fire-wood, which they collect in the neighbouring mountains, and sell to great advantage. If none, or only few of them, happen to be at Medina, no wood can be got even for money. They likewise serve as carriers or porters; and such of them as are not strong enough for hard work, make small mats and baskets of date-leaves. They usually live together in some of the huts of the public place called El Menakh, and remain till they have earned money enough for their journey home. Very few of them are beggars; of forty or fifty whom I saw here, only two or three resorted to mendicity, being unfit for any other vocation. In general beggars are much less numerous at Medina than at Mekka; and most of the foreign beggars, as at Mekka, are Indians. Few hadjys come here without either bringing the necessary funds, or being certain of gaining their livelihood by labour, the distance of Medina from the sea being much greater than that of Mekka, and the road through the Desert being dreaded by absolute paupers. It may be calculated that only one-third of the pilgrims who visit Mekka go also to Medina. The Egyptian caravan of pilgrims seldom passes by the town.* Medina has pilgrims during the whole year, there being no prescribed season for visiting the tomb; and they usually stay here about a fortnight or a month. They are in the greatest number during the months following the pilgrimage to Arafat, and likewise during the month of Rabya el Thany, on the 12th of which, the birth-day of Mohammed, or Mouled el Naby, is celebrated.

The Medinans make up for the paucity of beggars in their own town by going elsewhere to beg. It is a custom with those inhabitants of the town who have received some education, and can read and write, to make a mendicant journey in Turkey once or twice in their lives. They generally repair to Constantinople, where, by means of Turkish hadjys, whom they have known in their own town, they introduce themselves among the grandees, plead poverty, and receive considerable presents in clothes and money, being held in esteem as natives of Medina, and neighbours of the Prophet's tomb. Some of these mendicants serve as Imáms in the houses of the great. After a residence of a couple of years, they invest the alms they have collected in merchandize, and thus return with a considerable capital. There are very few individuals of the above description at Medina, who have not once made the grand tour of Turkey: I have seen several of them at Cairo, where they quartered themselves upon people with whom their acquaintance at Medina had been very slight, and became extremely disagreeable by their incessant craving and impudence. There are few large cities in Syria, Anatolia, and European Turkey, where some of these people are not to be found. For their travelling purposes, and for the duties incumbent upon them as ciceroni in their own town, many individuals learn a little Turkish; and it is their pride to

---

* Whenever the Egyptian caravan passes by Medina, it is always on its return from Mekka, and then remains, like the Syrian, for three days only. In going from Cairo to Mekka, this caravan never visits Medina.

persuade the Turkish pilgrims, that they are Turks, and not Arabians, however little they may like the former.

The Medinans generally are of a less cheerful and lively disposition than the Mekkans. They display more gravity and austerity in their manners, but much less than the northern Turks. They outwardly appear more religious than their southern neighbours. They are much more rigid in the observance of their sacred rites, and public decorum is much more observed at Medina than at Mekka : the morals, however, of the inhabitants appear to be much upon the same level with those of the Mekkans ; all means are adopted to cheat the hadjys. The vices which disgrace the Mekkans are also prevalent here ; and their religious austerity has not been able to exclude the use of intoxicating liquors. These are prepared by the negroes, as well as date-wine, which is made by pouring water over dates, and leaving it to ferment. On the whole, I believe the Medinans to be as worthless as the Mekkans, and greater hypocrites. They, however, wish to approach nearer to the northern Turkish character ; and, for that reason, abandon the few good qualities for which the Mekkans may be commended. In giving this general character of the Medinans, I do not found it merely on the short experience I had of them in their own town, but upon information acquired from many individuals, natives of Medina, whom I met in every part of the Hedjaz. They appear to be as expensive as the Mekkans. There were only two or three people in Medina reputed to be worth ten or twelve thousand pounds sterling, half of which might be invested in landed property, and the other half in trade. The family of Abd el Shekour was reckoned the richest. The other merchants have generally very small capitals, from four to five hundred pounds only ; and most of the people attached to the mosque, or who derive their livelihood from stipends, and from pilgrims, spend, to the last farthing, their yearly income. They outwardly appear much richer than the Mekkans, because they dress better ; but, not the slightest comparison can be made between the mass of property in this town and that in Mekka.

In their own houses, the people of Medina are said to live poorly, with regard to food ; but their houses are well furnished, and their expense in dress is very considerable. Slaves are not so numerous here as at Mekka; many, however, from Abyssinia are found here, and some females are settled, as married women. The women of the cultivators, and of the inhabitants of the suburbs, serve in the families of the town's-people, as domestics, principally to grind corn in the hand-mills. The Medina women behave with great decency, and have the general reputation of being much more virtuous than those of Mekka and Djidda.

The families that possess gardens go to great expense in entertaining their friends, by turns, at their country houses, where all the members, men and women, of the families invited assemble together. It is said that this fashion is carried to great excess in spring-time, and that the Medinans vie with each other in this respect, so that it becomes a matter of public notoriety, whether such a person has given more or less country parties, during the season, than his neighbours. A few families pass the whole year at their gardens; among these was the large family of a saint, established in a delightful little garden to the south of the town. This man is greatly renowned for his sanctity, so much so, that Tousoun Pasha himself once kissed his hands. I paid him a visit, like many other pilgrims, in the first days of my arrival, and found him seated in an arched recess or large niche adjoining the house, from whence he never moved. He was more polite than any saint I had ever seen, and was not averse to talk of worldly matters. I had heard that he possessed some historical books, which he would perhaps sell; but upon inquiry, I learnt from him that he did not trouble himself with any learning except that of the Law, the Koran, and his language. He gave me a nargyle to smoke, and treated me with a dish of dates, the produce of his own garden; and after I had put, on taking leave, a dollar under the carpet upon which I sat, (an act usual, as it was said, on such an occasion,) he accompanied me to the garden-gate, and begged me to repeat my visit.

Smoking nargyles, or the Persian pipe, is as general here as at Mekka; common pipes are more in use here than in other parts of the Hedjaz, the climate being colder. The use of coffee is immoderate. In the gardens fruit can be bought with coffee-beans as well as with money; and the fondness for tea in England and Holland is not equal to that of the Arabians for coffee.

The people of Medina keep no horses. Except those of the Sheikh el Haram, and a few of his suite, I believe there is not one horse kept in this town. In general, these parts of Arabia are poor in horses, because there is no fine pasture for them: the Bedouins to the N. and E. of the town, in the Desert, have, on the contrary, large breeds. The gardens of Medina might afford pasturage; and formerly, when there were warlike individuals in the town, horses were kept by them, and expeditions planned against Bedouins with whom they happened to be at war. At present the spirit of the Medinans is more pacific; and the few horses yet kept when the Wahabys captured the town, were immediately sold by their owners, to escape the military conscription to which principally the horsemen in the Wahaby dominions were subjected. Some of the richer families kept mules, and also dromedaries. Asses are very common, especially among the cultivators, who bring to town upon them the produce of their fields. They are of a smaller breed than those of Mekka and the Hedjaz. The wants of the Turkish army had caused a great diminution in the number of camels formerly kept by the cultivators, who sold them, under the apprehension of their being placed in requisition. The Bedouins of the eastern Desert, at three or four days' journey from the town, are rich in camels; a strolling party of the horsemen of Tousoun Pasha sent in, during my stay, seven hundred of them, which they had taken from a single encampment of the Beni Hetym tribe.

It is not unworthy of remark, that Medina, as far as I know, is the only town in the East from which dogs are excluded: they are never permitted to pass the gate into the interior, but must remain in the suburbs. I was told that the watchmen of the different quarters assemble once a year to drive out any of those animals that might have crept unperceived into the town. The apprehension of a dog entering the mosque, and polluting its sanctity, probably gave rise to their exclusion; they are, however, tolerated at Mekka.

Among the sheep of this neighbourhood, a small species is noticed with a white and brown spotted skin; the same species is likewise known about Mekka. It is of a diminutive size: they are bought up by foreigners, and carried home with them as rarities from the Holy Land. At Cairo they are kept in the houses of the grandees, who cause them to be painted red, with henna, and hang a collar with little bells round their necks, to amuse the children.

I believe the people of Medina have no other times of public rejoicing than the regular feast-days, except the Mouled el Naby or Prophet's birth-day, on the twelfth of the month of Rabya el Thany. This is considered a national festival: all the shops are shut during the day, and every one appears in his best dress. Early in the morning the olemas and a number of well-dressed people assemble in the mosque, where one of the Khatybs, after a short sermon, reads an account of Mohammed's actions, from his birth to his death; after which the company, at least the chief people present, are treated with lemonade, or liquorice-water. The zealous Muselmans pass the night preceding this day in prayer. The lady of Mohammed Aly Pasha, who, having performed the pilgrimage to Mekka, came here to visit the tomb, and see her son Tousoun Pasha, passed the greater part of the night in devotion at the mosque: when she returned to a house she had taken for that purpose, close by the gate of the mosque, her son paid her a short visit, and then left her to repose, while he himself ordered a carpet to be spread in the middle of the street, and there slept, at the threshold of his mother's dwelling; offering a testimony of respect and humility which does as much honour to the son, as to the character of the mother who could inspire him with such sentiments. The wife of Mohammed Aly is a highly respectable woman, and very charitable without ostentation. Her son Tousoun I believe to be the only one of the family, whose breast harbours any noble feeling; the rest are corrupted by the numerous vices inseparable from a Turkish grandee: but he has given, in many instances, proofs of elevated sentiment; and even his enemies cannot deny his valour, generosity, filial love, and good-nature. We must regret, that he is as much inferior in intellect to his father and his brother Ibrahim, as he is superior to them in moral character. His mother had appeared here with all the pomp of an eastern queen: from her donations to the temple, and to the poor, she was regarded by the people as an angel sent from heaven. She brought to her son presents to the value of about twenty-five thousand pounds sterling, among which were remarked twelve complete suits, including every article of dress, from the finest Cashmere shawl down to the slippers; a diamond ring worth five thousand pounds; and two beautiful Georgian slaves. In her retinue there was also a Georgian slave of great beauty and rare accomplishments, whom Mohammed Aly had lately married at Mekka; but as she had not yet borne any children, she was considered much inferior in rank to Tousoun's mother, who counted three Pashas as her own sons.* This slave had belonged to the Kadhy of Mekka, who brought her from Constantinople. Mohammed Aly, who had heard his own women praise her beauty and accomplishments, obliged the Kadhy, much against his will, to part with her for the sum of fifty thousand piastres, and soon after presented her with the marriage contract.

I can say little of any customs peculiar to the Medinans, having had so few opportunities of mixing with them. I may, however, mention, that in the honours they pay to the dead, they do not comply with the general rules observed in the East. I believe this to be the only town where women do not howl and cry on the death of a member of the family. The contrary practice is too generally known to need repetition here; or that, in other parts of the Levant, a particular class of women is called in, on that occasion, whose sole profession is that of howling, in the most heart-rending accents, for a small sum paid to them by the hour. There is no such practice here, (though it is known in other parts of the Hedjaz,) and it is even considered disgraceful. The father of a family died in a house next to that where I lived, and which communicated with it. His death happened at midnight, and his only boy, moved by natural feelings, burst into loud lamentations. I then heard his mother exclaiming, " For God's sake,

---

* Ismayl Pasha is the younger brother of the two mentioned above. It is reported that Ibrahim Pasha is not the son of Mohammed Aly, but was adopted by him when he married his mother, then the widow of an Aga of Karala, on the Hellespont, the native town of the present Pasha of Egypt.

do not cry: what a shame to cry! You will expose us before the whole neighbourhood;" and after some time she contrived to quiet her child. There is also a national custom observed at funerals: the bier, on issuing from the house of the deceased, is carried upon the shoulders of some of his relations or friends, the rest of whom follow behind; but when the procession advances into the street, every by-stander, or passenger, hastens to relieve the bearers for a moment; some giving way to others, who press forward to take in their turn the charge, which is done without stopping. The bier, thus unceasingly passes from shoulders to shoulders, till it is finally deposited near the tomb. If we could suppose for a moment, that this simple and affecting custom was the offspring of true feeling, it would prove much more sensibility than what is displayed in the funeral pomp with which Europeans accompany their dead to the grave. But in the East every thing is done according to ancient custom: it originated, no doubt, in the impulse of feeling, or a sense of duty and piety in those who introduced it; but has become, in these days, a mere matter of form.

The women of Medina never wear mourning; in which respect they differ from those of Egypt. It has been often stated by travellers, that the people of the East have no mourning dresses; but this is erroneous, as to Egypt at least, and part of Syria. The men, it is true, never indulge in this practice, which is prohibited by the spirit of the law; but the women, in the interior of the house, wear mourning in every part of Egypt: for this purpose, they first dye their hands blue, with indigo; they put on a black *borko*, or face-veil, and thus follow the funeral through the streets; and if they can afford it, they put on a black gown, and even a black shift. They continue to wear their mourning for seven, or fifteen, or sometimes for forty days.

As to the state of learning, I shall add that the Medinans are regarded as more accomplished olemas than the Mekkans; though, as I have mentioned above, there are few, if any, public schools. Several individuals study the Muselman sciences at Damascus, and Cairo, in both of which cities there are pious foundations for the purpose. As at Mekka there is no public book-market, the only books I saw exposed for sale were in some retail clothes-shops near the Báb es' Salám. There are said to be some fine private libraries; I saw one in the house of a Sheikh, where at least three thousand volumes were heaped up; but I could not examine them. As it often happens in the East, these libraries are all *wakf*, that is, have been presented to some mosque by its founder, or entailed upon some private family, so that the books cannot be alienated. The Wahabys are said to have carried off many loads of books.

Notwithstanding my repeated inquiries here, as well as at Mekka, I could never hear of a single person who had composed, or even made short notes of, the history of his own times, or of the Wahabys. It appeared to me, on the whole, that literature flourished as little at Medina as in other parts of the Hedjaz; and that the sole occupation of all was getting money, and spending it in sensual gratifications.

The language of the Medinans is not so pure as that of the Mekkans; it approaches much nearer to that of Egypt; and the Syrians established here continue for several generations to retain a tinge of their native dialect. It is common to hear natives talk, or at least utter a few words of Turkish. The gardeners and husbandmen in the neighbourhood have a dialect and certain phrases of their own, which often afford subject for ridicule to the inhabitants of the town.

ON THE GOVERNMENT OF MEDINA.

MEDINA, since the commencement of Islám, has always been considered as a separate principality. When the Hedjaz came under subjection to the Khalifes, Medina was governed by persons appointed by them, and independent of the governors of Mekka. When the power of the Khalifes declined, the chiefs of Medina made themselves independent, and exercised the same influence in the northern Hedjaz that those of Mekka did in the southern. Sometimes the chiefs of Mekka succeeded in extending a temporary authority over Medina; and in the fifteenth and sixteenth centuries this power seems to have been well established; but it often became dependent on the mighty Sultans of Egypt, whenever they assumed the sovereignty over Mekka. When the family of Othman mounted the Turkish throne, the Emperor Selym I., and his son Soleyman, (who paid, in general, more attention to the welfare of the Hedjaz than any of their predecessors,) thought it necessary to acquire a firmer footing in this town, which is the key of the Hedjaz, and became of so much importance to the great pilgrim caravans. They sent hither a garrison of Turkish soldiers, composed of Janissaries and Spahies, under the command of an Aga, who was to be the military commander of the town; while the civil government was placed in the hands of the Sheikh el Haram, or Aga el Haram, the prefect of the temple, who was to correspond regularly with the capital, and to have the same rank as Pashas in other towns. With the exception of a short period towards the end of the seventeenth century, when the Sheikh el Haram and the whole town fell under the jurisdiction of the Sherif of Mekka, this mode of government continued until the period of the Wahaby invasion. An Aga was at the head of a few soldiers, some of whom were in possession of the castle; and the Aga el Haram, who also had a small train of soldiers, was the nominal chief of the town. But great abuses had prevailed for the last century: the military commander was no longer chosen by the Sultans, but by his own people, and there were no longer any Turkish soldiers, but only the descendants of those originally sent hither, who had intermarried with the natives. This Aga had become the real master of the town, and his party was spread over all the first families. He had no other soldiers than the rabble of the town itself, and was chosen by the first officers of the garrison, whose employments were still kept up by their descendants, as they had been settled in former times, although the greater part of them had renounced the military profession. This tribe of soldiers, called *Merabetein*, had been enlarged to strengthen the Aga's party, and its privileges extended to many other inhabitants of the town, and foreigners who settled here. They were entitled to share in the yearly salaries originally fixed by the Sultan, for the pay of the garrison, and regularly transmitted from Constantinople; and had, besides, usurped a share of the surra or stipends sent to the mosque and to the whole town.

The Aga el Haram, together with the Kadhy, who was sent hither annually from Constantinople, to preside over the tribunal of justice, became, under the above circumstances, mere ciphers. The former was usually a eunuch, who knew nothing of Arabic, and who received the appointment rather in the way of exile, than as a preferment. His income, which he received from Constantinople, although handsome, did not enable him to keep up any military guard sufficient to cope with his rival, the Aga of the town; and he soon found himself only left in the charge of the temple, and the command of the eunuchs and

Ferráshyn. But the Aga of the town himself was not complete master; several of the chiefs of the different quarters had great authority; the Sherifs settled here had their own chief, called Sheikh-es'-Sadat, a man of great power; and thus, much disorder prevailed. The people of the town, and the gardeners and inhabitants of the suburbs, were often contending for months together: in the interior of the town itself bloody affrays often occurred between the inhabitants of the different quarters, on which occasions they sometimes barricadoed the streets, and kept up a firing upon each other from the tops of their houses. Instances are related of people firing even into the mosque upon their enemies, while engaged in prayer.

Within the last twenty years a man named Hassan had been appointed Aga of the castle, which gave him the surname of Hassan el Kalay. Born among the dregs of the people, his great skill and cunning, and determined hardihood, had raised him to this office. He was a man of a very short stature and a limping gait, but notwithstanding of great bodily strength; and his voice, when he was in anger, is said to have terrified even the boldest. After several years' hard struggle, this man succeeded in becoming complete master and tyrant of the town: he kept a guard of town's-people, of Bedouins, and Moggrebyns in his service, and had all the rabble on his side. He was guilty of the most flagrant acts of injustice; he oppressed the pilgrims, extorted money from them, confiscated the property of all the hadjys and foreigners who died here, withheld the surra brought from Constantinople by the Hadj, from the people for whom it was destined, and amassed great wealth. Instances are recorded of tyranny and brutality which cover his name with infamy. A rich old widow, with her daughter, having arrived at Medina, from Constantinople, to visit the tomb, he seized on her, and compelled her to marry him; two days after, she was found dead, her property was seized by him; and a short time after he forced the daughter to yield to his embraces. Many complaints were made at Constantinople against this man, but the Sultan had not power enough to dispossess him; and whenever the caravan arrived from Syria, Hassan el Kalay showed so imposing an attitude, that its chiefs could attempt nothing against him. He threw great obstacles in their way; and it is generally ascribed to him, that the last caravan from Damascus, which attempted to perform the journey after the Wahaby conquest, was obliged to return to Syria.

When the Wahabys began to make inroads into the Hedjaz, and to direct their forces against Medina, the conduct of Hassan became still more violent. During the two or three years which preceded the capture of the town, he set no bounds to his oppressions, and was often seen to inflict the severest punishments upon persons who happened to be laughing among themselves when he passed by, pretending that his limping gait was the cause of their mirth. During the night shops were robbed by the Arabs in his service, who patrolled the streets in large parties, and no justice could be obtained against them. When he saw the impossibility of holding the town longer against the Wahabys, after all the surrounding Bedouins, and Mekka itself, had surrendered, he gave up the place to Saoud, on condition that he should be continued in his command; this was promised, and the promise was kept: a Wahaby garrison was then placed in the castle; the Aga el Haram, with all the Turks residing in Medina, were obliged to leave the town, where he had been for several years a mere shadow; and Hassan el Kalay remained governor under the Wahabys. Being now unable to act with the same injustice as he had before done, he affected the greatest zeal for the new religion, and oppressed the inhabitants, by enforcing upon them, with the most scrupulous severity, the precepts of the Wahaby creed. Saoud showed much less respect for Medina than he had done for Mekka: the income of the latter town was left, as it was, in the hands of the Sherif, and the inhabitants were exempted from the *zekat*, or tribute, which the other Wahaby subjects paid to the chief, who here abandoned his right in favour of Ghaleb. The same conciliatory system was not observed at Medina: the inhabitants, who had never before known what imposts were, except the payment of some trifling land-tax, found themselves grievously oppressed; and Hassan el Kalay, with the tax-gatherers of Saoud, enforced the taxes with the utmost rigour.

The Hadj caravans now ceased; few pilgrims arrived by way of Yembo; Saoud, soon after, prohibited the passage to the town to all Turkish pilgrims; and the surra or stipends were of course withheld. Under these circumstances the Medinans felt most heavily the pressure of the times, and became exasperated against the Wahabys. Some further details on the subject will be found in my account of Mohammed Aly's campaign.

When Mohammed Aly first prepared an expedition against the Hedjaz, a strong garrison was placed in Medina, consisting principally of warlike Bedouins from Nedjed and the southern provinces, under the command of Medheyan, whom Saoud had named Sheikh of the tribe of Harb. Hassan el Kalay showed great zeal for the common cause; and, after the first defeat of Tousoun Pasha at Djedeyde, was confirmed in his situation at Medina; but when Tousoun returned a second time with a larger force, Hassan, foreseeing his success, entered into secret negociations with him, and received the promise of being continued in his office, provided he would facilitate the capture of the town by the Osmanlys. On their arrival before its gates, he joined them, and was received by Ahmed Bonaparte, the Turkish commander, with distinguished honours; the town was soon after attacked, and the castle taken by capitulation: but after the Wahaby party was totally suppressed in these parts, both Medheyan, to whom safe-conduct had been promised, and Hassan el Kalay, were seized, put in chains, and sent by way of Cairo to Constantinople, where they experienced the fate which, the latter at least, well merited, though his crimes can never excuse the treachery of those who seized him.

Soon after the above events, the Aga el Haram, a Kislar Agassi of Sultan Selym, returned, and partly recovered his authority; but the real command was now in the hands of the Turkish governor. Towards the end of the year 1814, Tousoun Pasha came here as governor, preparatory to his intended attack upon Nedjed; and here I found him on my arrival. His government was not bad, because his intentions were good, and he was liked by the inhabitants for his generosity and devotion; but his proceedings were foolish enough: he frightened away the Bedouins, by seizing their camels; he thus cut off the supplies from the town, created a general want of every kind of provision, and other necessaries; and his soldiers then soon began to commit excesses, which he neglected to suppress by punishment. After Tousoun's departure, his father, Mohammed Aly, arrived here in April, 1815, and with his more experienced judgment immediately took the proper measures for repairing the errors of his son.

Medina now continues under the government of a Turkish commander; a post filled for a few months by the Scotchman, Thomas Keith, or Ibrahim Aga, whom I have mentioned as being the treasurer of Tousoun Pasha. The Aga el Haram keeps about sixty or eighty soldiers, a motley crew of Turks, Arabs, Moggrebyns, and people of Medina; and all ecclesiastical affairs, and the pecuniary business of the mosque, are left in his hands. Next to him in importance stands the Kadhy, who, in the time of the Wahabys, had been obliged to retire. The Sheikh of the Sherifs, or Sadat, continues to enjoy great respect, as well as several other Sheikhs of the town; and I believe, after all, that the Medinans dislike their present masters, the Turks, less than any other class of the people of the Hedjaz, although they certainly have not yet been cordially reconciled to them.

Prior to the Wahaby invasion, the Sherif of Mekka kept an officer here of inferior rank, to receive some trifling duties upon vegetables, flesh, and other provisions brought to market; the only tax of the kind paid by the Medinans, and the last remnant of the jurisdiction once enjoyed by the Sherif of Mekka over Medina, and which, in later times, has been entirely lost. Sherif Ghaleb had no authority here whatever; but I believe, though I am not quite sure, that he still assumed the nominal superiority, or the title of Chief of Medina; and that Medina was supposed by the Porte to form part of the Hedjaz, under the command of the Sherif of Mekka.

Several respectable Arabian writers affirm, that Medina forms a part of Nedjed, and not of the Hedjaz, situated as it is on the eastern side of the great chain; and this opinion seems to be well founded, if the natural boundary be considered; but, in the common acceptation of the word on the coast, and at Mekka and Medina, the latter town is supposed to form part of the Hedjaz, although the Bedouins of the interior give quite a different meaning to this appellation.

CLIMATE AND DISEASES OF MEDINA.

I FOUND the climate at Medina, during the winter months, much colder than that of Mekka. Snow is unknown here, though I heard that some old people remembered to have seen it in the neighbouring mountains. The rains have no fixed period in winter, but fall at intervals, and usually in violent storms, which last for one day, or perhaps two days, only: sometimes a whole winter passes without more than one fall of rain, excepting a few light showers; the consequence of which is a general dearth. The Medinans say, that three or four gushes of rain are necessary to irrigate their soil; the water of the torrents then inundating many parts of the country, especially the pasturing grounds of the Bedouins. Uninterrupted rains for a week, or longer, such as often occur in Syria, are quite unknown here; and after every gush of rain, which lasts for twenty-four hours, the sky clears up, and the finest spring weather prevails for several weeks. The last storms are usually in April, but occasional showers are not unfrequent even in the middle of summer.

The Medinans, and many foreigners, assert, that the summer-heat is greater here than in any other part of the Hedjaz: I was not able to judge myself. I have already stated that the saline nature of the soil and water, the stagnant pools of rain-water round the town, and perhaps the exhalation and vapours produced by the thick date-groves

CLIMATE AND DISEASES OF MEDINA.

in its neighbourhood, render the air of Medina little favourable to health.

Fevers are the most common disease, to which many of the inhabitants themselves are subject, and from which strangers who remain here any time seldom escape, especially in spring. Yahya Effendi, the physician of Tousoun Pasha, assured me, when I was sick, that he had eighty persons ill of fever under his care; and it appeared that he was more fortunate in their cure than in mine. The fevers are almost all intermittent, and attended after their cure by great languor: relapses are much dreaded. When I went out after my recovery, I found the streets filled with convalescents, whose appearance but too clearly showed how numerous were my fellow-sufferers in the town. If not cured within a certain time, these fevers often occasion hard swellings in the stomach and legs, which are not removed without great difficulty. The Medinans care little about this intermittent fever, to which they are accustomed, and with them it seldom proves fatal; but the case is otherwise with strangers. In some seasons it assumes an epidemic character, when as many as eighty persons are known to have died in one week; instances of this kind, however, seldom happen.

Dysenteries are said to be rare here. Bilious complaints, and jaundice, are very common. There appears to be in general a much greater mortality here than in any other part of the East that I have visited. My lodgings were very near to one of the principal gates of the mosque, through which the corpses were carried when prayers were to be said over them; and I could hear, from my sick bed, the exclamations of "La illah il Allah," with which that ceremony was accompanied. During my three months' confinement one funeral at least, and often two, passed every day under my window. If we reckon on the average three bodies per day carried into the mosque through this gate, as well as the others, besides the poor Arabs who die in the suburbs, and over whose bodies prayers are said in the mosque situated in the Monakh, we shall have about twelve hundred deaths annually, in this small town, the whole population of which, I believe to be at most from sixteen to twenty thousand; a mortality which cannot be repaired by births, and would long ago have depopulated the place, did not the arrival of foreigners continually supply the loss. Of this population I reckon about ten or twelve thousand for the town itself, and the rest for the suburbs.

JOURNEY FROM MEDINA TO YEMBO.

April 21st. 1815. Our small caravan assembled in the afternoon near the outer gate of the town, and at five o'clock P. M. we passed through the same gate by which I entered, on my arrival, three months ago. Then I was in full health and spirits, and indulging the fond hopes of exploring unknown and interesting parts of the Desert on my return to Egypt; but now, worn down by lingering disease, dejected, and desponding, with no more anxious wish than to reach a friendly and salubrious spot, where I might regain my health. The ground leading to the town on this side is rocky. About three quarters of an hour distant, the road has a steep short descent, hemmed in by rocks, and is paved, to facilitate the passage of caravans. Our direction was S.W. by S. In one hour we came to the bed of a torrent called Wady el Akyk, which during the late rains had received so copious a supply from the neighbouring mountains, that it had become like a deep and broad river, which our camels could not attempt to pass. As the day was fine, we expected to see it considerably diminished the next morning, and therefore encamped on its banks, at a place called El Madderidje. Here is a small ruined village, the houses of which were well built of stone, with a small birket or reservoir, and a ruined well close by. Its inhabitants cultivate some fields on the bank of Wady Akyk, but the incursions of the Bedouins had obliged them to retire.

Wady Akyk is celebrated by the Arabian poets.* On its banks stand a number of ashour trees, which were now in full flower. We were accompanied thus far by a number of people from Medina, in compliment to one of the Muftis of Mekka, who had been on a visit to the town, and was now returning to his home, intending to leave our caravan at Szafra. He had several tents and women with him. My other fellow-travellers were petty merchants of Medina going to await at Djidda the arrival of the Indian ships, and a rich merchant from Maskat, whom I had seen at Mekka, where he was on the pilgrimage: he had ten camels to carry his women, his infant children, his servants, and his baggage; and he spent, at every station, considerable sums in charity. He appeared, in every respect, a liberal and worthy Arab.

April 22nd. The torrent had decreased, and we crossed it in the afternoon. We rode for an hour in a narrow valley, following the torrent upwards. At the end of an hour and half we left the torrent: the plain opened to the east, and is here called Esselsele; our road over it was in the direction W.S.W. The rocks spread over the plain were calcareous. At the end of three hours and a half we again entered the mountain, and continued in its vallies, slowly descending, for the whole night. At the break of day we passed the plain called El Fereysh, where I had encamped the day before I reached Medina; and alighted, after a march of twelve hours and a half, in the upper part of Wady es Shohada.†

April 23rd. We had no sooner deposited our baggage than a

---

* Samhoudy says, that this torrent empties itself into the same low ground called El Ghaba, or Zaghaba, to the west of Medina, in the mountains where all the torrents in this neighbourhood discharge themselves. He says also, that on the banks of this torrent, eastward, stood the small Arab fortification called Kasr el Meradjel; and from thence towards Ghaba the torrent crosses a district called El Nakya. About five miles distant from Medina was a station of the Hadj, called Zy'l Haleyfe, situated on the banks of Wady Akyk, with a small castle and a birket, which was rebuilt in A.H. 861. Perhaps this Madderidje is meant by it.

† The distances of this journey do not exactly agree with those given in coming to Medina; but I prefer stating them as I found them noted down in my journal.

heavy rain set in, accompanied with tremendous peals of thunder and flashes of lightning. The whole Wady was flooded in a moment, and we expected that it would be necessary to pass the whole day here. I found shelter in the tent of the merchant of Maskat. In the afternoon the storm ceased. At two P.M. we started, and at the end of an hour passed the tombs of the Martyrs or Shohada, the followers of Mohammed, forty of whom, it was said, lie buried there. We continued slowly descending in the Wady, mostly in the direction S.S.W. At the top of Wady Shohada, the granite rocks begin, the upper ranges of that chain being calcareous. At the end of five hours we issued from the Wady. In the night we passed the plains of Shab el Hal and Nazye; and, after a march of thirteen hours and a half, encamped in the mountains, in the wide valley called Wady Medyk, which lies in the road from Nazye to Djedeyde, two hours distant from the former, and which we had passed at night in my former journey. I heard that in these mountains between Medina and the sea, all the way northward, mountain-goats are met with, and that leopards are not uncommon.

April 24th. A few Arabs of Beni Salem here sow some fields with durra, which they irrigate by means of a fine spring of running water issuing from a cleft in the mountains, where it forms several small basins and pretty cascades—the best water I had drank since leaving the mountains of Tayf. We started from hence in the afternoon, and encountered more heavy rain from mid-day to sun-set. In the caravan were several sick and convalescents, especially women, who were all complaining. I had had a strong attack of fever during the night, which returned to-day, and lasted till I reached Yembo. It was particularly distressing to me, being accompanied by profuse perspiration during the night, followed by shivering fits towards day-break; and as the caravan could not halt on my account, I had no opportunity to change my linen. We were, moreover, obliged to encamp upon wet ground; and as the number of camel-drivers was very small, considering the quantity of baggage, I could not avoid assisting to load, my own Bedouin being one of the most ill-natured and lazy fellows I ever met with among people of his nation.

We rode in the winding valley for two hours and a half, to El Kheyf, the beginning of Wady Djedeyde, where the chief of the Turkish post stationed there inquired for news from head-quarters: he had been a whole fortnight without hearing what was done at Medina. During the whole Turkish campaign in the Hedjaz, no regular couriers had been any where established. Tousoun Pasha was often left for months at Medina, ignorant of the state of the army under his father; and even the latter usually received his intelligence from Mekka and Djidda by ordinary conveyances of caravans; expresses were seldom despatched, and still less any regular communication established over land between Cairo and Mekka. Not merely in this respect, but in many other details of warfare, the best Turkish commanders show an incredible want of activity or foresight, which causes the surprise even of Bedouins, and must expose their operations to certain failure whenever they encounter a more vigilant enemy with no disparity of force.

The camp of the soldiers at Kheyf was completely inundated, and the whole breadth of the wady covered with a rapid stream of water. Without stopping any where we passed Djedeyde at the end of three hours and a half, and further on Dar el Hamra, where the inhabitants had cultivated several new plantations, since I passed this way in January. The copious rains were a sure prognostic of a plentiful year, and the ever-recurring questions put to our guides by the people they passed on the road were, whether such and such a spot in the upper country was well drenched with rain. In seven hours we came to Szafra. The party from Mekka that was with us, separated here, having hired their camels only thus far, from whence they intended to take others for the journey to Mekka; and those which had carried them thus far, followed our party to Yembo. All those camels which are engaged in the transport and carriage between the coast and Medina, belong to the Beni Harb tribe.

We remained a few minutes only, about midnight, at Szafra, to drink some coffee in one of the shops, and then continued our road to the westward of the route by which I reached Szafra in coming from Mekka. Thick date-plantations form an uninterrupted line on both sides of the narrow valley in which we slowly descended. After nine hours and a half we passed a village called El Waset, built among the date-groves, and having extensive gardens of fruit-trees in its vicinity. At every step water is found in wells or fountains. A little beyond this village we left the valley to the right, and took our way up a steep mountain, this being a nearer road than that through the valley. The route over the mountain was rocky and steep; our guides obliged us to walk, and it was with difficulty that I mustered strength sufficient to reach the summit; from thence we descended by a less rough declivity, and, after twelve hours' march, again fell into the road in the valley, near a small village called Djedyd. The mountain we had crossed has the name of Thenyet Waset. The valley we had left to our right takes a western circuitous tour, and includes several other villages, of which I heard the following mentioned: Hosseynye, (nearest to Waset); then, lower down, Fara and Barake, in the vicinity of Djedyd. Below Waset the the valley is considered as belonging to Wady Beder, and above it to Szafra. Djedyd has very few date-trees and fields; it stands upon a plain, through which the torrent passes, after having irrigated the upper plantations of the wady. We continued on this plain for one hour, direction S. 50 W. After a thirteen hours' march we entered a chain of mountains, extending westward, the same which I have mentioned in my journey to Medina, as branching out westward from the great chain near Bir-es'-Sheikh. Our road lay in a broad sandy valley, with little windings, which brought us, after a very fatiguing march of fourteen hours and a half, to Beder.

April 25th. Beder, or as it is also called, Beder Honeyn, is a small town, the houses of which are built either of stone or mud, and of better appearance, although less numerous, than those of Szafra. It is surrounded by a miserable mud wall, ruined in many places. A copious rivulet flows through the town, which rises in the ridge of mountains we had just passed, and is conducted in a stone channel: it waters extensive date-groves, with gardens and fields on the southwest side of the place; and, although at a distance from its source, is still somewhat tepid. El Assamy, the historian of Mekka, says that El Ghoury, Sultan of Egypt, built a fine reservoir at Beder, for the Hadj; but I did not see it, and am ignorant whether it be yet in existence.

Beder is situated in a plain bounded towards the N. and E. by steep mountains; to the S. by rocky hills, and to the W. by hills of moving sand. The Hadj caravans usually make this a station; and we found the place where they had encamped just by the gate of the town, four months ago, still covered with carcases of camels, rags of clothes, and remains of broken utensils, &c. Beder is famous in Arabian history for the battle fought here by Mohammed, in the second year of the Hedjra, with a superior force of the Koreysh Arabs, who had come in aid of a rich caravan expected from Syria, which Mohammed intended to waylay on this spot. Although very ill, I walked out with the Maskat hadjys, to inspect the field of battle, to which we were guided by a man from Beder. To the south of the town, about one mile distant, at the foot of the hills, are the tombs of the thirteen followers and friends of the Prophet, who fell by his side. They are mere heaps of earth, enclosed by a row of loose stones, and are all close together. The Koreysh, as our guide explained to us, were posted upon the hill behind the tombs, while Mohammed had divided his small force into two parts, with one of which he himself advanced in the plain against the enemy, and the reserve was entrusted to Aly ibn Aby Taleb, with orders to take his post upon the sand-hill on the western side. The battle could not be won without the interposition of heaven; and three thousand angels, with Gabriel at their head, were sent to Mohammed's assistance. The above-mentioned thirteen persons were slain in the first onset. The Prophet, hard pressed, hid himself behind a large rock, which opened miraculously to admit him, and enabled him to reach his reserve; he then made a second attack, and with the heavenly auxiliaries was victorious, not losing another man, although seventy of his adversaries were killed on the spot. A handful of stones, or dust, which he (or according to the Koran, which God) threw towards his enemies, caused them to fly. After he had forced their position, he rested a little upon a stone, which, sensible of the honour, forthwith assumed the form of a seat. The rock and the stone are shown; and, at all events, answer one good purpose, which is to excite the visiter's charity towards the poor of Beder, who assemble at it whenever a caravan arrives. The position of Aly's troop upon the distant hill, that of the party of Mohammed close to the enemy, and the plain beyond that hill, where the caravan from Syria pursued its route during the battle, are made to explain the passage of the Koran, which alludes to it thus: "You were on the nearer side of the valley, and they on the further side, and the caravan was below," (Sur. 8.): but I could not well understand that passage, according to the usual interpretation; and rather believe that by the word *rukb*, which is taken here as synonymous with caravan, the party of horsemen under Aly must be understood, whose position, although upon a hill, was, with relation to Beder, a low one, the ground descending slightly. Several small domes, which had been erected here, were ruined by the Wahabys. In returning to the village, we walked, on its south side, into the mosque called Mesdjed el Ghemáme, built on the spot where Mohammed once sat exposed to the sun's rays, and prayed to God for a cloud which might overshadow him; this was immediately granted; and the mosque derives its name from the cloud. It is better built and more spacious than might be expected in such a poor place.

The market of Beder is furnished with the same articles as that of Szafra. Some water-melons, the produce of the gardens, were offered for sale. The Maskat merchant purchased, without my knowledge, five pounds of Mekka balsam, all that remained in the market, which he intended for a present to the Imám of Maskat. It was in the same adulterated state as that I had formerly seen at Szafra. The inhabitants of Beder are chiefly Bedouins of the tribe of Sobh, belonging to Harb, some of whom have become settlers here. Others only have their shops here, and return every evening to the tents of their family in the neighbouring mountains. Beder being a place much frequented by Bedouins and travellers, the houses are in great request, and a small shop in the market pays as much as twenty dollars a year rent. Some Sherif families are also established here, to whom the Hadj pays at passing considerable stipends.

In the evening several hundred camels belonging to Bedouins came to be watered at the rivulet, escorted principally by women, who freely entered into conversation with us. The Beni Harb established at Djedeyde, Szafra, and Beder, give their daughters in marriage to strangers, and even to settlers; and a few Turkish soldiers, attracted by the beauty of some Bedouin girls, had fixed themselves here, and married them: one of them, an Arnaut, who spoke good Arabic, and had been accustomed from his youth to the wild life of warlike mountaineers, intended to follow his young wife to the mountain. In the neighbouring mountains are immense numbers of the eagle (*rakham*); hundreds of them were constantly hovering about us; and some actually pounced down, and carried off the meat from our dishes.

April 26th. We had remained here the whole of yesterday. Some people of Beder kept watch at night over our caravan, for which they received a small compliment. This place abounds with robbers, and we were encamped outside the gate of the town. We left Beder in the evening, and took a direction N. 45 W. After proceeding for three quarters of an hour, we came to the ridge of sand-hills above mentioned, the highest summit of which is called Goz Aly, in memory of the position occupied there by Aly, during the battle of Beder. We crossed these hills for half an hour with difficulty, the sands being very deep, and then descended into the great western plain, extending as far as the sea, which is reached from Beder in one night's march, at a small harbour, south of Yembo, called Bereyke, much frequented by shipping. The plain, which we entered in the direction W. 1 N. is overgrown with shrubs. During our night-march we saw the fires of different Bedouin encampments. We met two negro pilgrims, who had started from Yembo by themselves, and were in great distress for water: we gave them both meat and drink, and directed them towards the Bedouin encampments. Without a compass, these enterprising travellers find their route across deserts: the direction of the road is shown to them at starting, and they pursue it in a straight line by night and by day, until they arrive at the destined spot. After a ride of ten hours from Beder, we encamped at the break of day in a part of the plain, where low acacia-trees grow, called *adheyba*.

April 27. I found myself in a very low state this morning. Violent vomiting and profuse sweats had rendered the last night one of the most disagreeable nights I passed in my travels. A quarrel with my guide, about victuals, further increased my fever to-day, to which perhaps the late relaxation of my nerves through illness contributed. To our right, northwards, about six hours distant, a chain of high mountains extends towards the sea. Nearer to us a lower ridge takes the same direction. The plain upon which we encamped is sandy, covered with small pebbles and petrosilex. We set out after mid-day. Four hours and a half, direction N. W. by N., trees and shrubs are no longer seen; a few saline shrubs only indicate the proximity of the sea; and a little further on, the ground becomes covered with a salt crust, while the air is strongly impregnated with sea-vapours. At the end of seven hours and a half, we again found some trees in the plain, interspersed with salt-incrusted spots. At fourteen hours, having travelled the whole night over bad ground, we saw Yembo at sun-rise; and after a ride of fifteen hours and a half, at a very slow pace, we reached the gate of the town: just before it we crossed an inlet of the harbour, it being then low water, but which extends to a considerable distance inland at high tide.

YEMBO.

It was with some difficulty that I could find a room in one of the okales or khans of the town, which were filled with soldiers, who had received permission to return to Cairo, after their last expedition against the southern Wahabys, and had come here from Djidda and Mekka; and, besides them, there were many hadjys, who, after their return from Medina, intended to embark for Suez or Cosseir. Among the latter was the lady of Mohammed Aly Pasha, who had arrived from Medina; for the transport of whose escort, suite, and baggage, four ships were in a state of preparation. After having deposited my baggage in an airy room, on the terrace of an okale, I walked towards the harbour, to inquire about a passage to Egypt. This, I soon understood, it was impossible to obtain at present. Positive orders had been given, that none should embark but soldiers, who had already engaged three or four ships, then ready to sail; and of whom upwards of fifteen hundred, including many Turkish hadjys, who passed for soldiers, being armed and dressed like them, were still waiting for conveyances.

While I was sitting in a coffee-house near the harbour, three funerals passed at short intervals; and upon expressing my surprise at this, I learned that many people had died within these few days of feverish complaints. I had heard, when at Beder, that a bad fever prevailed at Yembo, but then paid little attention to the report. During the rest of the day I saw several other funerals, but had not the slightest idea to what so many deaths were to be attributed, till night, when I had retired to my room up-stairs, which overlooked a considerable part of the town ; I then heard, in every direction, innumerable voices breaking out in those heart-rending cries which all over the Levant, accompany the parting breath of a friend or relative. At that moment the thought flashed upon my mind, that it might be the plague: I attempted, in vain, to dispel my apprehensions, or at least to drown them in sleep ; but the dreadful cries kept me awake the whole night. When I descended early in the morning into the okale, where many Arabs were drinking their coffee, I communicated to them my apprehensions ; but had no sooner mentioned the word plague, than they called me to order, asking me if I was ignorant that the Almighty had for ever excluded that disorder from the holy territory of the Hedjaz ? Such an argument admits of no reply among Moslims ; I therefore walked out, in search of some Greek Christians, several of whom I had seen the day before, in the street, and from them I received a full confirmation of my fears. The plague had broken out ten days ago : it had been raging at Cairo with the greatest fury for several months ; and at Suez a large part of the population had died : from that port two ships laden with cotton stuffs had carried it to Djidda, and from thence it was communicated to Yembo. No instance of the plague had ever before been witnessed in the Hedjaz, at least none within the memory of man ; and the inhabitants could with difficulty persuade themselves that such an event had occurred, especially at a time when the holy cities had been reconquered from the Wahabys. The intercourse with Egypt had not at any time been greater than now, and it was, therefore, no wonder that this scourge should be carried to the Hedjaz. While ten or fifteen people only died per day, the Arabs of the town could not believe that the disease was the plague, although the usual appearance of the biles upon the bodies of the infected, and the rapid progress of the disorder, which seldom lasted more than three or four days, might have been convincing proofs. In five or six days after my arrival the mortality increased ; forty or fifty persons died in a day, which, in a population of five or six thousand, was a terrible mortality. The inhabitants now felt a panic : little disposed to submit as patiently to the danger as the Turks do in every other part of the East, the greater part of them fled into the open country, and the town became deserted; but the disease followed the fugitives, who had encamped close together; and thus finding no remedy to the evil, many of them returned. They excused their flight by saying, " God in his mercy sends this disease, to call us to his presence; but we are conscious of our unworthiness, and feel that we do not deserve his grace; therefore, we think it better to decline it, for the present, and to fly from it :" an argument which I heard frequently repeated. Had I been myself in full strength, I should, no doubt, have followed their example and gone into the Desert; but I felt extremely weak, and incapable of any exertions. I thought also that I might escape the disease, shut up in my insulated room, and indulged moreover the hope of a speedy passage to Egypt; in the latter, however, I was deceived. By making a few presents, and a little bribery, I might perhaps have found means to embark forthwith; but the vessels now ready to sail were crowded to excess, and full of diseased soldiers, so that a stay in the infected town was to be preferred to a departure by such a conveyance. Some days after, I learnt that a small open boat, free from troops, was ready to sail for Cosseir, and I immediately agreed for a passage on board it; but its sailing was delayed from day to day, until the fifteenth of May, when I finally left Yembo, after a stay of eighteen days in the midst of the plague.

It was, perhaps, my own bad state of health, and the almost uninterrupted low fever under which I laboured, that preserved me; for, notwithstanding all my care, I was many times exposed to infection. The great street of Yembo was lined with sick, in the very agonies of death, asking for charity; in the yard of the okale where I lived, an Arab was dying; the master of the okale lost a sister and a son in his own family, and related to me, as he sat on my carpet, how his son died the preceding night in his arms. The imprudence of my slave likewise counteracted all my measures of precaution. Having missed him for several days early in the morning, I inquired the cause of his absence, when he told me that he had gone to assist in washing the dead bodies. The poor who died during the night were exposed in the morning upon biers, on the sea-shore, to be washed before the ceremony of praying over them in the mosque; and my slave thought it meritorious to join in this office, which had devolved upon several negro pilgrims, who happened to be at Yembo. I desired him to remain at home, for the future, at that hour, to prepare my breakfast; but I was as little able to prevent his walking out at other times, as I could myself dispense with that duty; and one could scarcely pass the bazar without touching infected people, or at least those who had been in close contact with them.

The sense of the danger which then threatened me is much greater, now that I find myself far removed from it, than I felt it at the time. After the first four or five days, I became tolerably familiarized with the idea of the plague, and compared the small numbers who died every day with the mass of the remaining inhabitants. The great many cases of persons remaining in full health, notwithstanding the closest connexion with the deceased, considerably removed the apprehensions of the malady being communicated by infection; and example works so powerfully on the mind, that when I saw the number of foreigners then in the town quite unconcerned, I began to be almost ashamed of myself for possessing less courage than they displayed. The disease seemed, however, to be of the most malignant kind; very few of those who were attacked, escaped, and the same was observed at Djidda. The Arabs used no kind of medicine; I heard of a few people having been bled, and of others having been cured by applying a drawing-plaster to the neck; but these were rare instances, which were not imitated by the great mass. As it is the custom to bury the dead in a very few hours after decease, two instances occurred during my stay at Yembo, of persons supposed dead being buried alive: the stupor into which they fell when the disorder was at a crisis, had been mistaken for death. One of them gave signs of life at the moment they were depositing him in the grave, and was saved: the body of the other, when his tomb was re-opened several days after his burial, to admit the corpse of a near relation, was found with bloody hands and face, and the winding-sheet torn, by the unavailing efforts he had made to rise. On seeing this, the people said, that the devil, being unable to hurt his soul, had thus disfigured his body.

The governor of Yembo took great care that the exact amount of the mortality in the town should not be known; but the solemn exclamations of " La illaha ill' Allah," which indicate a Moslim funeral, struck the ear from every side and quarter of the town, and I counted myself forty-two in one day. To the poor the plague becomes a real feast; every family that can afford it, kills a sheep on the death of any of its members, and the day after, the men and women of the whole neighbourhood are entertained at the house. The women enter the apartments, embrace and console all the females of the family, and expose themselves every moment to infection. It is to this custom, more than any other cause, that the rapid dissemination of the plague in Mohammedan towns must be ascribed; for when the disease once breaks out in a family, it never fails of being transmitted to the whole neighbourhood.

It is a common belief among Europeans, and even eastern Christians, that the Mohammedan religion forbids any precautionary measures against the plague; but this is erroneous. That religion forbids its followers from avoiding the disease if it has once entered a town or country; but it warns them at the same time, not to enter any place where the plague rages: and it accordingly forbids individuals to shut themselves up in a house, and to cut off all communication with the rest of the infected town, because this is the same as flying from the plague; but it favours measures of quarantine, to prevent the importation of the disease, or its communication to strangers upon their arrival. The belief in predestination, however, is so deeply and universally rooted in the minds of the eastern nations, that not the slightest measures of safety are any where adopted. The numberless extraordinary instances of the disease sparing those who have come into closest contact with it, confirm them in their opinion that it is not epidemic; and their prophet Mohammed has declared to them, " that the plague is caused by the demon's hostile attack upon mankind," and that " those who die of it are martyrs." The universal opinion prevails among Moslims, that an invisible angel of death, armed with a lance, touches the victims he destines for the plague, whom he finds out in the most hidden recesses. The trunk of a palm-tree lay in one of the streets of Yembo, and it had been observed that many people who had stepped over it, had soon after been seized with the plague; it was therefore believed that the demon had there taken his favourite stand, to wound the passer-by; and therefore the Arabs took a circuitous road, to avoid their foe, although they were persuaded that he was light-footed and could overtake them wherever they went.

That the Christians and Franks escape the disease by shutting themselves up in their houses, affords but a feeble proof to the contrary. Imprudence, and the tardy adoption of these measures, always cause a slight mortality even among them; and such cases are afterwards adduced in proof of the folly of attempting to oppose the decrees of Providence. Besides, there are many Christians in the East, who follow Turkish maxims, and, impressed with the same notions of predestination, think it superfluous to take any steps for their safety. Turks trifle with so many of the prescribed duties of their religion, that it might not, perhaps, be difficult, in this instance, to make them adopt rational opinions; and the more so, as the Koran is silent upon this head: but no private measures can be adopted, and rigidly observed, as long as every individual, almost, is convinced in his own mind of their folly and inefficacy. If this were not universally the case, the Turks themselves would, long ago, have found means of resorting to prophylactics, in spite of their religious doctrines; as the Arabs now did in the Hedjaz; and their olemas would have furnished them with *fetwas*, and quotations from the law, in favour of what their good sense might have led them to adopt. In the Hadyth, or sacred traditions, a saying of Mohammed is recorded: " Fly from the leprous, as thou flyest from the lion."

The case is different, respecting the means of preventing the plague from being imported, or to establish regular quarantines. This is a measure depending entirely upon the government. The most fanatic and orthodox Muselmans, those of the Barbary states, have adopted this system; and the laws of quarantine are as strictly enforced in their harbours, as they are in the European ports on the northern shores of the Mediterranean. That a similar system has not been introduced into Turkey is matter of deep concern, and may be attributed rather to motives of interest, than to bigotry. Constantinople, and the ports of the Archipelago, I have not visited myself; but I know that it would be easy for the governors of Syria, and still more for the governor of Egypt, to use their authority in introducing a system of quarantine on the coast, without any dread of opposition from their subjects. The governments of Syria, however, must be guided in such matters by the Porte, and would hardly attempt to establish quarantine, without the authority of their sovereign: but Mohammed Aly has often acted directly contrary to the orders of the Porte, even in matters affecting his sovereign's pecuniary interest; and we may believe that it is not solely the fear of displeasing his master, which has prevented him from listening to the frequent friendly advice and representations made to him on this subject by European powers; and, at the same time, his loose religious principles are too well known, to suppose that bigotry restrains him from yielding to their solicitations.

While for four succeeding years, from 1812 to 1816, the plague has every spring made ravages in Egypt, Mohammed Aly himself, with his family and principal officers, have been shut up in their palaces with scrupulous care; thus offering infinitely more scandal to the people than they would have done by the establishment of quarantine regulations. Wishing, however, to be considered by Europeans as a liberally-thinking man, devoid of any prejudices, he had really given orders, in 1813 and 1814, to establish a quarantine at Alexandria; but the shameful manner in which it was conducted, clearly proved that he had no sincere wish to guard his subjects from the horrors of infection; and the whole scheme was soon after abandoned. My own inquiries, and the opinion of many Turks themselves, who judge of the measures of their own government much better than is generally supposed, have led me to believe, that the Grand Signior, as well as his Pashas, tolerate the plague in their dominions, because the numerous deaths fill their purses: with respect to Egypt, I hold this to be indisputably the secret cause. The commercial towns of Cairo, Alexandria, and Damietta, are crowded with foreign merchants, and other strangers from all quarters of the East are established there: according to the law, the property of all persons who have no near heirs to claim it, falls to the Beit el Mál; a treasury, formerly destined for purposes beneficial to the subjects, but now entirely at the private disposal of the governors. The increased mortality thus causes great sums to fall into their hands. The prefect of every quarter of the town must, under the heaviest penalties, inform the government of any stranger or individual without heirs who dies within his district; and not only is the property of such people seized, but even that of those persons whose heirs, although known, are absent in foreign countries, and to whom no other privilege is granted, in return, than that of addressing their unavailing claims to the same governor, who converts the income of the Beit el Mál to his own use. The most flagrant injustice is committed with respect to the property of deceased persons, as well during the plague as at other times; and the Kadhy, with a whole train of olemas, officers, and people in inferior employments, share in the illegal spoil. In the same manner the property of military officers, and of many soldiers, is sequestrated at their death. Upon a moderate calculation, the plague this year in Egypt, which carried off in the city of Cairo alone from thirty to forty thousand, added twenty thousand purses, or ten millions of piastres, to the coffers of the Pasha, a sum large enough to stifle any feelings of humanity in the breast of a Turk. That the population has diminished, and consequently the regular revenues suffered, is a reflection which a Turkish governor never makes, who calculates merely the immediate consequences of an event; and, provided he be safe himself, and his wealth increasing, cares little for the fate of his subjects. As the plague seldom visits the open country, and therefore does not deprive the soil of its labourers, its effects are less dreaded by the Pasha. He will never be convinced that policy, as well as humanity, dictates a removal of the causes of plague, until he has seen a whole province depopulated, and the fields which yield him his revenues deserted.*

---

* The little care taken by the government in Egypt for preserving the lives of the sub-

It should seem as if Constantinople and Cairo were the great receptacles of plague in the East, communicating it mutually to each other, and to the neighbouring countries. How far the joint and energetic representations of European powers might induce the Grand Signior to adopt measures of safety for his capital, and to insure by that means the safety of the population of European Turkey and Anatolia, I am unable to decide; but I have little doubt, that a firm remonstrance from the English government would induce the Pasha of Egypt to obey the call of humanity, and thus benefit Egypt, as well as Syria and the English possessions in the Mediterranean.

The ravages of the plague were still more deplorable at Djidda than at Yembo; as many as two hundred and fifty persons died there per day. Great numbers of the inhabitants fled to Mekka, thinking to be safe in that sacred asylum; but they carried the disease with them, and a number of Mekkans died, although much less in proportion than at Djidda. Even the Kadhy of Djidda, an Arab, made his escape to Mekka, with all his olemas; but Hassan Pasha, then governor of the holy city, ordered him, under pain of death, to return immediately to his post; and he died on the road. The principal market-street of Djidda was quite deserted, and numbers of families were entirely destroyed. As a great many foreign merchants were then in Djidda, their property considerably increased Mohammed Aly's treasure; and I heard from eye-witnesses, that the only business then done in the town was the transport of corpses to the burial-ground, and that of the deceased's valuable property to the house of the commandant. Medina remained free from the plague, as did the open country between Yembo and Djidda.

I shall mention here a particular custom of the Arabs. When the

---

ject is evinced in an equally strange manner, by the neglect with which the small-pox is treated; a disease that makes as great ravages in Upper Egypt as ever the plague could do, which, itself seldom visits those southern provinces. The numerous representations made to Mohammed Aly for the introduction of vaccination have been of no avail, though, if he had chosen to inquire, he might have known that in 1813, in the small town of Esne alone, upwards of two hundred and fifty persons, adults and children, fell victims to the small-pox, the violence of which is much greater in these climates than in Europe.

plague had reached its height at Yembo, the Arab inhabitants led in procession through the town a she-camel, thickly covered with all sorts of ornaments, feathers, bells, &c. &c.: when they reached the burial-ground, they killed it, and threw its flesh to the vultures and the dogs. They hoped that the plague, dispersed over the town, would hasten to take refuge in the body of the camel, and that by slaughtering the victim, they would get rid at once of the disease. Many of the more sensible Arabs laughed at this; but it was so far of some use, that it inspired the lower classes with courage.

The town of Yembo is built on the northern side of a deep bay, which affords good anchorage for ships, and is protected from the violence of the wind by an island at its entrance. The ships lie close in shore, and the harbour is spacious enough to contain the largest fleet. The town is divided by a creek of the bay into two parts; the largest division is called exclusively Yembo; the other, on the western side, bears the name of El Kad, and is principally inhabited by seafaring people. Both divisions have the sea in front, and are enclosed on the other sides by a common wall, of considerable strength, better built than those of Djidda, Tayf, and Medina. It is flanked by many towers; and was erected by the joint labour of the inhabitants themselves, as a defence against the Wahabys, the ancient wall being ruined, and enclosing only a part of the town. The new wall comprises an area almost double the space occupied by habitations, leaving between it and the latter, large open squares, which are either used as burial-grounds, encamping-places for caravans, for the exercising of troops, or are abandoned as waste ground. The extent of the wall would require a large garrison to defend it at all points; the whole armed population of Yembo is inadequate to it: but Eastern engineers always estimate the strength of a fortification by its size; and with the same view a thick wall and deep ditch have been lately carried along the outskirts of the old town of Alexandria, which it would require at least twenty-five thousand men to defend.

Yembo has two gates towards the east and north; Bab el Medina, and Bab el Masry. The houses of the town are worse built than those of any other town in the Hedjaz. Their structure is so coarse, that few of the stones with which they are built have their surfaces hewn smooth. The stone is calcareous, full of fossils, and of a glaring white colour, which renders the view of the town particularly distressing to the eyes. Most of the houses have only a ground-floor. Except three or four badly-built mosques, a few half-ruined public khans, and the house of the governor on the sea-side, (also a mean building), there is no large edifice in the place.

Yembo is a complete Arab town; very few foreigners are settled here: of Indians, who have such numerous colonies at Mekka, Djidda, and Medina, two or three individuals only are found as shopkeepers; all the merchants being Arabs, except a few Turks, who occasionally take up a temporary residence. Most of the inhabitants belong to the Bedouin tribe of Djeheyne, in this neighbourhood, (which extends northward along the sea-shore), many of whom have become settlers: several families of Sherifs, originally from Mekka, have mixed with them. The settlers in this town, or, as they are called, the Yembawys, continue to live and dress like Bedouins. They wear the keffie, or green and yellow striped silk handkerchief, on the head, and a white abba on their shoulder, with a gown of blue linen, or coloured cotton, or silk stuff, under it, which they tie close with a leathern girdle. Their eating, and whole mode of living, their manners and customs, are those of Bedouins. The different branches of the Djeheyne tribe established here have each their sheikh: they quarrel with each other as often as they might do if encamping in the open country, and observe the same laws in their hostilities and their blood-revenge as the Bedouins.

The principal occupation of the Yembawys is trade and navigation. The town possesses about forty or fifty ships, engaged in all branches of the Red Sea trade, and navigated by natives of the town, or slaves. The intercourse between Yembo and Egypt is very frequent. Many Yembawys are settled at Suez and Cosseir, and some at Cairo and Kenne in Upper Egypt, from whence they trade with their native place. Others trade with the Bedouins of the Hedjaz, and on the shores of the Red Sea, as far Moeyleh, and exchange in their encampments the provisions brought to Yembo from Egypt, for cattle, butter, and honey, which they sell again at a great profit upon their return to the town.

The people of Yembo are less civil, and of more rude and sometimes wild behaviour, than those of Djidda or Mekka, but, on the other hand, their manners are much more orderly, and they are less addicted to vice than the latter, and enjoy, generally, over the Hedjaz, all the advantages of a respectable name. Although there are no individuals of great wealth in the town, every body seems to enjoy more ease and plenty than even at Mekka. Almost all the respectable families of Yembo have a country-house in the fruitful valley called Yembo el Nakhel, or Gara Yembo, or Yembo el Berr, about six or seven hours' distance from hence, at the foot of the mountains, in a N. E. direction. It is similar to the valleys of Djedeyde* and Szafra, where date-trees grow, and fields are cultivated. It extends about seven hours in length, and contains upwards of a dozen hamlets, scattered on the side of the mountain. The principal of these is Soueyga, the market-place, where the great Sheikh of the Djeheyne resides, who is acknowledged as such by the Bedouins of that tribe, as well as by the people of Yembo.

The valley of Yembo is cultivated exclusively by Djeheyne, who have either become settlers, and remain there the whole year, or keep a few labourers in their plantations, while they themselves remain encamped in the mountain, and reside in the valley only at the time of the date-harvest, when all the Yembawys who possess gardens there, likewise repair for a month to the same place. All kinds of fruits are cultivated there, with which the market of Yembo is supplied. The houses, I heard, are built of stone, and of a better appearance than those of Djedeyde. The Yembawys consider this valley as their original place of abode, to which the town and harbour belong as a colony. The Egyptian Hadj route passes by Yembo el Nakhel, from whence it makes one night's journey to Beder: this caravan, therefore, never touches the

* There is a road, of difficult passage, from Yembo el Nakhel to Djedeyde, over the mountains to the north of the great road.

harbour of Yembo, although many individuals of it, in returning from Mekka, take from Mastoura the road to Yembo, to transact some business in the town, and rejoin the caravan at one day's journey north of Yembo.

The trade of Yembo consists chiefly in provisions: no great warehouses of goods are found here; but, in the shops, some Indian and Egyptian articles of dress are exposed for sale. The ship-owners are not, as at Djidda, merchants, but merely carriers; yet they always invest their profits in some little mercantile speculation. The transport trade to Medina occupies many people, and all the merchants of that town have their agents among the Arabs of Yembo. In time of peace, the caravan for Medina starts every fortnight; lately, from the want of camels, it departed only every month. There are often conveyances by land for Djidda and Mekka, and sometimes for Wodjeh and Moeyleh, the fortified stations of the Egyptian caravan on the Red Sea. The people of Yembo are very daring smugglers, and no ship of theirs enters the harbour without a considerable part of its cargo being sent on shore by stealth, to elude the heavy duties. Parties of twenty or thirty men, well armed, repair to the harbour at night, for this purpose, and if detected, often resist the custom-house officers by open force.

The skirts of the town are entirely barren, no trees or verdure are seen, either within or without the walls. Beyond the salt-ground, next to the sea, the plain is covered with sand, and continues so as far as the mountains. To the N. E. is seen a high mountain, from whence the great chain takes a more western course towards Beder. I believe this to be the mountain of Redoua, which the Arabian geographers often mention. Samhoudy places it at one day's journey from Yembo, and four days from Medina. About one hour to the east of the town is a cluster of wells of sweet water, called Aseylya, which are made to irrigate a few melon-fields. Bedouins sometimes encamp there; at this time a corps of Turkish cavalry had pitched their tents near these wells.

In the town are several wells of brackish water, but no cisterns. The supply of water for drinking is obtained from some large cisterns, at about five minutes' walk from the Medina gate, where the rain-water is collected. Small canals have been dug across the neighbouring plains, to convey the streams of rain-water to these cisterns. They are spacious, well-cased, subterranean reservoirs, and some of them large enough to supply the whole town for several weeks. They are the property of private families, whose ancestors built them, and who sell the water, at certain prices, fixed by the governor, who also exacts a tax from each of them. The water is excellent, much better than that of any other town of the Hedjaz, where the inhabitants are not industrious enough to form similar cisterns. When the winter-rains fail, the inhabitants of Yembo suffer severely, and are obliged to fill their water-skins at the distant wells of Aseylya.

Yembo was formerly annexed to the government of the Sherif of Mekka, who ought to have divided the receipts at the custom-house with the Turkish Pasha of Djidda. Ghaleb appropriated it entirely to his own treasury, and kept here a vizier, or governor, with a guard of about fifty or sixty men. He appears to have had little other authority than that of collecting the customs, while the Arabs of the town were left to the government of their own Sheikhs, and enjoyed much greater liberty than the people of Mekka and Djidda. The powerful tribe of Djeheyne was not to be trifled with by the Sherif; and whenever a man of Yembo was unjustly persecuted, he flew to his relations in the Desert, who retorted the oppression upon some of the Sherif's people or caravans until the matter was compromised.

When Saoud, the Wahaby chief, attacked the northern parts of the Hedjaz, his first endeavours were to reduce the two great Bedouin tribes Beni Harb and Beni Djeheyne to submission; which was greatly facilitated by the hatred and animosity that had always existed between those tribes, who were frequently at war with each other. After the Djeheyne had surrendered, and Yembo el Nakhel had received a garrison of Wahaby soldiers, Saoud attacked Yembo, for the first time, in 1802, with a considerable force, which remained encamped before it for several weeks, and repeatedly attempted to carry it by assault. After his retreat, the Yembawys built the new strong wall round the town, by order of the Sherif, who made them bear the whole expense of the work. After Sherif Ghaleb himself had submitted to the superior power of Saoud, who took possession of Mekka, Yembo still held out for some months; and it was not till a strong army was preparing to attack it, and the Vizier himself had fled, that the Yembawys sent a messenger to Saoud, and capitulated, adopting at the same time his creed. The Wahabys did not place a garrison in the town; the Sherif continued to keep his governor there: but the Wahaby tax-gatherers came; and the inhabitants, who, except custom-house duties, had never before been subject to any imposts, found the government of the Wahabys press very heavily upon them.

In the autumn of 1811, when the Turkish army under Tousoun Pasha effected its first landing near the town, the Yembawys were very willing to shake off the government both of the Sherif and the Wahabys; and the officers of Ghaleb and Saoud then in the town fled, and, after a trifling show of resistance, the two first days, by Ghaleb's commander, who had but a few soldiers with him, and who soon saw that the spirit of the inhabitants was wholly against fighting, the town opened its gates, and experienced some slight injuries from the disorderly Turkish soldiers. Since that time Yembo has been garrisoned by them, and was made the commissariat dépôt of the Turkish army employed against the enemy in the neighbourhood of Medina. The soldiers, being at a distance from the Pasha, or his son, behaved with much more irregularity than they dared to do either at Djidda or Mekka. Every Bimbashy, or commander of a company, who landed here with his soldiers, assumed, during his stay, the government of the town; while the real governor, Selym Aga, who had but a few soldiers under him, was often reduced to a mere cipher. Several affrays happened during my stay, and the inhabitants were extremely exasperated. A Turkish officer shot, with his pistol, in the open street in mid-day, a young Arab, to whom he had for some time been making infamous proposals; he committed this murder with the greatest composure, in revenge for his refusal, and then took refuge in the quarters of a Bimbashy, whose soldiers were called out to defend him against the fury of the populace. The relations of the Arab hastened to Medina to ask the life of the aggressor from Mohammed Aly Pasha; I left Yembo before the affair was settled.

The Yembawys are all armed, although they seldom appear so in public, and they carry usually a heavy bludgeon in their hand. A few of them keep horses; the Djeheyne established at Yembo el Nakhel have good breeds of Nedjed horses, though in small numbers. Asses are kept by every family, to bring water to the town. The want of servants and day-labourers is felt here still more than in the other towns of the Hedjaz. No Yembawy will engage in any menial labour, if he has the smallest chance of providing for his existence by other means. Egyptian peasants, left on this coast after their pilgrimage, and obliged to earn money for their passage home, engage themselves as porters and labourers, bring wood, water, &c. I have seen a piastre and a half paid to a man for carrying a load the distance of five hundred yards from the shore to a house.

Yembo is the cheapest place in the Hedjaz with regard to provisions; and as it possesses good water, and appears to be in a much more healthy situation than Djidda, a residence in it might be tolerable, were it not for the incredible quantity of flies that haunt this coast. No person walks out without a straw fan in his hand to drive off these vermin; and it is utterly impossible to eat, without swallowing some of them, which enter the mouth the moment it is opened. Clouds of them are seen passing over the town; they settle even upon the ships that sail out of the harbour, and remain on board during the whole voyage.

FROM YEMBO TO CAIRO.

I EMBARKED at Yembo on the morning of the 15th of May, in an open *sambouk*, or large boat, bound to Cosseir, there to load with corn; the Reys or master was the son of the owner, a native of Yembo. I had agreed for my own and my slave's passage from hence to Cosseir at five dollars, two dollars being the usual charge paid by hadjys, and one dollar by poor people and servants. The government allowed the ship-owners only half a dollar per head for the transport of soldiers. As the partner of the commander of Yembo had a share in this boat, it was allowed to proceed without soldiers, and the Reys had told me that there were only a dozen Arab passengers on board. In making me pay two dollars more than the usual fare, he had agreed to let me have a small place behind the steerage to myself. When I came on board, however, I found that I had been deceived; above thirty passengers, principally Syrians and Egyptians, were crowded together in the boat, with about ten sailors. The Reys, his younger brother, the pilot, and the steward, had established themselves in the place behind the helm for which I had agreed. To revisit Yembo, the abode of death, was not advisable; and as I saw no appearance of plague on board, I submitted to my lot without any unavailing dispute. We immediately set sail, keeping close in shore. In the evening I saw that my situation was much worse than I had suspected it to be when I came on board; in the hold were lying half a dozen sick people, two of whom were in a violent delirium; the Reys's young brother, who had his seat close to me, was paid to attend the sick; one of them died on the following day, and the body was thrown overboard. Little doubt remained of the plague being actually in the ship, though the sailors insisted that it was a different malady. On the third day, the boy, the Reys's brother, felt great pains in his head, and, struck with the idea of the plague, he insisted on being set on shore. We were then in a small bay; the Reys yielded to his entreaties, and agreed with a Bedouin on shore to carry him back on his camel to Yembo. He was landed, and I am ignorant of his fate. The only precaution I could take against infection, was to place my baggage round me, so as to form an insulated spot in which I had just room enough to sit at my ease; but notwithstanding this, I was compelled to come in contact every moment with the ship's company. Very luckily the disease did not spread; we had only another death, on the fifth day from our departure, though several of the passengers were seized with the malady, which I cannot possibly affirm to have been the plague, as I did not examine the corpses, but every thing led me to that belief. The continual sea-sickness and vomiting of the passengers were, perhaps, to them a salutary operation of nature. As to myself, I was in a very low state of health the whole of the voyage, and frequently tormented with my ague, which was increased by the utter want of comforts on board. I had taken a disgust to all food, excepting broths: whenever we entered a port, I bought a sheep of the Bedouins, in order to have a dish of soup; and by distributing the meat among the ship's people, I obtained their good-will, so that in every instance I was well treated by them; and could command their assistance whenever I stood in need of it, either to raise a temporary awning every morning, or to fill my water-skins on shore.

The navigation is here the same as what I have already described in my voyage from Sowakin to Djidda. We went into a harbour every evening, never sailing during the night, and started again at day-break. If it was known that no small creek or harbour lay before us, near enough to be reached before sun-set with the then existing wind, we sometimes stopped at an anchoring-place soon after mid-day. Unfortunately, the ship's boat had been carried away by a heavy sea, in a preceding voyage; we therefore could seldom get on shore, excepting at places where we found other vessels, whose boats we took, as we usually anchored in deep water. The sailors showed as great cowardice here, as those of Sowakin on a former occasion. Whenever it blew fresh, the sails were taken in; the dread of a storm made them take shelter in a harbour, and we never made longer courses than from twenty-five to thirty-five miles per day. A large square cask of water was the only one on board, and contained a supply for three days for the ship's crew only. The passengers had each his own water-skin; and whenever we reached a watering-place, the Bedouins came to the beach, and sold us the contents of their full skins. As it sometimes happens that the ships are becalmed in a bay distant from any wells, or prevented from quitting it by adverse winds, the crew is exposed to great sufferings from thirst, for they have never more on board their boats than a supply for three or four days.

For the first three days we steered along a sandy shore, here entirely barren and uninhabited, the mountains continuing at a distance inland. At three days' journey by land and by sea from Yembo, as it is generally computed, lies the mountain called Djebel Hassány, reaching close to the shore; and from thence northward the lower range of the mountains are, in the vicinity of the beach, thinly inhabited throughout by Bedouins. The encampments of the tribe of Djeheyne extend as far as these mountains: to the north of it, as far as the station of the Hadj called El Wodjeh, or as it is also pronounced, El Wosh, are the dwelling-places of the Heteym Bedouins. In front of Djebel Hassány are several islands; and the sea is here particularly full of shoals and coral rocks, rising nearly to the surface; from the various colours of which, the water, when viewed from a distance, assumes all the hues of the rainbow. In spring, after the rains, some of these little islands are inhabited by the Bedouins of the coast, who there pasture their cattle as long as food is found: they have small boats, and are all active fishers. They salt the fish, and either carry it in their own boats to Yembo and Cosseir, or sell it to the ships which pass. One of these islands, called El Harra, belongs to the Beni Abs, once a powerful Bedouin tribe, but now reduced to a few families, who live mixed with the Beni Heteym, and, like them, are held in great disrepute by all their neighbours. Upon another island stands the tomb of a saint, called Sheikh Hassan el Merábet, with a few low buildings and huts round it, where a Bedouin family of the Heteym tribe is stationary, to whom the guardianship of the tomb belongs. The course of the Arab ships being usually close by this island, the crews often despatch a boat with a few measures of corn to those people, or some butter, biscuits, and coffee-beans, because they consider Sheikh Hassan to be the patron of these seas. When we sailed by, our Reys made a large loaf of bread, which he baked in ashes, and distributed a morsel of it to every person on board, who eat it in honour of the saint, after which we were treated by him with a cup of coffee.

In general, the Arab sailors are very superstitious; they hold certain passages in great horror; not because they are more dangerous than others, but because they believe that evil spirits dwell among the coral rocks, and might possibly attract the ship towards the shoal, and cause her to founder. For the same reason they observe the constant practice of throwing, at every meal, a handful of dressed victuals into the sea, before they sit down themselves to the repast; saying that the inhabitants of the sea must also have their morsel, otherwise they will impede the vessel's course. Our Reys once forgot this tribute; but on recollecting it, he ordered a fresh loaf to be baked, and threw it into the sea.

We met every day, during this voyage, ships coming from Egypt, and often lay in the same bay with three or four of them, in the evening. On such occasions quarrels frequently happen about water; and ships are often obliged to wait one or two days before the Bedouins bring a sufficient supply down to the coast. Butter, milk, honey, sheep, goats, salt fish, firewood, thin branches of the shrub Arák, of which the Arabians make their tooth-brushes, and which the Bedouins collect on this coast, are every where to be had in plenty, and are generally exchanged for corn or tobacco. These Bedouins are daring robbers, and often swim to the ships during the night, to watch for the opportunity of pilfering. The water on the whole coast is bad, except at Wodjeh and at Dhoba. Wodjeh, which is usually reckoned at three days' journey northward from Djebel Hassány, is a castle on the Hadj route, about three miles inland. Close by it is excellent spring water; and there are likewise copious wells of tolerable water in the vicinity of the small bay which serves as a harbour to the castle, and is therefore called Mersa el Wodjeh. Some Moggrebyn soldiers garrison the castle, which was said to be well stocked with provisions. Several of them were married to Bedouin women, and carried on a trifling trade in provisions with the ships that pass.

The neighbouring mountains of Wodjeh are inhabited by the Bedouin tribe of Bily. To the north of Wodjeh, and about two days' journey south of Moeyleh, lies the anchorage of Dhoba, renowned for its excellent wells. The anchoring-place is in a large bay, one of the best harbours on this coast, and the wells are about half an hour's distance inland, under a grove of palm and Doum date-trees. The route of the Egyptian Hadj passes here; and for its convenience, a birket, or reservoir, has been constructed. The ships that sail from Cosseir to Yembo generally make this point, and continue from thence their coasting voyage southwards. North of Dhoba two days, lies the castle and small village of Moeyleh, in the territory of the Howeytat and Omran Bedouins. We passed it at a distance; but I could see considerable plantations of date-trees near the shore. What is called the castle, appears to be a square building, upon the plain close by the water-side. The position of Moeyleh is distinguishable from afar by the high mountain just behind it; three pointed summits of which, overtopping the rest, are visible sixty to eighty miles off: I was told that in clear winter days they could be distinguished, from Cosseir, at the moment of sun-rise. Moeyleh is the principal position on this coast from Akaba down to Yembo. Its inhabitants, who are for the greater part Bedouins, become settlers, carry on a trade in cattle and fish with Tor and Yembo, and their market is visited by numerous Bedouins of the interior of the country. It is the only place on this coast where a regular market is kept, and where provisions are always to be found, and thus often affords timely relief to ships detained on their passage by contrary winds. Provisions being very dear in the Hedjaz, and very cheap in Egypt, ships, on leaving the Hedjaz harbours for Cosseir or Suez, never lay in more than is absolutely necessary; but the passage, which is usually calculated by them at twenty days, very often lasts a month, and sometimes even two months.

From off Moeyleh, the point of the peninsula of Sinai, called Ras Abou Mohammed, is clearly distinguished. Ships bound from Yembo to Cosseir generally make this promontory, or one of the islands lying before it, and thence steer south to Cosseir. They do this, in order to take advantage of the northerly winds that blow in these parts of the Red Sea for nine months of the year; and they prefer the tedious, but safer mode of a coasting voyage, during which they often enjoy a land-breeze, to the danger and fatigue of beating up, in open sea, against the wind, or of standing straight across from Djidda or Yembo to the African coast; with the harbours of which, south of Cosseir, very few Red Sea pilots are acquainted, and of the Bedouin inhabitants of which they all entertain great fears.

On reaching Ras Mohammed, they anchor near one of the small islands, or go into the harbour called Sherm, where they wait till a fair wind springs up, which usually carries them to Cosseir in one or two days. As for ourselves, we had not during the whole voyage any sort of disagreeable occurrence, though the wind, which was seldom fair, obliged us once to remain three days at the same anchorage; and I often expected the vessel to be wrecked, on seeing the pilot steer among the shoals in shore: a practice in which these people have acquired great experience, and in which they display as much boldness as they do cowardice in the open sea.

After twenty days' voyage we reached the neighbourhood of Ras Abou Mohammed, on the 4th of June: the boat was secured for the night with grapplings to some coral rocks, leeward of a small island ahead of the promontory; the pilot intending to strike across the next morning.

As I knew that Bedouins were always to be found in the harbour of Sherm, to transport passengers by land to Tor or Suez, I wished to be set on shore here. The road from hence to Cairo was much shorter than by way of Cosseir; and my low state of health rendered it desirable to leave the vessel where I had not the slightest accommodation, and where the fears of the plague had not yet subsided, though no person had died on board during the last fortnight. For the sum of four dollars given to the Reys, and one to the pilot, they were kind enough to go a little out of their course, and on the following morning, the 5th of June, we entered the harbour of Sherm.

Sherm is about four or five hours distant from the point called Ras Abou Mohammed, and is a good and spacious harbour, with anchorage for large ships; it lies at the entrance of the gulf of Akaba, and is the best harbour on the west side of that gulf. Under the name Sherm, or Sheroum, (the plural,) are included two harbours half a mile distant from each other, both equally good; but the southern is the most frequented. As a copious well is near, these harbours are often visited by ships coming from and going to the Hedjaz; and passengers who wish to save themselves a voyage up the Gulf of Suez, (which during the prevalence of the northerly winds is often of long duration,) land here, and are carried by the Bedouins upon camels to Tor and Suez. These Bedouins, living up in the mountains, see the ships from afar, and on their arrival hasten to the coast to offer their services. In former times, when the Pashas of Egypt exercised but a nominal power over the neighbouring Bedouins, the Arabs of Tor were much dreaded by the crews of ships; they enforced from them regular tributes whenever they entered their harbours, and conducted themselves in a very oppressive manner. At present, Mohammed Aly, through the means of the commander at Suez, has succeeded in overawing these Bedouins; their conduct is now very friendly, and travelling with them is perfectly safe: but if a ship happens to be wrecked on their coasts, or on the islands near them (no unfrequent occurrence), they still assert their ancient right of plundering the cargo.

In the evening a ship came in, laden with soldiers, which left Yembo six days before us; the commander of the soldiers, and four or five of his party, were set on shore, to proceed by land to Cairo, and both vessels continued their voyage the next morning for Cosseir.

There was no difficulty in obtaining camels; more than thirty were ready to be hired; and we started, on the evening of our arrival, in two parties, the one in advance composed of the soldiers, and the other, at about two hours' distance behind, composed of myself and slave, and two fellow passengers, men of Damascus, who were glad of this opportunity of shortening their journey home. We rode this evening about one hour and a half in a valley, and then rested for the night.

On the 6th of June we continued our road in barren valleys, among steep rocks, mostly of granite, till we halted, about noon, under a projecting rock that afforded us some shade. The Bedouins went to fetch water from a place up in the western mountains, called El Hamra, which proved to be of excellent quality. A poor woman with two goats lived in the valley quite alone. Among the Bedouins themselves the most perfect security prevails in this district, which is interrupted only by the scandalous behaviour of the Turkish soldiers who pass this way. I knew these men well from repeated experience, and therefore had declined joining their party. When we continued our route towards evening, we met on the road one of the Bedouin boys who served as camel-drivers to the party before us. His camel, upon which one of the soldiers was mounted, had not been able to keep up with the others, and its rider, furious at this delay, had drawn his sabre, and cut the animal to make it move at a quicker pace: when the boy remonstrated and seized the halter, he also received a cut on the shoulder; and as he persisted in keeping his hold, the ruffian discharged his gun at him; the boy then ran off, and waited for our coming up. At a few miles' distance we heard from afar the soldier's loud cursing, and found him walking behind the camel. As I expected an affray, I had loaded my gun and pistols. When he saw me riding in front of our people, he immediately ran towards me, and cried out to me in Turkish to descend and to change camels with him. I laughed at him, and told him in Arabic I was no fellah, to be addressed in that manner. In the usual style of those soldiers, who think that every person who is not a soldier must yield to their commands, he then turned towards my slave and ordered him to alight, swearing that he would shoot one of us, if we did not obey. On hearing this I took up my gun, and assured him that it was loaded with good powder, and would send a bullet to his heart better than his would to mine. During this altercation his camel had strayed a little into the valley, and fearing for his baggage, he ran after it, and we rode on. Not being able to follow us in the sands, he discharged his gun at me, from a distance, which I immediately answered, and thus the battle ended. Farther on we came up with his companions, who had alighted. I told them, that their friend behind was embarrassed with his camel, upon which they dispatched one of their Bedouins to fetch him, while I myself rode on, and encamped that night in a side valley out of the road, where the Bedouin boy again joined us, not wishing to be seen by the other soldiers.

We now conducted our journey in such a manner as not to fall in again with the soldiers; but two days after I met the man again at Tor. The governor of Suez was then there, to whom I might have addressed my complaints: this he was afraid of, and therefore walked up to me with a smiling countenance, and said he hoped that no rancour subsisted between us; that as to the shot he fired, it was merely for the purpose of calling his companions to assist him with his camel. In reply, I assured him that my shot had quite a different object, and that I was sorry it had missed; upon which he laughed and went away. There are not on earth more insolent, haughty, and at the same time vile and cowardly beings than Turkish soldiers: wherever they expect to meet with no resistance, they act in the most overbearing, despotic manner, and think nothing of killing an inoffensive person, in the slightest fit of passion ; but when they meet with a firm resistance, or apprehend any bad consequences from their conduct, there is no meanness to which they will not immediately submit. During my journey through Egypt from Cairo to Assouan, the whole of which was performed by land, I had several similar rencontres with soldiers; and I must lay it down as a rule for travellers, constantly to treat these fellows with great hauteur, as the most trifling condescension is attributed by them to fear, and their conduct becomes intolerable. We travelled this day about nine hours.

June 7th. We continued our course in valleys for about two hours and a half, when we came to a high mountain, where I was obliged to dismount. It was with great difficulty that I could reach the summit, for my strength was exhausted; and I had been shivering with a fever the whole preceding night. It took us about two hours and a half to pass the mountain, and to descend into the valley on the other side. From the top we had a fine view of the Gulf of Akaba. The upper part of this mountain is granite, and its lower ridges grünstein. In the afternoon we issued from this chain into the western plain, which declines slowly towards the sea of Suez, and encamped in it after a ride of about ten hours.

June 8th. We reached Tor, in about three hours and a half from our resting-place. Here we found every thing in a great bustle. The lady of Mohammed Aly Pasha, whom I had met with at almost every station on this journey, had arrived here from Yembo a few days before, and, as it blew strong from the north, had come on shore, that she might proceed by land to Suez. The governor of Suez and Mustafa Beg, her own brother, one of the Pasha's principal officers, had come to meet her, and her tents were pitched close by the little village of Tor. From four to five hundred camels were required to transport her suite and soldiers to Suez, and as that number could not soon be prepared, she had already been waiting here a whole week.

I had intended to stop at Tor a few days, merely to recover sufficient strength for my journey to Cairo; but when I learned that the plague was still at Suez, as well as at Cairo, I changed my plan, and determined to wait here some weeks, till the season for the disease should be passed. I soon found, however, that a residence at Tor was not very agreeable. This little village is built in a sandy plain, close to the beach, without any shelter from the sun; a few date-plantations are at some distance behind it. The houses are miserable, and swarms of flies and mosquitoes choke up the avenues of every dwelling. I remained at Tor for the night; and having heard from the Bedouins that at one hour's distance was another small village, in an elevated situation, with abundance of gardens and excellent water, I resolved to take up my quarters there.

It is surrounded by a half-ruined wall: the remains of a small castle are seen, said to have been constructed by Sultan Selym I., who fortified all the outposts of his empire. The French intended to rebuild it, but they left Egypt before the work was begun. Two small villages, about a mile distance, on both sides of Tor, are inhabited by Arabs, while in Tor itself none reside but Greeks, consisting of about twenty families, with a priest, who is under the Archbishop of Mount Sinai. They earn their livelihood by selling provisions to the ships that anchor here to take in water, which abounds in wells, and is of a good quality. Provisions are here twice as dear as at Cairo; and the people of Tor have their own small boats, in which they sail to Suez for those provisions. Were it not for the passage of Turkish soldiers, they would be rich, as they live very parsimoniously; but the rapacity of a few of these men often deprives them, in a single day, of the profits they have earned during a whole year. No garrison is kept here by the Pasha.

June 9th. In the morning I rode over the ascending plain to the above-mentioned village, which is called El Wady, after having laid in a sufficient stock of provisions at Tor. I easily found a lodging, and was glad to see that my expectations of the site of this village were not disappointed: it consists of about thirty houses, built in gardens, and among date-trees, almost every house having its own little garden. I hired a small half-open building, which I had covered with date-leaves, and enjoyed the immediate vicinity of a shady pleasure-ground, where grew palm, nebek, pomegranate, and apricot trees. A large well, in the midst of them, afforded a supply of excellent water, and I had nothing more to wish for at present. The people of the village, who are for the greater part Bedouins become settlers, could not suspect any motive I might have for residing here, as they saw that I was scarcely able to stand upon my legs: they treated me, in consequence, kindly; and little presents of meat and other provision, which I distributed among them, soon insured their good-will, and I had every reason to be satisfied with their conduct. Thus enjoying complete repose, and the good mountain air of this village, which lies so much higher than Tor, my strength soon returned.

For the last four years, since I had left the society of my friends Mr. Barker and Mr. Masseyk, and the delightful gardens of Aleppo, I had not found myself so comfortable as I did here; and even the first day that I passed in this retreat produced a visible improvement in my health. As I thought that slight exercise might be useful, I rode over to the Hammám, a warm bath, round the corner of the mountain, situated to the north of Tor, and about half an hour distant from El Wady. Several warm springs issue from the calcareous mountain, the principal of which has a roof built over it, and is visited by all the surrounding Bedouins. Some half-ruined buildings, probably as old as the demolished castle of Tor, offered, in former times, accommodation to the visiters. The water is of a moderate heat, and appears to be strongly impregnated with nitre. Close by the springs are extensive date-plantations. I have never seen a richer and more luxuriant growth of palm-trees than in this place; they form so thick a wood, that it is difficult to find one's way through it. These plantations belong to the Bedouins of the peninsula, who come here with their families at the date-harvest. The largest grove, however, is the property of the Greek priests of Mount Sinai, one of whom lives in an insulated tower in the midst of it, like a hermit, for he is the only constant resident in the place. The fear of the Bedouins keeps him shut up for months in this tower the entrance to which is by a ladder; and a waterman, who provides him every week with a supply of water, is the only individual who approaches him. The priest is placed here as gardener of the convent; but experience shows the inefficacy of all attempts to protect the trees from the pilfering Bedouins, and they have therefore given up the fruit to the first comer: so that this grove, the produce of which often amounts to the value of four or five thousand piastres, becomes public property.

I had some difficulty in providing myself with flesh-meat at Wady: sheep are very scarce in the whole peninsula, and no Arab is inclined to sell what he has. A flock had been sent from Suez to Tor, for the supply of Mohammed Aly's lady and her suite. I was obliged to pay twelve piastres here for a small kid.

The second week's residence at El Wady considerably improved my health. I was not thoroughly recovered, but only wished, at present, to acquire sufficient strength for the journey to Cairo, where the means of a complete cure might be found. I was the more inclined to hasten my departure, as it was said that all the Bedouins who had camels to spare, and had not given them up for the transport of the Pasha's women, were soon to leave this neighbourhood, with loads of coals for Cairo, when I should find it difficult to procure beasts of transport. I had been for eighteen months without any letters from Europe, and felt impatient to reach Cairo, where I knew that many awaited me. I knew too, that the plague would have nearly subsided by the time of my arrival, as about the end of June it always yields to the influence of the hot season. I therefore engaged two camels from hence to Cairo, for which I paid twelve dollars.

The Arabs of these parts have established particular transport customs: of those who inhabit this peninsula, the tribe of Sowaleha is entitled to one half of the transport, and the other half is shared by the two tribes of Mezeyne and Aleygat. As I wanted two camels, one was to be furnished to me by a Sowaleha, and the other either by a Mezeyne or Aleygat. If no individuals of those three tribes happen to be present, the business is easily settled with one of them, and the others have no after claim; but if several of them are on the spot, quarrels always arise among them, and he who conducts the traveller is obliged to give to the others a small sum of money, to silence their claims. The same custom or law marks out certain limits, which when the traveller and his guide have once passed, the countrymen of the latter have no more claims for the transport. The limit from Tor, northward, is half way between Tor and Wady. The Bedouin who had carried me from Tor to Wady passed this limit by stealth, none of his friends knowing of it: they pursued when they saw us on the road; but we had passed the limits before they came up with us, and I had thus fallen to the lot of this guide; when, on inquiring at Wady for a new guide to Cairo, I was told that no person could take the transport upon himself, without the knowledge or permission of the Bedouin who had brought me to Wady from Tor, and upon whose camel I had once crossed the limits. The man was therefore sent for, and as his own camels were not present, he ceded his right to another for two dollars; and with the latter I departed. These quarrels about transport are very curious, and sometimes very intricate to decide: in the mean while the traveller remains completely passive, but there is not much danger of imposition, for the amount of the hire is always publicly known, and one dollar is the largest sum he can lose.

I left Wady on the 17th of June. Our road lay upon an elevated plain, bounded on the east by the high summits of the Sinai mountains, and on the west by a low ridge of calcareous hills, which separate the plain from the sea, and run parallel with it for about five or six hours. This plain, which is completely barren, and of a gravelly soil, is called El Kaa, and is in bad repute with the Bedouins, from having no springs, and being extremely hot, from the nature of its position. Thus I found it myself. During this day we suffered much from one of the hottest winds I ever remember to have experienced. We alighted during the mid-day hours in the open plain, without finding any tree to afford shade. A Bedouin cloak, fastened to four poles, was erected as a tent, barely sheltering me from the sun, while my two guides and my slave wrapped themselves in their mantles, and lay down and slept in the sun. Instead of causing perspiration, the hot air of the Semoum chokes up every pore; and in the evening I again had the ague, which continued from hence, in irregular fits, till I arrived at Cairo. We encamped this night in El Kaa.

June 18th. We entered, in the morning, Wady Feiran, followed it down towards the sea, and then continued along shore for the rest of the day, till we reached the neighbourhood of the well called El Merkha, in front of the bay which bears the name of Birket Faraoun.

June 19th. From Merkha we again proceeded along shore, then entered the Wady Taybe, leaving to our left the mountains, which reach close to the shore, and in the midst of which lies the bath, called Hamam Seydna Mousa. Taybe is a valley full of trees, which were now withered for want of rain. Having reached its top, we continued over a high plain, passed Wady Osayt, and slept that night in Wady Gharendel.

June 20th. Passing by the brackish spring of Howara, we crossed a barren plain, reached Wady Wardan at mid-day, and encamped in the evening at Wady Seder. Our days' journeys were very long, and we travelled some hours during the night, that we might reach Suez in time to join the caravan, which was preparing there to conduct the Pasha's women to Cairo. As I shall speak in detail of this road in the journal of my visit to Mount Sinai, I forbear entering here into any particulars: the remarks I now made were, besides, very superficial.

June 26th. In the morning we passed Ayoun Mousa, and reached Suez in the afternoon. The caravan was just preparing to depart, and we started with it in the evening. There was a strong guard, and altogether we had about six hundred camels. We travelled the whole night without interruption, and on the morning of

June 22nd alighted at the place called El Hamra, the Hadj station between Cairo and Adjeroud. The ladies of the Pasha had brought two carriages with them from the Hedjaz, in which they had travelled all the way from Tor to Suez, the road being every where of easy passage. Two more carriages were sent for them from Cairo to Suez, one of which, an elegant English barouche, was drawn by four horses: they got into these at Suez, and quitted them occasionally for splendid litters or palanquins, carried by mules. We started again in the evening, and, travelling the whole night, reached Birket el Hadj on the morning of the 23rd, having thus made the whole journey from Tor in six days; a forced march which, from the heat of the season, had fatigued me extremely. At the Birket El Hadj the caravan was met by many grandees from Cairo: the ladies of the Pasha intended to encamp there for a few days among the date-groves. Being unable myself, from weakness, to proceed on the same day, (although Cairo is but four hours distant,) I slept here, and entered the city on the morning of the 24th of June, after an absence from thence of nearly two years and a half. I found that two letters, which I sent here from Medina, had not been received, and my acquaintances had supposed me lost. The plague had nearly subsided; some of the Christians had already re-opened their houses; but great gloom seemed to have overspread the town from the mortality that had taken place.

The joy I felt at my safe return to Cairo was considerably increased by flattering and encouraging letters from England; but my state of health was too low to admit of fully indulging in the pleasures of success. The physicians of Cairo are of the same set of European quacks so frequently found in other parts of the Levant: they made me swallow pounds of bark, and thus rendered my disease worse; and it was not till two months after that I regained my perfect health at Alexandria, whither I had gone to pay a visit to Colonel Missett, the British resident in Egypt, who had already laid me under so many obligations, and to whose kind attentions, added to regular exercise on horseback, more than to any thing else, I was indebted for my recovery. A delightful journey, in the winter months, through Lower Egypt, and by the Lake Menzaleh, restored me to my wonted strength, which I am happy to say has never since experienced any abatement.

APPENDIX.

APPENDIX.

No. I.

Stations of the Pilgrim Caravan, called the " Hadj el Kebsy," through the mountainous country between Mekka and Sanaa in Yemen.

MEKKA.

1st day. Shedád ; some coffee-huts.
2. Kura, a small village on the summit of the mountain so called.
3. Tayf.
4. Abbasa, in the district of the Thekyf Arabs.
5. Melawy Djedára, district of the Beni Sad Arabs.
6. Mekhra, district of the Naszera Arabs. The principal village of the Beni Sad tribe is Lagham, and of the Naszera tribe, Sour ; distant one day N. of the farthest limits of Zohran. In this district is also the fortified village of Bedjeyle.
7. Esserrar, of the Thekyf Arabs.
8. Berabrah, on the N. extremity of Zohran, a district inhabited by Arabs of the same name. This Zohran is one of the most fertile countries in the mountainous chain, although its villages are separated from each other by intervals of barren rock. It is inhabited by the Zohran tribes of Beni Malek and Beni Ghamed. The Zohran chief, Bakhroudj, having bravely resisted Mohammed Aly Pasha, was taken by surprise, in March 1815, and cruelly cut to pieces by that Turkish general's order.
9. Wady Aly, in the same district.
10. Meshnye, on the S. borders of Zohran.
11. Raghdan, a market-place of the Ghamed Arabs.
12. Korn el Maghsal, of the Ghamed Arabs.
13. Al Záhera, of the same Arabs. These two tribes of Zohran and Ghamed possess the Hedjaz (viz. the mountains) and adjoining districts in Tehama, or the Western plain

towards the sea, as well as the Eastern upper plain. The chief place of the Ghamed tribe is Mokhowa, a town not to be confounded with Mokha.

14. El Roheyta, of the powerful tribe of Shomrán.
15. Adama, of the Shomrán Arabs.
16. Tabala, of the Shomrán Arabs, who extend over both sides of the mountains in the W. and E. plain.
17. El Hasba, market of the Shomrán Arabs.
18. El Asábely, a village of the Asábely tribe.
19. Beni Shefra, a market-place of the tribe so called, formerly united with the Asábelys, but formed by the Wahaby chief into a distinct tribe.
20. Shat Ibn Aryf.
21. Sedouán: this place and Shat Ibn Aryf are inhabited by Arabs of the tribe called Ahl Aryef.
22. El Matsa.
23. Ibn Maan, which with El Matsa belong to the Ibn Katlan Arabs.
24. Ibl, in the territory of the powerful tribe of Asyr.
25. Ibn el Shayr, of the Asyr tribe.
26. Dahban, of the Kahtan Arabs, one of the most powerful tribes of the Eastern Desert.
27. Derb Ibn el Okeyda, a wady inhabited by the Refeydha tribe, who belong to the Asyr. They are strong in horses.
28. Derb Selmán, of the Refeydha tribe.
29. Wakasha, of the Abyda Arabs. In the district of Abyda is the town of Aryn, in a very fertile territory. From Aryn southward the Arabs keep on the mountains a few camels, but many sheep and goats, and are what the Bedouins call Shouáwy, or Ahl Sháh, or Ahl Bul.
30. Wady Yaowd, of the Abyda Arabs.
31. Howd Ibn Zyad, of the Abyda Arabs.
32. Thohran, a district and market-place of the tribe of Wadaa.
33. Keradh, of the Wadaa tribe.
34. Rogháfa, of the Sahhar Arabs.
35. Dohyán, of the Sahhar Arabs.
36. Sada, of the Sahhar tribe. From Sada the caravan, or Hadj el Kebsy, takes its departure; it is so called from the Emir, or chief of the Hadj, who is styled Kebsy. The pilgrims from all the interior parts of Yemen assemble at Sada: it is a large town, but much decayed, famous in Arabia Felix as the birth-place of Yahya Ibn Hosseyn, chief promoter of the sect of Zeyd, which has numerous adherents in that country. Of late a new saint has appeared at Sada; he is called Seyd Ahmed, and is much revered by the Zyoud, or sect of Zeyd, who entitle him Woly, or Saint, even during his life. Sada is governed by Arabs: the Wahaby influence extended thus far. From Sada towards Sanaa the country is inhabited by Arabs, under the dominion of the Imám of Sanaa.
37. Aashemye, of the Sofyan tribe.
38. A market-place, or Souk, of the Bekyl Arabs.

39. Another market-place of the same tribe. The Bekyl and Háshed Arabs of this district serve in the army of the Imám of Sana; many of them go to India, and are preferred by the native princes there to any other class of soldiers: Tipoo Saheb had several hundred of them in his service. They generally embark at Shaher, in Hadramaut; and their chief destination at present is Guzerat and Cutch.

40. Ghoulet Adjyb, of the Háshed Arabs.
41. Reyda, of the Omran Arabs.
42. Ayal Soráh, of the Hamdan tribe.
43. Sanaa. From Mekka to Sanaa, forty-three days' very slow travelling: for most of the pilgrims perform the whole journey on foot.

No. II.

Of the country through which the Kebsy pilgrims travel, and the extraordinary customs of some Arabian tribes.

THE route of this pilgrimage lies wholly along the mountains of the Hedjaz and Yemen, having the Eastern plain on one side, and Tehama, or the sea-coast, on the other. The road often leads through difficult passes on the very summit of the mountains. Water abounds, in wells, springs, and rivulets: the entire tract of country is well peopled, although not every where cultivated, enclosed fields and trees being only found in the vicinity of water. There is a village at every station of the Hadj: most of these villages are built of stone, and inhabited by Arab tribes, originally of these mountains, and now spread over the adjoining plains. Some are very considerable tribes, such as Zohran, Ghamed, Shomran, Asyr, and Abyda, of whom each can muster from six to eight thousand firelocks: their principal strength consists in matchlocks. Horses are but few in these mountains; yet the Kahtan, Refeydha, and Abyda tribes, who likewise spread over the plain, possess the good Koheyl breed. This country produces not only enough for the inhabitants, but enables them to export great quantities of coffee-beans, corn, beans, raisins, almonds, dried apricots, &c.

It is said that the coffee-tree does not grow northward beyond Meshnye, in the Zohran country; the tree improves in quality southward: the best coffee is produced in the neighbourhood of Sanaa. Grapes abound in these mountains. Raisins constitute a common article of food with the Arabs, and are exported to the towns on the sea-coast, and to Djidda and Mekka, where a kind of wine is made from them, as follows:—The raisins are put into earthen jars, which are then filled with water, buried in the ground, and left there for a whole month, during which the fermentation takes place. Most other fruits are cultivated in these mountains, where water is at all times abundant, and the climate temperate. Snow has sometimes fallen, and water been frozen as far as Sada. The Arabs purchase their cotton dresses in the market-places of Tehama, or on the coast: the passing pilgrims sell to them a few drugs, spices, and needles, and proceed on their way in perfect security, at least since the Wahabys have subjugated the whole country, by overpowering, after many sanguinary battles, the hostile Sheikhs, who were forced to pay an annual tribute.

Most of the Arab tribes south of Zohran belong to the sect of Zeyd: they live in villages, and are chiefly what the Arabs call Hadhar, or settlers, not Bedouins; but as they keep large herds of cattle, they descend, in time of rain, into the Eastern plain, which affords rich pasturage for cows, camels, and sheep. They procure clothes, drugs, utensils, &c. from the sea-ports of Yemen, where they sell dried fruits, dates, honey, butter, coffee-beans, &c. With the Bedouins of the Eastern plain they exchange durra for cattle. The Spanish dollar is current among them; but in their markets all things are valued by measures of corn. The dress of these Bedouins generally consists in cotton stuffs and leather.

Before the Wahabys taught them the true Mohammedan doctrines, they knew nothing more of their religion than the creed, *La Illaha ill' Allah, wa Mohammed rasoul Allah*, (There is no God but God, and Mohammed is the prophet of God); nor did they ever perform the prescribed rites. The El Merekede, a branch of the great Asyr tribe, indulged in an ancient custom of their forefathers by assigning to the stranger, who alighted at their tents or houses, some female of the family to be his companion during the night, most commonly the host's own wife; but to this barbarous system of hospitality young virgins were never sacrificed. If the stranger rendered himself agreeable to his fair partner, he was treated next morning with the utmost attention by his host, and furnished, on parting, with provisions sufficient for the remainder of his journey: but if, unfortunately, he did not please the lady, his cloak was found next day to want a piece, cut off by her as a signal of contempt. This circumstance being known, the unlucky traveller was driven away with disgrace by all the women and children of the village or encampment. It was not without much difficulty that the Wahabys forced them to renounce this custom; and as there was a scarcity of rain for two years after, the Merekedes regarded this misfortune as a punishment for having abandoned the laudable rites of hospitality, practised during so many centuries by their ancestors.

That this extraordinary custom prevailed in the Merekede tribe, I had often heard during my travels among the Syrian Bedouins, but could not readily believe a report so inconsistent with our established notions of the respect in which female honour is held by the Arabs; but I can no longer entertain a doubt on the subject, having received, both at Mekka and Tayf, from various persons who had actually witnessed the fact, most unequivocal evidence in confirmation of the statement.

Before the Wahaby conquest it was a custom among the Asyr Arabs, to take their marriageable daughters, attired in their best clothes, to the public market, and there, walking before them, to cry out, *Man yshtery el Aadera?* "Who will buy the virgin?" The match,

APPENDIX. 449

sometimes previously settled, was always concluded in the market-place; and no girl was permitted to marry in any other manner.

I heard that tigers and wolves abound in these mountains, but that there are not any lions. The Arabs have here a fine breed of mules and asses.

No. III.

Route from Tayf to Sanaa.

THIS itinerary was communicated to me by a poor man who had travelled with his wife, in 1814, from Sada to Mekka. He was a native of some place near Sanaa; and as the pilgrimage or Hadj el Kebsy had been for some years interrupted, and he could not afford a passage by sea to Djidda, he undertook this route, which is practicable even in these critical times to those who can pass unsuspected in the character of pilgrims. He was every where treated with hospitality. On his arrival at a village he proceeded to the Mesdjed or mosque, and recited some chapter of the Koran: the Arab inhabitants then inquired who he was, and supplied him with plenty of flour, milk, raisins, meat, &c. He was never stopped by robbers until he reached the advanced posts of Mohammed Aly's Turkish army; there he was plundered by some soldiers of all his provisions. He could not mark exactly each day's journey, because he loitered about from one settlement to another, waiting often several days that he might have companions on the road. The journey occupied him altogether three months. He supported himself at Mekka by singing, during the night, before the houses of wealthy pilgrims, some verses in honour of the prophet and of the pilgrimage. His route was as follows:—

El Tayf—Beni Sad, Arabs—Naszera, Arabs—Begyle (or Bedjele), a market-place—Rehah, a market-place—El Mandak, in the Zohran country—El Bekaa, in the Zohran country—Raghdan, in the district of the Ghamed Arabs—Ghamed, Arabs—Sollebat, inhabited by Ghamed Arabs and those called Khotham, a very ancient tribe that flourished in the beginning of Islám—Shomran, Arabs—Bel Korn—Ibn Dohman, an Arab tribe so called—Ibn el Ahmar, another Arab tribe—Ibn el Asmar, an Arab tribe—The country here is called after the inhabitants, which my informer had not forgotten, although he did not always recollect the names of the villages through which he passed in the districts of each tribe—Asyr; this tribe is now united with the three former under one head—The Asyr chief, El Tamy, proved the steadiest antagonist of Mohammed Aly: his principal residence was the strong castle of El Tor, situated upon a high level surrounded by mountains; he had also a smaller castle, called El Tobab, with a town, from four to five days' journey distant from Gonfode on the sea-coast.

In the Asyr district, the pilgrim passed the villages called Shekrateyn, Ed-dahye, Shohata, and Ed-djof. So far the road had always been on the very summit of the mountain: the traveller henceforward continuing along the valleys composing the lower chain of hills that intersect the Eastern plain.

Refeydha, Arabs—Abyda, Arabs—Harradja, a town in the district of the Senhán Arabs; which also contains the fertile wady called Ráha—-Homra, a place inhabited by the Senhán Arabs: at one day's journey eastward is Wady Nedjran, belonging to the tribe of Yam—Thohran, inhabited by the Wadaa tribe: this place is high in the mountain, but the Wadaa occupy also the low valleys—Bágem, a tribe of Arabs: eastward of them resides the powerful tribe of Kholán Arabs—Dohhyán, of the Sahhar tribe—Sada: from Sada the most usual stages to Sanaa are Beit Medjáhed—Djorf—Kheywan and Houth, two places in the district of the Háshed tribe—Zybein,—Omrán—Sanaa—Seven days from Sada to Sanaa.

No. IV.

Notices respecting the Country south of Mekka.

I HAVE already described the road from Mekka to Tayf. Four hours distant from Tayf, in a S.E. direction, is Lye, a wady with a rivulet, fine gardens, and many houses on the borders of the stream. About two hours S. of Lye, in the mountain, stands the celebrated castle of Byssel, built by the late chief of all the Hedjaz Arabs, Othman el Medhayfe, who was taken prisoner near it in autumn 1812. Here Mohammed Aly Pasha, in January 1815, fought his decisive battle with the united Wahaby forces. From Lye the road leads over mountains for about two hours, and then descends into the great Eastern plain, where, at a distance of seven or eight hours from Lye, and twelve from Tayf, lies the small town of Kolákh: here were the head-quarters of the Turkish army for several months in 1814. It is an open place, without trees or enclosures, with many water-pits. It lies from Tayf in the direction of E. S.E. About Lye and Kolákh, live the Arabs of the Ossama tribe, who form part of the great Ateybe tribe. Between Kolákh and Taraba, off the straight road, lies Abyla, once the residence of the great chief Medhayfe. By Kolákh passes the most frequented road from Nedjed to Zohran, and from thence to the sea-ports of Yemen. Continuing over the plain from Kolákh in a more southern direction for about eighteen hours, we come to the town of Taraba, as the people of Tayf and Mekka call it, or Toroba according to the Bedouin pronunciation. A soldier who possessed a watch told me that he had counted three hours on the march between Tayf and Taraba. This is a considerable town, as large as Tayf, and remarkable for its plantations, that furnish all the surrounding country with dates; and famous for its resistance against the Turkish forces of Mohammed Aly, until January 1815, when its inhabitants were compelled to submit. Taraba is environed with palm-groves and gardens, watered by numerous rivulets; near it are some inconsiderable hills, at the foot of which the Arabs cultivate durra and barley: the inhabitants are of the Begoum tribe, and their Sheikh is Ibn Korshán. One Ghálye, the widow of a deceased Sheikh, had immortalised her name by devoting her property to the defence of the town, and taking an active part in the council of the chiefs. The country about Taraba, and thence to Kolákh, is inhabited by the Ateybe Arabs, the most numerous of the Hedjaz tribes. The Begoums had enclosed Taraba with a wall, and constructed some towers: at present a Turkish garrison is stationed here, this being a principal position and the grand thoroughfare between Nedjed and Yemen.

Pursuing the road from Taraba southwards to the east of the great chain of mountains, over an uneven ground intersected by many wadys, we come, at two days from Taraba, to the town of Ranye, inhabited by the Arab tribe of Sabya, whose Sheikh is Ibn Katnán, a personage distinguished for his bravery in the campaign against the Pasha's Turkish troops. Three or four days from Ranye is the town of Beishe, the intermediate space being peopled by the Beni Oklob tribe. Beishe, the most important position between Tayf and Sanaa, is a very fertile district, extremely rich in date-trees. The Turkish army of Mohammed Aly, with its followers and allied Bedouins, amounting in all to ten or twelve thousand men, found here sufficient provisions for a fortnight's halt, and for a supply on their march of several days towards the south. The Arabs entitle Beishe the key of Yemen: it lies on one of the great roads from Nedjed to Yemen; and it was said that heavy-laden camels from Mekka to Yemen could not come by any other way, and that on the sea-shore beyond Beishe is an easy passage westward through the great chain of mountains. At Beishe many battles were fought between Sherif Ghaleb and Saoud the Wahaby general, who being victorious erected two castles in the neighbourhood, and gave them in charge to Ibn Shokbán, whom he also made chief of the Beni Salem tribe, the inhabitants of Beishe, who could furnish from eight to ten thousand matchlocks. Ibn Shokbán afterwards gallantly opposed the Turkish army. I believe that in former times the Sherifs of Mekka possessed at least a nominal authority over all the country, from Tayf to Beishe. In Asamy's history we find many instances of the Sherifs residing occasionally at Beishe, and having in their army auxiliaries of the Beni Salem tribe.

Beishe is a broad valley, from six to eight hours in length, abounding with rivulets, wells, and gardens. The houses here are better than those of Tayf, and irregularly scattered over the whole tract. The principal castle is very strong, with substantial and lofty walls, and surrounded by a ditch. About three or four days' journey to the E. and S.E. of Beishe, the plain is covered with numerous encampments of the Kahtan Arabs, one of the most ancient tribes, that flourished long before Mohammed, in the idolatrous ages. Some of these Beni Kahtan emigrated to Egypt, where the historian Mesoudi knew them as inhabitants of Assouan. The Wahabys found great difficulty in subduing this tribe, which, however, subsequently became attached to the conquerors, and still continues so. The Beni Kahtan possess excellent pasturage, and breed many fine horses: the vast number of their camels have become proverbial in Arabia. The tribe is divided into two main branches, Es-Saháma, and El Aasy. In December 1814 the Kahtans made an incursion towards Djidda, and carried off the whole baggage of some Turkish cavalry, stationed to protect the road between Djidda and Mekka: large parties of them sometimes pasture their cattle in the province of Nedjed.

From Beishe to Aryn, in the country of the Abyda Arabs, is a journey of five days, according to the Bedouin mode of travelling, but six or seven days as the Kebsy pilgrims march. Beishe itself is about two days distant from the western mountain. It is a journey of at least four days from Beishe to the district of Zohran: all the Arabs from Taraba to Beishe, and from thence westward, are cultivators or agriculturists; those due south and east, are Bedouins, or wandering Nomades.

South-east of Beishe, four or five days, live the Dowáser Arabs during the winter; but in summer they remove to the more fertile pasture-lands of Nedjed, the nearest frontiers of which are only eight days distant. They have no horses, but furnish to the Wahabys in their wars about three thousand camel-riders. The Dowáser are said to be very tall men, and almost black. In former times they used to sell at Mekka ostrich feathers to the northern pilgrims, and many pedlars of Mekka came here in winter to exchange cotton stuffs for those feathers.

Adjoining the Dowáser, but I cannot exactly ascertain in what direction, are the Beni Kelb, Bedouins of whom many absurd fables are related in the Hedjaz: thus it is said, the men never speak Arabic, but bark like dogs; a notion, perhaps, arising from the name *Kelb*, which signifies a dog. Their women, however, it is allowed, can speak Arabic; but the truth is, that the stranger who alights at their tents is entertained by the women, and not by the men.

Half way between Wady Dowáser, or the winter pasture-land of the Dowáser tribe, and Sanaa the capital of Yemen, a short day's journey east of Thohrán, (the territory of the Wadaa Arabs,) and four or five days from the town of Sada, lies the Wady Nedjrán, on the first of the great chain of mountains. It is a fertile valley between inaccessible mountains, in which the passes are so narrow that two camels cannot go abreast. The valley is watered by rivulets, and abounds with date-trees. Here reside the Beni Yam, an ancient tribe, distinguished lately by their opposition to the Wahabys: they consist of settlers and Bedouins ; the former being Shyas, or heretics of the Persian sect, followers of Aly, while the Bedouins are mostly Sunne or orthodox Muselmans. The latter are subdivided into the tribes of Okmán and El Marra, weaker than the disciples of Aly, and often at variance with them, although both parties unite whenever Nedjrán is attacked by a foreign enemy. The settlers can muster about fifteen hundred firelocks. They twice repulsed the Wahaby chief Saoud, who had subdued all the other Arab tribes except the Beni Sobh, of the Harb race, in the northern parts of the Hedjaz. The Beni Yam made a kind of treaty with the Wahabys, and were allowed to perform the pilgrimage annually. Some of them visit the tomb of Aly, at Meshebed Aly, but under circumstances of great difficulty; for their lives would pay the forfeit of their religious zeal, should they be detected on the road; and this frequently happens, as they are betrayed by their peculiar accent or dialect: one who has performed his devotions at Aly's tomb is regarded as a saint at Nedjrán.

When a man of this Beni Yam tribe undertakes a journey, he sends his wife to the house of a friend, who, it is understood, must in all respects supply the husband's place during his absence, and restore the lady to him at his return. It may be here remarked, that the name of *Nedjran el Yemen* is mentioned in the Catechism of the Druses; one of the questions being, " Is Nedjran of Yemen in ruins or not?" The tanneries of Nedjran are famous throughout Arabia.

The less mountainous districts mentioned here, south of Mekka, are even in time of peace accessible only to Bedouins, or Bedouin merchants, and have not any regular communication with Mekka by caravans—Taraba excepted, the inhabitants of which carry their dates in monthly caravans to Mekka and Djidda. The people of Nedjed pass continually through this district in search of coffee-beans, and during the Wahaby dominion there was no other intercourse between Yemen and the northern provinces of Arabia. This country seldom enjoys peace, the mountaineers being hostile to the pastoral inhabitants of the low districts, and often at variance among themselves. They are all very warlike, but the Wahabys have succeeded in checking their private feuds.

The country from Mekka southwards near the sea-shore, to the west of the chain of mountains, is flat, intersected with hills that gradually disappear as we approach the sea, of which the shore presents a level plain in almost every direction at the distance of several hours. In time of peace the land road is most frequented by caravans, which either proceed along the coast close to the harbour, or by the foot of the mountains. The former way affords but little water. The first inhabited place south of Djidda is Leyth, four days distant, a small harbour, which the people were now deserting through dread of the mountaineers. The inhabitants of Leyth are mostly of the Beni Harb tribe, numerous and powerful in the country between Mekka and Medina. On this coast are many encampments of the Heteym Arabs. From Leyth up the mountains to the district of Zohrán, is a journey of three days and a half: from Leyth to Shagga, a small town, is one day's journey: from thence to Doga, the same distance. Doga lies near the mountainous region, and is a considerable market-place; but its houses, or rather huts, are constructed only of brush-wood and reeds, not of stone. The inhabitants are mostly Sherifs, connected in kindred with the Sherif families of Mekka, to whom they often granted an asylum in the late civil wars. It is a journey of one day from Doga to Gonfode, the well-known harbour. One day and a half south of Gonfode, is the small harbour of Haly: this was the southern limit of the territory belonging to the Sherif of Mekka, who kept custom-house officers at Gonfode and Haly. The Wahaby chieftain, Othman el Medhayfe, in 1805 (or 1806), took Gonfode from the Sherif, and the whole coast from thence to Djidda fell under the Wahaby dominion. In 1814 the Turkish troops of Mohammed Aly Pasha endeavoured to establish themselves there, but were soon dislodged with considerable loss by Tamy. Gonfode, however, was retaken in 1815 by Mohammed Aly himself, after his return from the expedition against Tamy, the Sheikh of Asyr.

The caravan distance from Djidda to Gonfode along the coast is seven days, easy travelling. From Djidda to Leyth, another more eastern road, somewhat mountainous, five days' journey, yielding plenty of water: while on the coast road, but one well is found between the two towns.

The other road from Mekka to Yemen, close along the western foot of the great mountains, is much frequented in time of peace: there are weekly arrivals of caravans, chiefly from Mokhowa, which is distant fifteen hours from Doga, and one day from the district of Zohrán in the mountains. Mokhowa is a large town, nine days' journey from Mekka, for caravans travelling slowly : it has stone buildings, and is the market where the husbandmen of Zohrán and the neighbouring districts sell the produce of their labour to the merchants of Mokhowa, who send it to Mekka and Djidda. The country about Mokhowa is very fertile, and inhabited by the three tribes of Beni Selym, Beni Seydán, and Beni Aly: the two latter had submitted to the Wahabys, and were commanded by Tamy, the Sheikh of Asyr. There are likewise at Mokhowa many of the Beni Ghamed tribe. In time of peace the intercourse between this town and Mekka is very considerable; perhaps one third of the supplies of Mekka in grain of different kinds come from this place. Between these towns the road lies chiefly through valleys, and crosses but few hills: on it are some villages, of which the huts are inhabited by Bedouins as well as agriculturists. I must here repeat that Mokhowa is not to be confounded with Mokha.

The two first days' journeys lie in the territory of the Djehádele tribe, whose boundary on the S. is Wady Lemlem, a fertile valley with springs. Beyond that live the Beni Fahem, an ancient tribe, now much reduced in numbers: they are celebrated throughout the Hedjaz for having retained the purity of their language in a higher degree than other tribes; and those who hear one of their boys speak, will be convinced that they deserve this praise.

The country west of the great mountainous chain down to the sea is called Tehama; an appellation not given, at least in this part of Arabia, to any particular province, but assigned generally to the comparatively low grounds towards the coast; and the Bedouins extend this appellation northwards as far as Yembo. The people of Tehama are poor, those excepted who engage in trade; for the country has few fertile spots, and less pasturage than the mountains, where rain falls more abundantly. In the lower Tehama there are sometimes, during a whole year, but three or four days of rain. The Tehama Bedouins south of Mekka had mostly retired up into the mountains, when Mohammed Aly invaded the Hedjaz, not from dread of the Turks, but because, in such an unsettled state of affairs, weak tribes were not secure, in the open country, from being surprised by straggling Bedouins from the more powerful hostile tribes, who during the power of the Wahabys did not venture to show their enmity, and now impatiently broke loose. Among the Bedouins of Tehama are many tribes of the Beni Heteym, a tribe more widely spread than any other in Arabia.

The Great Desert, east of Beishe and Wady Dowáser, and south of the province of Nedjed, extending eastwards to the frontiers of Oman, is called by the Bedouins *Roba el Khaly,* " the empty or deserted abode." In summer it is wholly deserted, being without any wells. In winter, after rains, when the sands produce herbage, all the great tribes of the Nedjed, Hedjaz and Yemen pasture their flocks in the parts of this desert bordering respectively on their own countries. The sandy soil is much frequented by ostriches, which

APPENDIX. 455

are killed by the Dowáser Arabs. Several Bedouins assured me, that in the Robá el Khály there are many parts which have never yet been explored; because towards the east it does not, even in winter time, afford the slightest vegetation. The only habitable spot on this dreary expanse of sand is the Wady Djebryn. There the road passes, by which, in winter, the Arabs of Nedjed travel to Hadramaut: it is a low ground with date-trees and wells; but the pestilential climate deters people from residing there. The dates are gathered by the passing travellers.

No. V.

Stations of the Hadj or Pilgrim Caravan from Cairo to Mekka.

THE following account refers to the route of the caravan in 1816; but formerly, as I learn from Arabian authors, the stations differed in many instances.

The caravan assembles for several days at a place eastward of the Gardens near Cairo, about one hour distant, called El Hassoua, and then proceeds to Birket el Hadj, four hours distant, where they remain two days. From this place the caravan starts on the 27th of the month Showál: it travels only by night, generally setting out at four o'clock in the afternoon, and alighting soon after sun-rise at the station where they encamp, until evening.

From the Birket el Hadj—

1st night—To Dár el Hamra.

2. To Adjeroud: here they halt the whole day and following night. The caravan is supplied with water from Suez, that which Adjeroud furnishes being extremely bad.

4. To Roos el Nowatyr, a plain in the mountain, without water: here they halt only a few hours, and proceed

5. To Wady Tyh, the entrance to the Desert of Tyh: here they halt a few hours, but, not finding any water, go on

6. To the castle of Nakhel: here they repose, after their forced march, during the whole day and following night, supply themselves with water, and set out next evening.

8. To El Alaya, where they remain one hour, but find no water.

9. To Sath el Akaba, the summit of the western chain of Akaba: here is a small village. The road up and down the mountain is very difficult. From this station they march a whole night, to descend in the narrow passes to the plain and castle of Akaba.

10. Here they remain the day and night.

12. Thaher el Homar, a rocky ground, with bad water and numerous date-trees.

13. (Night,) To Shorafa, a barren long extended valley, without water.

14. To Moghayr Shayb: many wells of sweet water, date-plantations, and trees among the rocks, render this one of the most agreeable stations on the route; but it is infested by robbers.

15. To Ayoun el Kassab, a plain ground with date-trees, and water. It belongs to the territory of Moeyleh.

16. To El Moeyleh, where are fine pasture-grounds and good water: here the caravan halts for the night, and remains till the next evening.

18. To Selma, a place yielding water.

19. To Kalat Ezlam.

20. To El Astabel, or Astabel Antar: the only water here is in a few holes dug in the sands of the valley,

21. To Kalat el Wodjeh, where there is good water: they halt this night, and next evening proceed

23. To Akra; a very long march; they arrive at Akra in the evening: here the water is of a most offensive smell. The caravan halts one hour.

24. To El Houra, likewise called Dár el Ashreyn, because it is the twentieth station from Cairo. Between Akra and Houra lies El Hank, a valley without water. At Houra are many trees; also the shrub Arak, of which the pilgrims cut branches, to use as toothbrushes. The water here is bad, and of a strong aperient quality.

25. To Nabt.

26. To El Khedheyra, where the caravan stops one hour in the morning, and marches the rest of the day, the whole night, and next day till evening.

27. To Yembo el Nakhel, where they remain the night, and proceed

29. To Beder: here they remain that day and night; and set out early next morning, and arrive at El Kaa in the afternoon, where they halt till evening, and then proceed

31. To Rábegh.

32. To Djereynát.

33. To Akabet e' Sukar.

34. To Kholeys.

35. To Asfán.

36. To Wady Fatme.

37. To Mekka.

Thirty-seven days on the road—thirty-one nights marching—seven days halt.

No. VI.

Geographical Notices of the Country northward and eastward of Medina.

THE stations of the caravan between Damascus and Medina are well known. The most interesting spot on this road, within the limits of Arabia, appears to be Hedjer, or, as it is sometimes called, Medayen Saleh, seven days north of Medina. This place, according to many passages of the Koran, (which has a chapter entitled Hedjer,) was inhabited by a gigantic race of men, called Beni Thamoud, whose dwellings were destroyed because they refused to obey the admonitions of the prophet Saleh. In circumference Hedjer extends several miles; the soil is fertile, watered by many wells and a running stream: here are generally large encampments of Bedouins. The Wahaby chief, Saoud, intended to build a town on this spot; his olemas deterred him, by declaring that it would be impious to restore a place that the Almighty had visited with his wrath. An inconsiderable mountain bounds this fertile plain on the west, at about four miles' distance from the ground where the pilgrim caravan usually encamps.

In that mountain are large caves or habitations cut out of the rock, with sculptured figures of men and various animals, small pillars on both sides of the entrances, and, if I may believe the testimony of Bedouins, numerous inscriptions over the doors; but I am inclined to think that the Arabs may have mistaken sculptured ornaments for letters. The rock is of a blackish colour, probably volcanic, for there is a lukewarm well in the vicinity. My illness at Medina, and subsequent weakness, prevented me from visiting this spot, from whence I might, in a straight direction, have proceeded to Akaba, on the extremity of the eastern gulf of the Red Sea.

The Bedouins call the whole country between Hedye and Oela (a more northern station of the pilgrims) the district of Sheffa. From thence to Akaba el Shám, or the Syrian Akaba, (likewise a Hadj station), the country is called Essafha. It is this Akaba that may be properly described as the boundary of Arabia towards Syria. Here a steep mountain extends for several days' journey westward towards the Red Sea, and eastward towards the interior of the Desert. On the north of that mountain we enter the higher or upper plain, which continues to Damascus. Between the Syrian Akaba and the Egyptian Akaba is another pass through the same mountain, called Báb el Nedjed, or the "Gate of Nedjed," because here the Bedouins of southern Syria (or, as they are called by the Arabian Bedouins, *Ahl el Shemál*, "People of the North,") pass on their way to Nedjed. In those passes the Wahabys, when they make excursions against the Bedouins, leave strong guards, to secure their own retreat.

The Hadj route from Medina direct to Syria is not much frequented even in time of peace. Sometimes a few Bedouin merchants take camel-loads of coffee-beans by this road to Damascus; but it is infested by strolling parties of the Beni Omran and Howeytat tribes, who live in the western mountain, and frequently descend to rob travellers in the plain. The most frequented route to the north of Medina is towards the country of Kasym, which, as I have already mentioned, supplies Medina in time of peace with all sorts of provisions. The route to Kasym lies between the Hadj route on one side, and the straight road to Derayeh (the Wahaby capital) on the other. The direction of the province of Kasym, as well as of Nedjed, was often pointed out to me at Medina, and I always found it to be

E. ¼ N. for Kasym
E. by S. for Derayeh
} bearing from Medina.

Between the Hadj road and that to Kasym lies a third route, leading straight from Medina to the province of Djebel Shammar, which in peaceable times is much frequented; but the most common way from Medina to Djebel Shammar is by Kasym, two days longer than the last route, but less fatiguing for camels, because there is abundance of water on this road, and very little on the other.

Caravans going from Medina to Kasym visit the following stations:—

Medina.—At one hour's walk beyond the gardens (the road passing E. of Djebel Ohod) is an open space called El Areydh, with the tomb of a sheikh, having a cupola over it. Near this is a well, named Byr Rasheyd.

3 hours from thence is El Hafná, with the bed of a torrent.

19 hours. Soweyder. The road from Hafná to this place is rocky, with two ascents, difficult for camels, and wholly without water. Soweyder lies between two mountains, and has some wells of brackish water dug in the ground; also Doum date-trees. The road from Medina to this place is inhabited by Mezeyne (or Omzeyne) Arabs, of the Beni Harb tribe, and by the Heteym and Beni Safar Arabs, also of the same tribe.

4 hours. A valley, with wells and Doum date-trees.

7 hours. Hanakye, in the plain, with many ponds and wells of sweet water dug in the ground. At a certain depth water is always found here. The ruins of an ancient castle, in the Saracen style, are visible; and here date-trees grow. This important position is frequently visited by the Bedouin tribes.

6 hours. Abou Khesheyb. The road from Hanakye to this place is on a sandy plain. Abou Khesheyb lies between two mountains, and affords good well-water.

12 hours. El Heymedj, a station having sweet and saltish water.

8 hours. El Máwát. The road from Heymedj to this place is sandy, with low mountains, no trees; the herb called *adjref* grows here. The pasture-ground of the Beni Harb tribe extends as far as Heymedj: then begin the pastures of the Meteyr Arabs. El Máwát has the best water on the whole route: it is a sandy spot in an inlet of the mountains.

16 hours. El Badje. The road from Mawát to this place is without water, on a sandy plain, having mountains on both sides: the chain on the left is called Taáye. Badje is an extensive tract, with trees and herbage, and wells both of sweet and brackish water.

3 hours. Neffoud, or, as it is called from the soil, Gherek-ed-Dessem, a plain of deep

sand, four hours long, after which the road becomes less sandy and difficult, being covered with small stones.

14 hours. Djerdáwye, a plain with wells of good water; from thence in 7 hours, to Dát, the first town of Kasym.—In all, one hundred hours.

From Dát to Rass, one of the chief towns of Kasym, is four or five hours. From Rass to a place called Khabara, five hours; and from Khabara to Shebeybe, four hours.

According to the night-journies of the Bedouins, one hundred hours are equal to ten or eleven marches by day. The journey here detailed was performed by Tousoun Pasha's army at night. Three days from Medina to Hanakye, and eight days from thence to Dát. A person belonging to the court of Tousoun Pasha measured the distance by his watch. The caravans, loaded with corn, are generally ten or eleven days on the road between Medina and Rass.

Kasym, which is the most fertile district in the province of Nedjed, begins at Dát. The name of Nedjed, signifying high or elevated ground, is given to this country in opposition to Tehama or " low lands," applied to the sea-coast. It seems to be an oblong tract, extending between three and four days' journies from west to east, and two journies in breadth south to north. Within this space are above twenty-six small towns or villages, well peopled, in a cultivated territory, irrigated by water from numerous wells. The chief town is Bereyda, where resides the Sheikh of Kasym, an old man named El Hedjeylan, once an enemy to the Wahabys, now a convert to their doctrine. The neighbourhood of Rass produces the most corn; and that part of Kasym about Dát and Rass lies nearest to Medina. In time of peace, regular caravans arrive every month at Medina from Rass. Tousoun Pasha's army found plenty of provisions in the few villages of Kasym which they occupied.

The most considerable place in Kasym is Aneyzy, said to be equal in size to Siout in Upper Egypt, which contained, according to the French computation, three thousand houses. Aneyzy has bazars, and is inhabited by respectable Arab merchants. Of the other towns and villages, the following are most noted:—Es' Shenáne, Balgha, Heshashye, El Helalye, El Bekeyrye, Batah el Nebhanye, Ashebeybe, Ayoun, Kowár, and Mozneb.

Small tribes of the Aenezes, of Ateybe (whose chief seat is on the Hedjaz mountains inhabited by the Beni Harb), of Meteyr, and others, encamp during the whole year among the plains of Kasym, which afford excellent pasturage.

Between Kasym and Derayeh, the capital of Nedjed, the intermediate district, mostly a desert, is called El Woshem: from the eastern extremity of the district of Kasym to Derayeh is a distance of five days. The last place in Kasym, on this side, is Mozneb: then begins Wady Sarr, a broad sandy valley with pasturage, which continues for several days towards Derayeh through the district of Woshem.

Nedjed, near Derayeh, assumes the name of El Aredh, a district once separate from Nedjed, but now considered as belonging to it. El Aredh is less fertile than El Kasym, from which, in fact, it is partly supplied with provisions. Its principal town, Derayeh, has always been a place of note, but much increased since it has become the capital of the Wahaby power and sect. Its direction was often indicated to me; and I found it to bear from Medina E. by S. (variation not computed); the bearing of Kasym from Medina,

E. ¦ N. Derayeh is situated in a valley, the inlets and outlets of which on the N. and S. sides are very narrow, admitting only one camel at a time. The houses (many built of stone) are placed on the declivities of both mountains, the valley itself being throughout very narrow. The town is not walled. The number of inhabitants may be estimated, according to the report of the Bedouins, who state that the town furnished three thousand men armed with firelocks to the Wahaby chief: they are composed of different tribes, principally the Mekren, a branch of the Messalykh, part of the great Aeneze race. All the inhabitants of Nedjed trace their pedigrees to some ancient Bedouin tribe; thus the people of Rass claim descent from the Beni Yam, who now reside at Nedjran, in Yemen. The smaller tribe of Beni Lam (related to those of the same name on the river Tigris, but not, like them, of the sect of Aly), and the small tribe of Essehoun, dwell in the Aredh, and seldom encamp beyond its limits. Derayeh is supplied with water from wells. Ibn Saoud, the late Wahaby chief, discovered a spring behind this house, which he built, and wished to persuade the people that God had inspired him on the occasion. The mansion of the Wahaby chief stands on the mountain, at about ten minutes' walk from the town: it is spacious, but without any splendid apartments: all the married members of the reigning family have their own chambers; and there are many rooms for guests, with whom the house is constantly filled; for all the chiefs of tribes who come to Derayeh on business are invited to the mansion or palace of the great Sheikh. There are not any khans or public inns, so that every stranger quarters himself upon some inhabitant; and the people of Derayeh are proverbially hospitable. The immediate neighbourhood is barren, yielding only some date-trees. Derayeh is supplied with provisions chiefly from Dhoroma, a large and populous village, one day's journey towards the E. or N.E., which has gardens and orchards well watered from copious wells.

From Derayeh to Mekka is a distance of eleven or twelve long caravan days' journies. For three days beyond Derayeh are found cultivated spots and small settlements of Arabs; the rest of the road is through a desert country, as far as Wady Zeyme, two days from Mekka. The distance from Rass (in Kasym) to Mekka is also computed at twelve days' journey. This latter road abounds more with water than the former, and likewise passes by Wady Zeyme.

A straight road from Nedjed to the mountains of Hedjaz (I use this word here in the Bedouin sense, meaning the mountains south of Tayf), and to the country of Beishe and Yemen, passes by the village of Derye, on the southern extremity of Nedjed, on the great road from Kasym to Mekka. The road from Derye to Beishe lies four or five days east of Mekka. Between Derye and Taraba (above mentioned) is a pasture-land, with many wells, called El Bakarra, a well-known halting-place of all the Bedouins of these countries. It belongs to the Kereyshát tribe, a branch of the Sabya Arabs inhabiting Ranye.

Nedjed is celebrated throughout Arabia for its excellent pastures, which abound even in its deserts after rain: its plains are frequented by innumerable Bedouins, who continue there for most of the year, and purchase corn and barley from the inhabitants. During the rainy season these Bedouins retire towards the interior of the Desert, where they remain until the rain-water collected in the hollow grounds is consumed by their cattle. Previous to the Wahaby establishment, the pasturage of Nedjed belonged exclusively to the Aenezes,

APPENDIX.

which I have already mentioned as the largest of all the Bedouin tribes of Arabia. Great numbers of them frequented this territory in spring, and kept off all the other tribes, except the powerful Meteyr, who reside in the Desert between Kasym and Medina. These strengthened their party by an alliance with the Kahtan Arabs, while the Aenezes were assisted by the Beni Shaman. Between these tribes an inveterate hatred subsisted, which every spring was the cause of much bloodshed, and checked the commercial intercourse with the Hedjaz; and both parties levied contributions on the settled inhabitants of Nedjed: but this custom has been abolished by the Wahabys, whose chief, instead, receives a regular tribute, and has reconciled the hostile parties, and opened the pastures of Nedjed to any tribes of Wababys who may choose to frequent them. A Bedouin assured me that twenty encampments of different tribes may now be seen here in the course of one day's march—such is the security maintained by the Wahaby chief, who is inexorable in the punishment of robbers.

The fine pastures of Nedjed have produced an excellent breed of camels, more numerous here than in any other Arabian province of equal extent. The Arabs call this country *Om el Bel*, or " the mother of camels," and resort to it from all quarters for the supply of their own herds; and it constantly furnishes not only Hedjaz, but Syria and Yemen, with camels, of which useful creatures an ordinary one is sold for about ten dollars in Nedjed. In this country there is also a most excellent breed of horses, so remarkable that the finest blood Arabs are properly denominated *Kheyl Nedjade*, or Nedjed horses. But the Wahaby power has caused a diminution of this breed; for many Arabs have sold their best horses in foreign parts, lest they should be forced to attend the Wahaby chief, who, in his wars, frequently required cavalry.

Nedjed, however, is often subject to scarcity, caused by the failure of rain, and consequently of herbage: this soon affects the cattle of the Bedouins, who seldom expect, in this country, more than three or four successive years of plenty, although absolute famine does not occur above once in ten, or perhaps fifteen years. It is generally accompanied by epidemical diseases, much like the plague, consisting of violent fevers (but without biles or buboes,) that prove fatal to great numbers. Nedjed is peopled by small tribes of Bedouins, who never leave it, and by settlers intermarried with them, and often travelling as merchants to Damascus, Baghdad, Medina, Mekka, and Yemen: they export camels and woollen cloaks (abbas), of which the best are manufactured at El Hassa; and from Baghdad they receive rice, (the produce of the banks of the Tigris), and articles of dress, especially the keffies, or handkerchiefs, striped green and yellow, of cotton, wool, or silk: these the Bedouins wear over their bonnets. From Mekka they get coffee, drugs, andperfumes, much used among them, particularly the perfume called *Arez*, which comes from Mokha. In general there is a spirit of commerce very prevalent in Nedjed, where the merchants are wealthy and of better repute for honesty than most of the Eastern traders. The settlers here are armed with matchlocks, and constitute the best portion of the Wahaby infantry: they are generally successful against the Bedouins who invade their crops or pastures; and, as saltpetre is found in Nedjed, every family makes its own yearly provision of gunpowder.

In Nedjed are many ancient wells, lined with stone, and ascribed by the inhabitants to a primeval race of giants. They are generally from twenty-five to thirty fathoms deep, and mostly the property of individuals, who exact a certain contribution from the tribes whose cattle they supply with water. Here likewise are numerous remains of ancient buildings, of very massive structure and large dimensions, but in a state of complete ruin. These are attributed to a primitive (or perhaps a fabulous) tribe of Arabs, the Beni Tamour, of whose supposed works some vestiges are likewise seen in the Syrian deserts eastward of the plains of Hauran.

Of all the Bedouin tribes that exist in Arabia, some few families at least may be found in Nedjed, to which refugees fly for security against their enemies. This country, in fact, is not only the seat of the Wahaby government, but seems the most important of the interior districts of Arabia, from its fertility and population, its central position, and facility of intercourse with other provinces. To acquire a perfect knowledge of the Bedouins, it would be necessary to examine them in Nedjed, where their manners continue unaltered by conquest, and retaining all their original purity: nor have they been contaminated by an influx of strangers; for, except the Hadj caravan coming from Baghdad, no foreigners ever pass through Nedjed. For this reason I consider Nedjed and the mountains between Tayf and Sanaa as the most interesting portion of Arabia, affording more objects of inquiry to a traveller than any other part of the peninsula.

From Derayeh eastward towards the Persian Gulf, the country is called Zedeyr, as far as the limits of the province of El Hassa, six days distant from Derayeh, of which three days are without water. The district of Hassa (or, as it is sometimes written, El Absa) is celebrated for its numerous wells, and extends for about two days' journey parallel with the sea-coast, from which it is distant, inland, fifty or sixty miles. In breadth it is about thirty-five miles. The abundance of water enables the Arabs to cultivate clover, which serves to feed their finest horses. The Wahaby chief sends all his horses to this place every season.

The town of El Hassa (built by the Karmates in the tenth century) is populous; in it reside some wealthy merchants. It has walls and towers, and was successfully defended against the Pasha of Baghdad in 1797. It is one of the principal strongholds of the Wahabys; and their chief derives from this fertile district the greater part of his income. The sea-port for El Hassa is Akyr, a small town on the Persian Gulf, much frequented by the Arabs of Maskat and the pirates of the Kowasem (qy. Jowasem) tribe, who inhabit the port of Ras el Kheyme. The woollen cloaks, or abbas, made at El Hassa are in great demand all over Arabia and Mesopotamia: they cost from ten to fifty dollars each.

The territory of Hassa contains about twenty villages: the principal Bedouins that inhabit it are the Beni Khaled (a tribe extended over many parts of Arabia), the Bisher Arabs, a tribe of the Benezes, and the El Zab tribe. Here also, as well as in Nedjed, are some of the Beni Hosseyn, a tribe belonging to the Persian sect of Moslims.

Between El Hassa and Basra, water abounds. The road from Derayeh to Baghdad leads through the provinces of Kasym and Djebel Shammar, taking a western direction, because in a direct line no water is found in the Desert. Having reached Kowar, a small town on the frontiers of Kasym, towards Djebel Shammar (eight days from Derayeh), the traveller proceeds one day's journey to Kahfe, a village within the territory of Djebel Shammar. The road continues two days in the cultivated parts of this province as far as the well of

Shebeyke, which bounds Shammar on this side. From thence is one day's journey to Lyne, famous for its numerous and abundant wells, that supplied the whole Wahaby army with water: this place is much frequented by the Aeneze Arabs. Between Nedjed and the Euphrates a well in the Desert furnishes sulphur to the powder manufactories of Nedjed.

From Lyne three days' journey, in a desert without water, brings the traveller to the well of Shebekka, and from that one day to the town of Meshehd Aly. This is the summer route: in winter, when the rain-water is collected in ponds on the way, the Arabs travel from the well of Shebekka by the road called Derb Bereydha, the ancient Hadj route of the Khalifes when they went on pilgrimage. Here are many tanks, cased with stone, constructed by the Khalifes to supply the pilgrims with water; and the road passes straight on from Meshehd Aly towards Djebel Shammar, without touching at Lyne. From Meshehd Aly to Djebel Shammar the distance is reckoned eight days, and the traveller from Baghdad to Nedjed always passes by the tomb of Aly. This route is much frequented, especially by the Ageyl Arabs of Baghdad, of whom many are from Nedjed, which they often visit as pedlars. All the Arabian Bedouins settled in the suburbs of Baghdad are comprised under the name of Ageyl. This was once a powerful tribe, but it has much degenerated.

Through the province of Djebel Shammar, or, as it is commonly called, El Djebel, lies also the road from Nedjed to Damascus. It is a mountainous tract to the N.E. of the province of Kasym, bearing from Medina E.N.E. Its inhabitants are the powerful Beni Shammar, a tribe of which some have passed over to Mesopotamia. Their Sheikh, Ibn Aly, is a main supporter of the Wahaby government. They are said to muster seven thousand matchlocks; and, like their neighbours in Nedjed, they cultivate palm-trees by means of water drawn up from wells in leathern buckets by camels. One of the principal towns in Djebel Shammar, is El Mestadjedde: the chief town is said to be El Hayl; and the next in size, Kofár.

From Djebel Shammar to Damascus the road passes by the district El Djof, which is five days distant from it. The road is of deep sand, without any water but what is afforded by the well of Shageyg, four days from Djebel Shammar, and one from Djof. I believe that there is no other station of equal length entirely destitute of water, in any part of Arabia frequented by caravans, like the four days between Djebel and Shageyg. The well of Shageyg belongs to the Aenezy tribe of Rowalla; and whoever wishes to go from Southern Syria to Nedjed, must necessarily pass here. There is not any water from Djof southwards, in a direct line towards Khaibar and Medina; the road is therefore not frequented. Arabs going from Djof to Medina must pass by Shageyg and Shammar and Kasym, taking a circuitous route.

My residence at Medina in time of war, when the eastern and northern Bedouins were hostile, and did not come into the town, prevented me from acquiring as much information as if a peaceable intercourse had subsisted. Whenever this is the case, small caravans from Khaibar and Teyme frequently repair to Medina. Khaibar is well known in Arabian history, as the scene of early Muselman wars under Mohammed, Aly, and their successors. It is said to be four or five days (some say only three) from Medina, the road passing between the Hadj route to Damascus and the route to Kasym. The Arabs of Khaibar, in time of peace, bring their dates for sale to Medina. They are said to be of a darker complexion than the surrounding Bedouins: this may be caused by the great heat in the low situation of that place. Khaibar is about six hours distant from the Hadj route to Syria, and lies, I believe, in a direction N.E. from Medina. It appears in former times to have formed part of the territory of the Sherif of Mekka. When the Sherif Hassan Abou Nema was installed in 966, (A. H.) his territory, as we learn from Asamy, comprised Mekka, Tayf, Gonfode, Haly, Yembo, Medina, and Khaibar. The present inhabitants of Khaibar are the Wold Aly, a tribe of Aenezes mustering about three hundred horsemen, whose sheikh Aleyda distinguished himself in the Wahaby war. Another branch of the Wold Aly inhabit the deserts near Hauran, south of Damascus. At Khaibar also are encampments of the Oulad Soleyman, a tribe of the Bisher Arabs (likewise of the Aeneze nation); but the Wold Aly possess the ground and the date-plantations.

A colony of Jews formerly settled at Khaibar has wholly disappeared. It is commonly believed at Mekka and Djidda, that their descendants still exist there, strictly performing the duties of their religion; but, upon minute inquiry at Medina, I found this notion to be unfounded, nor are there any Jews in the northern parts of the Arabian Desert. The Jews who were formerly settled in Arabia, belonged to the tribe of Beni Koreyta (Caraites). They came to Medina after Nebuchadnezzar had taken Jerusalem; when Kerb Ibn Hassan el Hemyary (one of the Toba kings of Yemen who had possessed themselves of Mekka) made an inroad towards Medina, which he besieged, and on his return from thence carried some of the Beni Koreyta with him to Yemen. These are the first Jews who settled in that country, and their descendants still remain at Szanaa. (See Samhoudy's History of Medina.)

The small town of Teyme is three days from Khaibar, and as many from Hedjer, in an eastern direction. It is inhabited by the Aeneze Arabs, and abounds with dates. It belongs neither to Nedjed nor Kasym, and, like Khaibar, was an independent Bedouin settlement before the time of the Wahabys. Those small towns in the interior of the Arabian Desert, are like the Oases in the Libyan; and serve as points of intercourse between the Bedouins and the neighbouring cultivated countries. Their Bedouin inhabitants are agriculturists, and mostly petty merchants who sell to their wandering brethren of the Desert the goods which they purchase at the first cost in the Syrian or Arabian towns. Beginning northward with the small town of Deir on the Euphrates, we can trace a line of these oases that form advanced points towards the Desert all the way south as far as Medina. Deir, Sokhne, Tedmor, Djof, Maan, Ola, Khaibar, and Teyme, are all inhabited by Bedouins, who cultivate the soil, and form an intermediate class between Bedouins and peasants. These positions would be highly important to those who might wish to subdue, or at least to check the Bedouins; and they might become of still greater importance, in being rendered the means of inspiring the whole Bedouin nation with more amicable sentiments towards the Syrian and Hedjaz inhabitants.

No. VII.

Postscript to the Description of the Beitullah or Mosque at Mekka—(See p. 161.)

THE law forbids that blood should be shed either in the mosque or town of Mekka, or within a small space around it: neither is it lawful there to cut down trees, or to kill game. This privilege of the mosque is generally respected in common cases of delinquency, and many criminals take refuge in the Beitullah accordingly; but it is also frequently violated. I have myself seen Mohammed Aly's soldiers pursue a deserter, seize and carry him off from the covering of the Kaaba to which he had clung; and the history of Mekka cites numerous examples of men killed in the mosque,—among others the Sherif of Mekka, Djazan Ibn Barakat, assassinated while he performed the towaf round the Kaaba. Sanguinary battles (as in A. H. 817.) have even been fought within its sacred precincts, which afford the most open spot in the town for skirmishing. Horsemen have often entered and passed a whole night in it. Therefore we may say that the privilege is generally useless in those cases where it would be most valuable; such as the protection of fugitives from the powerful oppressor. As to the sanctity of the territory, it is but a name, and seems to have been little respected even in the first ages of Islám. The extent of the sacred territory is variously stated by the three historians whose works I possess, and who were themselves Mekkans. The four Imáms or founders of the orthodox sects also disagree upon the subject. At present the privilege of the sacred territory seems almost forgotten; and it has been crossed in every direction by infidel Christians employed in the army of Mohammed Aly or Tousoun Pasha, who, though they have not entered Mekka, have visited Mount Arafat. Contrary to the precepts of Mohammed, wood is now cut in the mountains close behind Mekka, and no one is prevented from shooting in the neighbouring valleys. The plain of Arafat alone is respected, and there the trees are never cut down. The sacred district, or, as it is called, *Hedoud el Haram* (the limits of the Haram), is at present commonly supposed to be enclosed by those positions where the ihram is assumed on the approach to Mekka: those are, *Hadda* to the west, *Asfan* to the north, *Wady Mohrem* to the east, and *Zat Ork* to the south. Aly Bey el Abbassi has represented this district, in his map, as a particular province or sacred territory called Belad el Harameyn: but in fact, no such province has ever existed; and the title of Belad el Harameyn is given, not to this sacred space, but to both the territories of Mekka and Medina.

No. VIII.

Philological Observations.

MANY Arabic terms which have become obsolete in other places, and are found only in the good authors, many expressions even of the Koran, no longer used elsewhere, are heard at Mekka in the common conversation of the people, who retain, at least in part, the original language of the Koreysh. Some neighbouring Bedouin tribes, especially those of Fahm and Hodheyl, use a dialect still more pure and free from provincialisms and grammatical errors. I sometimes attended the lectures of a Sheikh in the mosque, who to his own excellent native Arabic had added the result of his studies at Cairo: and I never heard finer Arabic spoken. He prided himself in sounding all the vowels, not only in reading, but even in conversation; and every word he uttered might be noted as of standard purity.

It is to their extensive commerce with foreigners that we must ascribe the corruption of the Mekkan dialect when compared with that of the neighbouring Bedouins, though it still serves as a model of softness to the natives of Syria and Egypt. In pronunciation, the Mekkans imitate the Bedouin purity—every letter has its precise and distinct sound: they pronounce ك like *k*, and the ق like a soft *g*, (as in the word *going*); although in the public service of the mosque, and in reading the Koran, they express that letter with the guttural aspiration given to it in Syria, and which is therefore regarded as the true pronunciation. The ج is pronounced *djem*; but in the mountains to the south, and the interior of Yemen, it is sounded *gym*, as at Cairo. The guttural pronunciation of the *elif* ا, often neglected in other places, is here strictly observed. The only fault in the Mekkan pronunciation is, that in common with the Bedouins they sometimes give, in words of two syllables, too great an emphasis to the last: thus they say *Zāhāb*, (ذهب) *Sāfar*, (سفر) *Lāhēm*, (لحم) *Mātār*, (مطر) *Sābȳ*, (صبي) and others.

The people of Yemen whom I saw at Mekka pronounced and spoke Arabic almost equally well as the Mekkans: those from Szanaa spoke with purity, but a harsh accent; but the Hedjazi, like the Bedouin accent, is as soft as the language will admit.

It has been said that the dialects of Arabic differ widely from each other; and Michaelis, one of the most learned orientalists, affirms that the Hedjazi is as different from the Moggrebyn dialect as Latin from Italian; and a noble Sherif traveller makes a strong distinction between Moorish and Arabic, pretending to understand the latter and not the former; and even the accurate and industrious Niebuhr seems to have entertained some erroneous notions on this subject. But my own inquiries have led me to a very different opinion. There certainly exists a great variety of dialects in Arabic; more perhaps than in other languages: but notwithstanding the vast extent of country in which Arabic prevails, from Mogador to Maskat, whoever has learned one dialect will easily understand all the others. In respect to pronunciation, whoever can spell correctly will feel little em-

APPENDIX. 467

barrassment from the diversity of sound, and soon become familiar with it. The same sense is often expressed by different terms; but this is applicable rather to substantive nouns than to verbs. Many words are used in one country and not in another: thus *bread* is called *khobs* in Syria, and *aysh* in Egypt; both terms being genuine Arabic, a language rich in synonyms: but the Syrian dialect still retains what has become obsolete in the Egyptian. From the specimen given by Niebuhr of the Egyptian and Hedjazi dialect, I could show, word by word, that there is not one provincialism in the whole. If the Egyptian says *okod*, and the Arabian *edjles*, they both use genuine Arabic words to express the same thing, one of which is more common in Arabia, the other in Egypt, when both terms are well understood by all who have mixed in the busy crowd, or have had even an ordinary education. An Englishman is justified in using "steed" for "horse;" thus the Moggrebyn calls a horse *owd*, the eastern Arab *hoszán*; but many poets use the word *owd*, which is at present unknown to the vulgar in Egypt. This variation of terms arose probably from the settlement of different tribes, each having their peculiar vocabulary; for it is known that Feyrouzabády compiled the materials of his celebrated Dictionary (the *Kámous*) by going from one tribe to another. The Arabs spreading over conquered countries took their idioms with them, but the joint-stock of the language continued known to all who could read or write.

Pronunciation may have been affected by the nature of different countries, retaining its softness in the low valleys of Egypt and Mesopotamia, and becoming harsh among the frozen mountains of Barbary and Syria. As far as I know, the greatest difference exists between the Moggrebyns of Marocco, and the Hedjaz Bedouins near Mekka; but their dialects do not differ more from each other than the German of a Suabian peasant does from that of a Saxon. I have heard learned men of Syria express their ignorance of many Bedouin terms used by tribes in the interior of the Desert, especially the Aenezey, who, on the other hand, do not comprehend certain words of the Syrian town-language; but the wants and habits of a Bedouin are so different from those of a town-person, that the one frequently cannot find terms to express the ideas of the other.

As to pronunciation, the best is that of the Bedouins of Arabia, of the Mekkans, and people of the Hedjaz; that of Baghdad and of Yemen is next in purity. At Cairo the pronunciation is worse than in any other part of Egypt; after which I should rank the language of the Libyan Arabs, who have a tinge of the Moggrebyn pronunciation mixed with the Egyptian. Then comes the Arabic spoken in the eastern and western plains of Syria, (at Damascus, Aleppo, and on the sea-coast); then the dialect of the Syrian mountaineers, the Druzes, and Christians; next, that of the Barbary coast, of Tripoly, and of Tunis; and lastly, the rough articulation of the Marocco and Fez people, which has a few sounds different from any other, and is subdivided into several dialects. The Arabs, however, of the eastern side of Mount Atlas, at Tafilelt, and Draa, pronounce their Moggrebyn tongue with much less harshness than their western neighbours. But I must acknowledge, that of all Arabic dialects, none appeared to me so disagreeable and so adulterated as that of the young Christian fops of Cairo and Aleppo.

No. IX.

*Topographical Notices of the Valley of Mekka and its Mountains; extracted from the History of Azraky, showing the names assigned to every part.**

THE different mountains forming the southern chain of the valley of Mekka are:— *Djebel Fádeh*, on the lower part of Djebel Kobeys, nearest to the town—*El Khandame*, likewise part of Djebel Kobeys—*Djebel el Abyadh*, called among the Pagan Arabs *Mestebzera*, belonging also to Djebel Kobeys—*Mozazem*—*Korn Meskale*, lower ridge of Shab Aamer—*Djebel Benhán*, ibid.—*Djebel Yakyán*, on the side of Shab Aamer—*Djebel el Aaredj*, near the latter—*Djebel el Motábekh*, or Shab Aamer; so called because the Toba kings of Yemen, when they invaded Mekka, established here their kitchen—*Shab Abou Dobb*—*Shab e' Szafa*, or *Djebel Ráha, Shab Beni Kenáne*—*Shab el Khor*—*Shab Athmen*.

On the northern side are:—*El Hazoura*; here was formerly the market of Mekka—*El Djethme*—*Zogág el Nár*—*Beit el Ezlám*—*Djebel Zerzera*, in the Djehelye called *El Káym*—*Djebel Omar*, in the Djehelye called *Da Aasyr*—*Djebel el Adkhar*,† in the time of the Djehelye called *El Mozhebát*, or *El Aadhad*—*Djebel el Hazna*—*Shab Arny*—*Thenyet Keda Batn Zy Towa*—*Djebel el Mokta*—*Fah*, a valley beyond the Djidda gate—*El Momdera*—*El Moghesh*, from whence was cut the white marble used in the mosque—*El Herrowra*—*Istár*—*Mokbaret el Noszára*, the burial-ground of the Christians—*Djebel el Beroud*—*Thenyet el Beydha*—*El Hashás*—*Da el Medowar*—*Djebel Moslim*—*Wády Zy Towa*—*Thenyet Om el Harth*—*Djebel Aby el Keyt*—*Fedj*—*Shab Ashras*—*Shab el Motallęb*—*Zát Khalilyn*—*Djebel Kabsh*—*Djebel Rahhá*—*El Bagheybagha*—*Djebel Keyd*—*El Ark*—*Zát el Hantal*—*El Akla*—*Shab el Irnye*—*El Alká*—*Shab el Leben*—*Melhet el Ghoraba*—*Melhet el Herouth*—*Kaber el Abd*.

On the lower side of Mekka are:—*Adjyád*, or *Djyad*—*Ras el Insán*, between the Djebel Kobeys and Adjyád—*Shab el Khatem*, near Adjyád—*Djebel Khalife*—*Djebel Oráb*—*Djebel Omar*—*Ghadaf*—*El Mokba*—*El Lahdje*—*El Kadfade*—*Zát el Lahá*—*Zou Merah*—*Es Selfeyn*—*El Dokhádekh*—*Zou el Shedyd*—*Zát e' Selym*—*Adhat el Nabt*, so called from some Nabateans who resided there, and were sent by Mawya Ibn Aly Sofyán to make mortar at Mekka—*Om Kerdan*.

On the north side of the Mala are—*Djebel Deylamy*—*Djebel Sheyb*—*Djebel Habeshy*—

---

* It may be here remarked, that the Bedouins of the present day continue to bestow on the smallest hill, projecting rock, or little plain, a distinct and particular name; which circumstance renders the history of Arabia often obscure, as the names have, in the course of ages, sometimes changed.

† *El Adkhar* is a shrub or plant, mixed by the Mekkans with mortar in the construction of their houses. *El Aadhad* a thorny tree, common in Arabia.

Shab el Mokbera—Abou Dedjáne—Djebel el Lyám—El Ghoráb—Shab el Akhnes, also called *El Khowaredj*, or *El Gheyshoum—El Káad*.

On the road towards Mekka are:—*El Mofdjer*, or *El Khoder—Shab Howa—Er Rebáb. Zou el Aráke—El Ambara*, in the Djehelye called *Semyra—E' Seder.*

On the road towards Djebel Thor, southward of Mekka, are:—*Zát el Lakhob—Zát Ardjá—El Kaflye—Thor—*and *El Bána*.

No. X.

ADDITIONAL NOTES.

Mokhowa, مخوات mentioned in pp. 112, 189, &c. must not be confounded with *Mokha*, مخا on the sea-coast. *Mokhowa* is a town ten days distant from Mekka at the western foot of the great chain of mountains.

The word *Hedjer*, حجر mentioned in p. 139, is not to be mistaken for *Hadjar*, a stone: the space of ground is called *Hedjer* "because it is separated from the Kaaba or Beitullah;" حجر بسبب انه محجور من البيت—

Page 299—The *Beni Amer*—The word *Amer* عامر in this place must not be confounded with *Amer* عمر another tribe of Harb. The damma in عمر is never pronounced by the Arabians, who say *Amr Ibn el Lás*, (الاص ابن عمر) and not *Amrou Ibn el Lás*, placing the damma merely to distinguish the word from عمر *Omar*.

INDEX OF ARABIC WORDS.

Names of Countries and Cities frequently mentioned. —
Hedjáz, حجاز—Mekka, مكة—Medina, مدينه—Tayf, طايف—
Djidda, جده—Yembo, ينبع—Nedjed, نجد &c.

PAGE		PAGE	
xxii.	Asamy, عصمي	56.	Shemeysa, شميسه
3.	Seyd Mohammed el Mahrouky, سيد محمد المحروقي	57.	Djerouel, جرول
		58.	Moábede, معابده—Wady Muna, وادي منى
4.	Araby Djeylani, عربي جيلاني		
6.	Seyd Aly Odjakly, سيد علي اوجقلي	59.	Sebyl - es - Sett, سبيل الست — Mohsab, محصب—Mezdelife, مزدلفه
29.	Homar, حمر—Ruteb, رطب		
30.	Baklawa, بقلاء—Gnáfe, تنافه		
31.	Bastorma, بسطرمه	60.	Kazeh, قزح—Dhob, ضب—Mazomeyn, مازمين — Medyk, مضيق—Nimre, نمره
34.	The wants of a man, حاجت الرجل		
37.	Yosser, يسر		
44.	Hosh, حوش	61.	Arafat, عرفاة—Kebákeb, كباكب—Ryshye, ريشيه
52.	Khayn, خاين — Khán, خان — Ykhoun يخون		
		63.	Kora, كرا
53.	Ragháme, رغامه — Beyadhie, بياضيه—Feráyne, فراينه	65.	Nakeb el Ahmar, نقب الاحمر—Beled, بلد
54.	Bahhra, بحره—Hadda, حده	84.	Ghazoan, غزوان

INDEX OF ARABIC WORDS.

86. Thekyf, تثقيف—Hamde, حمد—Themále, ثماله
87. Zeyme, زيمه
91. Mashrabe, مشربه
94. Metowef, مطوف
95. Meltezem, ملتزم
96. Szafa, صفي—Say, سعي—El Myleyn el Akhdereyn, الميلين الاخضرين
98. Motam, مطعم—Nehyk, نهيك
107. Ayn Arf, عين عرف—Shámekh, شامخ
109. Háret, حارت—Shebeyka, شبيكه
110. El Khanduryse, الخندريسه
112. Hadjela, هجله—Mesfale, مسفله—Mokhowa, مخواه
113. Aabedye, عابديه—Birket Mádjen, بركت ماجن
115. El Djyad, الجياد
116. Mesaa, مصعي
118. Soueyga, سويقه
121. Keffie, كفيه—(plural, كفاني)
122. Garara, قراره—Lala, لعلع
123. Keykaan, تعيقان—Rekoube, ركوبه—Modaa, مدعه—Gesháshye, تشاسيه—Shab el Moled, شعب المولد
124. Ghazze, غزه—Mala, معلا
125. Wady el Naga, وادي النقي
126. Zokak el Merfek, زقاق المرفق
128. Shab Aamer, شعب عامر—handmills, (rahha) رحا
129. Hazna, حزنه
130. Moabede, معابده
136. Kaaba, كعبه
138. Madjen, معجن—Myzab, ميزب
139. El Hatym, الحطيم—Hedjer, حجر
140. Kesoua, كسوة
141. Uryán, عريان
145. Kobbateyn, قبتين
151. Kotob Muhbat o Kuboul, كتب محبت و قبول
152. Báb el Zeyt, باب الزيت—Baghle, بغله—Medjahed, مجاهد—Zoleykha, زليخه—Om Hany, ام هاني—Wodaa, وداع—Beni Sheybe, بني شيبه—Djenaiz, جنايز—Sertakát, سرطاقات—Bazan, بازان—Makhzoum, مخزوم—Dokhmase, دخمسة—Sherif Adjelan, شريف عجلان—Hazoura, حزورة—Kheyatyn, خياطين—Djomah, جمح
153. Al Omra, العمرة—Beni Saham, بني سهم—Ateik, عطيق—Bastye, باسطيه—Kotoby, قطبي—Zyáde, زياده—Dereybe, دريبه—Sedra, سدرة—Adjale, عجله—Zyade Dar el Nedoua, زيادة دار الندوة
157. Greek Surra, صرة الرومي
158. Agat el Towáshye, اغاة الطواشيه
171. Mokhtaba, مختبا
172. Kobbet el Wahy, قبة الوحي
173. Umna, امنه
174. Abou Kobeys, ابو قبيس

INDEX OF ARABIC WORDS.

175. Mogharat el Hira, مغارة الحجرة— Djebel Hirá, جبل حرا
176. Thor, ثور—Bir Tinaym, بير تنعيم—Ahlyledge, اهليلجة
183. Meshale, مشاله—Beden, بدن
184. Fan used at Mekka, مروحه
185. Habra, حبرة—Borko, برقع
195. Muhallil, محلل
200. Rukub el Medina, ركب المدينه
205. "In el Haram fi belád el Harameyn," ان الحرم في بلاد الحرمين
216. Djok, جوق
220. Dwy Barakát, دوي بركات—Abou Nema, ابو نمي— Abadele, عبادله—Ahl Serour, اهل سرور—Herázy, حرازي—Hamoud, حمود— Souamele, سوامله— Shambar, شنبر— Thokaba, ثقبة—Djazan, جازان—Báz, باز
230. Mowaly, موالي
231. Morabby, مربي
248. Mekowem, مقوم
257. Kánoun, كانون
262. Sabbák, سباق
275. Djamrat el Owsat, جمرة الاوسط— Sofaly, سفلي — El Aksa, الاقصي
277. Muna, مني
278. Kheyf, خيف
281. Medjna, مجنة — Zou el Medjáz, ذو المجاز—Hásha, حاشة

284. Towaf el Ifadhe, طواف الافاضه
292. Meymounye, ميمونيه — Wady Fátme, وادي فاطمه— Djemmoum, جموم—Medoua, مدوة— Merr, مر—Serouat, صروعة— Rekany, ركاني
295. Barka, برقا—Kara, قرة— Ma Wardy, ما ء وردي
296. "But their government is good," ولكن حكمهم طيب
297. Bir Asfán, بير عسفان—Owla, عولا—Kholeys, خليص
299. Wady Khowar, وادي خوار — Thenyet, ثنية
300. Kolleya, كليّه—Kobeyba, كبيبه—Abou Shyh, ابو شيح—Agál, عقال—Ateybe, عتيبه
301. Rábegh, رابغ—Owf, عوف
304. Mastoura, مستورة
305. Medjbá, مجباه—Sobh, صبح
306. Wady Zogág, وادي زقاق
307. Wild chesnut-trees, شجر ابو فروة
309. Beshem, بشم
311. El Kharma, الخرمة — Dár el Hamra دار الحمرة — Howaseb, حواسب
312. Mokad, مقعد
313. El Názye, النازية
315. El Fereysh, الفريش — El Hamede, الحامده
316. El Djohfe, الجحفة
322. Tahama, تهامه

INDEX OF ARABIC WORDS.

323. Sabbak, سبك
324. El Belát البلاط — Es' Saha, الساحة — Komet Hasheyfe كومة حشيفه — Zogág el Towal, زقاق الطوال — El Dhorra, الضرة — Sakyfet El Shakhy, سقيفة شخي — El Bakar, البقر—El Hamáta, الحماطه—El Habs, الحبس—Ankyny, عنقيني—Semáhedy, السماهدي—Háret el Meyda, حارت الميضة — Shershoura, شرشورة — Bedour, بدور — El Agowat, الاغوات — Derwán, درون—Es' Salehye, الصالحيه—Zogag Yahou, زقاق ياهو—Ahmed Heydar, احمد حيضر—Besough, بسوغ—Sakyfet, سقيفة—Er' Resás, الرصاص—Zerendy, ذرندي — Kibreit, كبريت
325. Hadjámyn, حجامين — Kamáshyn, قماشين
326. Monákh, مناخ—Hosh, حوش
327. El Ambarye, العنبريه—Wájeha, واجها—Es' Sahh, السم—Abou Aysa, ابو عيسي—Masr, مصر—El Teyár, الطيار—Nefyse, نفيسه — Hamdye, حمديه — Shahrye, شحريه — Kheybarye, خيبريه — El Aala, الاعلي—Zobáb, زباب—Sola, سلع

328. Seyl el Medina, سيل المدينه—Bathán, بطحان—El Ghába, الغابة—Zaghába, زغابة
334. Kokab ed' durry, كوكب الدري
336. Mahbat Djybrail, مهبط جبريل
337. El Rodha, الروضة—"Between my tomb," &c. مابين قبري ومنبري روضة من رياض الجنة
339. "Destroy our enemies," &c. — دمر اعدابنا و لهم عذاب النار Shobák en' Neby, شباك النبي — Fátme e' Zohera, فاطمة الزهرة
341. Es' Sháme, الشامه—Báb Merouan, باب مروان
342. Ed' Djeber, الجبر—El Nesa, النسا
344. Ferráshyn, فراشين
354. Nowakhele, نواخله
356. Djebely, جبلي—Heloua, حلوه—Heleya, حليه—El Syhány, صيحاني
357. Birny, برني—Djeleby, جلبي—Kalayd es' Shám, تلايد الشام—Rotab, رطب
358. Ithel, اثل—El Medshounye, المدشونبه
359. El Shathat, الشطات — Wayra, وعيرة
360. Thor, ثور
362. El Bekya, البقيع
364. El Goreyn, القرين

INDEX OF ARABIC WORDS.

367. Kheroa, خروع — Mobrak el Náka, مبرك الناقة
368. Ayn Ezzerka, عين الزرقا
370. Ows, اوس—Khezredj, خزرج
371. Nowakhele, نواخله
378. Fera, الفرع
392. Merábetein, مرابطين
401. Wady el Akyk, وادي العقيق—Al Madderidge, المدرجه
402. Esselsele, السلسله—El Ghaba, الغابه—Zághaba, زغابه—Kasr el Merádjel, قصر المراجل—El Nakya, النقيع—Zy'l Haleyfe, ذي الحفلفه
403. Wady Medyk, وادي مديق
405. El Waset الواسط — Thenyet Waset, ثنية واسط—Fára, فارع—Barake, بَرَك—Beder Honeyn, يدرحنين
407. Rukb, ركب — El Ghemáme, الغمامه
408. Goz Aly, قوز علي—Bereyke, بريكه
409. Adheyba, عضيبة
412. "God in his mercy," &c. هذا رحمة من الله ولكن نحن ما لنا مستحقين الرحمة و نهرب منها
415. "Fly from the leprous," &c. فرّ من المجذوم كفرارك من الاسد
419. El Kad, القعد
420. Djeheyne, جهينه — Moeyleh, مويلح
421. Yembo el Nakhel, ينبع النخل—Gara Yembo, قرا ينبع [قرا] instead of قري or [قرايا]
Yembo el Berr, ينبع البرّ
422. Redoua, رضوي—Aseylya, عسيليه
428. Hassáni, حساني — Djeheyne, جهيني—El Wodjeh, الوجه—Heteym, هتيم—El Harra, الحرة
429. Arak, اراك
430. Mersá el Wodjeh, مرسا الوجه—Bily, البلي—Dhoba, ضبا—Moeyleh, مويلح
432. Sherm, شرم—Sheroum, شروم
433. El Hamra, الحمرة
439. El Merkhá, المخا
440. Osayt, اصيط—Gharendel, غرندل—Seder, سدر
445. Kebsy, كبسي—Shedád, شداد—Kura, كرا—Abbasa, عباسه—Mellawy Djedára, ملاوي جدارة—Mekhra, مخرة—Naszera, ناصرة—Lagham, لغم—Sour, صور—Bedjeyle, بجيله—Esserar, السرار—Berahrah, برحرح — Zohran, زهران — Meshnye, مشنية Raghdan, رغدان — Ghámed, غامد — Korn el Maghsal, قرن المغسل—Al Záhera, ال زاهرة
446. El Roheyta, الرهيطه—Shomrán, شمران — Adama, ادمه — Tabála, تبالة—Hasba, حصبا—Asábely, عسابلي—Beni She-

INDEX OF ARABIC WORDS.

Sedouan, سدوان—بني شفره fra,
—Ahl Aryef, اهل العريف—
El Matfa, المطفا—Ibn Maan,
Asyr, عسير--Ibl, عبل--ابي معان
—Ibn el Shayr, ابن الشاير
—Dahbán, دهبان—Kahtan,
تحطان — Derb Ibn el
Okeyda, درب ابن العكيده —
Refeydha, رفيضة—Wakasha,
وكشه—Abyda, ابيده—Aryn,
عريي—Shouáwy, شواوي—Ahl
Sháh, اهل شاه—Ahl Bul, اهل
بل—Yaowd, يعوض—Howd
Ibn Zyád, حوض ابن زياد—
Thohran, ظهران — Wadaa,
وادعة—Keradh, كراض—Ro-
gháfa, رغافه—Sahhár, صحار
— Dohyán, ضحيان — Sa-
da, صعده — Woly, ولي —
Aashemye, عاشميه — Bekyl,
بكيل

447. Háshed, حاشد — Ghoulet
Adjeyb, غولة عجيب—Reyda,
ريده — Omrán, عمران—Ayál
Soráh, عيال سراح—Hamdán,
حمدان—Sanaa, صنعه

449. Beni Sad بني سعد — Begyle,
بقيله — Rehah, رحاح — El
Mandak, المندق — Bekaa,
بقاع—Sollebát, صليات—Kho-
tham, ختم — Bel Korn,
بل قرن—Ibn Dohmán, ابن
دهمان — Asmar, اسمر — El
Tor, الطور

450. Shekrateyn, شترتيي — Ed-
dahye, الضحيه — Shohata,
شوهطه — Ed-djof, الجوف —
Refeydha, رفيضه—Harradja,
حرجه — Senhán, سنحان —
Ráha, راحه—Homra, حمره—
Bágem, باقم—Kholan, خولان--
Beit Medjahed, بيت مجاهد
— Djorf, جرف—Kheywán,
خيوان--Houth, حوث--Zybein,
ذيبين—Lye, لية—Byssel, بسل
— Kolákh, كلاخ — Ossama,
عسمة—Abyla, ابيله

451. Begoum, بقوم—Ghálye, غاليه—
Ranye—رنية—Sabya, سبيعة
—Beishe, بيشه—Oklob, اقلب

452. Dowaser, دواسر — Nedjran,
نجران

453. Leith, ليث—Doga, دوقه—Haly
حلي

454. Mokhowa, مخواه—Djehádele,
جهادله — Lamlem, لملم —
Fahem, فهم — Roba el
Khaly, ربع الخالي

455. Djebryn, جبريى — Hassoua,
حصوة—Dar el Hamra, دار
الحمرة—Adjeroud, عجرود—
Rous el Nowatyr, روس
النواطير—Tyh, تيه—Nakhel,
نخل — El Alayá, العلايا—
Sath el Akaba, سطح العقبه
Thaher el Homár, ظهر الحمار

456. Shorafa, شرفه — Moghayr
Shayb, مغاير شعيب—Ayoun

INDEX OF ARABIC WORDS.

el Kassab, القصب عيون— Moeyleh, الموبلع — Selma, سلما — Kalat Ezlam, قلعة ازلم—Astabel Antar, اصطبل عنتر—Akra, عكرة—Howra, حورة—El Hank, الحنك Nabt, نبط — Khedheyra, خضيرة—Yembo el Nakhel, ينبع النخل — Beder, بدر — El Kaa, القاع—Djereynat, جرينات—Akabet e' Sukar, عقبة السكر—Kholeys, خليص —Asfán, عسفان

457. Medayen Saleh, مداين صالح— Sheffa, الشفّه — Essafaha, الصفحا

468. Areydh, عريض—Hafna, حفنا— Soweyder, الصويدر — Mezeyne, مزينه — Hanákye, حناكيه — Abou Kheshyeb, ابو خشيب—Heymedj, هيمج — El Mawát, الماوات — El Badje, البعجة—Taâye, طاعية —Neffoud, نفود—Ghereked-Dessem, غرق الدسم

459. Djerdáwye, جرداويه—Dat, الذات —Rass, الرص—Kasym, قصيم —Es-Shenáne, الشنانه—Balgha, بلغا — Heshashye, حشاشيه — Helálye, هلاليه— Bekeyrye, بكيريه—Batah el Nebhánye, بطاح النبهانيه— Ashebeybe, الشبيبه—Ayoun,

عيون—Kowár, قوار--Mozneb, الوشم El Woshem — مذنب العارض El Aredh,--سرّ‎ Sarr,— درعيه Derayeh,—

460. Mekren, مكرن — Essehoun, السحون—Dhorama, ضرمه— Derye, دريه—Bakarra, بقرة —Kereyshát, قريشات

461. Meteyr, مطير—Om el Bel, ام البل — Kheyl Nedjadi, خيل نجادي—Arz, ارز

462. Tamour, تعمور—Zedeyr, زدير— Hassa, حسا—Ahsa, احسا— Akyr, اكير—Bisher, بشر— El Zab, الزعب—Kahfe, كهفه

463. Lyne, لينة — Mestadjedde, مستجدة — Hayl, حايل — Kofár, كفار—Shageyg, شقيق Teyme, تيمه

468. Fádeh, فاضح — Khandame خندمه—Mestebzera, مستبزره —Mozazem, مزازم — Korn Meskale, مسقله قرن—Benhán, بنهان—Yakyán, يقيان —Aaredj, اعرج—Motabekh, متابخ—Shab Abou Dobb, شعب ابو دب — Khor, خور —Athmen, عثمن—Káym, قايم — El Adkhar, الادخر —Arny, ارني—Keda, كدا— Batn Zy Towa, بطن ذي طوي — Momdera, ممدره— Moghesh, مغش — Hashás,

INDEX OF ARABIC WORDS.

Fedj, قيط — Keyt, حصاص —
Kabsh, اشرس—Ashras, فج
بغيغة ,Bagheybagha — كبش
Ark, ارق—Keyd, كيد —
—عقلا Akla,—حنطل ,Hantel
علقا Alká, — ارنيه ,Irnye
Orab, عراب—Ghadáf, غدان
Mokba, متبعه — Lahdje,
لاحجه—Kadfade, قدندء —
A- — ضخاضخ ,Dokhadekh
dhat el Nabt, اضات النبط—
Om Kerdan, ام قردان

469. Dedjáne, دجانه—Lyam, ليام—
Akhnes, اخنس — El Kaad,
القاعد — Mofdjer, منجر —
Khoder, خضر—Shab Howa,
شعب حوا—Rebáb, رباب—Zou
al Aráke, ذو الاراكه—Ambara, انبره — Semyra, سميره —
Sedr, سدر—Zát el Lakhob,
ذات اللخب—Ardjá, ارجا —
Kaflye, قفلية—Thor, ثور—
El Bána, البانه*

THE END.

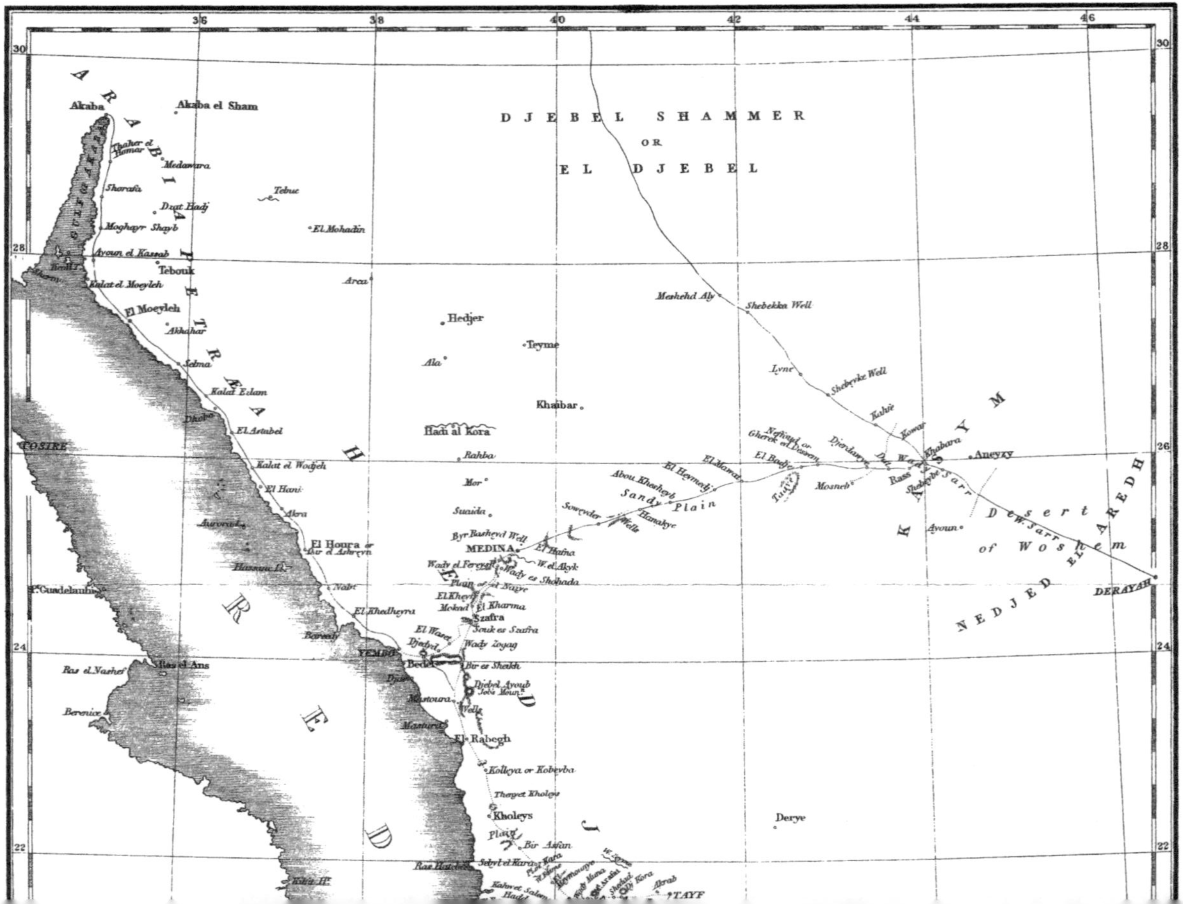

36
38
40
42
44
46
30
28
26
24
22
DJEBEL SHAMMER
OR
EL DJEBEL
ARABIA PETRÆA
HEDJAZ
RED SEA
NEDJED
KASYM
Desert of Woshem
EL AREDH
Akaba
Akaba el Sham
Medawara
Sharafa
Daat Hadj
Moghayr Shayb
Ayoun el Kassab
Tebouk
Tebuc
El Mohadin
Kalat el Moeyleh
El Moeyleh
Akhahar
Selma
Kalat Eslam
Dhoba
El Astabel
Kalat el Wodjeh
El Hani
Akra
Auvenat
El Houra or Bir el Ashreyn
Hassani I.
Nabt
El Khedheyra
Boreydy
YEMBO
Arca
Hedjer
Teyme
Ala
Khaibar
Hadi al Kora
Rahba
Mor
Suaida
Byr Bashyed Well
MEDINA
El Hafna
W. el Akyk
Wady es Shohada
Wady el Fereysh
El Kheyf
Mokad
El Kharma
Szafra
Souk es Szafra
Wady Zogag
El Waset
Djedyd
Beder
Bir es Shakh
Djebel Ayoub
Job's Moun.
Dyar
Mastoura
Wells
Mastura
El Rabegh
Kolleya or Kobeyba
Theyet Kholeys
Kholeys
Plain
Bir Asfan
Ras Hatiba
Sebyl el Kara
TAYF
Akrab
Derye
COSIRE
P. Guadelauhi
Ras el Ans
Ras el Nashef
Berenice
Meshehd Aly
Shebekka Well
Lyne
Shebeyke Well
Kahfe
Kowar
Khabara
Aneyzy
Nefhayd or Gherek el Dawem
Djerdawye
Dat
El Bady
El Mawat
El Heymedi
Abou Khesheyb
Sandy Plain
Sowerder
Wells
Hanakye
Mosneb
Rass
Shebeybe
Ayoun
Dew Sarr
DERAYAH

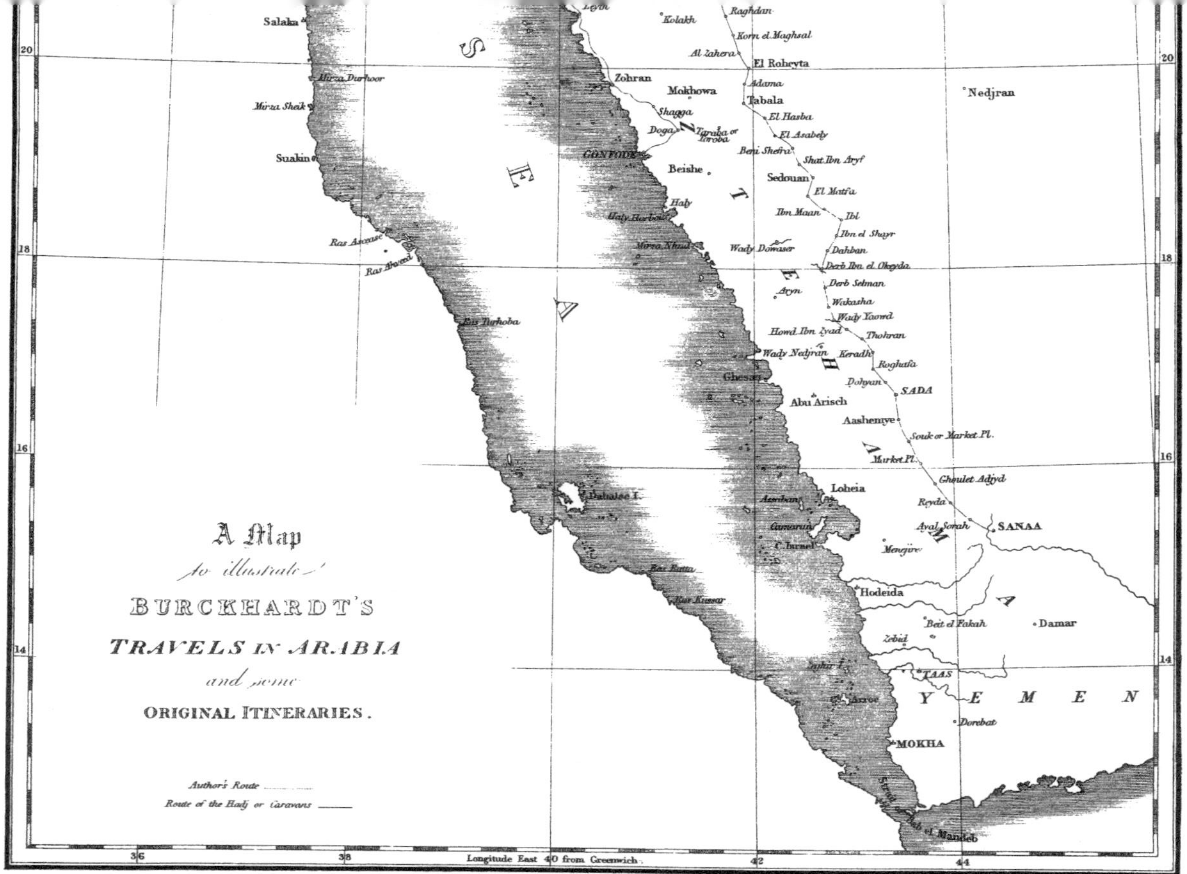

London, Published by Henry Colburn, New Burlington Str.t Feb.y 1829.

Sid.y Hall, sculp.t Bury Str.t Bloomsb.y